Geography of Britain:

Perspectives and Problems

D A Kirby & H Robinson

University Tutorial Press

Published by University Tutorial Press Limited
842 Yeovil Road, Slough, SL1 4JQ

© D. A. Kirby & H. Robinson

ISBN 0 7231 0810 2

Published 1981

Text set in 10/11 pt Linotron 202 Bembo, printed
and bound in Great Britain at The Pitman Press,
Bath

Preface

We have written this book in the belief that social, economic and environmental problems, illustrated by systematic studies, are best understood in the context of a specific place and in relation one to another. We also believe that an important educational characteristic of geography is its elucidation of a student's own country and the place in which he lives. The book is intended for students taking A-level courses in geography, BEC economic geography, college-based environmental studies courses, and general or complementary studies. It should also be a suitable introduction to geography for students in higher education approaching the subject for the first time.

Over the past decade geography has broken out of the introspection which characterised the period of the 'quantitative revolution'. A search for relevance has built upon a strong tradition of applied geography, and continues to interest many in matters of social concern and regional and land-use planning. A wider awareness of resource limitations has once more demanded that geographers should understand the characteristics of natural as well as social systems. Finally, reaction against a strictly mechanistic view of the subject has encouraged an interest in decision-making processes, and a re-assertion of such subjective concepts as sense of place and regional personality. This book seeks to illustrate these themes within the context of Great Britain and Northern Ireland.

D A Kirby
H Robinson

August 1980

Acknowledgements

The authors are particularly grateful to their colleague C. G. Bamford, who contributed the chapter on Economic Policy.

Thanks are also due to the following for kind permission to use copyright material on which maps and diagrams in this book are based:

Sir L. D. Stamp & S. H. Beaver, *The British Isles* (Longman), **3.1, 3.2, 3.3, 3.5, 4.1, 4.3, 9.3, 9.5**; J. W. House, *U.K. Space* (Weidenfeld & Nicolson), **18.3**; Land Decade Educational Council & Graham Moss (for diagram first published in *Architectural Journal,* Jan. 1978), **14.5**; J. Wreford Watson & J. B. Sissons, *The British Isles: Systematic Geography* (Thomas Nelson), **4.3**; P. Hunter Blair, *Roman Britain & Early England* (Thomas Nelson), **5.5**; National Coal Board, **2.8**; Hugh Clout, *Changing London* (U.T.P.), **19.5**; M. Beresford, *Deserted Medieval Villages* (Lutterworth Press), **6.3**; W. J. King, *The British Isles* (Macdonald & Evans) **19.8**; E. H. Cooper, *Introduction to Economic Geography* (U.T.P.), **10.4**; J. Glasson, *Introduction to Economic Planning* (Hutchinson), **18.1**; P. Hall, *Containment of Urban England* (George Allen & Unwin), **13.5**; *Geographical Magazine* & D. Q. Bowen, **2.6**; *Geographical Magazine* (May 1977) & J. Booth, **3.6**; *Geographical Magazine* (June 1978) & R. J. Tyler, **11.1**; *Geography* (The Geographical Association) & Judith Rees, **3.7**.

Crown Copyright Sources (Crown Copyright reserved): The Director, Institute of Geological Sciences, **2.1a**; Department of Energy, **2.12**; HMSO, **16.1, 16.2, 16.3, 16.4, 19.6**; Department of Industry, **18.4**; Ordnance Survey and Second Land Utilisation Survey, **14.1, 14.2, 14.3**.

The following gave kind permission to reproduce photographs:

Aerofilms Ltd., **2.2, 2.4, 2.7, 5.1b, 5.2, 6.2, 12.2, 13.3, 13.8, 15.2, 19.3a, 19.3b, 19.4, 19.13, 20.2, 20.6, 20.8, 20.13, 21.9, 21.11**; Cambridge University Collection (Copyright Reserved) **2.3a, 6.1, 7.1, 9.1, 9.2, 19.14**; British Tourist Authority, **5.1a, 5.7, 6.6, 15.1, 15.3, 20.12, 21.5b**; John Topham Picture Library, **9.4**; Forestry Commission, **9.6**; Scottish Tourist Board, **2.5, 3.4, 20.3**; British Petroleum Co. Ltd., **2.10, 20.5**; Sussex Archaeological Society, **5.3**; Durham County Council, **5.4**; Dr. D. A. Kirby, **6.5a**; City of Newcastle-upon-Tyne, City Engineer's Photographic Section, **6.5b**; Plus Pleasures Ltd., **7.2**; Crown Copyright, National Railway Museum, **7.4**; Beamish North of England Open Air Museum, **7.6**; Crown Copyright, Office of Population Censuses & Surveys, **8.1a, 8.1b**; British Airports Authority, **11.4**; J. Allan Cash Ltd., **12.4, 13.9a, 19.9, 19.11**; Camera Press Ltd., **13.9b**; English Industrial Estates Corporation, **13.10**; Milton Keynes Development Corporation, **13.11**; Leonard & Marjorie Gayton, **14.4**; Scottish Postal Board, **14.6**; British Steel Corporation, **20.10, 21.2**; ICI Petrochemicals Division, **21.4**; British Nuclear Fuels Limited, **21.5a**; Rochdale Metropolitan Borough Council, **21.7a, 21.7b**.

Contents

v

Illustrations

Tables

1

Location and Spatial Relationships

THE NATURE OF LOCATION

Location is a fundamental geographical concept. Many of the problems which are considered in this study of Great Britain and Northern Ireland are related to, if not always attributable to, location and we should do well to consider this important idea. First of all we have to appreciate that location is comparative. Places are given their location only in relationship to other places or points on the earth's surface. Thus, although the position of the British Isles between latitude 49° 90′ N (the Isles of Scilly) and 60° 90′ N (the Shetland Isles) and between longitude 10° 50′ W and 1° 70′ E could be regarded as an absolute location, it is really a location related to the Equator and the Greenwich meridian.

A more meaningful description of the location of the British Isles would *relate* its position to the neighbouring land mass of Europe and the waters of the North Atlantic. Yet even to say that the British Isles lie in the north-eastern part of the North Atlantic, on the continental shelf of Europe but detached from the main European land mass by the narrow waters of the English Channel and the North Sea, is also an inadequate definition of their location. The significance of any position depends upon the natural systems at work in the area, e.g. major patterns of atmospheric circulation or the advance or retreat of polar ice, as well as the changing fortunes of human history.

The significance of location also rests upon accessibility, and certainly the importance of the British Isles (and for that matter North-west or Atlantic Europe of which it is a part) has grown in relation to the extent of the world known at different periods to the peoples of the Mediterra-

nean basin. In antiquity the only part of Europe that formed part of the literate world, and in which technology and urbanisation were of a relatively high order, was limited by the Alps. Even after the Roman conquest of Gaul, the British Isles lay on the very edge of the vaguely known world. *Ultima Thule* was the name given to the lands of North-west Europe – a name which means 'the ends of the earth.' The great navigations of the fifteenth and sixteenth centuries revealed the presence of the 'New World', and helped to shift the centre of gravity, as it were, from the Mediterranean to the marginal lands and seas of North-west Europe. Subsequent history, of course, has changed the significance of Britain's position, although we can see a number of enduring factors.

First, Britain is situated in the centre of the continental land masses of the world. It lies near the middle of what is known as the 'land hemisphere', i.e. that half of the earth's surface which contains the maximum possible amount of land. Nantes, in France, has been calculated by van Zandt to lie at the exact centre of the land hemisphere. Britain is displaced only slightly from this focus, hence it shares with neighbouring Western Europe a fortunate location with respect to most other continental areas. One has only to compare Britain's location with that of New Zealand, situated at the middle of the 'water hemisphere' and detached, remote and isolated, to appreciate the enormous advantages which accrue to the former. Britain is, then, in spite of the radical technological transformation of Japan and other countries of the Far East, still in easy reach of the most economically developed and some of the most populous regions of the world. We should however note that such a position does not necessarily confer economic benefit upon her.

Secondly, Britain has an insular position on the wide submarine platform which extends westwards and northwards from the European mainland. This continental shelf is nowhere very deep – less than 100 fathoms (190 metres) – and the North Sea and the English Channel are quite shallow: if the sea level fell by as much as 95 metres the British archipelago would find itself attached, as in fact it once was, to the European mainland. Insularity has not resulted in isolation, however. Although free contact with the continental mainland has been hindered (to Britain's strategic benefit from the Norman Conquest to the development of aerial warfare) successive cultural influences have been received from the mainland, coming principally from three directions:

(i) from the south-western approaches, e.g. early 'Mediterranean' cultural influences and Phoenician contacts;
(ii) from across the Channel, e.g. Neolithic, Bronze Age and Iron Age cultures, Roman influences, Christianity, the Normans and Renaissance influences;
(iii) from across the North Sea, e.g. Mesolithic culture, Anglo-Saxon and Scandinavian invasions and influences.

More recently, of course, influences have been much wider in origin, e.g. technological innovations from America and Japan, or migrants from the New Commonwealth countries. It is important to remember that the significance of location varies according to the tide of events in other parts of the world as well as, in our own case, events in Great Britain and Northern Ireland.

Thirdly, the location of the British Isles has ensured a temperate climate, at least over the last 8,000 years or so. Open on the west to the ameliorating influence of the warm North Atlantic Drift and the South-west winds which blow from warmer latitudes, Britain and the neighbouring continental coasts enjoy more favourable climatic conditions than any other area so far distant from the equator. Winters are, in general, especially mild, in contrast to the ice-bound coasts of North America, in comparable latitudes. Again, lying on the fluctuating polar front, the British Isles are subject to frequent mid-latitude

depressions which bring stimulating variability to the climate.

Fourthly, it is important to remember that there are significant differences in location within the British Isles. These will become apparent in subsequent parts of the book, but it is important to note here that, in a general way, proximity to Europe combines with physiographic and climatic factors to favour the southern and eastern parts of Britain. Areas to the north and west are less accessible, more rugged, and less conducive to the settlement and occupation of dense concentrations of population. Part Four of this book amplifies this concept within a core-periphery framework. However, because the national core in south-eastern Britain is related to the European core area it is important that we note at this point the major features of the recent relationships with Europe. This point is further developed in Chapter 17.

BRITAIN AND EUROPE

It has been said in the past that Britain is in, but not part of, Europe; in other words, although Britain is geographically part of the continent, it has seldom concerned itself politically with European affairs except when its security has been threatened. The development of an overseas empire led to social and economic bonds, as well as political ties, being developed in a global context, at the expense of mainland Europe. Even after World War I, Britain released itself from its European obligations and gave its political support to the newly-founded League of Nations. Already, though, the English-settled Dominions had secured self-government, and after World War II the independence of India and Burma pointed to a loosening of the old Imperial ties. In Europe, on the other hand, there was a growing tendency to closer collaboration.

At the end of World War II much of Europe lay in ruins, and bankrupt. Victor and vanquished alike faced acute problems of reconstruction and recovery, and it was soon realised that the best approach to these essential tasks lay in co-operation and collaboration. There were two fundamental issues: first, the need for economic rehabilitation and development to repair the shattered economies of the European protagonists and, second, to devise some formula which would ensure that Western Europe would never again tear itself apart.

The first economic development was the setting up of the Organisation for European Economic Co-operation (O.E.E.C.) in 1948, to distribute the substantial funds provided by the United States through the 'Marshall Plan' to assist European recovery. In 1961 the O.E.E.C. was replaced by the Organisation for Economic Co-operation and Development (O.E.C.D.), which aimed to achieve the highest sustainable economic growth, full employment and improved living standards in the member countries. It is of interest now to recall that even before the war ended, Belgium, Luxembourg and the Netherlands had realised that their mutual economies would stand to gain from the creation of a custom's union. It was agreed that, if it was to be effective, it was necessary first to attempt to co-ordinate their financial, economic and social policies. By 1948 sufficient progress had been achieved for the three countries to abolish internal tariffs and to establish a common external tariff. 'Benelux' thus came into being.

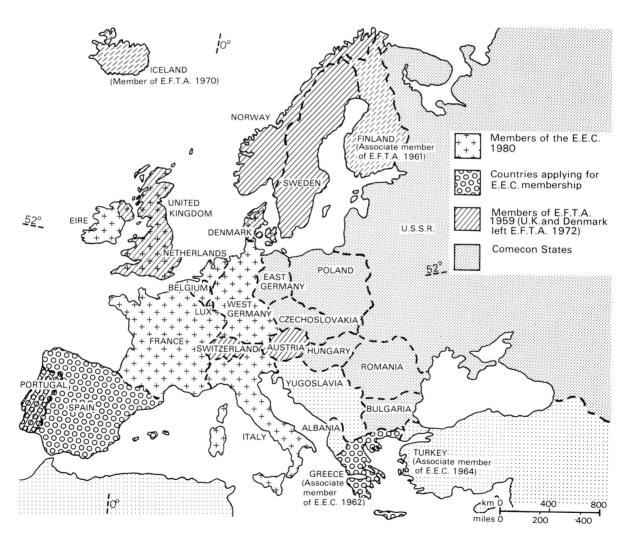

Fig. 1.1   The EEC and other groupings in Europe. In January 1981, Greece becomes a full EEC member

The first major step in the direction of European unity was the establishment, in 1952, by Belgium, the Netherlands, Luxembourg, West Germany, France and Italy, of the European Coal and Steel Community (E.C.S.C.). Membership of the E.C.S.C. was open to other European countries but, at that time, Britain felt unable to join. In 1955 the Foreign Ministers of the six members of the Community, encouraged by the success of the E.C.S.C., met to discuss further possibilities of integration. Their proposals for the setting up of a wider common market and also an atomic energy pool led to the signing of two treaties in Rome in March 1957. Britain had been invited to participate in the discussions but withdrew from them since she did not feel able to accept all the conditions and obligations which were inherent in the type of union envisaged by 'the Six'. The principal difficulties which faced Britain, and for that matter certain other European countries, were (i) the erection of a common external tariff, (ii) the degree of economic integration and supranational control implicit in the proposed union, and (iii) the implication of ultimate political integration. For Britain, in particular, the long-standing relationships and tariff arrangements with the rest of the Commonwealth still presented special difficulties.

The European Economic Community (E.E.C.) came into existence at the beginning of 1958 with the original Six participating members. Neverthe-less, links with Europe continued to grow in significance and in the following year seven O.E.E.C. countries – Austria, Norway, Denmark, Sweden, Switzerland, Portugal and Britain formed the European Free Trade Association (E.F.T.A.). Subsequently, Finland became an associate member, and Iceland a full member. E.F.T.A.'s objective was free trade arrangements between its members and the promotion of closer economic co-operation. For more than a decade the two groupings, E.E.C. and E.F.T.A., operated and developed independently of each other.

In Britain, however, the Commonwealth connection began to appear less important in the face of the neighbouring E.E.C.'s market of 200 million people (Fig. 1.1). The growing success of the E.E.C. persuaded the British government to apply for membership in 1961, and again in 1967, but on both occasions the opposition of France resulted in defeat. Success came only in 1973 but Britain was not in a position to shape the fundamentals of policy, particularly on agriculture, which had already been established. Nevertheless, since 1973 Britain has become more closely, perhaps irrevocably, bound to mainland Europe. Its peripheral location to European affairs contrasts with its former centrality within the Commonwealth, and as such will inevitably affect its economic and social development for the foreseeable future.

Part One

The Human Habitat

2

Physiography and Resource Endowment

GEOLOGY AND STRUCTURE

The British Isles are unique geologically for they contain rocks which are representative of almost the entire geological column. In the extreme north-west of Scotland are to be found Lewisian schists and gneisses, Torridonian sandstones and conglomerates of Pre-Cambrian age, the oldest rocks in the country, while in the south-east of England occur deposits of alluvium, sands and gravels of geologically recent times. Between lie rocks of intermediate age, but it is well to remember that much of the British Isles lies on a basement or foundation of ancient Pre-Cambrian rocks and that occasionally these basal rocks break through the overlying newer rocks, as happens in the case of Anglesey, Charnwood Forest and the Wrekin.

The present features of the land surface and the coast are the result of a long and complex geological history. It has involved continental movement as a result of plate tectonics, a series of great earth movements or orogenies, and extreme climatic changes giving at one time hot, arid conditions, at another glacial conditions. These mountain-building phases and climatic changes are closely linked with plate tectonics. For example, the changes in climate which took place over geological time are the result not so much of oscillations in the climate itself, although there may have been some of these, as of continental drifting through a wide range of latitudes having different climates. The proto-continental area of which the British Isles now forms a part lay somewhere in the southern hemisphere in early geological times. We must think of it as slowly migrating northwards during past geological time and in so doing moving through a series of climatic zones.

Changes in the Palaeozoic

Taking a broad view, it is possible to think of Britain's geological history in terms of alternating 'continental' and 'marine' episodes. It may be assumed that the first episode was a continental one, when part of Britain belonged to an ancient land mass which subsequently broke up and became dispersed. Remnants of this old Pre-Cambrian land mass still remain in the far north-west of Scotland, as previously mentioned. Much of the Scottish Highlands, too, are composed of old rocks such as gneisses and schists, which are hard, tough and resistant to erosion. This first continental episode (Pre-Cambrian) was followed by the first marine episode (Cambrian), when slow subsidence resulted in most of the then existing land area being invaded by the sea. Vast accumulations of sediments were laid down in the submerged areas, which subsequently were compressed and hardened to form the Cambrian rocks which include shales, slates, sandstones and quartzites. During the following Ordovician period, vulcanicity occurred which produced great volcanoes, the remnants of which form the present mountains of Snowdon and Cader Idris. Later, during Silurian times, limestones were laid down (Fig. 2.1a).

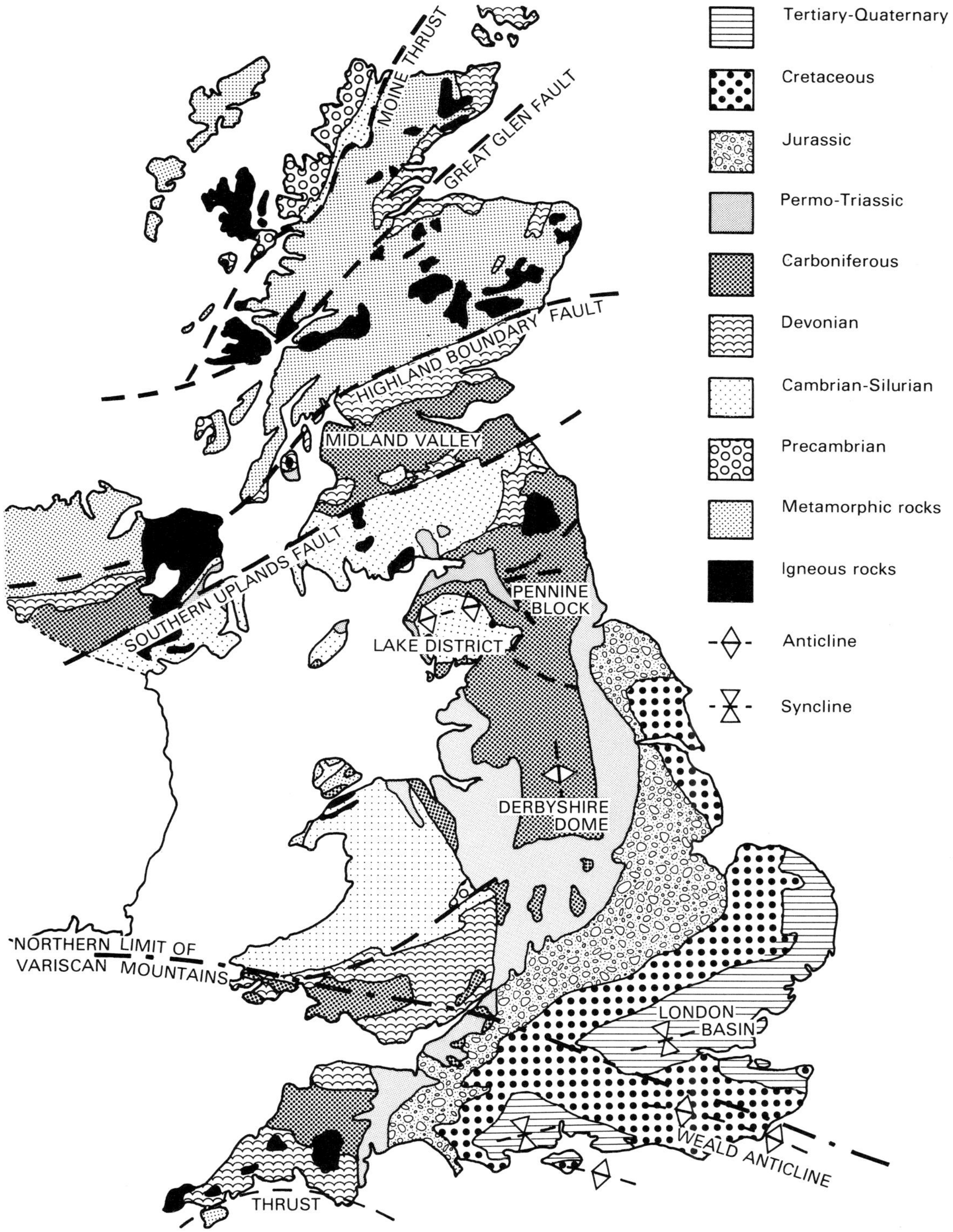
MOINE THRUST
GREAT GLEN FAULT
HIGHLAND BOUNDARY FAULT
MIDLAND VALLEY
SOUTHERN UPLANDS FAULT
PENNINE BLOCK
LAKE DISTRICT
DERBYSHIRE DOME
NORTHERN LIMIT OF VARISCAN MOUNTAINS
LONDON BASIN
WEALD ANTICLINE
THRUST
Tertiary-Quaternary
Cretaceous
Jurassic
Permo-Triassic
Carboniferous
Devonian
Cambrian-Silurian
Precambrian
Metamorphic rocks
Igneous rocks
Anticline
Syncline

Fig 2.1a A simplified geological and structural map of Britain (Crown Copyright Reserved)

After this first prolonged marine episode, a second continental episode (Devonian) set in. At this time plate movements, the first tremors of which had appeared in the Ordovician period and had been responsible for the volcanic activity just mentioned, led to a mighty upheaval, the Caledonian orogeny, which produced a series of narrow mountain chains now oriented south-west to north-east. Their eroded remnants are to be seen in the Scottish Highlands, the Southern Uplands and their continuation in Ireland as the Mountains of Mourne, and in the mountains of North and Central Wales and their continuation in the Wicklow Mountains of south-eastern Ireland. While this orogenic movement was in process, intense volcanic activity accompanied it to produce the lava hills of the Ochils, Sidlaws and Renfrews, and the Cheviots. In the long narrow depressions between the mountains, accumulations of sands were compressed and converted into Old Red Sandstone rocks. These Old Red Sandstones occur

in the Orkney Islands, in Caithness, around the Moray Firth, and in a belt immediately south of the Helensburgh-Stonehaven fault line in Scotland, in the eastern borderlands of Central and South Wales, and in north Devon (Fig. 2.1b).

The Carboniferous Period

Approximately 350 million years ago the Carboniferous period began and lasted for about 65 million years. The Carboniferous is correlated with the second marine episode, when marine transgression and a dramatic change in the climatic conditions took place giving hot, wet, equatorial-like conditions. Early in the Carboniferous, vast accumulations of marine organisms led to the formation of the massive Carboniferous Limestone, which now covers large areas of the Pennines and gives rise to highly distinctive karst scenery (Fig. 2.2). Later, increasing rainfall

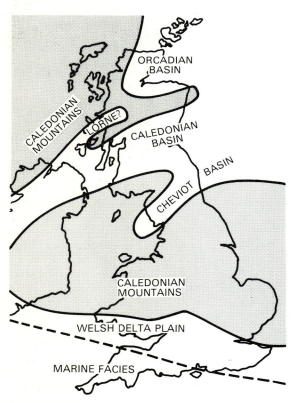

Fig 2.1b Devonian palaeogeography of Britain

Fig 2.2 Eglwyseg Mountain, Clwyd

Fig 2.3a The Midland Valley, Stirling. The Ochil Hills here form a dramatic northern boundary to the Midland Valley. The Forth meanders across the post-glacial valley floor

scoured the land surface and the great rivers of that time transported the coarse gritty material which accumulated to produce the Millstone Grit Series. The extensive delta areas so formed were covered in swamp forests which came to form the Coal Measures. In the early Carboniferous and towards the end of that period, there was some tectonic activity accompanied by considerable vulcanicity; for example, basaltic lavas were poured out in the Midland Valley of Scotland (Fig. 2.3a).

The Hercynian Orogeny

At the end of the Carboniferous and the beginning of the Permian, the disruptions which had punctuated the Carboniferous period culminated in another great mountain-building episode: the Armorican or Hercynian orogeny. As the African 'plate' moved northwards, the sediments which had been laid down in the seas were crushed and elevated into a range of mountains stretching widely across what is now central Europe. In Britain, the strongest effects of this orogeny are seen today in the South-west Peninsula and South Wales, where the Devonian and Carboniferous strata came to be folded into a series of east-west trending folds with similarly aligned faults. Further north the effects were less pronounced although the Pennines were folded and faulted at this time. Igneous activity was also widespread and the granite bosses that were to become Dartmoor and Bodmin Moor were produced as, too, was the Great Whin Sill in Northumberland.

As had happened after the Caledonian orogeny in Devonian times, the palaeogeography again underwent a change. It is well to remember that at this point in time the present continental area of Europe was part of the great super-continent of Pangea which was gradually migrating northwards. After the Hercynian orogeny, the ocean waters withdrew from embryonic Britain, the climate became increasingly arid, and the Permian and Triassic Periods were largely marked by the deposition of continental deposits: the varied rocks known as the New Red Sandstone. The

Permian rocks are mostly red or yellow breccias, conglomerates, sandstones and siltstones, and it is believed they were deposited in desert basins since some of the sandstones reveal fossil dune structures. However, in the area of north-east England there existed a saline sea, one of a series of basins which stretched across the present North Sea area to link with the German Zechstein basin, and it was in this north-eastern evaporating sea that the Magnesian Limestone and evaporite salts associated with it were laid down. The natural gas and oil deposits of the North Sea are intimately associated with the salts laid down in the Zechstein Sea. During the following Triassic period the climate, at least during the early phases, continued warm and arid, and sediments of essentially the same kind as those of the Permian period were laid down; these are known as the Bunter sandstone and the Keuper marl and sandstone.

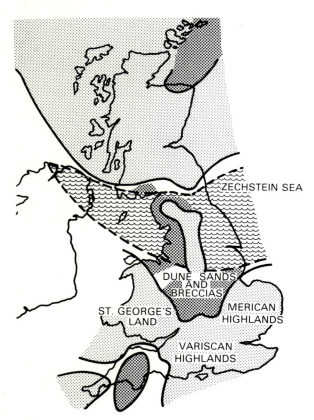

Fig 2.3b Permian palaeogeography of Britain

Changes in the Mesozoic

Throughout the Permo-Trias age, the Hercynian uplands underwent fairly rapid denudation and the basins were gradually filling with the eroded debris. By late Triassic times, therefore, the relief had been substantially reduced and the Keuper deposits helped to bury the former Hercynian landscape. In parts of northern England and the Midlands, shallow lakes seem to have developed in which red marls and evaporites accumulated. The salt deposits of Cheshire were formed in this way.

During the ensuing Jurassic and Cretaceous periods, which together spanned some 100 million or more years and were the age of development of the great reptiles, a third marine episode developed. In Jurassic times the seas once again spread in to cover much of the now flattened landscape, and a variety of shales, sandstones, limestones and ironstones were deposited. In Cretaceous times various sedimentary rocks, including Greensand, Gault Clay and finally Chalk were laid down. It was during the Upper Cretaceous that a widespread transgression of the sea occurred, which probably inundated most of England and in which vast quantities of Chalk, a remarkably pure and fine-grained, white limestone, were deposited. In many areas, more particularly in the north of England, the Chalk has been eroded away but in the south it is common over wide areas. In places the Chalk is over 300 metres thick and contains very little terrigenous material, perhaps suggesting very stable conditions and very little erosion of any neighbouring land masses (Fig. 2.4).

The Tertiary Period

The Tertiary period, which began about 75 million years ago, saw yet another great change as a major elevation occurred and a fourth continental episode set in. The dominant event of the period took place in mid-Tertiary times when the African plate, moving northwards, squeezed, crumpled and uplifted the thick sediments which had accumulated in the geosyncline of the Sea of Tethys, and gave rise to the Alps and its associated ranges. The ripples of the Alpine orogeny were felt as far north as Britain, where the Mesozoic and Tertiary sediments of south-eastern England were squeezed into a series of east-west trending folds, e.g. the

Fig 2.4 The South Downs, north of Brighton. Scrub vegetation marks the availability of moisture at the foot of the chalk escarpment

Wealden pericline and the gentle folds of the Isle of Wight. Further north there was renewed movement along old faults, and areas such as the Pennines, the North York Moors, and the Lake District were flexed and elevated. Tertiary rocks occur mainly in the London and Hampshire Basins, the strata consisting largely of unconsolidated sands and clays. They represent a mixture of fluviatile and marine sediments deposited where rivers were draining from western land masses to the sea in the south-east. Many of Britain's planation surfaces were also probably cut late in Tertiary times by river or, in some cases, marine action.

Thus, to summarise, Britain's structure, at least in its main features, developed through a series of stages or cycles of orogenic activity. These gave rise to the folding of rock strata and their uplift followed by long periods of relative quiescence, though minor crustal adjustments seem always to

have taken place throughout the long span of geological time. Very early folding – the Charnian of Pre-Cambrian times – is represented only by outcrops of very ancient rocks in the extreme north-west of Scotland. The Caledonian folding of the Primary era greatly affected the northern and western parts of Britain. The much worn down remnants of this former great mountain range, which extended into Scandinavia, now form the Scottish Highlands north and south of the Great Glen fault (Fig. 2.5), the Southern Uplands, and, in Northern Ireland, the Mountains of Mourne. The Hercynian orogeny of the Secondary or Mesozoic era, followed a long period of comparative quiescence. This affected south-west Ireland, south-west England, South Wales and the Pennines. Finally, the Tertiary Alpine folding, though not directly affecting Britain, had important secondary effects, for the pressures which the orogeny created resulted in the gentle folding of the Weald

Fig 2.5 Mam Ratagan, Wester Ross. Note the accordant summits of this ancient mountain mass, the ice-scarred hills and glacial profile

and the Chalk hills, and renewed movement along old fault lines. Since this last orogenic cycle there has been a long period of denudation and, to all intents and purposes, Britain's structural evolution has ceased, though physiographical changes continue to occur. In Quaternary times a major glaciation took place which has left an indelible mark on the landscape, and to this momentous happening we must now turn our attention.

THE PLEISTOCENE GLACIATION

Traditional ideas about the last great Ice Age have been radically upset in recent years through modern research. Perhaps the two most important facts that have emerged are (i) the Ice Age lasted longer than was hitherto believed, and (ii) there have been many more glacial phases than was formerly imagined; Bowen (1977) has suggested that there were perhaps twenty-one. Recent research has indicated that a prolonged but gradual period of cooling set in, perhaps beginning in later Tertiary times and culminating during the Pleistocene period. In this long period of intermittent refrigeration, vast accumulations of ice developed over northern and much of central Europe. There were, incidentally similar ice-sheets in the northern parts of North America and in Siberia. These ice-sheets did not simply grow in extent and then melt away: rather they oscillated, advancing and retreating many times. Long and careful study of the Pleistocene glaciation in Europe has shown that periods of ice advance were separated by interglacial phases when the ice, due to ameliorating climatic conditions, melted and retreated, perhaps even disappearing almost entirely except in higher altitudes and higher latitudes. In the Alps five different phases of ice advance had been distinguished, while in northern Europe at least three had been clearly recognised and these were broadly correlated with the Alpine advances.

However, modern research, particularly oxygen isotope studies, has shown that there were numerous glacial phases. It is known that eight glacials occurred during the past 700,000 years alone, but only the most recent have left their impact clearly on the landscape. The whole story of the Ice Age is very complex and, it must be

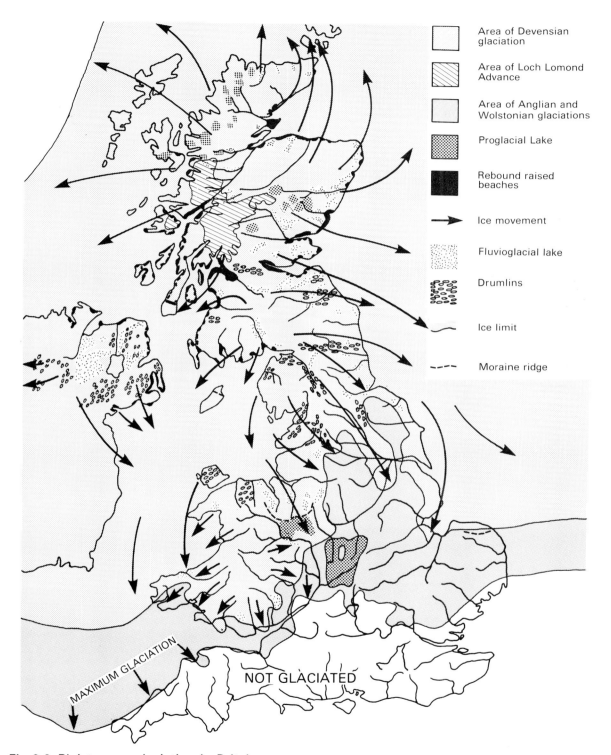

Legend:

- Area of Devensian glaciation
- Area of Loch Lomond Advance
- Area of Anglian and Wolstonian glaciations
- Proglacial Lake
- Rebound raised beaches
- → Ice movement
- Fluvioglacial lake
- Drumlins
- Ice limit
- - - Moraine ridge

MAXIMUM GLACIATION

NOT GLACIATED

Fig 2.6 Pleistocene glaciation in Britain

said, very confused; opinions vary and the whole picture awaits clarification. Here is not the place to enquire more deeply into this specialised and tangled glacial era, and it must suffice to pick out a few salient points.

The British Isles were clearly affected by some of these glacial phases, although it is not entirely clear how many major glacial advances actually occurred. There is good evidence from many parts of England of at least two glaciations, and some authorities would claim three. One major problem is that the effects of the more recent glaciations often obscure or even obliterate the evidence of the earlier ones. In Britain the penultimate glaciation was more extensive than the last and its extent – roughly to the line of the Thames – can be traced by the occurrence of deposits of glacial drift which extend from East Anglia across the Midlands to South Wales. The fact that the last glaciation, which took up most of the last 100,000 years, ended only 10,000 years ago, has meant that its effects upon the landscape remain remarkably fresh. During this glaciation, ice caps developed in the highland regions and sent out tongues of ice which flowed into the surrounding lowlands. Ice also crossed the North Sea from the Scandinavian ice sheet and reached the eastern coast of Britain. (Fig. 2.6).

The following Table shows the phases of ice advance during the Pleistocene glaciation, with the British phases correlated with those in northern Europe and in the Alps.

ALPINE REGION	NORTHERN EUROPE	BRITISH ISLES
WÜRM	WEICHSELIAN	DEVENSIAN
	Eemian	Ipswichian
RISS	SAALE	WOLSTONIAN
	Holsteinian	Hoxnian
MINDEL	ELSTER	ANGLIAN
		Cromerian
GÜNZ		
DONAU		

Field mapping and radiometric dating, however, have cast considerable doubt upon the validity of some of these stages. In East Anglia, deposits previously assigned to the Anglian and Wolstonian glaciations have been shown to be the product of only one glacial period (probably the Saale) with the Hoxnian deposits post-dating them. The correlation of the Hoxnian with the Holsteinian would, therefore, appear to be erroneous.

The morphological consequences of glacial erosion and deposition are great, and the landscape has been much modified in many areas. Indeed, land which has been under ice cover is always modified in one way or another, and shows certain features and landforms which distinguish it from land which has not been affected by ice action. Two distinctive processes occur: 'ice-ploughing' which is erosional and transportational in character, and deposition which results in the dumping and spreading of eroded material. The ice, through its scratching and scraping action, and its associated meltwater, produced considerable erosion, especially in upland areas such as the Highlands of Scotland, the Lake District, the Northern Pennines and in Northern and Central Wales. Valleys were deepened and straightened, and cirques were incised into mountain sides to produce arêtes and allied features. The Lake District and Snowdonia provide classic examples of the erosional activity of ice (Fig. 2.7). In the lower lying parts of these two areas the chief legacy of the ice was the boulder clay spreads and terminal moraines. Elsewhere in Britain, spreads of hummocky or drumlinoid till are found, as in the Yorkshire Dales, the Vale of York and the Solway Plain. Hence, a great variety of both erosional and depositional landforms, such as moraines, drumlins, eskers, kames, lake beds, glacial spillways, glacial troughs, cirques, arêtes, roches moutonnées, crag-and-tail and hanging valleys can be seen in the British landscape as a result of the past glaciations.

The ice, too, interfered with the drainage pattern which had established itself, and led to river capture, the displacement of rivers, the diversion of streams and the creation of numerous lakes. For example, the Thames, which originally followed a more northerly course, was displaced by the ice front and sought its present more southerly outlet. Again, the Yorkshire Derwent, which rises within a few miles of the coast north of Scarborough, had its outlet barred by the North Sea ice and was diverted southwards to carve out a new course for itself through the Kirkham Gorge, to join the Ouse south of Selby. These are but two of many glacial interferences with the drainage system.

The oscillations in climate and the development of ice sheets also caused variations in sea level. These, in turn, led to the formation of river

Fig 2.7 Great Langdale, Cumbria. The ice-scarred dome of the Lake District, looking north over Grasmere Common to Skiddaw and Blencathra in the distance

terraces and of raised beaches – the latter can be clearly seen around many parts of the coast such as in western Scotland. The subsequent final retreat and disappearance of the ice resulted in a rise of sea level which, in addition to creating such coastal features as fjords, rias and estuaries, led to the breaching of the Straits of Dover (probably as recently as 7,000 years ago) which gave Britain its present-day configuration.

Finally, mention must be made of the effects of periglaciation. The importance of periglaciation in producing landscape effects and features has only been realised relatively recently. Although the consequences of periglaciation are nothing like so obvious as those arising from glaciation, periglacial action has played a not insignificant role in many areas. Stone polygons on high summit areas; hill slopes patterned by stone stripes or mantled by screes now stabilised; fossilised landslips and solifluction deposits such as the 'head' deposits occurring in the dry valleys of Chalk country, are all legacies of periglacial action.

15

SURFACE RELIEF

The late Sir L. Dudley Stamp in his book *Britain's Structure and Scenery* drew attention to the fact that Britain epitomised in miniature the geological history of the earth and that this geological spectrum was responsible to a considerable extent for the extremely varied, if small-scale, physical conditions and scenery. It is this assemblage of 'landscape miniatures' which provides Britain with such varied scenery. The landscape is never so vast as to become monotonous and satiate the viewer.

A line drawn between the mouths of the rivers Exe and Tees broadly separates the higher and more rugged northern and western parts of the country from the lower and topographically more gentle parts to the east and south. This Tees-Exe line roughly separates the outcrop of the old Palaeozoic rocks (ancient igneous, metamorphic and hard sedimentary rocks) from the younger Mesozoic, Tertiary and Quaternary rocks (which consist chiefly of limestones, sandstones and clays). Old, hard rocks are usually tougher and more resistant to weathering and erosion than younger rocks which yield more readily to destructive processes; thus, in Britain, the older rocks tend to form the highlands, the younger the lowlands. Again, whereas old hard rocks when subjected to pressure and stress tend to fracture and break up into blocks, often bounded by great faults, younger rocks, especially sedimentaries, tend to fold under pressure producing great upfolds and downfolds (anticlines and synclines). Hence, 'Highland Britain' to the north and west of the Tees-Exe line, together with N. Ireland, consists in the main of upstanding, and sometimes tilted, upland blocks, frequently marked by fault lines. However, 'Lowland Britain' to the south and east consists mainly of lowland, diversified by low ridges and composed of young, and in some places very recent, rocks which rest upon an underlying platform of older rocks.

Highland Britain

In the highland region of Britain large and continuous stretches of country more than 300 metres (1,000 feet) high are common; plains and valleys do occur, it is true, but they are limited in extent and tend to form interruptions in the typically upland nature of the country. Although the land is rugged in some areas, the mountains were worn down and their outlines rounded as a result of ice scouring the surface. The Scottish Highlands, the largest mountain mass in the country, are divided by the Great Glen tear or wrench-fault into two parts: the North-west Highlands and the Grampians. The Grampian mountains generally lie at elevations of between 600 metres (2,000 feet) and 900 metres (3,000 feet); however, in the west they culminate in Ben Nevis which reaches 1,343 metres (4,046 feet), while in the Cairngorms, Ben Macdhui and Cairngorm exceed 1,200 metres (4,000 feet). South of the Central Lowlands or Midland Valley, a major trough-faulted area or graben, are the Southern Uplands, a dissected plateau, much like the Highlands to the north but generally lower in elevation. Smooth in outline, a number of hills reach over 600 metres (2,000 feet), e.g. Merrick in the west, 843 metres (2,764 feet) and Broadlaw, 839 metres (2,754 feet). Over to the south-east and physically, if not geologically, continuous with the Southern Uplands are the Cheviot Hills which rise up to 816 metres (2,676 feet) in the peak Cheviot.

The Pennines, traditionally spoken of as the 'backbone' of England, a fractured, tilted and eroded anticline, were uplifted in Hercynian times. Tilted up on the western faulted side, they drop sharply on their western flank but slope gradually eastwards; hence most of the Pennine rivers flow eastwards. Transverse faulting, marked by the Aire and Stainmore Gaps, has provided main routeways across the uplands and divided the Pennines into three blocks. The Pennines constitute the largest outcrop of Carboniferous rocks in Britain. In the northern and southern sections there are extensive areas of Carboniferous Limestone, with spectacular scenery in the Malham area. All the features of karst landscape – limestone pavements, crags and gorges, swallow holes, potholes, caves, dry valleys, Vauclusian springs, etc. – manifest themselves in this fascinating region. Whereas the Millstone Grit capping rock was worn away in the northern Pennines to expose the limestone, in the central Pennines the Millstone Grit remains to give a very different type of scenery with up-standing tor-like outcrops rising out of the moors – sombre and wild in winter, but where heather grows, turned to pink and mauve in summer. Further south, in Derbyshire, the limestone re-appears to give some very beautiful scenery, especially where rivers, such as the Derwent and the Dove, have carved out steep-sided, deep gorges. Cross Fell, 893 metres (2,930 feet) in the far north of the range is the highest point, but three mountains in Yorkshire – Whernside, Ingleborough and Pen-y-Ghent – reach around 700 metres elevation, while the High Peak in Derbyshire is 636 metres (2,088 feet) high.

The Cumbrian Mountains of the Lake District form the eroded remnants of a huge dome of very old rocks and volcanic extrusions; this central core of old rocks is almost completely encircled by Carboniferous Limestone. The highest mountains occur in the eroded dome, e.g. Scafell, at 978 metres (3,210 feet) the highest peak in England, and at Helvellyn and the Langdale Pikes; these eroded lavas have produced sharp, jagged outlines and provide spectacular scenery. The dome gave rise to radial and superimposed drainage; it was initiated on the outer covering of sedimentary rocks and then, before these were eroded away, the streams etched themselves into the older rocks beneath, thereby maintaining the original drainage pattern. The disposition of the numerous lakes, largely glacial in origin, brings out the radial pattern very well.

Except for its peripheral lowlands, most of Wales is upland country composed of Cambrian, Ordovician and Silurian rocks, with intrusions and extrusions of igneous rocks in the north, and of softer Silurian sandstones and mudstones in the centre which give way to the Carboniferous basin of the South Wales Coalfield in the south. In the core of the massif in the north, hard volcanic rocks have helped to create the peaks of Snowdonia and Cader Idris. Snowdon itself, which attains a height of 1,086 metres (3,560 feet) is the highest mountain in England and Wales. Here in north Wales, as in Cumbria, there are clear signs of ice erosion. Although, in general, the hill region of central Wales gets steadily lower towards the south, the Black Mountains and the Brecon Beacons stand up boldly, the latter reaching nearly 900 metres (3,000 feet).

In the South-west Peninsula, though there are residual remnants of older rocks in the headlands of Lizard Point and Start Point, most of the rocks are of Devonian times or later. Topographically, the South-west is made up of scattered uplands of varying sizes separated by plains and river valleys.

In north Devon, Exmoor, which culminates in Dunkery Beacon, 521 metres (1,708 feet), and its eastward extension, the Quantocks in west Somerset, are composed of Devonian sandstones, which also occur in Cornwall. The granite masses of Dartmoor, Bodmin Moor, Hensbarrow and Carn Menellis are exposed bosses giving bleak plateaus with distinctive rocky outcrops or tors, some of which, like Yes Tor and High Willhays in northern Dartmoor, reach around 600 metres (approximately 2,000 feet). The largest areas of lowland are the Plains of Somerset, the Vale of Taunton, and the Plain of Devon which occupies a syncline between Exmoor and Dartmoor and is filled with Culm rocks of Carboniferous times. The coasts, particularly of Cornwall and south Devon, are cliffed and much indented, and famous for their raised beaches. In Northern Ireland the only substantial area of lowland is around Lake Neagh and along the Bann Valley.

Lowland Britain

Turning now to Lowland Britain we find that south and east of the Tees-Exe line are the broad plains or low-lying plateaus of the Midlands, built up of the younger Triassic rocks, pierced here and there by inliers of ancient rocks. The Midland Plains give way to the scarplands – parallel belts of limestone and chalk, with their alternate scarps, dips and shallow vales – which give an essential unity to lowland England. As a result of the earth movements of the Alpine age, the rocks have been gently tilted towards the south-east but it is only in the extreme south that the beds have undergone real folding. Geologically, the lowland zone is a region of fewer rock types – mainly soft sandstone, limestone and chalk – while topographically it is a region of plains and gently sloping hills. As a result of differential erosion, the relatively harder rocks in the sequence stand up to form escarpments facing the north-west which are separated by 'strike' valleys floored with clays.

The post-Carboniferous deposits are, first, Permian deposits, including the band of Magnesian Limestone, east of the Pennines, which are extensive but largely covered by superficial deposits of drift; west of the Pennines in Lancashire there are sandstones and breccias. Second, Triassic deposits extending from Devon along the lower Severn valley floor cover almost the whole of the Midland Triangle, with a north-westward extension into Cheshire and western Lancashire, and a north-eastward extension along the Trent valley into the Plain of York. Third, Jurassic outcrops extend in a great arc from Lyme Regis, in Dorset, to Redcar, in north Yorkshire, with their northerly extremities running parallel with the Pennine axis. The Lower Jurassic, or Lias, forms a broad belt of low-lying land across the southern and eastern portions of the Midland Plain. Some of the Middle Jurassic Oolitic Limestones have produced bold scarps as in the cases of the Cotswolds, the Lincoln Edge and the Cleveland Hills. Above the Lias and the Oolitic Limestone are the Upper Jurassic Beds, showing bands of Corallian limestone and intervening Oxford and Kimmeridge clays, which form flat country with locally diversified relief resulting from the presence of harder limestone bands.

Fourth, are the Cretaceous deposits. The Wealden sandstones and the clays of Kent and Sussex are the oldest Cretaceous formations. Surrounding the Wealden Beds is a narrow band of Lower Greensand which forms escarpments. It appears again in central England, along with the Gault Clays, as a narrow outcrop between the Jurassic and Chalk escarpments. The Chalk, however, dominates much of south-eastern England, the main formation running in parallel with the Jurassic rocks. Beginning in Dorset, it widens out to form Salisbury Plain and then bifurcates, the northern limb extending north-eastwards to form the Chiltern Hills, the Berkshire Downs, the Norfolk and Suffolk Downs, and the Lincolnshire and Yorkshire Wolds, while the southern limb of the Chalk itself divides to form the North and South Downs which enclose the Weald.

Fifth, and finally, are the Tertiary and Quaternary deposits of the London Basin, eastern Norfolk and Suffolk, and the southern part of the Hampshire Basin, chiefly sands, clays and alluvium.

The limestones, including the Chalk rocks of south-eastern England, have produced some of the loveliest country in the kingdom. The Cotswolds, with their warm, buff-coloured rock, have given rise to some of the finest domestic architecture in the land and to wander through the Cotswold Country, out of season, is a joyous experience. The swelling, turfed downs of the Chalk lands, with their occasional hill-top clumps of trees, give a different scenery with an airy spaciousness about it.

RESOURCE ENDOWMENT

A large part of Britain's resource base – energy, minerals, water, soils, forests, scenery – is intimately related to the geology and physiography of the country. These resources will be discussed more fully in subsequent chapters, but a general account of the country's resource endowment and its significance is useful at this stage.

About half a century ago James Fairgrieve, a well-known geographer, wrote *Geography and World Power,* the underlying theme of which was that throughout history peoples had advanced and become powerful in relation to the energy resources they possessed, developed and utilised. Today, the amount of energy used by a people or country is a fairly sure guide to the stage of its economic development. The United States, which is the most economically advanced country in the world and whose people, in general, enjoy the highest standard of living is the greatest user of energy: in the early 1970s energy consumption per capita in terms of kilograms of coal per year was 10,900 kg (cf. Britain 2,450 kg) and each American had at his fingertips, on average, the equivalent of the personal energy expended by 500 human slaves.

Coal

The Coal Measures were greatest on the Pennine flanks, for the Pennines formed the largest outcrop of Carboniferous rocks in Britain, and here are found a whole series of coalfields running from the Lancashire and North Midlands fields to the Yorks-Derby-Notts, and Northumberland and Durham fields. There are two other important areas: the fields of the Central Lowlands of Scotland and the South Wales field. In addition, there are half a dozen or so other fields of lesser importance: the Cumberland, North Wales, Shropshire, South Staffordshire, Cannock, Forest of Dean, Somersetshire fields and Kent field. It is worth noting that not all of these are on the exposed Coal Measure series. In the mid 1970s two significant extensions to the Pennine fields were discovered: the rich Selby field in Yorkshire and that in the Vale of Belvoir in north Leicestershire (Fig. 2.8). Since World War II there has been a considerable amount of open-cast mining for coal but it would appear that this phase of exploitation is now drawing to a close.

Fig 2.8 Coalfields in Great Britain

A century ago Britain was the largest producer of coal and she maintained this lead until the beginning of the present century, when she was overtaken by the United States. Peak production in Britain was reached in 1913 with 292 million tons, a substantial proportion of which was exported. After World War I a rapid decline in output set in: the change-over in shipping from steam to oil propulsion, the rapid developments in the use of electricity, and more recently natural gas, have all been important contributing factors

in the shrinkage of the British coal industry. But there were other factors too: most of the more easily worked seams had become exhausted and the industry was slow to mechanise, with the result that after World War II Britain could not compete, for example, with cheaper Polish coal. In 1946 the industry was nationalised. When the rationalisation of coal production got under way in 1957 there were marked changes over the next twenty years: the labour force was reduced from over 700,000 in 1957 to about one-third of this number, 245,000 in 1975; the number of mines in operation dropped from around 800 to less than 300; output per man increased over this period from 300 metric tons to 480, while the mechanised output grew to in excess of 90 per cent as against 23 per cent in 1957. For a long time the industry was hampered by surplus production, but since 1968 demand has been outrunning supply, particularly due to the 1973 oil crisis. Rather more than half of current production goes to supplying the demands of thermal electric production. Britain's coal reserves (despite the fact that much of the best coal has been worked out) are still very substantial and there is enough coal to meet the country's demands through the twenty-first century, and perhaps considerably beyond that time.

Oil

Although exploration for petroleum has long been carried on in mainland Britain, very little has been found and the grand total amounted to about 80,000 tonnes annually. This is a tiny fraction of the country's total needs – over 100 million tonnes a year in recent years, all of which had to be imported at heavy cost until 1975 when Britain's North Sea fields began to yield. Exploration in the North Sea commenced in 1970–71, and since then several major fields have been discovered, e.g. Brent, Forties, Brae and Ninian. Although the first oil was piped ashore in June 1975, it was not until two years later that Britain really began to feel the benefits. The capital investment has been enormous – the development of the Forties field alone cost £800 million – but something of the order of 30 million tonnes was brought ashore in 1977, 79·9 million tonnes in 1979, and it is generally believed that during the 1980s output from the North Sea will be between 100 and 150 million tonnes a year. Certain grades of light oil formed a

19

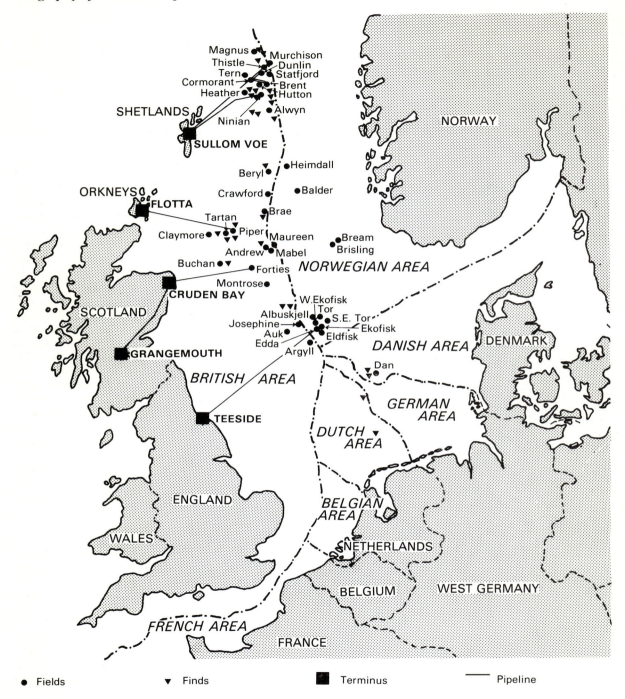

Fig 2.9 North Sea oilfields and pipelines

● Fields   ▼ Finds   ■ Terminus   —— Pipeline

significant export item by 1979, and although other grades will continue to be imported for the foreseeable future, Britain will be a net exporter of oil throughout the 1980s. The known reserves of oil in the North Sea (in 1977) amounted to an estimated 22 billion barrels, of which Britain owned 16–17 billion barrels. In the British sector of the North Sea, 14 fields had been developed by 1978 which in total contain approximately 9 billion barrels of oil. The major fields mentioned above between them share two-fifths of Britain's reserves. Fig. 2.9 shows the oilfields and pipelines in the North Sea. The success of the North Sea explorations has encouraged drilling operations elsewhere, and prospecting is going on in the areas to the west of the Orkneys and Shetlands, and in the Celtic Sea (Fig. 2.10).

Fig 2.10 North Sea oil recovery. B.P.'s drilling rig *Sea Conquest* off the Shetland Islands, with supply vessel alongside

Natural Gas

The exploitation of natural gas from the North Sea began shortly before that of oil. The discovery of a large natural gas field in the north of the Netherlands in 1959 stimulated interest in the possibility of locating further deposits in the North Sea basin. By 1970 nine commercial gas fields had been located, six of which lay in the British sector: West Sole (the first to be discovered, in 1965), Leman Bank (the most productive so far), Hewett, Indefatigable, Viking, and Rough, a more recently discovered field. Fig. 2.11 shows the location of these fields, and those subsequently discovered in the mid 1970s. A series of submarine pipelines pump the gas to the terminals at Easington in Holderness, Theddlethorpe in Lincolnshire, and Bacton in Norfolk. Gas pipelines now distribute natural gas widely throughout the country, with the result that whereas in 1960 95 per cent of the gas used in Britain was made from coal, by 1970 95 per cent of the gas used was natural gas. Just how rich the North Sea reserves of natural gas are is problematical: although large quantities of gas have been found in the North Sea, the initial discoveries, such as the southern group of fields, have probably already reached their peak production and it is unlikely that present production levels will be maintained after 1985. Moreover, it is generally believed that after the end of the century yields from the fields will begin to decline, perhaps sharply. Britain's newest gas field in Morecambe Bay is expected to come on stream by 1984.

Hydro-Electric Power

Only a small fraction of Britain's energy supplies comes from hydro-electric power. With the exception of three small schemes on Dartmoor, five in Wales, chiefly in the Snowdon area including the pumped-storage at Ffestiniog, and two in southern Scotland, most of the hydro-electric power generated comes from the Highlands of Scotland where there are ten main schemes. The essentials for H.E.P. generation are ample rainfall to provide a constant flow of water and a steep gradient to give a 'head' of water. Since large reservoirs or natural lakes are frequently required for storing water, large schemes can, usually, be located only where there are large, empty spaces

Fig 2.11 North Sea gasfields and pipelines

Table 1:   Total Inland Energy Consumption (in million tons coal equivalent)

	1951	1969	1973	1974	1975	1976	1977	1978
Coal	207·8	161·1	131·3	115·0	116·0	120·0	122·0	121·0
Petroleum	24·8	135·7	159·4	149·0	114·7	132·0	132·0	133·0
Natural Gas	–	9·2	43·5	52·1	44·6	58·0	62·0	66·0
Nuclear Electricity	–	10·5	9·9	11·9	12·0	} 15·0	} 16·0	} 17·0
Hydro-Electricity	1·0	2·0	2·0	2·1	2·1			
Total	233·6	318·5	346·1	331·0	289·4	325·0	332·0	337·0

and the Highlands are well-suited in this respect. While we receive enough rainfall, our total catchment area is not big enough to allow much extension of H.E.P. The power generated by the above schemes is fed into the national grid.

Nuclear Power

Finally, Britain is steadily increasing its use of nuclear electricity. Although there are no native supplies of uranium, apart from a small amount in the Orkneys, Britain is now able to produce nuclear fuel in the form of plutonium. There are a dozen nuclear power stations, mostly occupying estuarine or coastal sites because of the nuclear power industry's need for vast quantities of water but partly, too, for safety reasons.

Table 1 gives a breakdown of Britain's total energy consumption for selected years over the past three decades. The drop in 1974 was due to the oil crisis which demanded that the country try to make savings in its consumption of energy. Fig. 2.12 shows in graphical form the contribution of the various forms of energy to the total of Britain's inland energy consumption (1973–78).

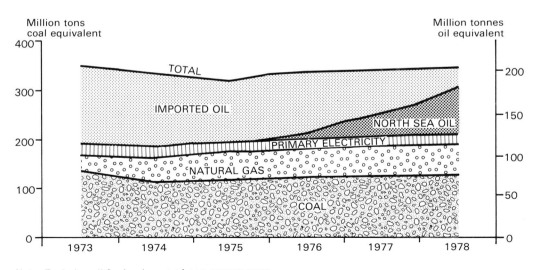

Note: Excludes oil for bunkers and non-energy uses

Fig 2.12 Inland energy consumption of primary fuels 1973–78

Mineral Resources

Geologically there is great variation in the origin and in the nature of mineral deposits, but from the geographical point of view a simple five-fold grouping can be made: (i) rocks, used for building stones, brick and cement making, ceramics, etc; (ii) non-metallic minerals, e.g. salt, sulphur, potash; (iii) metals, e.g. gold, copper, lead, iron; (iv) mineral fuels, e.g. coal, petroleum; and (v) water. The whole of the earth's crust, of course, is composed of mineral matter but a mineral resource, like any other kind of resource, is of potential value to man only when it occurs in quantity in concentrated form, when he can find ways and means of extracting it, and when he has a use for it. Although mineral substances are widely, if erratically, spread throughout the crust, in general, few occur in sufficiently concentrated quantities to justify their commercial exploitation. For this reason, mining is usually confined to localised areas.

Broadly, at least in Britain, minerals may be said to have formed in one of three ways. First, during times of tectonic disturbance (when magma was squeezed into the crust or metamorphism took place) the crystallisation of minerals directly from the magma occurred, as in the case of copper. What are known as *pegmatitic* deposits arise as a result of residual magmatic fluids penetrating fissures, either in the cooled igneous rocks or in the adjacent 'country' rock; the tin deposits of Cornwall were formed in this way. Secondly, sedimentary or bedded ores occur in horizontal sheets or layers, e.g. the black-band and clay-band iron ores of the Coal Measures, the Jurassic iron ores, common salt, and potash salts. Formation of these beds takes place in different ways: some deposits are due to precipitates being deposited on lake floors; others are the result of the evaporation of saline waters which leave the dissolved salts behind; others again are due to percolating water dissolving mineral matter out of rocks and then re-depositing it again, at depth, in concentrated form; and yet others, such as coal and oil, result from organic matter becoming trapped, squeezed and changed between layers of rock. As we saw in the early part of this chapter, the salt and potash deposits of the Tees area are evaporites, as also are the salt deposits of Cheshire. Thirdly, some mineral deposits result from the decomposition of the surface rocks: soluble matter is washed away

leaving behind a residual deposit. Bauxite (the ore of aluminium) is the best example of this although, excepting some in Eire, there are no bauxite deposits in Britain. Kaolin, or China clay, found in Cornwall, also occurs as a residual deposit.

Some of the baser metals, e.g. tin, copper, lead and zinc, have a long history of exploitation in Britain; indeed, our history books would have us believe the *Cassiterides* was Cornwall and that the Phoenicians voyaged to Britain some three thousand years ago for Cornish tin. The home-produced ores of these metals is now negligible, but this does not necessarily mean they have become entirely exhausted; what it does mean is that under present conditions it is uneconomic to mine them. And yet it is interesting to recall that 150 years ago the copper mines of Anglesey were the most productive in the world!

Britain's reserves of iron ore occurred in a variety of situations. Associated with the Coal Measures was the clay-band ironstone, found in the Forest of Dean, in South Yorkshire and Durham; and although this was exhausted early, the black-band ores (nodules found in the Coal Measure shales) were worked in North Staffordshire until 1956. For over a hundred years high-grade haematite, found in the Carboniferous Limestone rocks of Furness and Weardale (the only non-phosphoric ores in the country) played an important role in the steel-making industry in the days of the Bessemer process. The Jurassic iron ore fields stretch in a great arc from Redcar to Banbury: the Cleveland ironstone, which became the main source of ore until 1920, ceased to be mined with the closure, in 1964, of the North Skelton mine; the Frodingham ore near Scunthorpe in north Lincolnshire, continues to be mined by open-cast methods and helps to supply Scunthorpe's needs; the lower Oolite of Northamptonshire, which lies at the surface or under a thin overburden, gave rise to the Corby steel-works. All the Jurassic ores have a low iron content; moreover, they were phosphoric ores and so could not be used for steel-making until the basic-hearth process was introduced. In the early years of the present century Britain was mining some 15 million tons of iron ore annually; today home sources provide only a very small fraction (less than 1 million tons) of the iron ore used, and the country is dependent for more than 90 per cent of its needs upon imported ores.

It is not possible to mention all the mineral resources at our disposal but a brief reference should be made to some of the more prosaic, though not necessarily less important, mineral resources. Building stones are widely spread except in the south-east, but stone is expensive and increasingly brick is being used for domestic building purposes. Bricks are made from clay fired in kilns and some 7,000 million bricks are produced annually. The Oxford clay belt is one of the most important areas, the region around Peterborough being particularly well known. Roughly one-third of all the bricks in the country come from this region. Cement production, amounting to some 20 million tons annually, is also important; the industry has grown rapidly with the increasing use of concrete – a mixture of gravel, sand and cement – for constructional purposes. Kaolin or China Clay is soft white residual clay produced by the complex chemical weathering of aluminium silicates, especially the felspars in granite. It is much used in the manufacture of porcelain, tiles, toothpaste, paper, etc. The finest kaolin deposits in the world occur in Devon and Cornwall and, in addition to the large quantities sent to the North Staffordshire Potteries where some three-quarters of Britain's pottery is made, large quantities are exported. About one million tons of China clay are mined every year.

References

Potter, A.W.R. & Robinson, H., *Geology* (Macdonald & Evans, 1975).

Warwick, G.T., 'Relief and Structure', in *The British Isles: A Systematic Geography,* ed. Watson & Sissons, (Nelson, 1964).

Stamp, Sir D. & Beaver, S.H., *The British Isles,* 6th ed., (Longman, 1971).

Bowen, D.Q., 'Hot and cold climates in prehistoric Britain', *Geographical Magazine,* Vol. XLIX, No. 11, August 1977, pp. 685–98.

Wright, P., Supplement on 'Energy' in *The Times,* Tuesday October 24th 1978.

Manners, G., *The Geography of Energy,* 2nd edition (Hutchinson, 1971).

Resources for Britain's Future, ed. M. Chisholm (Pelican Books, 1972).

Manners, G., 'The changing energy situation in Britain', *Geography,* 61, 1976, pp. 221–31.

Fernie, J., 'The development of North Sea oil and gas resources', *Scottish Geographical Magazine,* Vol. 93, 1977, pp. 75–85.

3

Climate and the Water Budget

WEATHER AND CLIMATE: CHARACTERISING FEATURES

While climate is the average of weather conditions, the changeable characteristics of the British weather, and its lack of clear cut and emphatic seasonal change, reduces the value of statements relating to mean values. Prolonged cold winters, such as those of 1947, 1963 and 1978–9, and prolonged hot, dry summers, such as that of 1976, are relatively unusual, although it is now being suggested that cyclical patterns may be detectable. The outstanding features of Britain's weather and climate are its variability, its mildness, and its humidity. The climate belongs to the Temperate Western Margin type but possesses special qualities not found in other regions classed within this climatic type, qualities which might perhaps be best summed up in the term 'extraordinary equability'.

Several factors have a determining influence on the weather and climate of the British Isles:

(i) They are located between latitudes 50° and 60° N., i.e. in the temperate zone, hence temperatures are never very high nor very low; with rare, and usually brief exceptions, temperatures are characteristically moderate.

(ii) They have a maritime situation. Oceanic, onshore winds have a moderating effect, but of greater significance is the high specific heat of water. Land heats up and cools down more quickly than the sea in a given time, thus in summer the sea's influence is cooling, in winter warming; as a result, the temperature range is small.

(iii) The shores, more especially on the western side, are influenced by the warm waters of the North Atlantic Drift, which is a continuation of the Gulf Stream. This warm drift exerts an important ameliorating effect upon winter conditions and prevents the coasts from becoming ice-bound.

(iv) The British Isles lie wholly within the Westerly Wind belt. Blowing from warmer latitudes and over a warm ocean surface, they are warm and moisture-laden. Since they are the prevailing winds and are heavily charged with moisture, they bring warmth and rain to the British Isles.

(v) The British Isles come under the influence of an almost constant procession of 'depressions' or 'lows', punctuated by ridges of high pressure, which are characteristically travelling in a south-west to north-east direction. On average, a depression reaches the British Isles every ten days. The weather owes its characteristic variability to this stream of depressions and intervening ridges of high pressure.

(vi) The coastal configuration, especially the existence of numerous inlets, permits oceanic influence to penetrate well inland. The disposition also of the main hill masses across the path of the chief rain-bearing winds causes an appreciable difference in the amount of precipitation received on the western and eastern sides of Britain.

The Influence of Air Masses

The variety of weather conditions likely to be experienced in Britain is due to the effects of a number of air masses and the atmospheric systems associated with them. Not only do these air masses possess the characteristics of their source regions but they are likely to be modified as they move towards Britain. For example, Polar maritime (P.m.) air, originating over the North Atlantic, becomes warmed as it moves southwards and hence picks up water vapour; as a result, by the time it reaches Britain it has become unstable and moist. The air turbulence which is generated is prone to give gusty winds, broken cloud, and sharp, heavy showers, punctuated with periods of sunshine, which may occur at any time of the year but which are characteristically of frequent occurrence. P.m. air is likely to bring below average temperatures in the summer season, but the degree of instability engendered is dependent upon the distance over which the air mass moves and the path it takes. In winter the eastern side of Britain may be affected by Arctic maritime (A.m.) air; this is also unstable because of its journey over the North Sea and gives rise to strong north winds, hail and snow showers and low temperatures. Occasionally in winter, cold, dense, dry Polar continental (P.c.) air comes from the east bringing stable, severe conditions to Britain. In 1947, for example, a tongue of P.c. air emanating from the Eurasiatic anticyclone extended across the North Sea to cover England; heralded by a heavy snow, stable conditions with keen frost persisted for six or seven weeks without a break. Tropical continental (T.c.) air, moving northwards from the continent, occasionally invades southern Britain for short periods bringing fine weather, blue skies and high temperatures – sometimes over 32° C (90° F) – in summer. The summer of 1976 saw a prolonged hot, dry period as a result of persisting T.c. air. Tropical maritime (T.m.) air, flowing from the Azores high pressure area, is also fairly stable but it has a high relative humidity, giving rise to the frontal rain in depressions or relief rain when it reaches elevated areas. In winter, T.m. air brings mild conditions commonly associated with poor visibility and much cloud.

Atmospheric Systems

The stream of mid-latitude depressions which influence Britain's weather conditions mostly develop along an oscillating line of contact between cold polar air and warm maritime tropical air, known as the *polar front*. When a wedge of warm tropical air thrusts itself into the cold air, the mass of warm air rises over the adjacent cold air to give a warm front. As the warm air overrides the cold air, instability sets in to produce cloud and then rain. The amount of cloud experienced and the duration of the rain will depend upon the rates of movement of the system and the front; moreover, the form of the cloud and the heaviness of the rain mainly depends upon the warmness of the air. For example, the appalling storm which brought torrential rain and high winds during the period of 16th and 18th September 1979, and caused the disaster of the Fastnet yacht race, resulted from a tropical cyclone finding its way into mid-latitudes and bringing very warm air with it. As depressions move north-eastwards, cold air attacks and undercuts the rear, forming a cold front and bringing short, heavy downpours – 'clearing showers' as they are often called. It should be remembered that the adjacent air masses are separated by sloping boundaries, so that the passage from one air mass to another is marked by a zone of transition rather than an abrupt line. This zone may vary from only a few miles to over 100 miles in width, depending on the slope of the frontal layer. Consequently, our experience of the change will vary with the steepness of the front and the speed at which it is moving. But it is this procession of 'lows' separated by wedges of high pressure which cause the highly changeable conditions of much of the weather we experience.

Temperature

A location in mid-latitudes implies that temperature must vary seasonally, but the seasonal range in Britain is much less than latitude alone would suggest. The insular character of Britain means that the warm sea surface has a moderating influence, especially during the winter period. Furthermore, the dominant westerly winds, warmed as they move over the North Atlantic Drift, bring relatively warm air to Britain in winter. A map of sea-level isotherms for January indicates quite emphatically, through the general north-south alignment of the isotherms, that the mean midwinter temperature is a result of location rather than of latitude. The 4° C isotherm for January roughly bisects Britain: to the west temperatures are slightly higher – the 6° C isotherm runs through Devon and the Pembroke peninsula –

clearly indicating the ameliorating influences of the sea and the westerly winds; to the east temperatures are slightly lower – 3° C in parts of eastern Scotland and in Lincolnshire and East Anglia – reflecting the chilling effect of the land in winter and the fact that the shallow North Sea is colder than the ocean water to the west of Britain. Thus, in general, winter temperatures decrease from west to east: along the western and southern coasts the mean temperatures are 5–7° C (41–44° F) with the higher values occurring over the Welsh and Southwest peninsulas, whereas along the northern coast of Scotland and most of the east coast of Britain as far as the Thames estuary, the mean temperatures are about 4·5° C (40·5° F). (Fig. 3.1).

Winter weather conditions are highly variable. In the period 1946–56 there were several winters of keen frost and heavy snowfall, but during the past decade there has been a run of exceptionally mild winters, although in the winter of 1978 there were periods of heavy snowfall especially in northern Scotland and, quite exceptionally, in south-western England.

In summer, latitude exerts a much stronger influence and the July sea level isotherms run generally east-west, but tend to show a slight northwards bulge over the land since the land is warmer than the sea. In July the mean monthly temperature is lower than that in most other temperate-latitude countries. Mean temperatures are appreciably higher in the south than in the north; sea level values range from about 17° C (62° F) in the south, especially in the London Basin, to about 13° C (56° F) in the extreme north of Scotland. At any given latitude, temperatures are slightly higher at inland locations than on the coast. In almost all parts of Britain, except for far north-west, mean maxima exceed 16° C (60° F) and attain 21° C (70° F) or more in parts of southern England, more especially in inland areas.

Fig 3.1 Mean sea-level temperatures for January (after E G Bilham)

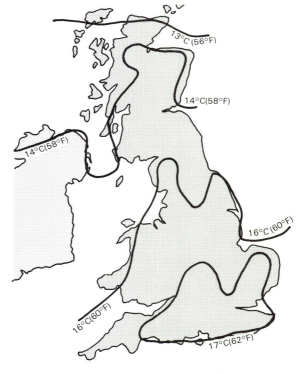

Fig 3.2 Mean sea-level temperatures for July (after E G Bilham)

"High temperatures are exceptional features", says Gregory (1964), "but nearly all lowland areas have experienced values above 27° C (80° F). In the southern two-thirds of England more than 32° C (90° F) has occurred in many areas, while temperatures of above 35° C (95° F) have been recorded in some places." Summer conditions do vary widely however; the summers of 1975 and 1976 brought high temperatures and prolonged sunshine, whereas those of 1978 and 1980 proved to be the cloudiest for nearly seventy years. (Fig. 3.2).

The incidence of frost is of considerable significance: the length of the frost-free period affects the growing period and unexpected late frost can spell disaster for the fruit-grower, while keen frost may hamper transport in various ways. Three factors principally affect the incidence of frost: altitude, the occurrence of ground hollows, and nearness to the sea. Elevation undoubtedly induces frost, for the Grampians and the Southern Uplands have only four months free from frost, although, as Rees has commented, "Altitude, in itself, does not seem to be the decisive factor: Sheffield at 429 feet has only 69 frosty days, while Cambridge, at only 41 feet, has 111 days of frost." Ground hollows, i.e. enclosed basins, or river valleys, may function as sinks into which cold air drains; as a result, in many fruit-growing areas the orchards are planted on the hill sides or valley slopes to evade the downslope creep of cold, dense air which accumulates in the hollows. Coastal districts are less likely to be frost affected; for example, a frost-free period of up to nine months characterises the Isle of Anglesey, the Lleyn Peninsula, the Cardigan Bay coastlands, Pembrokeshire, Cornwall and the south coast of England as far as the Isle of Wight. Along the eastern section of the Channel coast the frost-free period is reduced to some seven months and along the east coast to about six months. Over most of the English Plain, except in some restricted areas prone to 'frost-drainage', the period free from frost is about six months.

Precipitation

Precipitation embraces rainfall and snowfall. The highest falls of rain occur as orographic rain on the highlands of the north and west, but to the west of the central axis of the highland rather than on its most elevated parts. Over the low ground, too, the amount of rain decreases from west to east.

Precipitation varies much more widely between one locality and another than does temperature, with average annual amounts ranging from a maximum in excess of 5,000 mm (200 in.) in some mountain areas to as little as 500 mm (20 in.) along the Thames estuary (the lowest mean annual rainfall occurs at Shoeburyness with 490 mm (19·2in)). Higher rainfall on the western side of Britain is a result not only of higher relief but also because most of the depressions approach from the west bringing frontal and warm-sector rain. Convectional rainfall, associated with unstable air conditions which develop in summer, is more especially common over the English lowlands and East Anglia which are subject to thunderstorm downpours. (Fig. 3.3).

There are three important and noteworthy features of the rainfall of Britain: first, it is well-distributed throughout the year nowithstanding monthly variations; secondly, there is a tendency for the western half to receive the greater part of its precipitation in winter, the eastern half in summer; and, thirdly, there is in general an autumn maximum, usually reached in October. Although prolonged dry spells, such as were experienced in the summers of 1947 and 1976, are by no means unknown, particularly in the English Plain, they are not typical. Rainy periods are most frequent in the west, especially in the highland areas; on the other hand, dry periods are most common in the lowland areas of the east and south-east. There is no rule, however, concerning the occurrence of dry periods and wet spells which are highly irregular in their incidence. In Essex the number of days on which rain falls is around 150, but travelling westwards and northwards the number steadily increases until in the extreme north-west of Scotland they reach 250. In eastern England the highest rainfall usually occurs in July or August, followed by October; February is the driest month. In southern and western England, October is commonly the month of highest rainfall; March of least. In Wales and western Scotland, December and January are the months of highest rainfall, May or June of least.

Snow and associated phenomena, such as hail and sleet, are most frequent in the north of Britain; over the higher upland areas some of the precipitation falls as snow and remains as snow for considerable periods. The heaviest snowfalls come with easterly and north-easterly winds which bring Polar continental and Arctic maritime air to

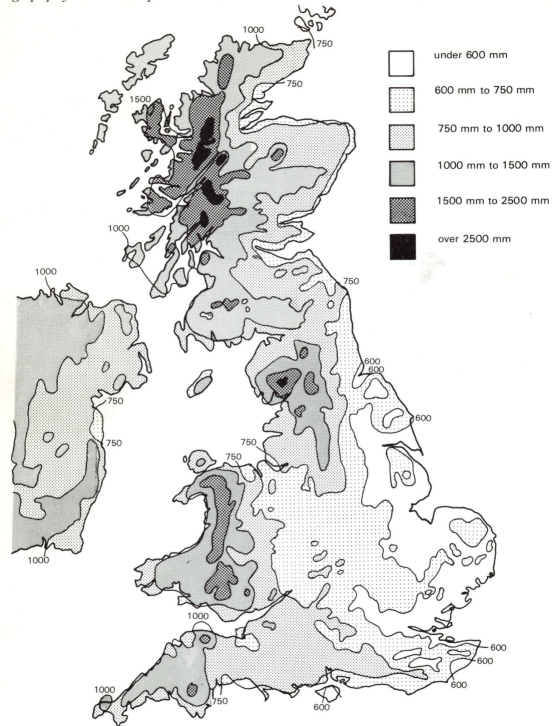

Fig 3.3 Average annual rainfall of the British Isles (after Stamp & Beaver)

Fig 3.4 Ski-lift, Glenshee. One of the closest ski runs to the Midland Valley, Glenshee is popular with week-end skiers, but has a shorter season than the Glen More slopes on Cairngorm itself

the east and north of Britain. The likelihood of snow increases from the south-west to the north-east: in the Scilly Isles snow is unlikely to fall on more than 3 or 4 days a year; in Norfolk it falls on about 15 days; in northern England from 20 to, in places, 50 days; and in the Highlands of Scotland snow may lie on the ground for 100 days or more a year, which has enabled the development of major ski resorts at Aviemore in the Grampian region, and at Glenshee (Fig. 3.4). Actual conditions are very variable from year to year; for instance, heavy snowfalls with long ground lay are unusual in the south-west of England but in the winter of 1978 a particularly heavy snowfall made many roads impassable and isolated many settlements for several days.

Sunshine and Cloud

Considering Britain as a whole, cloud, haze or fog prevent the sun from being visible for approximately two-thirds of the time when it is above the horizon; sunshine diminishes from about 40 per cent of the possible amount in Cornwall to about 26 per cent in the Orkneys.

Cloudiness is a characteristic of the British climate. Cloud is least common in the south-eastern parts of the country. Northern Britain and much of Wales are areas with a great proportion of highland, and therefore a consequently greater incidence of cloudiness. Sea mists coming up the Channel often affect the south coast, while the low-lying parts of eastern England are prone to suffer from mists, especially at the change of the seasons. Fog, less common nowadays as a result of smoke abatement policies, is more especially associated with the industrial towns and results from smoke being emitted into a humid atmosphere.

The mean daily duration of bright sunshine clearly indicates the advantage of a situation along the south coast and the east coast. A point to take into consideration is that the longer winter days in the south of Britain result in a slightly larger proportion of winter sunshine. The average bright

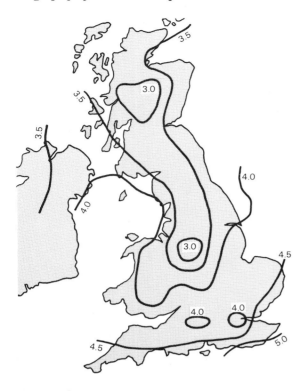

Fig 3.5 Mean daily hours of bright sunshine

sunshine in January ranges from 2 hours and more along the south coast to less than 1 hour in the extreme north of Scotland. In July and August the south and south-eastern coasts, approximately from Plymouth to Cromer, average 7 hours or more; the English Plain and coastal Wales, between 5½ and 7 hours; the Pennines and the Southern Uplands, 4½ to 5 hours; and Scotland north of a line joining Ayr to Peterhead, under 4½ hours. The mean daily duration of bright sunshine is highest in the coast region of East Sussex where it reaches 5 hours and lowest in the Grampians and the north-western Highlands where it is only 3 hours. (Fig. 3.5).

WATER RESOURCES

In Britain, people tend to take water very much for granted: it is only during occasional long, dry summers, as in 1947, 1959 and 1976, when springs begin to dry up, rivers are greatly reduced, reservoirs sink to critically low levels and the problem of water supply becomes serious, that public attention is focused upon the water problem. But of all the natural resources, water is the most important for the welfare of mankind. It is the basis of life: indeed, man himself consists of about 70 per cent of water and requires five to six pints per day to maintain essential bodily functions. Water is equally vital to almost all animals and plants. Apart from sustaining all forms of life, the value and uses of water are manifold: for domestic and municipal requirements, for agricultural and irrigation purposes, for industrial demands, for power resources, for navigation and transport, for sewerage, for fisheries, and for recreation and amenity purposes.

The demands placed upon these various uses and needs vary considerably from place to place and sometimes there is a conflict of interests, especially if the available water supplies are restricted.

Incredible as it may seem, Britain has a growing water problem resulting primarily from (i) the irregular distribution of rainfall in the country, (ii) the increase until recently of the population, combined with a changing distribution of population, (iii) the rapidly growing demand for water, and (iv) the inadequate management of the resources we possess.

It is possible roughly to divide Britain into two rainfall provinces by using the 750 mm isohyet. To the east and south of this line, the average annual rainfall amounts to between 500–750 mm, but it is precisely in this area of the Midlands and the South-east that the demand for water is greatest and is expanding most rapidly. To the north and west of the 750 mm isohyet the rainfall varies but is broadly between 750–1,500 mm and there is, generally speaking, a surplus over demand.

Of greater significance than the total rainfall is the net precipitation, i.e. that which is left after evaporation has been accounted for. The evaporation rate varies regionally to an appreciable extent, largely depending upon temperature and wind, but over most of the country it amounts approximately to 500 mm of rainfall a year. This evaporation is of great significance since it substantially diminishes the net amount of water available. It will be clear that if loss through evaporation is subtracted from the total amount of moisture received, the actual surplus of water running off the land surface to the rivers or percolating into the ground will vary from 0–250 mm in the south-east, and from 250–750 mm or more in the north-west.

Another factor which must be taken into consideration is that the seasonal precipitation in Britain is variable and unpredictable, and it is this that contributes most to present problems of trying to provide a reliable water supply cheaply. Broadly speaking, rainfall is highest in the cooler months and lowest in the warmer months; it is, therefore, unfortunate that the demand for water is greatest in summer when the rainfall is least and the evaporation rate highest, and that most of the rainfall comes at that time of year when it is least needed.

It will be clear from what has been said that in some years the amount of water remaining after evaporation has taken place will be negligible, particularly in the south-eastern part of England. It will be apparent, too, that if the steady increase in demand upon supply – estimated to be at the rate of 1·78 per cent per annum – continues, in some years parts of the South-east will be in deficit and that, as time goes on, such deficiencies will become progressively greater. Fortunately, however, other parts of the country have unused surplus water resources and these can be used to make good the shortages in the south-eastern part of England. Viewing Britain's water problem as a whole there is no overall shortage of water and it should be possible to maintain supplies; such problems as exist relate to its storage, distribution and management.

Source of Supplies

Britain's water supplies are obtained from three sources: (i) from rivers which have flows sufficient to meet the demands imposed upon them; (ii) underground supplies, used either directly from springs or abstracted from bore-holes which tap artesian supplies (Fig. 3.6); and (iii) from reservoirs which impound water collected in wet periods for use in dry. The bulk of Britain's supplies – about four-fifths – comes from rivers or from gathering grounds whose water is stored in either natural lakes or man-made reservoirs. Most of our larger rivers have a more or less regular flow and water is frequently abstracted

Fig 3.6 Regional Water Authorities and sub-surface water supplies in England and Wales

from them directly and merely passed through filtration plants before being distributed. At other times water is drawn off and put into storage reservoirs where it is treated before being released for human consumption. In the case of London, more than two-thirds of its water supply is derived from the Thames (upstream from Teddington) and the Lea, and the water is stored and treated before use since effluent has been discharged into the rivers. (Gross river pollution is one of the great problems affecting the use of rivers as suppliers of water). Almost one-fifth of the country's water supplies comes from underground sources, which are estimated to yield around 180 million gallons annually. Subsurface supplies are of particular importance in southeastern England, though they are also tapped in other parts of the country. However, in some areas (e.g. under London) the underground resources are being used up more quickly than they are being replenished. Accordingly, water engineers are now having to turn their attention to the possibility of artificially recharging natural underground stores which are being depleted.

In the more northerly and hillier parts of the country, where there are extensive collecting grounds, much use is made of reservoirs, and the Millstone Grit and Coal Measure areas of the Pennines are peppered with them. In the more densely populated and highly industrialised parts of the Midlands and Northern England, there have often been battles among the more powerful city corporations to secure water collecting rights over the more sparsely inhabited moorlands and hills of the Pennines, the Lake District and central and northern Wales. The larger towns, unable to assuage their thirst locally, have been compelled to seek water far afield, e.g. Bradford built a series of reservoirs in upper Nidderdale, Manchester went to the Lake District (Thirlmere and Haweswater), Liverpool to North Wales (Lake Vyrnwy), Birmingham to Central Wales (Elan and Claerwen Reservoirs). These and other civic schemes, however, have created much ill-feeling since they have in the past involved depopulation, usually involved the loss of farmland, the drowning of villages, the destruction of amenities or have cut across other interests. Feelings have run particularly high in Wales against the supplying of English water needs; but proposals in 1979 to raise the level of Wastwater and Ennerdale water in Cumbria for supplies to the nearby nuclear industry met equally fierce opposition.

The constantly rising demand for water due to increasing population, higher standards of living, increasing demands from industry (both energy supply and manufacturing), and increasing demands by agriculture, especially in relation to the growing practice of irrigation in England, has placed the water authorities under great strain. It should also be borne in mind that the utilisation of Britain's water resources is not merely concerned with supplying the country's domestic, agricultural and industrial needs but also with the demands from five other interests, viz. land drainage, inland water transport, hydro-electric power, fisheries and recreation. Since these varying interests frequently conflict, the water management problem may be a complex matter. Largely because of these conflicting interests and the growing demands for more water, the Water Act of 1973 was passed; but before outlining the provision of this Act it will be useful to trace briefly the chief landmarks in water legislation over the past fifty years.

Institutional Framework

The Land Drainage Act of 1930 resulted in the division of England and Wales into 47 catchment areas. At that time there were around 1,000 statutory water authorities (borough, urban and rural councils), together with a similar number of water supply companies. The 1930 Act was a significant development, but it was only with the Act of 1945 that the foundations of a national water policy were laid. Since that time the number of water undertakings dropped from around 1,000 to about 270, two-thirds of which were local authorities, most of them responsible for their own local supplies and frequently catering for populations of less than 100,000, although some of the larger cities, e.g. Birmingham, Manchester, Liverpool, were important exceptions. The largest authority was the Metropolitan Water Board which served the needs – some 360 million gallons daily – of six and a half million people living in the London area.

The regrouping of the water authorities made for more efficient planning but, though they were able to supply their own particular water needs, they were still not large enough to undertake and organise the necessary complex, long-term planning of new and greatly augmented supplies. The situation was aggravated by the fact that related problems such as drainage and flooding, river navigation, the control of effluents and pollution, together with agricultural, fishing and recreational rights lay outside their control. These were controlled by other authorities and interests such as the River and Drainage Boards, Public Health Authorities and the Ministry of Agriculture. To assist and rationalise the water supply position, the Water Resources Act was passed in 1963, which set up a new central authority, the Water Resources Board, whose task was to co-ordinate at national level the conservation and distribution of water resources and to undertake research into the water problem. The Act also established 26 new River Authorities in England and Wales who took over the powers and duties of the River Boards. The water and river authorities thus came to be responsible to the Water Resources Board. The new situation, however, was far from satisfactory since the Board was really only an advisory body: it had neither the authority nor the finance to act upon its investigations and recommendations.

The latest development in the history of the water industry is the Water Act of 1973. This Act, which coincided with the new local authority re-organisation, transferred control from some 1,600 assorted bodies to 10 massive new regional water authorities (R.W.A.s), who have control of rivers, reservoirs, water supply treatment and distribution, sewers and sewage disposal (See Fig. 3.6). One hopes that the new organisation will indeed provide a more efficient and effective water service, but we have long come to realise that bigger is not necessarily better, and of one thing we can be certain – water will be much more expensive.

The Water Resources Board in planning for future demand envisages that conservation and distribution arrangements will have to be vastly augmented. If one ignores the increased tapping of underground resources and the desalinisation of sea-water, additional supplies of water can be obtained in two main ways: by barrage schemes and by further reservoir construction. Schemes for barrages across the Wash, Morecambe Bay, the Solway Firth, the Dee and the Severn have all been mooted and serious studies of some of these

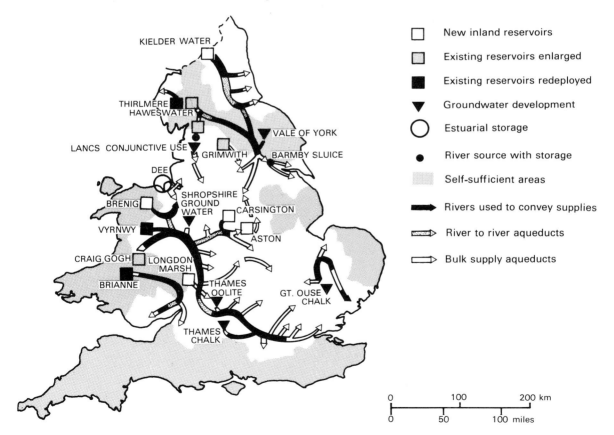

Fig 3.7 Water planning strategy for England and Wales

suggested projects have already been made. All these schemes, however, would prove to be very costly. The Water Resources Board sees that it may be necessary to embark upon barrage schemes sooner or later but comes to the conclusion that, "not more than two estuary sites should be developed in this century and not more than one at a time." The alternative to barrage schemes is to build more reservoirs but it is estimated that at least 30 would be required. The construction of large reservoirs, however, would be likely to meet with much opposition since a high proportion of them would have to be sited in the National Parks, and others would make heavy demands upon agricultural land. The upper Teesdale scheme, Rutland Water, and the suggested Dartmoor reservoirs have all incurred strong opposition.

The Water Resources Board Report comes to two main conclusions: (i) the management of water obtained from various sources must be done in a fully integrated way and (ii) there is a need to move water massively from the wetter to the drier areas of the country. The Board's strategy is illustrated in Fig. 3.7. The intention is, as far as possible, to use the rivers as natural aqueducts to carry water to the consuming areas. The transfer of water from one river to another could be effected by a measure of environmental engineering.

Lastly we must not forget that flooding is the most significant natural hazard in Britain. Heavy rain and melting snow frequently causes limited flooding in low-lying areas. Considerable areas were flooded in the West Country in the winter of 1979–80. Coastal flooding, often produced by the coincidence of high tides (particularly at the spring equinox) cyclonic rainstorms and on-shore winds, have produced damaging floods at irregular intervals, particularly along the east coast. A recent example was at Cleethorpes and the North Lincolnshire coast in the winter of 1977–8. Particularly at risk in this regard is London itself. Rapid urbanisation in the region has ensured that storm run-off reaches the river far more rapidly than was the case 75 years ago, so that flood levels are higher. Combined with strong tides this puts considerable areas behind the waterfront in central London at a high risk of particularly damaging and expensive flooding. The Thames barrage is the major response to this hazard, as a means of controlling tidal surges.

References

Miller, A.A. and Parry, M., *Everyday Meteorology* (Hutchinson, 1958). Chapters 4, 5 and 6.

Brooks, C.E.P., *The English Climate* (English Universities Press, 1954).

Gregory, S., 'Climate', in *The British Isles: A Systematic Geography,* ed. Watson & Sissons (Nelson, 1964).

Isaac, P.C.G., *Water, waste and wealth,* (University of Newcastle upon Tyne, 1965).

Rees, J., 'Water Resources', in *Resources for Britain's Future,* ed. M. Chisholm, (Pelican Books, 1972).

Rees, J., 'Money down the drain', in special feature on Water in *Geographical Magazine,* Vol. XLIX, No. 8, May 1977, pp. 493–7.

Rees, J., 'Rethinking our approach to water supply provision', *Geography,* 61, 1976, pp. 232–45.

Smith, K., *Water in Britain* (Macmillan, 1975).

Hanna, L.W., in *The U.K. Space,* ed. J.W. House. (Weidenfeld and Nicolson, 2nd edition, 1977) pp. 224–27.

4

Biotic Processes and Resources

ECOLOGICAL CHARACTERISTICS

Although Britain's ecological history is quite short – effectively only beginning with the final retreat of the ice after the Pleistocene glaciation – very little now remains of the natural pattern of vegetation established over the period between *c.* 10,000–3,000 B.C., largely because of the impact of agriculture. Since the introduction of farming techniques in the Neolithic (outlined in Chapter 5), natural processes of change attendant upon climatic fluctuation have been obscured by the hand of man. We can postulate that most of Britain, without man's interference, would have remained covered with woodland.

By the Roman period most of upland Britain had been cleared of forest; by A.D. 1000 the lowland deciduous forests had been seriously depleted, by 1500 they had been largely cleared and by 1800 virtually exterminated. At the present time only 8·1 per cent of Britain is occupied by woodland, the vast majority of which are afforestations of the last 150 years. Arable land currently occupies 29·3 per cent, pasture land 46·1 per cent, and other land uses account for the remaining 15·5 per cent. It is against this background, then, that we must view the three-fold division identified by Tansley in 1950.

Forest and woodland

Pine and birch were among the first trees to colonise Britain. Exceptionally hardy, the birch is capable of withstanding considerable exposure and now dominates woodland at the higher elevations (up to 600 metres). The Scots pine (*Pinus sylvestris*) has practically disappeared from Scotland, but paradoxically, being introduced into southern England, it has thrived on the heaths supported by soils such as the Bagshot Sands. The heavy soils of lowland Britain formerly supported oak forest (*Quercus robur*), with *Quercus sessiliflora* in drier situations. Ash is a common companion, still to be found in parts of the Lake District, where oak-ash woodland is a characteristic. Ash is dominant in the limestone districts of northern England, but in the chalk and limestone country of lowland Britain the beech (*Fagus sylvatica*) is very common, thriving in the well drained conditions of the Chilterns, and the Downland of southern England. The elm, where it has survived widespread Dutch Elm Disease, is more at home on the damper clays and loams, while along water courses moisture-tolerant species such as alder (*Alnus rotundiflora*) and the willow (*Salix*) are common.

Heathland and Moorland

Research suggests that most areas now covered by heath and moor were cleared of their woodland in the prehistoric period. They are, then, largely unnatural. The heathlands are generally dry, found on the acid, sandy soils typical of the Tertiary sandstones such as those in south-east England. The most abundant species is heather or ling (*Calluna vulgaris*). Moorland is generally wet, often supported on deep organic soils of almost pure peat. In upland situations, cotton grass (*Eriophorum vaginatum*) is common, along with *Sphagnum* in the boggier areas, also found in the lowlands.

Grassland

Britain's grasslands are composed of either deliberately sown pastures, or else relict vegetation resulting from woodland clearance. Former damp oakwood is marked by a *neutral grassland* of close turf and herbaceous plants; dry oakwood by *acidic grassland* dominated by bents. In higher areas we can distinguish between the spongy turf of the *basic grassland* of the Downs, the *nardus* and *molinia* grasslands on the acid soils of upland Britain, and the *arctic-alpine grassland* in the highest parts of northern Britain. In addition we should note the occurrence of locally significant areas of salt-tolerant species (e.g. *Salicornia*) common in coastal zones.

FORESTRY AND AFFORESTATION

By the beginning of the present century Britain found herself in a unique position compared with her continental neighbours: while most of the countries of Europe had between roughly 20 to 30 per cent of their area under forest and woodland and were more or less self-supporting in timber, Britain had only about 5 per cent of her area under forest and was supplying less than 10 per cent of her growing requirements. The First World War focused the attention of the Government on the country's timber resources, and in 1916 a Forestry Sub-Committee was set up to consider plans for ensuring that in a time of national emergency the country could be assured of sufficient home-grown timber supplies for a three year period. One of the recommendations put forward was that a Forestry Commission should be established (set up in 1919). Since that time a census of woodlands has been made at roughly twenty-year intervals and the Commission has done much not only to increase the area under forest but to rescue such woodlands as existed from the neglect into which they had fallen. Its work, though not completely free from mistakes, has been commendable and our forests and woodlands are now under capable management. Table 2 shows the distribution of woodlands by types and sub-types in 1965, the year of the last census made by the Forestry Commission.

The Second World War wreaked a heavy toll on Britain's timber resources, especially useful timber, i.e. mature enough to be cut. As a result, since 1945 there has been a vast amount of planting by the Forestry Commission. The heavy increase in death duties and capital transfer tax led to the break up of large landed properties and has in many cases discouraged private landowners from large scale planting of trees. Increasingly, planting is becoming a matter for the State. Nevertheless, some 60 per cent of Britain's woodland remains under private ownership, as against 96 per cent in 1924. Most of the broadleaved high forest is in private hands. On the other hand some two-thirds of the coniferous high forest is owned by the Forestry Commission. Since the economic demand is mainly for softwood, the Commission's policy has been to plant quick-growing conifers

Table 2: Distribution of woodlands by types and sub-types, 1965

FOREST TYPE	ENGLAND			WALES			TOTAL SCOTLAND			GREAT BRITAIN		
	'000 ha	'000 acres	%	'000 ha	'000 acres	%	'000 ha	'000 acres	%	'000 ha	'000 acres	%
High Forest												
Coniferous	332	822	38	131	323	65	453	1121	69	916	2266	53
Broadleaved	285	705	32	25	63	13	39	97	6	349	865	20
Total High Forest:	617	1527	70	156	386	78	492	1218	75	1265	3131	73
Coppice	29	73	3	–	–	–	–	–	–	29	73	2
Scrub and felled	283	590	27	44	110	22	163	402	25	490	1102	25
Grand Total:	884	2189	100	200	496	100	655	1620	100	1739	4305	100

Source: Forestry Commission, 1965

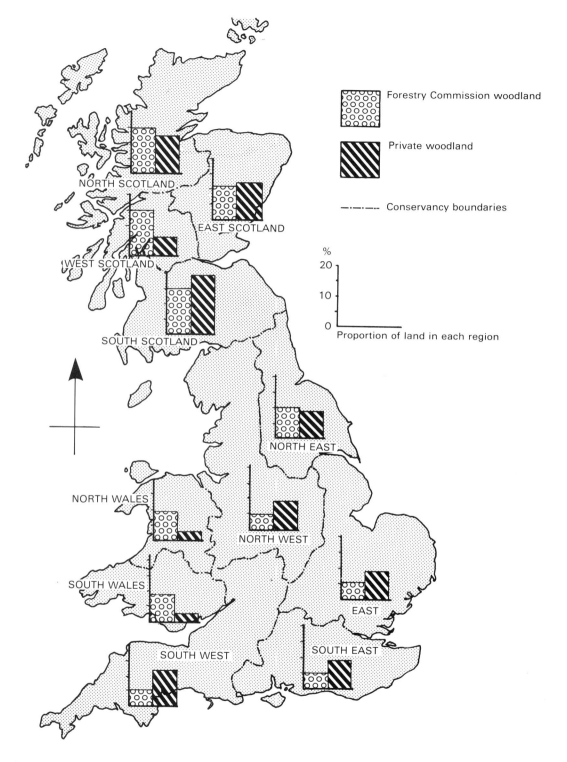

Fig 4.1 Relative proportion of Forestry Commission Conservancy to private woodland in Great Britain

such as Sitka spruce, Norway spruce, and lodge-pole pine. This policy proved unpopular with the public who disliked the great regimented areas of drab conifers. Now, partly because people have become familiar with them and partly because the Commission has begun to mix species to give variety, the antagonism is much less pronounced. Furthermore, with the adoption of a policy of limited public access, the Commission's work is beginning to be increasingly appreciated. The

State forests are widely distributed but there tends to be concentrations in Wales, northern England, the Southern Uplands and in the Grampians. Five of the largest forests – each over 10,000 ha (25,000 acres) – are in England, in the New Forest, Thetford Chase, Allerston in north-east Yorkshire, and Kielder and Wark in Northumberland. The Commission employs some 10,000 people, roughly half of the total forestry workforce in the country. However, despite these important developments, the amount of timber and by-products produced is only a small fraction of the country's total needs; for instance, in 1975 Britain spent £1,344 million on imports of timber and timber products, including paper and pulp.

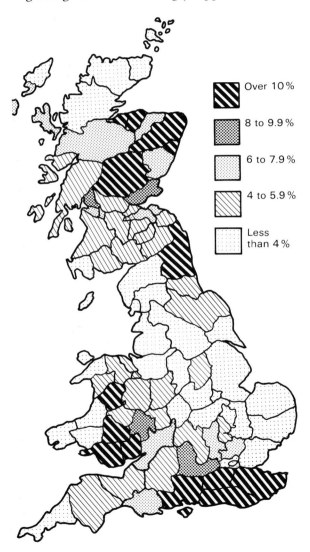

Over 10%

8 to 9.9%

6 to 7.9%

4 to 5.9%

Less than 4%

Fig 4.2 Wooded areas of Great Britain as in 1965

SOILS: GENERAL CONSIDERATIONS

Soil, the uppermost layer of the land surface, consists of weathered bedrock or transported rock-derived material which has been influenced and changed over a long period of time by the action of climate, the vegetation cover, and biological activity. At one time soil was looked upon as an inert mass of comminuted rock material, but nowadays we think of it as a dynamic substance which undergoes continuing change as a result of climatic variations, organic action and, not least, of human interference. Many soils develop *in situ*; others have been laid down by natural agencies, e.g. alluvial soils which have been deposited by running water; aeolian or loessic soils deposited by the wind; and glacial drifts by ice-sheets. Broadly speaking, British soils may be said to fall into three main categories according to their origin: soils derived from the underlying parent rocks whether these be the old, hard rocks of the north and west or the younger sedimentaries of the south-east; soils derived from drift deposits, the alluvium of river flood-plains, and marine silts; and soils derived from organic deposits such as the black, peaty fen soils and the acid, infertile moorland peat soils. The process of soil formation is normally a slow one and, in temperate latitudes, it is estimated that it takes about a century for one inch of soil to accumulate, but soil is very easily lost and in many parts of the world large areas have suffered soil erosion, i.e. the partial or total loss of the fertile top-soil. Fortunately, in Britain, soil erosion is not serious although it may occur locally as, for instance, on slope land which may be affected by rain-wash during torrential showers, or by prolonged drought as happened in parts of East Anglia during the hot, dry summer of 1976, when the soil became baked, cracked and crumbled, so that strong winds blew the powdered soil away.

From the farmer's point of view, the value of a soil depends (a) upon its chemical composition, that is whether it is acid, alkaline or neutral and whether or not it contains adequate amounts of the various mineral substances essential to plant growth; and (b) upon its physical character, that is whether it is coarse, fine, heavy, light, crumby, cloddy, etc., which affects its workability and its suitability for specific crops. Much can be done to modify soils: if they are acidic they can be limed, enriched if they are poor, lightened if they are too heavy, and drained if they are wet. The characteristics of a soil are important. Fineness of grain, or texture, for instance, determines the moisture-retaining capacity of the soil. The spongy character of the decayed organic matter of vegetable and animal origin which is present in most soils is also of considerable importance in this respect. Fine-textured soils, such as clays, are stiff and heavy and difficult to work; moreover, they are usually slow to warm up and so are 'cold' soils. On the other hand, a soil which is coarse-grained will have a fairly open texture which not only permits rapid drainage but enables air and warmth to circulate more freely; hence, gravelly and sandy soils warm up fairly quickly. Such light soils encourage earlier growth than heavier clay soils, though they have the disadvantage of drying out more quickly. Light, porous, sandy soils are usually very productive under irrigation. The best soils, generally speaking, are loams which are more permeable than clays, have a firm texture and are easier to work; these characteristics make them very favourable for cultivation.

Plants use the soil for two main purposes: as an anchorage and seedbed, and as a source of water and mineral salts. Unlike animals, plants manufacture their own food from water and carbon dioxide using sunlight as the source of energy. In order to do this they require small amounts of various mineral substances containing nitrogen, potassium and phosphorus, as well as certain trace elements. The plant secures these essential mineral

constituents from the soil solution (i.e. the soil moisture which holds dissolved salts) since plants cannot absorb minerals in their solid form. It follows, therefore, that the amount of moisture entering and held in the soil is of much significance. Abundant precipitation, or moderate rainfall with low evaporation, leads to soil infertility since, as the moisture percolates downwards, it absorbs the soluble substances present in the soil and carries them into the lower layers or *horizons* out of reach of plant roots. This process of *leaching* characterises the soils developed under coniferous forest. Pronounced leaching produces *podzol* soils, particularly in boreal forest. The plant litter – needles, cones, twigs – forms a thick layer of vegetable material which breaks down only slowly owing to the poverty of soil fauna and low temperatures, to form a strongly acid type of humus. Strong leaching gives these soils an ash-grey 'A horizon', but lower down they become iron-stained and brown, and a hardpan may develop which inhibits drainage and so may eventually lead to peat formation. Conversely, light rainfall and a high evaporation rate induce calcination, for salts are brought up to the surface by capillary action and deposited there. Excessive accumulation gives rise to saline encrustation.

Virgin land is commonly fertile and when put under crops will yield well for a number of years, but sooner or later the yield falls off. The soil can be kept fertile and productive only by careful management and systematic enrichment. Most of the cultivable soils of Britain have been used for several hundreds of years yet their fertility remains high. This continued fertility has been achieved in the past by resting the soil periodically and by the use of crop rotation, as well as by the application of animal manure, and, at present, by scientific crop rotation and the use of artificial fertilisers such as nitrates, potash and phosphate. The soils of Britain have been tilled and modified for so long that in many areas they have lost completely their original characteristics and qualities. Some soils, which in their natural state were poverty-stricken and difficult to work, have been so patiently worked, mixed, treated and fertilised that they bear little resemblance to the original soil and now yield prolific crops of high quality. In other words, the character of the soils at the present time is due as much to the modification wrought by man as to the originating factors of parent rock, climate, slope etc.

SOILS OF BRITAIN

For some of the reasons given above, it is not easy to classify soils in Britain. However, the British Soil Survey, in order to comply with the needs of the International Soil Map of Europe, and using the universally accepted soil classification based on the processes by which soils are developed, drew up a small-scale map which recognised six main categories:

(i) Podzolised soils of the uplands, e.g. the high-lands of Scotland, the higher parts of Wales, much of the Pennines and the Lake District, the North York Moors, Exmoor and Dart-moor in the south-west.

(ii) Podzolised soils of the lowlands, e.g. those of the north-east coastal areas of northern Scot-land and the coarse sandy areas of the north-west Midlands and the Hampshire basin, together with Bagshot Heath in Surrey.

(iii) Acid Brown Forest soils which occur mostly in upland areas and on their margins where the annual rainfall is more moderate; they are dominant in much of south-west Scotland, the coastal margins of Cumbria, and over most of Wales and the Southwest Peninsula.

(iv) Grey-Brown Podzolic soils found over much of the Central Lowlands of Scotland, north-eastern England, Yorkshire and the West Midlands: areas formerly under deciduous forest but which have long been cleared and cultivated.

(v) Grey-Brown Podzolic and Brown Forests soils mixed, which occur over much of south-eastern England, e.g. the Oxford Clay Vale, Bedfordshire, Huntingdon, much of East Anglia and north Kent.

(vi) Brown Forest soils and Rendzinas (shallow, dark, humus-rich soils developed on lime-stones in damp conditions or on Chalk); they are found on the limestone areas of the Cots-wolds and on the Chalklands of the south-east.

This classification does not take into account the many localised and specialised soils such as the organic soils of upland peats or lowland fens, or the meadow soils on alluvial flood plains, or various soils derived from varied drift deposits. Fen or mild peat accumulates when the water is rich in lime which neutralises the acids released by the decomposition of plants. When these low-lying peats are drained they give a thick, black, spongy soil of great fertility, and the Fenlands have become one of the most important arable farming areas in the country. The Fens and the Somerset levels illustrate particularly well the beneficial effects of human interference. The fine-grained alluvial deposits of river flood plains are widely distributed. Usually alluvial soils are rich in lime and humus, but where they are constantly flooded the lower levels may become waterlogged to give a gley soil.

There are many soils derived from the extensive drift deposits, e.g. boulder clay, glacial sands and gravels and brick earth. Spreads of boulder clay are common, but especially so in parts of eastern England where there is frequently an admixture of Chalk; such chalky boulder clay is often very fertile. Some fine loamy soils come from deposits of brick earth, a material related to loess, but deposited under more humid conditions. The soils derived from brick earth are mostly confined to the southern parts of England and are very fertile. In some places there are patches of sands and gravels, as around Sheriff Hutton in Yorkshire, which are of variable value but frequently infer-tile. Finally, mention may be made of a special type of deposit called 'Clay-with-Flints' which occurs on the chalk hills of Kent more particularly; it is a stiff, brownish clay with sharp, angular flints which is lime-deficient, in spite of its origin as a residual deposit from the weathering of chalk.

The leached siliceous soils of the upland areas and those developed on blanket peat are infertile and of little use for cultivation; in all probability they have altered but little over the centuries. The lowland soils, more especially those long given over to arable farming, show considerable divers-ity and, though they reflect the influence of the parent rock material, topography and climate, the influence of man is often clearly discernible. In some areas the soils have been altered very sub-stantially by ploughing, draining, fertilisation and crop rotation.

LANDSCAPE CONSERVATION AND USE

The physical landscape is dynamic rather than static in its character, but sometimes the changes are so gradual that in the countryside at least there

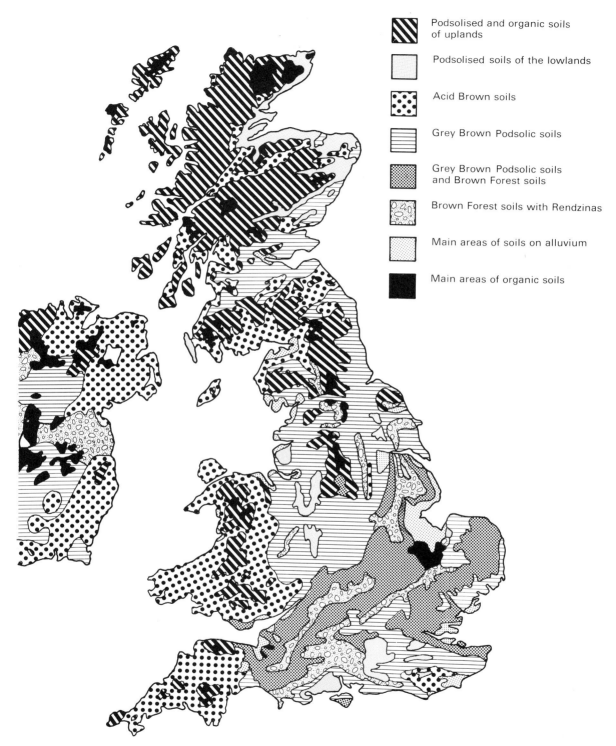

Legend:

- Podsolised and organic soils of uplands
- Podsolised soils of the lowlands
- Acid Brown soils
- Grey Brown Podsolic soils
- Grey Brown Podsolic soils and Brown Forest soils
- Brown Forest soils with Rendzinas
- Main areas of soils on alluvium
- Main areas of organic soils

Fig 4.3 Generalised soil types of the British Isles

43

seems to be no change. Those who live in urban areas are, in contrast, usually very aware of landscape changes for since the end of World War II there has been much re-building of town centres, slum clearance, and major highway construction.

Before 1945 there were relatively few motor cars and the urban dweller had little impact upon the rural landscape. Today the situation has changed dramatically: with 15 million cars on the roads and a highly developed system of motorway and primary roads, there are many areas which suffer from mass invasion in the summer or on fine weekends. Mobile man, indeed, is becoming a menace. As a result, the countryside, even in the more remote areas, is no longer sacrosanct and caravan sites, camping sites, second homes, broken walls, well-trodden paths, etc., attest to this new social pressure upon the rural landscape. But the impact is not wholly one of social pressure, for modern economics is also contributing to the changing landscape; for example in the interests of more economic agriculture, field hedgerows are being uprooted at the rate of about 1,600 km (1,000 miles) a year to create large fields more suited to mechanised farming. Slowly but surely the arable landscape is approaching the character it had in medieval times before the great enclosure movement began. Partly arising from these and other pressures on the landscape, and a growing consciousness among many that the traditional, inherited character of the countryside is being eroded away, a new appreciation and awareness of the environment has developed and something in the nature of a crusade for conservation and preservation has emerged.

Man's interest in, and concern for, the countryside is a relatively new development – although, of course, there have always been lovers of the countryside and of the wildlife which uses it as a habitat. The 'back to Nature' trend effectively had its beginnings in the Romantic movement when Wordsworth and the other Romantic poets called man's attention to the beauties of the natural landscape and quiet, unspoiled places. This idea became widely adopted and the countryside has as a result been increasingly viewed as an antidote to the pressures and problems of urbanisation (see Chapter 14).

The first official action in support of leisure time recreation and nature conservancy was the passing of the National Parks and Access to the Countryside Act in 1949, which led to the setting up of the National Parks Commission for England and Wales and of the Nature Conservancy. The first park, the Peak District National Park, was designated in 1951. There are now ten National Parks covering an area of 13,618 km or 9 per cent of the area of England and Wales. In 1966 the Countryside Commission took over the functions of the National Parks Commission and was given powers to promote further public enjoyment of the countryside.

With the spread of the motorway network which has increased their accessibility, the National Parks have become very popular since not only do they provide fine, and often spectacular, scenery but they provide a suitable location for a wide range of outdoor activities which include bird watching, pony trekking, fishing and, where there are stretches of water, boating, water skiing and other water-based sporting activities. In the Yorkshire Dales and Peak District parks there are opportunities for climbing, pot-holing and other strenuous activities. The very popularity of some, usually the more accessible, of the National Parks has created serious problems especially during the summer holiday season and on fine weekends when they are subject to overcrowding. The deluges of visitors not only lead to traffic jams and delays on roads which are not meant to carry heavy traffic, but to the need for parking and picnic areas in the principal beauty spots. Over-use, indeed, is tending in many cases to destroy the amenities for which the Parks were designated. Streams are often polluted, picnic waste is often left to litter the countryside, visitor's dogs often harass cattle and sheep, while farmers wage a constant battle against trespassers who tramp over their fields, knock down walls and leave gates open. In the Lake District, the lakes are becoming polluted and the rural quiet shattered by the drone of motor boats and water skiers. In many hamlets and villages properties are being snapped up by more affluent urban dwellers and converted into second homes.

There are other conflicting interests. Because many of the National Parks are in well-watered upland areas, they have tended to become valuable water catchment areas, and in the Lake District, the Peak District and Dartmoor for example, many lakes and man-made reservoirs store water for urban and industrial needs. Formerly such bodies of water were frequently out-of-bounds to the general public but now a more relaxed approach is being adopted by the Water Authorities and re-creative activities are being allowed on many stretches of water. Many National Parks offer valuable sites for afforestation and considerable areas have been planted with conifers. The Forestry Commission, however, has opened up certain restricted areas and provided leisure facilities for motorised visitors. Although Scotland has not as yet any National Parks, there are seven Forest Parks including Argyll, Glen More, Queen Elizabeth and Glen Trool Forest Parks. (See Fig. 15.4, on page 192).

Continued pressure from the 30 million annual visitors to the National Parks and Forest Parks has led to the suggestion that certain areas – core areas – within the Parks should be 'cordoned off'. In other words, these core areas, often mountainous or wild waste, should be forbidden to the motor car, rendered accessible only to the walker and placed out-of-bounds to any form of commercial enterprise. Only by such stringent measures, it is claimed, will the natural beauty and tranquillity be kept sacrosanct and the landscape preserved from degradation. Such areas – the High Peak, Snowdon, the central Lake District, central Dartmoor – would be cherished and rendered as inviolate as it is possible to make them.

In addition to the National and Forest Parks there are other areas of variable size which have been officially designated Areas of Outstanding Natural Beauty (A.O.N.B.s). In England and Wales there are over thirty such areas covering some 14,245 sq. km. (5,500 sq. miles) which include areas of mountain, fell and dale, cliffs, sand-dunes and tidal flats, with woods and wildlife, historic remains and delightful villages. While in theory the A.O.N.B.s are protected against desecration, uncontrolled building and industrial development, in practice, as in the National Parks, there is relatively little which can be done to conserve existing patterns of land use. Normal planning procedures for development control can be applied more rigorously, but the practice of agriculture – including forestry – falls outside planning legislation. While building developments connected with farming and forestry can be carefully monitored, the enlarging of fields to suit modern farming practice can go ahead regardless of any loss of landscape quality; similarly afforestation, as we have noted, can make massive changes in the landscape even in cherished areas.

References

Clark, J.G.D., *Prehistoric Europe* (Cambridge University Press, 1952).

Tansley, A.G., *The British Islands and their Vegetation* (Cambridge University Press, 1950).

Eyre, S.R., *Vegetation and Soils* (Arnold, 1963).

Robinson, H., *Biogeography* (Macdonald and Evans, 1972).

Bracey, H.E., *People and the Countryside* (Routledge and Kegan Paul, 1970).

Furmidge, J., 'Planning for Recreation in the Countryside', *Journal of the Town Planning Institute,* Vol. 55, 1968.

Board, C. & Morgan, B., 'Parks for People', *Geographical Magazine,* Vol. XLIII, June 1971, pp. 640–8.

Burnham, C.P., 'The Regional Pattern of Soil Formation in Great Britain', *Scottish Geographical Magazine,* Vol. 86, 1970, pp. 25–34.

Stamp, Sir L.D. and Beaver, S.H., *The British Isles* (Longman, 6th ed., 1971) pp. 103–133, 134–147, 148–159.

Part Two

Environmental History

5

Pathfinders and Settlers: The Peopling of the British Isles

INTRODUCTION

In the 1960s and early 1970s the people of the British Isles became conscious of a new population movement among them, as holders of British passports overseas exercised their right to come to the 'mother country' most of them had never seen. Almost two million people of African, Caribbean and Asian descent immigrated to Britain to add their talents, their culture, and their genes to those of the native population. Over the next few decades it is also likely that migrant workers from our partners in the EEC will take up residence in Britain, just as citizens of the Irish Republic already do in the United Kingdom. These are just the latest of a whole series of folk migrations that have brought people to the British Isles, migrations which have occurred since before the dawn of history, and helped fashion our environment to a greater degree than we might imagine. So, although this book is concerned with the contemporary British scene we must extend the scope of our study to include a short analysis of the peopling of the British Isles, and the way successive groups of migrants introduced new ideas which were to change the environment they found, and condition the landscape we can see today.

Although the British Isles were inhabited during the Pleistocene glaciation, the peopling of these islands effectively took 10,000 years, from the last retreat of the ice, to the conquest by the Normans who were the last significant group of migrants until relatively recent times. The folk movements had not come to an end, however, for although increases in the population were subsequently the result of natural increase rather than of im-

migration, there was much movement within the British Isles as colonists broke away from the original settlements to found new ones; or when groups of settlers left England or Scotland for plantations in Ireland; or later still when country folk moved to coalfield areas to man the growing industries of the eighteenth and nineteenth centuries. In each of these examples we can see the environment being modified and new living conditions being created, as settlement was progressively extended across the face of Britain, and as in recent times population was drawn more closely together to form the urbanised society that we know today.

However, our analysis begins in the cold and barren wastelands just being recolonised by plants and animal life 12,000 years ago. Over the succeeding millennia we can see many different groups of folk, whose names are unknown to us. We identify them either by their characteristic artifact or implement, like the *Beaker Folk*, or *Battle Axe Folk*, or else by the place where their culture was first investigated, like *La Tène culture* (La Tène is a site on Lake Neuchatel). However, it is important to remember that the fact that a group of people are identified with a place name does not mean that they necessarily originated from there, nor was that place their most important centre. It is simply a convenient label. In each of the major cultural successions – Mesolithic, Neolithic, Bronze and Iron ages – we can see distinct environmental changes taking place, many of which show to some extent the hand of man. How significant man was in either instigating or enhancing the rate and extent of change is, however, to a large degree problematical, and in some cases entirely hypothetical.

The problems stem both from the nature of the evidence and its interpretation. The evidence is in general slight, fragmentary and unevenly distributed. It falls into two categories: pollen analysis and other mechanical analyses such as lake sediment examination, and archaeological evidence. Pollen analysis is usually conducted on filaments of bog deposit extracted by a core. Obviously, then, such analysis can only take place where there are bogs, and these are not randomly distributed over the country. In fact their present distribution is skewed in favour of less habitable areas, at either very high or very low altitudes, which have not been the scene of more recent clearing and draining. A further distortion of the total spread of evidence is the activity of researchers. For a variety of reasons, for instance, the Lake District and the North York Moors have been more heavily worked over than some other areas, such as the Lancashire lowlands. Similar difficulties arise from the archaeological evidence. Once again we have to remind ourselves that the distribution of archaeological evidence does not accord to a representative sample. Stevenson reminds us that, "archaeological data contained in a distribution map are the product of two processes: first those that determined the original (i.e. real) distribution and secondly the factors that have affected the real distribution since its formation". We can add a third process – the actual techniques available for discovery, and the regional imbalance of research. A further problem, which relates to the evaluation of the evidence is that we have to take into account also all the other processes that were simultaneously at work in any given situation. Do changes in pollen counts, for instance, represent human, animal or climatic influences; and indeed, to how wide an area can be ascribed the typicality of a pollen count from a particular site?

PREHISTORIC ADVANCES

Although *Palaeolithic*-style hunters and collectors were present in the tundra waste of Britain over 12,000 years ago, it is only with the advent of the *Mesolithic* period, about 8,000 years ago, that we can tentatively detect the first signs of systems of land use that may have involved deliberate manipulations of the pattern of vegetation (Table 3). By this time climate had undergone very rapid warming during the Boreal period, tending towards a pronounced dryness. Successive plant colonisation had led to the establishment of elm, oak, hazel, birch and pine, and mature soil profiles had emerged. Over the succeeding 2,000 or 2,500 years, climate reached something of an optimum during the 'Atlantic' period, with a warm and wet oceanic type. Over this period Simmons (1975) envisages woodlands which are quite different from those we know today. They would have a "more or less unbroken canopy, below which tall unbranched trees would stand amongst a relative lack of shrubs and ground flora". This woodland may have extended up to between 250 m and 350 m according to local topographic conditions. In northern England the peat bogs of the Pennine plateaus were perhaps already forming, but between the high level bogs and the woodland cover lay a transition zone of mixed grass, scrub and open woodland that offered a good browse for herbivores and potentially a rewarding habitat for man.

Archaeological evidence for early human settlement comes mainly in the form of small assemblages of flints associated with hearths, suggesting small and temporary encampments. To begin with it seems likely that small family groups engaged in seasonal hunting forays, returning to more permanent base camps at lower altitudes in the winter. A celebrated Mesolithic site at Starr Carr in the Vale of Pickering may represent one of these sites. Subsequently, though, it is quite possible that there was a deliberate burning of the woodland cover to improve the quantity and quality of browse for the red and roe deer that were being hunted. Evidence from pollen studies certainly suggests interference by man, and a sharp rise in hazel pollens is a common occurrence at Mesolithic sites, perhaps a result of hazel recolonisation after burning. However, the numbers of people involved at this time were very small, and it is not until the Neolithic period that we can detect considerable environmental change that was almost certainly effected by man in both upland and lowland areas.

Neolithic folk were still stone users but they had assimilated the techniques of animal domestication and the cultivation of plants. The effect of Neolithic man on vegetation in the British Isles is a controversial subject, not least because the spread of the Neolithic arts coincided with climatic change, as the wet Atlantic phase passed into a drier period known as the sub-Boreal. Turner

Table 3:   Environmental change in the Glacial and post-Glacial period in Britain

CLIMATIC PERIOD	TIME	TENDENCIES	VEGETATION	SOILS	HUMAN OCCUPATION
Modern	*c.* 450 A.D.		Oak limit 1500 ft O.D.	Progressive modification by man	
Sub-Atlantic	*c.* 500 B.C.	Cool moist oceanic	Increase in birch and in s. beech and hornbeam	Acceleration of peat formation especially in uplands	
Sub-Boreal	*c.* 3,000 B.C.	Warm dry continental	Decline of elms. Increase of ash spread of birch and heather	Increased deforestation encourages soil leaching and podsolisation	Bronze Age. Settlement in English uplands
Atlantic	*c.* 5,500 B.C.	Warm wet oceanic (optimum?)	Mixed oak forest. Birch limited in N. and W. tree 2,500 ft	Beginning of peat growth in Pennines above above 1,200 ft	Neolithic farming
Boreal	*c.* 7,600 B.C.	Fairly warm and dry	Elm/oak/hazel birch and pine	Mature soil profiles	Mesolithic
Pre-Boreal	*c.* 8,500 B.C.	Sub-arctic	Birch, pine and juniper forest	Accumulations of humus begins soil profiles on stable sites	
Younger Dryas	*c.* 8,800 B.C.	Sub-arctic with local glaciation	Treeless tundra	Frost-affected raw mineral soil	

outlined two ways in which these early farmers seriously modified the natural processes of the climax forest. First was by shifting cultivation in which small plots of land were cleared by ring barking, felling and burning – demanding incidentally the use of the heavy stone axes for which the period is known – and then used for a few cereals, mainly wheat. The plots were abandoned after a few seasons and allowed to return to natural woodland. At least that is what would normally have happened in a stable ecosystem, but at a time of ecological stress, such as when climate changes, clearing such as this could have led to quite rapid soil erosion. A second way in which the woodland cover was affected was through the selective browsing of stock. In very many pollen diagrams there is a sudden and marked decline of elm pollens, and occasionally also lime and pine pollens, that has been attributed to the use of leaves and young shoots for cattle fodder.

Early Farmers

Radiocarbon dating now suggests that farming communities were established in many localities at least five thousand years ago, and the earliest migrants may have been established in Britain by 3,750 B.C. Archaeologists are now less interested than formerly in assigning sites to particular cultural types such as 'Windmill Hill' or 'Peterborough', and it is becoming increasingly clear that flint mines in southern England and axe factories in Highland Britain were providing the raw materials for a mixed farming economy in many parts of Britain, that adapted itself to local natural conditions. The most striking monuments left by late Neolithic and early Bronze Age folk are undoubtedly the standing stones, alignments and circles of megaliths that are found scattered throughout Highland Britain, and form part of a distribution scattered along the Atlantic fringes

Fig 5.1a Avebury Ring, Wiltshire. The celebrated stone circle at Avebury lies close to Windmill Hill and Silbury Hill which together form one of the most important Neolithic sites in Britain

of Europe. Once thought of as post-dating the monumental architecture of Egypt and Mycenaean Greece, corrected C_{14} dating has shown that they came first, and if there really is cultural diffusion linking the two areas the direction of the diffusion was from west to east, and not east to west. Thom has suggested that these arrangements were constructed on a basic unit, the 'megalithic yard', and that they were used for very sophisticated astronomical purposes, implying a mathematical understanding that pre-dated that of classical Greece by a thousand years. Such scientific understanding clearly demanded a degree of stratification in society, while the technology needed for the erection of the stones implies a high degree of control and organisation that must have had implications for the whole resource base of the people (Figs. 5.1a and b).

Fig 5.1b Silbury Hill. Dwarfing the passing traffic, the exact purpose of this Neolithic mound has yet to be satisfactorily explained

The Bronze Age

About four thousand years ago, the use of metal spread to Britain in the form of bronze, an alloy of copper and tin, and preceded, certainly in Ireland, by a copper-using phase of uncertain duration. Bronze was an expensive metal, and was more useful for ornament and armament than for common implements like hoes and axes. Its use seems to have been spread by in-breeding groups of smiths who penetrated a host culture. In Britain the host culture was overwhelmingly that of the *Beaker Folk*, originally a stone-using group who had established themselves several generations earlier. They were given their name by the archaeologist, Peake, because their most common artefacts were beaker-shaped vessels of various sizes that were used for a variety of purposes, including the burial of the cremated remains of the dead. There is a suggestion that they might have been responsible for the introduction of barley, and the use of barley for the drinking of beer, but very little is known about the day-to-day life of the early Bronze Age, as so many of their remains are associated with mortuary practices rather than day-to-day activities. Bronze Age finds are widely distributed throughout the country, with concentrations in the Eden valley, on the Northumberland lowlands, in North Yorkshire, Norfolk, and the South coast counties of Hants, Dorset and Sussex. During this period the sub-Boreal climate was drier than before, and this had considerable implications for colonisation and settlement. It seems likely that the permeable chalk and limestone uplands became too dry for cultivation, and were mainly used for extensive grazing, while areas like the North York Moors, or the valley terraces of the Midlands which had formerly been too wet to attract settlement, became the scene of new colonisation and clearance. The southern fringes of Dartmoor were used for both pastoral farming and grain cultivation by groups of people who had a close appreciation of soil quality. We must remember, though, that the numbers we are dealing with are small, even though they may have had an influence on the landscape out of all proportion to their size. On the North York Moors, for instance, Fleming has suggested that a population of less than 500 shifting cultivators was able to reduce wooded uplands to the heather-clad moors we know today within a span of 200 to 400 years.

The Iron Age

By about 500 B.C. damper and less sunny conditions came to prevail in a climatic period known as 'sub Atlantic'. Into these cooler conditions moved iron-bearing, horse-riding people with a knowledge of the wheel. These folk had been a major disturbing factor all over Eurasia. Wherever they moved their powerful combination of technical and military superiority had given them mastery over existing settled communities. From China to Spain these aristocratic warriors, bearing skills that had been developed in south-west or south-central Asia, carried all before them. Around 500 B.C. the Iron Age began in south-east England. Advance further west and north into the British Isles was hindered by the tangled topography of north-west Britain, an area less accessible to horsemen, and bronze-age cultures were to survive much longer in the more remoter areas of Britain. In the eastern coastlands of Scotland, around Dundee, for instance, although iron-age forts may have been established as early as 600 B.C., late bronze-age traditions survived almost until the arrival of the Romans, a situation similar to that which held in the north-east of England. Further north in Grampian, the degree of bronze-age persistence was much stronger, although there was a strong movement of population from the south into the north during the last centuries B.C. It is, perhaps, appropriate at this point to remind ourselves that what was happening in one part of the British Isles at any one stage during this early period was by no means happening in others, and that there was a great range in the level of material culture which was not necessarily a simple gradation from relative sophistication in the south-east to low levels of barbarism in the north-west. Nevertheless, Sir Cyril Fox was right in ascribing to the Highland Zone of Britain in general the characteristic of receiving new cultures later than the rest of Britain, and assimilating them into an already existing framework of ideas and techniques, rather than substituting the new techniques for the old. Certainly Freeman suggests that this is a fruitful idea in relation to Ireland. He points out that Ireland was not within such easy reach of the iron-age migrants who so revolutionised environmental techniques in eastern Britain, and that iron was only introduced into Ireland during the early years of the Christian era.

Iron as a raw material was much more accessible

than the copper, tin, or lead that were used to produce bronze, and it was, moreover, stronger and harder. As Gordon Childe pointed out, it was not bronze, but iron axes that cleared the forests of the Mediterranean, and the same is true for Britain. Iron could be used for axes and hoes, and for plough tips, as well as for armaments. With iron, man was given far better tools to exploit his environment. In a period of wetter climate the nutrients lost through leaching in the soil could best be returned to the surface by heavy ploughing, and the ploughman therefore prospered. With their new weapons the iron-using ploughmen could take by force if necessary, territory that was occupied by others, and in many parts of Britain heavily ramparted forts, often on promontory hills, proclaim to this day the military and economic triumph of the incoming iron-using folk (Fig. 5.2). All over southern and eastern Britain, forest pollens decline rapidly around 400–200 B.C., while grain pollens rise. On the slopes of the limestone and chalk hills we can today detect the faint traces of small square fields associ-

ated with clusters of circular huts, sometimes in the shadow of a nearby hill fort. The great attack upon the woodlands of Europe which was to characterise the Middle Ages had a herald in the later developments of the iron age, when perhaps far more of today's settlements were founded than an earlier generation of archaeologists would have thought likely.

New techniques and new ideas spread very slowly in a pre-industrial world, however, and at the beginning of the Christian era, when the *Romans* turned their attention to the British Isles, they found a variety of peoples living in a variety of environments, and exhibiting a range of cultures. The most advanced peoples were those that lived in south-eastern England, and in particular in the Essex region, although they had already penetrated into the Midlands. They were a relatively recent arrival, whom we know as the *Belgae*. They had arrived early in the first century B.C., and it is significant that they had established themselves in what had previously been a relatively untractable country of woodland and heavy soils. The Belgae

Fig 5.2 Maiden Castle, Dorset. Though inhabited earlier, the present fort owes its characteristics to Celtic invaders of the 1st century B.C.

had brought with them a heavier plough than previous settlers had possessed, a plough that was mounted on wheels, and was much more suited to tilling the heavier, but rewarding soils of the claylands. They were successful cultivators, able to raise up to 750 kilos of grain per acre, and so they prospered and expanded not only in area, but in numbers. Thus the Romans found a fairly thickly populated countryside of agricultural villages interspersed with a few larger centres. Without doubt earlier prehistoric folk had had tribal centres, associated with ritual and with the clan chief; undoubtedly, too, they had indulged in trading, sometimes of a very long distance nature, but never, as far as we can see, had they possessed anything like what we would recognise as a town – a permanent centre of substantial buildings devoted to trade, exchange, and craft working. The Belgae had a system of administration, and coinage quite beyond anything known further north in the remote fastnesses of highland Britain, and they influenced much of south-east Britain. Other tribes in eastern Britain, such as the Iceni of East Anglia, were at a high stage of development, if not equivalent to the Belgae; but further west and north, tribal groups appear to have been less advanced. In parts this is because we know less about them, in part also they were probably more inclined towards pastoral farming than widespread grain production, and thus they have left fewer material remains for us to find and investigate. The Brigantian group of folk, for instance, who occupied a large stretch of the Pennines are very largely an unknown quantity. In the far north, the Romans made little contact with people living in the Scottish highlands, and similarly never effectively encroached upon Ireland at all.

THE ROMAN CONTRIBUTION

The introduction of effective urbanisation to the furthest corners of the Empire was one of the greatest achievements of Rome. Associated with towns, of course, are the Roman roads – lines of communication that linked towns to their hinterland. Together these two elements without doubt engendered an environmental revolution, so that Britain was firmly tied into an international matrix of trading routes and sources of raw materials. Such a state of affairs lasted for ten generations or

so, but after the end of the fourth century A.D. much was lost, and the longer-term impact of Roman administration is a much more tenuous thing. Something that is certainly with us to this day is the addition of new genetic combinations as Roman troops from distant parts of the empire were brought to Britain and mixed with the native population. Another element is the Roman road network. More than 6,000 miles of Roman road are known to us, many, particularly the major trunk lines, still used as principal lines of communication. Over the succeeding centuries the Roman road network was to be used by invading peoples, with the consequence that Dark Age settlements usually shunned the zone along the line of the roads, which were often later to be used as township and parish boundaries.

Towns

Towns encouraged the development of trade, and stimulated agricultural production. Through the town, political control and magisterial government could be exercised, and the Roman arts of gracious living passed on to rude provincials. The most important Roman town in England was without doubt London (*Londinium*) with a population of *c* 25,000 one of the foremost cities of the Empire, and the hub of the British road system. It had some notable industries, especially glass making and pottery, but it was as a port and market that it flourished and then, as now, we can see London being specially concerned with service industries. The number of other Roman towns was relatively small: four *coloniae* (or colonies of Roman citizens, often retired soldiers), 12 tribal capitals and 50 or so other towns, like spas and garrison centres; and they were overwhelmingly found in lowland south-eastern Britain. Most towns were grouped around a central square where were found many of the principal buildings. On the central square converged the cardinal routeways through the town, bringing traffic from gateways in the walls. These gateways frequently conditioned the planning of subsequent cities on the sites of these Roman towns, for often the old Roman walls were used as a basis for medieval defences; and so the Roman road pattern of Chester and Chichester, for instance, is preserved today, passing through the city gates laid out in ancient times.

Countryside

Beyond the towns, and developed after them, was a scattering of villas – large farmsteads belonging to Romanised folk, where some of the comforts of urban life were reproduced out in the countryside (Fig. 5.3). Like the towns they are mainly found in lowland England, but recent work has detected a number of sites in the frontier zone of northern England. They varied greatly in size and sophistication. During the first two centuries of Roman rule they were relatively simple and tended even to decline during the third century A.D., but thereafter they enjoyed a remarkable renaissance. In some senses they were rather like the manor house of the Middle Ages, and alongside them there was often an associated group of huts which presumably housed the agricultural labourers. In two areas of lowland England the villa is unknown, although there are many crude villages of poor-quality housing. These are in the Fen margins of East Anglia and in Dorset, and it is thought that these areas were the basis of large state farms whose job was to supply the frontier troops of the north and west respectively with grain supplies. Certainly the Romans were responsible for increasing the area under cultivation, particularly for wheat, barley and oats, grown in small square fields and cultivated with a small light plough. The land was kept in good condition by application of organic waste and by liming. Domestic animals were kept, and the upland areas were

Fig 5.3 Model of the Roman palace at Fishbourne, Sussex. Not all Roman villas were as grandiose as this magnificent house constructed in the first century A.D.

already acting as a reservoir for stock. Wool was a principal export, particularly from south-west England.

Because material remains of mining and smelting activities tend to survive, there is a danger that we over-estimate the importance of Roman mineral working within their overall use of British resources. Nevertheless, mining was a common activity, particularly for iron. Ores from the Carboniferous, Jurassic and Cretaceous series were mined wherever they were found, but major areas of Roman iron-working were the Forest of Dean, and the Weald. Copper was mined in Wales, and tin in Cornwall, although Cornish tin was not so important as some writers in the past have tended to suggest. Above all, lead was important, particularly as it was a source of silver. All the known lead fields were exploited from Alston in the north Pennines to the Mendips in Somerset. The ore was mainly exported, but much was used to serve a growing pewter industry. Coal, too, was mined on most outcrops, and from the north-east, Tyne coal was carried back to East Anglia in the grain barges supplying the garrisons of the wall.

The level of environmental technique organised by the Romans was not to be achieved again for perhaps a thousand years, and meanwhile the British Isles was to be profoundly affected by the great European migration of peoples that has been called the *Völkerwanderung*, the folk wandering.

THE MIGRATION AND EARLY MEDIEVAL PERIOD

In a period of massive folk migration, often associated with warfare and tribal hostility, there was little hope of the settled values of Roman life surviving in any but the most attenuated form. However, the folk wandering did not start with the withdrawal of the Romans. Around the turn of the millennia peoples all over Europe were on the move, with clans and tribes migrating in a number of directions, but mainly to the west. Even Rome was sacked in the second century B.C., and the arrival of the Belgae in south-eastern England is not unconnected with these early movements. The expansion of the Roman Empire halted these movements for a while, but the pressure gradually built up behind the frontiers, and by the beginning of the fifth century A.D., Rome was finally obliged to withdraw her legions from Britain in order to protect the Empire nearer home.

Germanic Settlers

Throughout the third century A.D., the south-eastern shores of Britain had been subjected to raiding from across the North Sea. The Roman response to this had been the building of a series of coastal defences from the Wash to the Isle of Wight, along what came to be known as the Saxon Shore. During this same period the Scottish Uplands were reduced to protectorate areas, rather than being a continuously policed part of the Empire. A century later these territories, divided between the Damnonii of Strathclyde and the Votadini of the Lothians and Northumberland, were given the status of treaty states in their own right. At one and the same time this shows the increasing development of the marginal areas of the Empire, and the weakness of the central authority itself in the face of outside pressures. During the fourth century the defences of the Saxon Shore were extended northwards in a chain of signal stations lining the Yorkshire and Lincolnshire coast. In addition a further innovation was made. The Romans converted the Saxon raiders into Saxon wardens by giving them lands along the eastern margins of Britain on the understanding that they would prevent subsequent landings. This practice, begun under Roman rule, was continued afterwards and proved disastrous for the native British of lowland England. Despite the attempts of individual tribal chiefs, possibly commanders-in-chief like the romanticised Arthur, Germanic peoples under the general names of Angles, Saxons and Jutes penetrated lowland England during the fifth and sixth centuries. Controversy still rages on the process and effects of Germanic colonisation. There is now increasing opinion that the Germanic invasions were not so cataclysmic for the existing inhabitants as had been once thought. In some instances there must undoubtedly have been peaceful co-existence and eventually intermarriage. In other areas there must have been sporadic hostility and even genocide. A simplified model of colonisation has three stages. First, groups of mercenaries or tributary settlers are established in vulnerable areas. These groups then act as magnets for new settlers who eventually penetrate beyond the original area of occupation, to provide in the second stage a Germanic sphere of influence. In a third stage we can detect the overthrowing of the local British chiefs and vigorous military campaigns over the surrounding countryside, with the eventual establishment of Anglo-Saxon kingdoms. Thus were formed Bernicia and Deira, later to become Northumbria, founded by Anglian folk, like neighbouring Mercia, and East and Middle Anglia. Wessex, Essex and Sussex were colonised by Saxons, with Jutes in Kent and the Hampshire basin. Further west, Germanic influence becomes progressively weaker towards the 'Celtic' territory of Cornwall and Wales, while in the northeast of England a strong sub-stratum of Celtic customs persisted well into the Middle Ages.

Today, of course, we can see very little of the earliest settlements for they were very frail and have been rebuilt on or around the same site many times since their original foundation. Occasionally a pre-Christian cemetery is discovered, and in a few places like Escomb in Co. Durham and Wareham in Dorset we can see the remarkable survival of small late Saxon churches, not important of themselves at the time of their building, but interesting to us as small links with a long-distant past (Fig. 5.4). Because of the very scant archaeological remains we know very little about the form of these early settlements. The pattern of natural vegetation that existed at that time must have been a guide to settlement location, but to us it now seems that these early settlers had an unerring eye for finding the driest sites in wet lowlands, along with patches of more rewarding soils in the mixed glacial deposits of the eastern lowlands. Of course settlements which were not founded in such advantageous positions may have perished.

Fig 5.4 Escomb Church, Bishop Auckland, Co. Durham. A rare survival from the Anglian period, this little church was built of squared masonry robbed from the nearby Roman fort at Binchester (*Vinovia*)

Much of our understanding of this colonisation formerly sprang from place-name study. It was argued that areas with Anglo-Saxon names were occupied by Anglo-Saxons, etc. By the same means the generalised sequence of settlement could be discovered, for the earliest settlements were usually referred to by the name of the occupying group. The suffixes *ing* (*ingas* in Old English), meaning 'people (of)', *ham* meaning 'home', and *ton* meaning 'township', show the gradual gradation of first settlement, then homestead and later increasing territoriality of the early colonists. However, while the absence of place names belonging to a particular ethnic group may mean that that group was not present in an area, the reverse is not necessarily the case. A complete matrix of Anglo-Saxon place names for instance does not necessarily mean that every place was

founded by Anglo-Saxon colonists and that no Celtic or subsequent Scandinavian settlers were present (Fig. 5.5).

What is clear is that the seventh and eighth centuries saw an expansion of population, probably based on natural increase as much as migration, for a period of climatic amelioration prolonged the growing season, increased the number of good harvests and helped reduce the susceptibility of the population to disease and famine. With an increasing population, more settled conditions and an expansion of settlement, this period is seen as one of great cultural efflorescence, as Christian missionaries united England once more to the cultural mainspring of Rome and the Mediterranean.

Scandinavian Settlers

The Anglo-Saxons were not to be the last group of invaders, for towards the ninth century a new wave of people swept down from Scandinavia. Just as climate was helping the Anglo-Saxon/Celts to prosper in England, so also cultivation in more northerly latitudes had become more successful, and population had increased. An improvement in climate also allowed easier sea travel, and an increasing population in Scandinavia, newly equipped with fast sea-going vessels, expanded west over the sea. They colonised Iceland, the Faroes, Greenland and even Newfoundland, but they also turned south and made landfalls in Britain, northern France, Sicily and southern Italy. We can divide them into three groups, Danes, Norse, and Norman.

The Danes first appeared on the eastern coasts in 787/9 A.D. They continued raiding the coasts for half a century and in 850 A.D. wintered on the Isle of Thanet. Over the following 150 years much of southern Britain was harried by sporadic warfare during the course of which the Danes gained control of much of northern and eastern England. The dramatic events of the ninth century are recorded in the Anglo-Saxon chronicle, and by the end of the century the Danes had established themselves over a wide area roughly north and east of a line from the Thames to the Mersey. Danish settlement, today marked by the preponderance of Danish elements in place names (*by*, *thorpe*), was particularly strong in Yorkshire, Lincolnshire and Norfolk. In many areas Anglo-Saxon place names were Scandinavianised – and

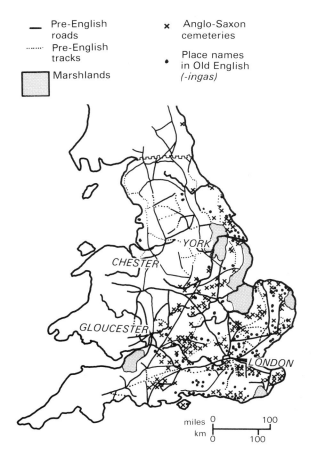

Fig 5.5 Anglo-Saxon Settlements

occasionally re-Anglicised – a fluid situation involving the substitution of landlords rather than populations; but in other areas, Danish settlement occupied quite distinct areas. The movement of the war bands along the line of Roman roads, for instance, is marked in Kesteven by the preponderance of Danish names within four miles of the road from Stamford to Lincoln (Fig. 5.6).

Scandinavian settlement in western Britain, however, was largely accomplished by Norsemen from western Scandinavia, sailing around the northern tip of Scotland and moving into the Celtic Sea by way of the North Channel. They made landfalls on the Irish coasts in the last years of the eighth century, and as the Danes in England

they ravaged and pillaged – and settled the land – intermittently for two hundred years. Just as the Danes had been responsible for developing the 'Five Boroughs' in England (Lincoln, Stamford, Leicester, Nottingham and Derby) so the Norse later fostered town life in Ireland, establishing trading ports at Dublin, Waterford, Cork and Limerick. The Norse used Ireland as a springboard for colonisation in Britain, both in southwestern Scotland and northern England. These migrants were not specially warlike and tended to occupy areas that had not previously been settled. Thus Norse place names are today associated with remote land of only marginal agricultural value, the low-lying coastlands of Lancashire and

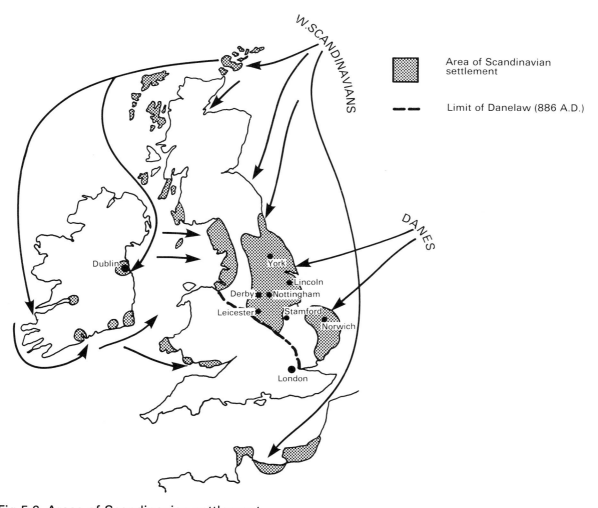

Fig 5.6 Areas of Scandinavian settlement

Cheshire, the higher lands of the interior of the Lake District and the Pennines. From here Norse settlement spilled over the watershed into the Pennine Dales, where the scattered field barns of Swaledale in particular still give the area a Scandinavian character that is quite different from the nucleated settlements with Anglian names in the lower parts of more southerly dales. The trading interests of these people should not be overlooked, however, for under them York became not only a capital city but a major hub of trade.

The last group of Scandinavians to reach the British Isles came by such a roundabout route, that they were barely recognised as Scandinavian at all, for they brought with them a Romance language and a largely Latin society. The Normans, though, were certainly Scandinavians who had established themselves in northern France early in the tenth century, where the fair-headed folk of Calvados are their descendants today.

From there two further expansions were promoted first south again, across the Mediterranean to Sicily and southern Italy, and secondly across the Channel to England, where the Norman royal line and a ruling aristocracy were established by force over the period 1066–72. The impact of this ruling minority group with its military might and administrative capabilities had a distinct, and long-lasting effect on the landscape of England and Wales, which was much greater than the castle-building and cathedral-founding that are their visible remains today (Fig. 5.7). We shall examine these effects in detail in the next chapter.

The Domesday record of William I (1086) gives us a unique picture of parts of England at the close of this period of folk migrations. The Domesday Books are not easy to interpret for they are a tax collector's record, and not a geographical field report. They are deficient in that the four northern counties are not included, and we now know that

Fig 5.7 Durham Castle. The massive stronghold of the Bishops of Durham when they were not only great landlords but also the King's regent. The castle was begun in 1075

some existing settlements were omitted. Similarly, the returns from some towns, and particularly London, are either absent or incomplete. Comparisons are very difficult to make because, for example, land measurements in 'carucates', 'bovates' and acres vary across the country, and woodland is sometimes measured in leagues and sometimes in terms of the number of pigs it would support! Nevertheless, the picture that is presented shows a countryside which is being vigorously exploited. With the exception of the undrained marshlands that were to be reclaimed much later, most of the better-quality land was under the plough, while uncleared land was used for pasturing. Population densities were highest in southern and eastern England, with more large villages and very many more churches. Unfortunately the picture in Yorkshire is confused because of recriminations against insurgents, but even there it is clear that the best-quality land was supporting population densities and providing tax returns as high as other good agricultural regions.

The Normans were the last major infusion of new blood into the British Isles for almost nine hundred years, but the succeeding centuries were to see the descendants of these early pathfinders and settlers taking possession of the whole land of Britain.

References

Stevenson, J.B., 'Survival and Discovery', in *The Effect of Man on the Landscape: The Highland Zone,* eds. J.G. Evans, S. Limbrey and H. Cleere, C.B.A. Research Report No. 11, London, 1975.

Simmons, I.G., 'The Ecological Setting of Mesolithic Man' in *The Highland Zone, ibid.*

Pennington, W., 'Vegetational History in the NW of England: a Regional Synthesis', in *Studies in the Vegetational History of the British Isles,* eds. D. Walker and R.G. West (Cambridge University Press, 1970).

Turner, T., 'Post-Neolithic Disturbance of British Vegetation', in D. Walker and R.G. West, *ibid.*

Thom, A., *Megalithic Sites in Britain* (Oxford University Press, 1967)

Fleming, A., 'Bronze Age Agriculture on the Marginal Lands of North East Yorkshire', *Agricultural History Review*, Vol. 19, 1971, pp. 1–24.

Fox, Sir Cyril, *The Personality of Britain*, 4th edition (National Museum of Wales, 1959).

Freeman, T.W., *Ireland: a General and Regional Geography*, 4th edition (Edward Arnold, 1969).

Jones, G.R.J., 'Multiple Estates and Early Settlements', in *Medieval Settlement*, ed. P.H. Sawyer, (E. Arnold, 1976).

6

Pre-industrial Environments: Making the Land their own

Until the nineteenth century, the British Isles were occupied preponderantly by a rural population and only a small minority gained their living other than directly from the land. The greater part of the British Isles is still countryside, of course, but now only a minute proportion of the population (less than two per cent) is directly dependent upon the land for their living. The environment of our pre-industrial ancestors was therefore very different from ours in almost every respect. Even the surface of the land was different. Although the mountains of Scotland and the uplands of England were as surely there as they are today, their covering of vegetation was in many places quite different. Much of midland England, for instance, was covered with thick oak woodland, and considerable areas of coast and estuary land was made up of marsh and fen which were to be drained during the Middle Ages and afterwards. Thus, settlement was at first funnelled along corridors of more easily tillable land, and it was only as population increased, sometimes encouraged by slight climatic change, that the woodlands, the fenlands and the highlands were effectively penetrated and permanently settled.

The present day pattern of rural settlement owes much to this early medieval occupation, although there is now growing evidence that township or parish areas are more significant than village sites. The specific siting of a present day village may well relate as much to now vanished vegetation patterns as to individual springs, or patches of dry ground evident today. Nevertheless, in parts of lowland England the regular spacing of villages along scarp foots, or on elevated valley terraces, is a well known and characteristic feature. In many parts of midland,

northern and western England, though, the more common settlement form is the hamlet or individual farmstead. It is now realised that the settlement history of such districts is very complex, and often too ancient to be glibly ascribed to a pastoral tradition rather than a tradition of co-operative village arable farming.

AGRICULTURAL TECHNIQUES AND RURAL LAND-USE

Arable Farming

A characteristic feature of medieval agriculture was the use of the heavy mould-board plough, which needed up to four pair of oxen to draw it through the ground. With this was produced a long sinuous strip of ploughland, the relics of which we can still see in many places today as 'ridge and furrow' (Fig. 6.1). The ploughed land around a medieval township was made up of 'bundles' of parallel ridges, and the bundles themselves were arranged into fields. The ridges of ploughed land and the bundles were called by different names in different parts of the country, but the ridges were commonly called *lands,* or *selions,* and the bundles were sometimes called *shotts,* or *flatts.* We often refer to this system of agriculture as open field farming, for there were no permanent walls or hedges around strips, or groups of strips, but only grass walkways or balks which allowed access to the various parts of the fields. The system is also sometimes referred to as 'common-field' farming, for this is another aspect of the system which was found in some areas, at some period. In such cases the whole area of cultivable land was used by the whole community and *lands* might change hands from year to year. All the holders of *lands* in a particular *flatt*, or even in a whole field, would grow the same crop, either winter or spring sown grain, along with peas and beans. After the harvest the entire stubble area would be thrown open for the grazing of all the village stock in common 'horn by horn and bite by bite'. Most striking of all, however, was that the land would be tilled only for two successive years before being allowed to lie fallow and recover its fertility for a year. The system of open common field farming was far more flexible than was once thought. There were often more than three fields and the unit of rotation may not always have been an entire field. Indeed there were regional variations on the basic two or three course crop rotations. Gradually the system of strip distribution and common arrangements came to be modified and degrees of permanency and privacy were introduced, until in some places,

particularly in northern England, the system gradually faded away to be replaced by the now familiar system of private farms. In other areas, particularly in the south Midlands, the system fossilised and could only be changed at one fell swoop in an agreed Act of Enclosure.

However, medieval farming was not just a matter of ploughing, for stock were kept, often in considerable numbers. Unfortunately, we know less about peasant animals than we do about peasant ploughing. Sheep and, especially, cattle were the major animals. The horse was not generally used for draught, but was mainly kept by the wealthy for riding. Just as some land was reserved for tillage, then so also some land was reserved for stock. Although stock had use of the fallow land, and the stubble after the harvest, this was not enough, and other land had to be provided. The plough oxen which were so important were often provided with pasture reserved for their sole use, and there are many field names today which

Fig 6.1 Ridge and furrow, Padbury, Bucks. The medieval pattern of ridges and furlongs is here overlain by more recent field boundaries. Note the sinuous strips to the right of the road

reflect this – Ox-Close, Ox-Pasture, etc. Second-ly, there had to be provision for winter feed, and this was mainly met by meadow hay. Meadow-land was often land that was too wet for the plough. From early spring until the grass was cut stock were not allowed to graze the meadowland, but after the hay making the animals were folded on the meadow so that their droppings would fertilise the ground, and by eating the old stubble, new growth would be encouraged the following year. Lastly, around the improved land would often be found uncleared and uncultivated land that could be used for extensive grazing. Open pastures on permeable land were ideal for sheep grazing, and woodland was used for swine, but animal manure was so important as a fertiliser, that stock were often brought in for the night so that their droppings could be saved.

Pastoral Farming

It would be quite wrong to think that this mixed arable system was followed all over Britain, for it was mainly confined to lowlands, and even here there were many differences in technique and stock-grain ratios that matched variations in the quality of the land. However, wherever the En-glish migrated they took with them their practices of open field common farming, and so in the 'Englishrys' of the Welsh borders and in areas of Norman settlement in Ireland, elements of this system of agriculture were to be found. In the majority of these western and northern areas, though, quite different systems obtained. In west-ern districts of Ireland, for example, the plough itself was a much more primitive implement, described by Estyn Evans as little different from the plough of the bronze age. In many places in these districts, the very stony quality of the soil made the spade and the *caschrom* (or digging stick) much more useful implements, with the result that fields were little more than small cultivated plots. One important characteristic of Irish farm-ing was the *lazy bed,* still used for potatoes, but formerly used for other crops. Its name derives from the fact that the potatoes are simply placed on the ground, and the soil piled over them in long rows. The sod underneath the lines of potatoes is thus not broken. The system was mainly tooled with spades and was also known in the Scottish Highlands.

The pastoral tradition was particularly impor-tant in the uplands of the peripheral regions. But even here agriculture was more important than has perhaps been suggested, and it now seems clear that the basic unit of settlement in medieval Wales, for instance, was a small township of co-operating farmers, using some kind of open field system. In many parts of highland Britain, and particularly in Scotland, an 'infield-outfield' system of agriculture was practised. By this means a relatively small area of land immediately about the settlement was permanently tilled. This was the *infield,* and its fertility was maintained by folding stock upon it. The yields of this area were supplemented from temporary fields which were opened up in the extensive wastelands which surrounded the village, the *outfield.* These tempor-ary clearings would be cultivated for one or two seasons, and then allowed to revert back to 'natu-ral' conditions, while another area was cleared. By this means the land was allowed to regain its fertility. In the passage of time some of these temporary clearings came to be permanently established settlements, offsprings of the parent village.

Monastic Granges

Such, then, were some of the diverse practices by which the medieval environment was harnessed, but this was not a static system, and there were a number of elements in it which made for change. One of these was the monastic tradition, and in particular the growth of the Cistercian order in England in the twelfth century. For various reasons, not always pious, many monastic houses were endowed with land and so became major landholders. Often grants of lands were made up of small peasant holdings, and so subject to all the common customs of land in a village community. These could be rented out, or else tilled by lay brothers, but they often became the core of a farm as we know it today – an area of land that was set apart from the communal system, with all its land together, and not spread about a number of fields; if this happened, they were tilled individually, not according to village custom. Indeed, it is from such ventures that we get our name farm, for these areas of land, called by the monasteries *granges,* came to be leased or *farmed out* to a tenant. The

Fig 6.2 Fountains Abbey, North Yorkshire. Beyond the ruins of the Cistercian Abbey can be seen Fountains Hall built by Sir Stephen Proctor from Abbey stone in 1610

tenant was thus a *farmer,* and his holding a *farm.* In a more spectacular way, however, the Cistercian order was responsible for settling considerable upland areas in western England and Wales, harnessing rough grazing land for commercial sheep farming. The ascetic character of the Cistercian order encouraged communities of monks to establish themselves in remote areas, and undertake manual work. The zeal and piety of these monks commended itself to landholders, who were often willing to make grants of quite extensive tracts of empty, apparently poor quality land. Over the

succeeding two centuries, the monks and their tenants were to make this land much more rewarding, and their hand can be seen upon the landscape even today. In remote valleys like the Rye and Skell in Yorkshire, the grand remains of Rievaulx and Fountains Abbeys testify to the effectiveness of monastic land holding (Fig. 6.2). The Cistercians were not alone in improving land, for Benedictine Abbeys like Glastonbury and Crowland were responsible for draining fenland in Somerset and Lincolnshire respectively, and making it very fertile.

Climatic Change

Another quite unexpected element of change was climate. We must remember that the medieval farmer was much more dependent upon the weather than are farmers today. When agricultural technology was at a relatively simple stage, subtle changes in climatic conditions could have a profound effect upon crop yields. Let us briefly examine the slight climatic changes that occurred during the medieval period, and see how they had a crucial effect. First, the climate tended to improve towards the latter half of the twelfth century, and during the thirteenth century. Winters became milder, and summers drier. Thus, the growing season for grass was prolonged, grain harvests became more substantial, and thus more food could be produced. This tended to promote an increase in population. Similarly, the mild winters meant that more of the vulnerable sections of the community – the very young, the old and infirm – would survive the winter, for we must remember that the standard of housing and clothing for the mass of the population was very low indeed. As the population expanded, so there was a need to grow more food, and this was satisfied not by improving agricultural techniques, but by bringing more land into cultivation. During the twelfth and thirteenth centuries, then, we can see a great colonisation of land taking place. Great inroads were made upon woodlands and also upon marginal lands, for climate had a role to play here too. As the winters became milder, and the summers drier, land which was previously too exposed, or too wet for cultivation became open for ploughing. During this period we see a marked thrust into the uplands of Britain, and in many places, like county Durham, for instance, newly-laid out villages were planted by great landlords. This period saw a great flowering particularly of the English countryside, and the accumulated wealth we see displayed today in the splendid parish churches and cathedrals of England, was achieved in part during this period of rather better climate.

However, climate could, and did change for the worse, and during the fourteenth century colder winters and wetter summers took away much of the benefits of the earlier period of better climate. Settlements on or near the margins of cultivation were the first to suffer, and we can see a perceptible retreat of cultivation to rather more congenial areas.

The Black Death

At this critical time, however, a dreadful event occurred. A particularly virulent form of the plague, the *Black Death,* struck western Europe as a whole. Plague was endemic in medieval society but this particular attack was more severe than most, and coming in conjunction with poor climatic conditions its effect was drastic. It swept through a population weakened by a period of poorer harvests and severe winters, killing not just directly, but also indirectly through pneumonia. Indeed, Shrewsbury has argued that more people died of pneumonic plague, than of the bubonic plague itself. The effect of the Black Death was to reduce the population as a whole by about one third. The plague reached into every region of the country, but its effect was varied. Some communities were completely wiped out, while others escaped infection altogether. Nevertheless such a massive loss of the working population obviously affected the way in which the environment could be harnessed. When labour was short, then less labour intensive techniques had to be adopted, and in many places the old system of peasant farming was dealt a major blow. When landlords were faced with depopulated villages their response was sometimes to give over all the former plough land to wide pastures for sheep grazing. Another alternative was to till all the land as one unit, needing only labourers, and not tenant farmers. Either way the demand for labour was less, while the general profitability of the land was often raised. In the century and a half in which the population recovered from the massive onslaught of the Black Death, many other landlords saw the advantages that could be gained from turning their lands over to sheep farming. The result was that many once-thriving villages were abandoned as the peasants were either killed off by the plague, moved to other settlements, or were evicted by their landlords. Research has now proved the existence of over 2,500 *deserted medieval villages* although not all of these desertions can be attributed to the Black Death (Fig. 6.3). In some ways this is fortunate for the archaeologist, for by careful excavation, much can be learned of every

Fig 6.3 Distribution of deserted medieval villages in England (sites known in 1968)

day life in medieval England. Elsewhere, more modern developments have obscured what a village was like in the fourteenth or fifteenth centuries.

Over the medieval period we have seen how there was first of all an advance over the country-side, as more and more land was cleared. Then during the fourteenth century we can see a retreat partly due to poorer climate, partly due to the Black Death and its aftermath, but partly also due to the quickening pulse of urban life, industry and trade, each of which offered alternative means of making a living, and it is to these elements of medieval life that we must now turn.

TOWNS AND TRADE

The conventional view of medieval agriculture as a broadly self-sustaining system still holds good in great measure. The inference from this is that towns were not of very much significance and certainly in terms of the numbers of people involved this is very true. A county town would perhaps have no more than two or three thousand inhabitants, a local market town less than one thousand. Nevertheless towns did exist, and their main function was to act as points of exchange, in some cases as centres of industry, and also as points of consumption.

Urban Genesis

The towns that were established during Roman rule of Britain did not survive the turbulent years of post-Roman colonisation. Although some of the most important medieval towns were established on or near the sites of these Roman centres, there is very little evidence to suggest that there was continuous *urban* life at these places although there is likely to have been some sort of continuity at places such as York, London and Carlisle. We can expect that town life lingered longest in those parts of south-eastern Britain where it was most strongly established, but the fact remains that during the post-Roman period recognisable towns all but vanished, and it is only in the eighth and ninth centuries that we can see a resurgence in England. Wales and Scotland were at least a century behind, and indeed, the town was almost an alien cultural form in Wales, Ireland and the Scottish highlands during the Middle Ages.

When towns were re-established it was once again south-eastern Britain that was in the forefront. Attempts to resist the Danish armies encouraged the Anglo-Saxon kings to organise their lands into a central place system based upon the common defence of a fortified place – a *burh*. Some of these *burhs,* like Wareham in Dorset, later grew into proper towns, with permanent buildings and periodic markets. Some came to have mints for producing the small money needed for small scale trading. On the other hand the Danes themselves promoted towns. As Danish armies wintered at particular places they established permanent bases, and from these grew the five boroughs of Lincoln, Derby, Stamford, Nottingham and Leicester. With the exception of Stamford, these all became shire towns. Shire towns apart, though, other urban centres were overwhelmingly located in south-eastern England, until well into the Middle Ages, London, Canterbury and Winchester were important centres, and during the course of the twelfth century urbanisation became stronger in northern and western England. More systematic royal taxation over this period enables us to see the relative wealth of places. During the first quarter of the twelfth century London's nearest rival in importance was Winchester, contributing two thirds as much as London to the royal coffers. By the third quarter of the same century, though, Winchester had been displaced by York, and London had increased its lead in importance. We can see two trends here. The first is that London is re-asserting its Roman dominance, and becoming overwhelmingly large. The overcrowded conditions of south-eastern England are a major feature of our times, yet London has been disproportionately large for most of its recorded history. The second trend is the moving of the urban tradition further out into northern and western Britain. Chester, Newcastle and Bristol, as well as York, Lincoln, Coventry and Norwich begin to assume importance. In part this is a reflection of population expansion and colonisation in these formerly marginal areas during the period of climatic amelioration. With a busier countryside, clearly more towns were needed. In addition, though, these towns expanded because of an expansion of trade and industry. Figure 6.4, for instance, shows that in northern England at the beginning of the Norman period boroughs were confined to the lowlands. Subsequently they were established at garrison towns on the major routeways, especially along the main north-south drifts either side of the Pennines. Western regions tended to be provided with boroughs much later than the east, while the medieval penetration of the Pennine valleys is reflected by the foundation of boroughs during the later thirteenth and early fourteenth centuries.

Both trade and industry were based upon wool. Newcastle, York, Lincoln and Norwich were *staples* at some time during the medieval period, and so were centres through which the trade in raw wool to the low countries and to Italy was concentrated. In addition, Coventry, York, Lincoln and Norwich were important centres of cloth manufacture, although only Norwich was able to maintain its industrial function into the later middle ages. At York, the introduction of the fulling mill and the close restrictions of the guilds forced the cloth workers out into the southern Pennines. At Norwich new specialist techniques, introduced from the continent, allowed Norwich in particular, and East Anglia in general, to capture the major part of the English production of better quality woollen cloth. The expanding wool textile industry had a profound effect upon the English landscape. We have already noted how stretches of ploughland were turned into sheep walks. The wealth that was gained by trade and manufacture alike was turned into handsome houses and the exceptionally fine churches that are to be found in the Cotswolds, East Anglia, and parts of the

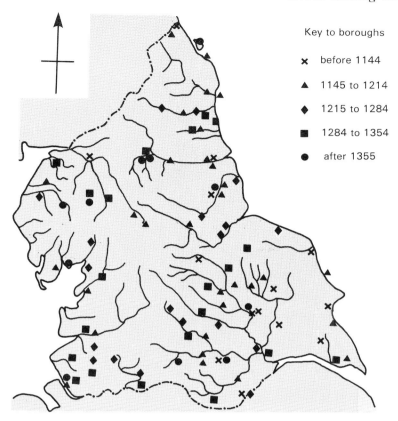

Key to boroughs

✕ before 1144

▲ 1145 to 1214

◆ 1215 to 1284

■ 1284 to 1354

● after 1355

Fig 6.4 Borough foundation in Northern England in the Middle Ages

Yorkshire Pennines – all areas participating in the wool textile industry. Apart from their continuing religious significance these churches now provide an element of the cultural landscape that is particularly attractive to the growing tourist industry of our own time. Another important aspect of urban industry was the trade in cattle products – leather goods of all kinds including harnessing, wearing apparel and utensils.

Markets and New Towns

However, a major function of medieval towns was to act as market centres, points of exchange for the local countryside. Indeed, town and market were virtually synonymous in the medieval mind. Thus, just as we can see a flowering of the countryside during the twelfth and thirteenth cen-turies, we can also see a flowering of towns, and this is specially shown in the number of new towns that were deliberately promoted during this period. We often think of New Towns as a creation of the twentieth century, yet as Beresford has shown, far more towns were founded and laid out in the middle ages than since. As the country became more settled politically, and the land was used more intensively, the existing network of market centres was insufficient for local needs and it became possible for new market towns to be located between the older centres. These new markets became the object of speculation on the part of landholders, for it could be a very profit-able venture. Landlords who developed a new market town were able to levy tolls on the market trade, they could charge rents for the building plots that would be taken up, and there was the general quickening of the local economy that could be encouraged by the provision of local

Fig 6.5a Town Hall, Newtown, Isle of Wight

marketing facilities. Income from tolls and rents never amounted to a majority of a landholder's income, but it was a supplement that had needed little investment.

Not all new towns lived up to the profitable hopes of their founders, for not all were endowed with a favourable location. At Newtown in the Isle of Wight, the town hall now stands forlornly empty, looking rather like a little Quaker meeting house to the side of a little used road. Other towns did prosper, some, like Liverpool and Newcastle upon Tyne, to become some of the more important centres in the country (Fig. 6.5). The new foundations which were successful were generally those that lay on routes which funnelled trade to their doors. Towns like Boroughbridge, in Yorkshire, for instance, which were located at a new bridge over a major river, or towns founded on a Roman road, a natural highway for travellers, were towns that succeeded in the way that their

founders had hoped. Towns which also had a built-in chance of success were those that were established outside the gates of great religious houses, like Bury St. Edmunds in Suffolk, or at major castle strongholds, like Conway in North Wales, for these places offered a ready market for consumables and were also natural gathering places for pilgrims and travellers alike. Indeed, the very concept of the towns was largely introduced into Wales, especially North Wales, by the founding of new towns or *bastides,* a combination of fort and market established by Edward I of England. Writing in the seventeenth century John Taylor gave this description of Caernarfon:

". . . so to Caernarfon, where I thought to have seen a Town and a Castle, or a Castle and a Town; but I saw both to be one, and one to be both; for indeed a man can hardly divide them in judgement or apprehension."

Fig 6.5b The Civic Centre in modern Newcastle upon Tyne—the heir to a successful medieval new town—in contrast to the rustic solitude of Newtown, Isle of Wight, a failed medieval new town

One of the characteristics of these new towns is their regular lay-out. Because the towns were often founded on completely open green-field sites, they were often laid out in rectilinear patterns. This might simply take the form of regularly-spaced building plots facing onto a main street widened out to take a market, as at Leeds. Another very popular method was what Beresford calls 'chequors', that is a regular series of squares, as at Winchelsea in Sussex, but also found at Stratford-on-Avon and Liverpool. Often the squares were arranged to give a single larger square, say sixteen squares arranged four by four. In other places the squares would be arranged asymmetrically to fit the exigencies of the site. This rectilinearity is recognisable today and offers a clue to the origin of many towns. The principal difference between the new towns of the medieval period and the new towns of the present century, though, is that the only 'planning' that was undertaken was the initial choosing of the site and the laying out of the building plots, upon which tenants could build whatever sort of property suited their need. The landlord might provide a corn mill and a bake-house, and perhaps even a chapel dependent upon the church in whose parish the town was established, for parochial boundaries had already been fixed by this period. There was no thought of planning the industrial and economic structure of the town, nor of maintaining a balanced population structure. Lastly we must remember that many existing settlements were raised to urban status by the provision of a market during this period, and cannot be thought of as new towns in our sense; and these represent the more typical element in urban expansion at this time.

Fig 6.6 Lavenham, Suffolk. Raised to prosperity on the wool trade, the little town of Lavenham still testifies to the great rebuilding which characterised England between the 15th century and the early 17th century

THE MEDIEVAL CONTRIBUTION

The medieval world seems far removed from our own, and yet the hand of medieval man lies heavier on the landscape than we might at first imagine. To begin with this period saw the identification of all but a small proportion of the settlements that are to be found in Britain. Secondly, the fixing of patterns of landholding at both large and small scales during this period has had a formidable effect in conditioning subsequent developments in town and country alike. Not a few great country estates were built up during this period and have remained more or less intact until very recent times, even though their ownership may have changed. Before the days of compulsory land purchase, property boundaries, often the same as plot boundaries, endured intact for many centuries, as Conzen has shown in Alnwick in Northumberland. In our own period we are much concerned with conservation, and the preservation of ancient buildings that have survived from past periods. Towns like York, Durham, Salisbury, Chester and Lavenham offer difficult problems in reconciling past building and layout techniques with the pressures of twentieth century traffic and urban life (Fig. 6.6). Even in less obviously historic centres, the presence of an occasional medieval building such as a church or ancient gateway are today seen as important elements in urban planning schemes, often conditioning urban land use for some distance round about them. Lastly, a word on rural conservation. The setting up of National Parks, and areas designated as being of outstanding natural beauty, in an attempt to conserve the landscape attractions of certain areas, is by no means new. From at least early Norman times considerable stretches of countryside were laid out as 'forests', not necessarily wooded areas, but areas in which great lords could preserve 'natural' conditions for hunting game. Present discussion as to whether access to National Parks should be carefully controlled lest the natural conditions that are being conserved should be spoilt, would have a very familiar ring to a medieval keeper! Not surprisingly, the areas of 'unspoiled natural' beauty today are often areas where development was controlled in the past. The New Forest in Hampshire is an obvious example, but much of the Snowdonia and Yorkshire Dales National Parks were also once conserved as medieval game reserves.

The pre-industrial medieval past, then, lives on in our landscape today, but most of us live most of our lives amongst a very different environment which is largely the product of the past two hundred years. During this period both landscape and environment have undergone revolutionary changes, and it is these that must be the subject of our next chapter.

References

Baker, A.R.H., and Butlin, R.A., *Studies in Field Systems in the British Isles* (Cambridge University Press, 1973)

Jones, G.R.J., 'Settlement Patterns in Anglo-Saxon England', *Antiquity*, Vol. XXXV, 1961, pp. 221–32.

Platt, C., *The Monastic Grange in Medieval England*, (Macmillan, 1969).

Shrewsbury, J.F.D., *A History of the Bubonic Plague in the British Isles* (Cambridge University Press, 1970).

Beresford, M.W., and Hurst, J., *Deserted Medieval Villages* (Lutterworth Press, 1971).

Beresford, M.W., *New Towns of the Middle Ages* (Lutterworth Press, 1967).

Conzen, M.R.G., 'Alnwick, Northumberland, a study in town plan analysis', *I.B.G. Publications*, 27, 1960.

7

Environment, Landscape and Revolution

During the eighteenth and nineteenth centuries, the British Isles were the scene of a series of economic and social changes that profoundly affected the way of life of all the people in them, and the landscape in which they lived. It is now commonplace to talk of the Industrial Revolution, or the Agricultural Revolution, or the revolution in commerce, transport and almost every other sphere of our lives. Unfortunately it is not so easy to say *precisely when* these revolutionary changes occurred, nor *precisely where*. Economic historians have for long tried to interpret the chronology of change. Did the agricultural revolution precede the industrial revolution? What relationship did the transport revolution have to other spheres of economic life? (The geographer would probably say that it was crucial). For our purposes, though, it is best for us to see all these threads as inextricably intertwined, and although we shall examine the various aspects of revolutionary change individually we must remember that they are linked one to another, and are not isolated events.

PROLOGUE TO CHANGE

In our last chapter we left the British Isles at the time of the middle ages. The period between then and this time of revolutionary change, though, was of itself one of the most significant in human history. Without a doubt the seeds of change were sown in this period. From the end of the fifteenth century to the beginning of the eighteenth century, western Europe in general and the British Isles in particular, found itself launched into new worlds of discovery and understanding. Not only

was more of the surface of the earth discovered by navigators from western Europe, but man's understanding of nature was vastly increased. These two aspects of man's understanding go hand in hand, but while geographers have always paid attention to voyages of discovery, we have not always taken account of the intellectual climate of the day, which was equally important.

Hand in hand with the spread of *Renaissance* learning went a spirit of criticism which reacted against the formalised, almost fossilised structure of a 1,500 year-old church. The effect of the *Reformation* in England at least was relatively painless, but the ferment it induced aided the rapacious Henry VIII to dissolve the monasteries and other religious houses, and so produce a redistribution of land and property. The new landlords took the lead in large-scale farming, just as the monasteries had done three hundred years before. More land was given over to sheep, many peasants were evicted while many landlords sought to regulate the use of the commons and extensive grazing areas. More profitable farming techniques like these were not lost on village communities, and many villages outside the English midlands abandoned or modified their common field systems at this time.

The most spectacular movement of the period, though, was the effective discovery of North and South America, and of the sea routes to the East Indies. The ensuing development of commercial navigation revolutionised the spatial relations of Europe. The British Isles, formerly a relatively insignificant group of off-shore islands, found themselves sharing the focus of the world's trade routes with the Low Countries, a position which has not been radically changed to this day. The opportunities for speculative commerce were not lost, particularly in England, and the profits were applied to the purchasing and development of country houses and estates, and to investments in further commercial ventures. In these expanding commercial horizons *capitalism* was born, and capitalism has been one of the most formative influences in harnessing the earth's resources for man's own ends.

The development of contacts with the New World, however, had other more immediate and local effects. The western ports of Bristol, Liverpool and Glasgow were given a great boost, although London never lost its superiority. More importantly, perhaps, the potato was introduced. First commercially grown on Merseyside in the mid-seventeenth century, the potato was to become one of the principal agents in feeding an increasing population. The development of commercial navigation, though, along with its attendant naval strength demanded a great deal of timber. Timber was also being increasingly used in house construction and the production of furniture, hitherto a comparative rarity. Timber was also being used to fuel a growing iron industry, whose products were demanded by the navy, house builders and craftsmen alike. All over England the woodlands were coming under great pressure, until by the seventeenth century there was a massive timber shortage. Quite simply, men had been cutting down trees since the Mesolithic period, and now there were very few left, except in the less accessible parts of the country. Seventeenth century England was barer of trees than at any time before or since. This shortage of timber induced an energy crisis, particularly in London and the south-east of Britain. This was relieved only by the development of coal mining, itself made possible by the introduction of better techniques of shaft mining developed in Germany during the sixteenth century.

All these themes, philosophical, economic, environmental and religious, are in evidence in the development of the export trade in coal from the river Tyne in the sixteenth and seventeenth centuries. It was the religious reformation which enabled the merchants of Newcastle to exploit the coal reserves of the south bank of the Tyne which were held by the Bishop of Durham. It was the applied mathematics and logical observation of the Renaissance which enabled better mining techniques to be introduced. It was the discovery of the

New World which precipitated the energy crisis, and so created the demand for coal. The techniques of credit and money exchange that were developed between the Newcastle exporters, London agents and wholesale customers was a formative exercise in commercial expertise. The merchants of Newcastle were among the first industrial capitalists, making profits out of coal, the raw material of the industrial revolution.

AGRICULTURAL CHANGES

The agricultural revolution was a series of changes that ultimately produced an increase in the output of food and industrial crops without increasing the number of people on the land. As population increased, then the relative number of food producers decreased. Eventually developments in agricultural techniques reduced this number absolutely. Both men and the land were made more productive, and this was made possible by a number of factors.

Increasing the Areas of Cultivated Land

The increase in population during the Middle Ages was supported by the taking in of more land for cultivation. This process continued well into the nineteenth century and was perhaps the most important single factor in increasing the productiveness of the land. We can see reclamation taking place at both the upland and the lowland limits of cultivation. In County Durham and Northumberland the ancient common moorlands were under pressure in the seventeenth century, and many were enclosed and brought into cultivation. In the Yorkshire Pennines piecemeal enclosure of the moorlands had been going on since the sixteenth century, mainly associated with a mixed clothworking/pastoral farming economy. Large scale enclosure and improvement came in the eighteenth and nineteenth centuries when Acts of Parliament were sponsored to enclose vast tracts of upland grazing. In the last forty years of the eighteenth century between two and three million acres were brought into cultivation, mainly in northern England. This pushing up of the altitudinal limit of cultivation produced new improved grassland for pasture. The pushing down of the limits of cultivation into the fen and marsh land produced quite different land.

The Romans and, later, some of the great medieval landlords like the Cambridge Colleges, and monasteries such as Glastonbury and Crowland, had been responsible for draining marshland. During the seventeenth century, though, great advances were made, often using techniques developed in the Netherlands. One of the foremost engineers was *Cornelius Vermuyden,* who is specially associated with draining the Humberhead levels in Yorkshire, and the fenland of Norfolk, Lincolnshire and Cambridgeshire. Here, the Duke of Bedford was a great entrepreneur who is remembered in the twenty mile long new course for the Ouse, called the Bedford Level to this day. Throughout the eighteenth and nineteenth centuries further advances were made into the marshlands. The most spectacular gains in land were in East Anglia and the Lancashire mosses, but extensive drainage operations also took place along the banks of the Severn, in the Thames estuary, and along the Firth of Forth. These lowland reclamations were much more productive than the marginal lands of the uplands. Whereas many of the upland enclosures have now been abandoned, the former fen and marshland remain amongst the most profitable agricultural land in the country. Root crops and other vegetables are important products of the East Anglian fens and the west coast areas, along with first class grain lands in some eastern districts.

In the north and west of Scotland, quite different reclamation was taking place. Here, instead of large scale reclamation of land for commercial farming, small scale improvement was taking place for peasant farming in the most unrewarding of environments. In the Scottish Highlands many tenants were evicted by new landlords after the rebellion of 1745. As the demand for wool rose in the last years of the eighteenth century, Cheviot sheep were introduced, the tenants' grazing rights were taken away from them, and they were either forced to settle in new crofting communities on the western coasts or to emigrate. The 'Highland Clearances' resulted in great deprivation for the native highlander, in the depopulation of the Highlands, and in a greatly altered pattern of land use in the area.

Using the Land More Efficiently

During this period a whole range of new techniques and tools were introduced which enabled the increased amount of land we have already noted to be used more effectively than before. These innovations were propagated by such enthusiasts as Arthur Young and William Marshall. They included:

(i) *Enclosure:* three-quarters of the cultivated land of Britain was already enclosed by the beginning of the eighteenth century, and it now seems strange that such great importance has been attached to enclosure during this period. The reason undoubtedly is the great number of *Parliamentary Enclosures* that took place, and which have caught both the historian's and the geographer's eye in the past. Many of the Parliamentary enclosures were concerned with the enclosure of common wastelands, particularly in the north of England and so have already been mentioned. Others, particularly concentrated in the English midlands, were concerned with the re-allotment and enclosure of land previously within an open or common field system. More than anything else this gave agricultural change a 'revolutionary' flavour, for here was the substitution of the 'new' for the ancient. Nevertheless, whether enclosure was taking place on cultivated land or open moorland, its effect was to enable the land to be used much more flexibly. Unenclosed open moorland could be used only for grazing. Unenclosed open cropland could be used only for pasture in a fallow year. Communal obligations had to be maintained. Where all the land of a township was divided into enclosed fields belonging to private owners, then *all* the land could be used for either tillage or pasture according to the wishes of the farmers. Instead of having areas permanently devoted to grazing, and areas permanently devoted to tillage, a system of *ley farming* was introduced, so that any field could be used for tillage, and then put down to grass. This had an important effect. By increasing the area of improved pasture, more stock could be kept. This increased the quantity of animal manure, and so in turn raised the productivity of land under tillage. The whole quality of the land was raised, and agriculture had burst out of the fundamental limitations of medieval agriculture, the lack of fertiliser.

76

(ii) The introduction of *new crops* into British farming was a second element in using the land more efficiently. The great majority of these crops were not really new to the British Isles, but they had not been used as part of an agricultural system in quite the same way before. One crop *was* new, however, and that was the *potato*. Its most spectacular impact was in Ireland where it was universally adopted as a staple food by the rural population. It sparked off a massive population increase, for a diet of potatoes and milk products proved to be extremely nutritious, if monotonous. Between the 1770s and the 1840s the population of Ireland more than doubled to 8,175,000. The potato, though, was a foodstuff, and as such was an exception, for the 'new' crops were very largely used as feedstuffs for animals. They were the new *ley crops*. First, were the roots (turnip, carrot, beet, etc.) and the coles (cabbage, rape, kale, etc.). The roots, and especially the turnip were sown on light and deep soils. First developed in High Suffolk during the mid-seventeenth century, turnip husbandry spread to almost all areas of light soils within the next hundred years. Where the soil was shallow, or too heavy for roots, then the coles were sown instead. Secondly, there were the artificial grasses, like sainfoin and clover, which were found to be specially good for improving new pasture in the uplands. All these new crops gave the farmer more flexibility in his tillage, they provided useful winter fodder, while also putting some basic plant nutrients – nitrogen for instance – back into the soil

(iii) As well as new crops, this period saw the development of *new breeds and strains of existing stock*. The main advances were made on the better grasslands of the newly-enclosed English midlands during the later eighteenth and nineteenth centuries. Of several regions where enterprising farmers were beginning to draw out particular characteristics from their animals, the Tees lowland has a special place. This area produced one of the biggest strains of English sheep, the Teeswater, the Durham shorthorn cattle, and the Cleveland Bay horse. This is another change we should note – more and more horses were kept, displacing oxen as the principal draught animals.

(iv) Lastly we must remember the *improved tools* that were introduced. Every farming region in the British Isles had its own styles of farm implements. The shape and weight of hoes, for instance, varied a great deal, reflecting the nature of the soil and the system of tillage commonly used. They reflect thought about how the soil can be most easily worked. Formerly a great deal of emphasis used to be given to Tull's seed drill which sowed seed in straight lines sufficiently far apart for a horse hoe to clean the soil in between, but the greatest innovations did not come until well into the nineteenth century. One major introduction was the Rotherham plough which allowed one man and two horses to do what had formerly taken two men and up to eight oxen to achieve. Another innovation was the steam plough which was used on the larger estates. There were many other refinements and improvements made available as iron working and engineering techniques themselves improved. Another important innovation was the development of the *mole plough,* which enabled wet land to be drained, and so more land could be brought into the general system of tillage.

Non-Agricultural Factors

It would be wrong for us to think that the agricultural revolution was engendered solely by itself. Agricultural change was also encouraged by a whole array of other elements. The most important single group were the changes in transport which we shall look at in more detail shortly. First of all, improvements in roads led to improved local marketing conditions. Secondly, the development of first the canal network, and then the railways, enabled large bodies of fertiliser and marketable crops to be moved around the country relatively cheaply. In the latter half of the nineteenth century, improvements in external communications were to expose the British farmer to European and American competition, and well nigh ruin him.

The world of politics and the world of the soil are not always linked by the geographer, yet changes in both national and international politics have important effects on farming profitability. The Act of Union with Scotland in 1707, for example, increased the flow of Scottish cattle to England. The famine conditions of the Napoleonic Wars encouraged the ploughing up of land that would not normally have been cultivated, and gave an increased impetus to the taking in of marginal hill land. At the end of our period of agricultural expansion, the repeal of the Corn

Laws in 1848 encouraged a move away from wheat towards grass cultivation.

Lastly, cost and profit margins are crucial determinants of change. As agriculture was made more profitable, so landlords were more willing to invest in the land. It was usually the larger landholders who took the lead in enclosure, not for their direct interest in the land, but for their interest in their rent roll.

However, if the economist has a special interest in prices and profitability, the geographer has a special interest in the landscape and we must note the changes that were effected on the British landscape by these changes in function. The most massive single change was the substitution of an artificial pattern of vegetation for a natural one over much of upland Britain, and the low-lying marsh lands. Secondly this period saw a rapid development in enclosing land, whether it be with stone walls in the uplands, or thorn hedges in the lowlands (Fig. 7.1). These newly enclosed fields had a regularity and rectilinearity that had not been seen in the landscape before, the product of a surveyor's skill, and not the convenience of a colonist's spade. In addition, in many lowland areas, the countryside was peppered with small copses for fox covers and game preservation.

Agricultural change did not always mean agricultural prosperity, but all over the British Isles at this time we can see a great process of rebuilding

Fig 7.1 Pettril Valley, Cumbria. An enclosure landscape of rectilinear fields and game covers flanks the Roman road between Carlisle (*Luguvallium*) and Brougham (*Brocavum*)

that dwarfs any previous period. Although the great new houses of the eighteenth century were not always the product of agricultural prosperity, they are often regarded as the symbol of it. Equally we can see in villages across the length and breadth of Britain the hand of the eighteenth and nineteenth century builder, as primitive cabins were replaced by more substantial houses, now the dream of many suburban dwellers. Out in the newly-enclosed countryside wide straight roads gave access to the new land, where often new farmsteads were built. These were quite separate from the mother township, and are a symbol of the total and final breakdown of communal, subsistence agriculture, and the substitution of the new commercial farming.

TRANSPORT CHANGES

We can look at changes which occured in transport during the eighteenth century in two ways. First, there were a number of changes in the *technology of transport:* roads were improved, canals were built and during the second half of the nineteenth century the railway network was constructed. These are obvious, though in a way, superficial changes. Secondly, we can see the more fundamental changes that these technological innovations induced. The real importance of changes in transport was that distances between places were effectively shortened, and the relative location of individual places changed. In the middle of the eighteenth century, Birmingham occupied a relatively inaccessible position in the centre of England; by the middle of the nineteenth century it was at the heart of a communications network linked equally with the fast growing centres of northern England, London, and ports on both the west and east coasts, as well as the south.

Obviously changes of such magnitude had far-reaching effects not only upon the local community and its hinterland, but also upon the national and ultimately the international scene. Nowadays it is often a central feature of the policy of governments to foster economic growth by investing in large scale public works. These often take the form of developing communications, whether a new motorway in north-east England, or a new railway and port development in an east African country. If such ventures are deliberately undertaken today, we can see why far reaching changes in transport over the course of little more than a century were so important to the pace of economic development and landscape formation during the industrial revolution.

Roads

The Romans had constructed an excellent network of roads – direct, well engineered and durable. Fifteen hundred years later, at the beginning of this period of environmental change, they were still the only roads that had been deliberately engineered. Some stretches of road were still well maintained and passable, but the mast majority were in a very poor condition. Most were badly constructed, and maintained on a parish basis, employing local labour for a week or so each year, under the direction of temporary constables with no technical expertise whatever. They were badly rutted and potholed, and unequipped with drainage facilities, so that in wet weather and during winter they were quite impassable. Roads in England were judged to be the worst in Europe.

Improvements came with the Highways Acts of 1767 and 1783, and the formation of *Turnpike Trusts* throughout the eighteenth century, in particular between 1791 and 1810. The two Acts were in reality only gestures. Among their more significant features were that cartways into market towns had to be maintained at least 20 feet wide, and certain regulations were placed upon users as to axle weight and wheel width. The Turnpike Trusts were in general more successful, but advances here were far from uniform. The trusts were mainly local affairs which took over the responsibility of maintaining a stretch of road in return for the right to collect tolls. Unfortunately in the vast majority of cases the tolls themselves were insufficient to maintain the roads, and by the beginning of the nineteenth century many were being used to service loans. Traffic was far too heavy for most of the road surfaces, and rather than build roads capable of taking the traffic the Turnpike Trusts vainly attempted to regulate the sort of wagons that used their roads. Eventually advances were made in highway engineering that produced a surface approximating to those we know today. The innovators were a small number of surveyors, the most notable of whom were Thomas Telford and Robert Macadam. In the event the new techniques (which were not so very different from those used by the Romans) were almost too late, for the great road building triumphs were during the first quarter of the nineteenth century on the very eve of the railway age.

The most famous of the new roads was the road connecting London and Dublin – via Holyhead. Engineered by Telford and completed in 1830, it cost almost three-quarters of a million pounds. Until this time Telford had been the principal engineer of his day. He had been responsible for opening 900 miles of road in the Scottish Highlands, but the great cost of the Holyhead road rather reduced his appeal to government. Most of the traffic that used the roads was commercial rather than passenger. Pickfords had their roots in the early seventeenth century, but during the latter half of the eighteenth century many substantial haulage firms developed, carrying out regular scheduled services between the major towns. By 1835 there were well over 14,000 regular wagon services each week in all parts of England, and more than 800 public carriers operating from London alone. Passenger traffic was served by the increasingly competitive stage coach services. As major highways were improved so the frequencies and time of journeys between major cities were speeded up. Journeys from London to the north of England which had taken three or four days in the mid eighteenth century were reduced to 18 or 20 hours by the 1830s. Such improvements were more important for speeding up postal communication than for passenger or goods transport, for while these services obviously benefited, the number of travellers involved was very small, and the cost was relatively high.

Although there was a considerable amount of long distance road traffic generated during the later eighteenth and early nineteenth centuries, improvements in road communications mainly benefited the local and regional community. Larger scale, longer distance movements were really facilitated by the canals.

Waterways

Whatever the success of the road makers, the busiest highway during the eighteenth century was the sea route along the eastern coast of Britain, from London north to Scotland, just as it had been since the time of the Romans. For both goods and passengers, water transport was still the most reliable and the speediest. Only a few would travel from London to Newcastle by road: most travellers would go by sea. The Tyne coal trade had long demonstrated that water transport was the only feasible way of moving heavy goods economically about the country, and Tyne coal had been able to penetrate into the heart of England by way of the many estuaries and rivers of the east coast, which were navigable for boats of shallow draught. It was largely the demand for coal which stimulated much of the early canal building. River dredging and improvement had been widely undertaken since the Middle Ages, but the building of new waterways was a novelty. The first commercial canal was the Sankey Canal completed in 1757 by Liverpool merchants who wished to tap the coalfield at St. Helens. Three years later the Duke of Bridgewater constructed a canal to carry coal from his mines at Worsley to Manchester. The entrance to the Duke's mines and the Bridgewater Canal can still be seen, now overshadowed by the M 62 motorway. This juxtaposition of two forms of transport is most evocative. By the side of the busy highway of the 1970s, the canal has a rustic air that does not befit the revolutionary role it played. The canal was an instant success, halving the price of coal in Manchester, and becoming the direct inspiration for half the Navigation Acts passed over the next forty years. (One of the plans laid was a canal from the river Tees to the south Durham coalfield; the scheme never came to fruition, but the idea anticipated the Stockton and Darlington railway.)

Of all the areas in Britain none benefited more than the English Midlands. The Grand Trunk Canal joined the Trent and Mersey, while the Staffordshire and Worcestershire Canal joined the Trent and Severn. At the junction with the Severn a mini new town arose, Stourport, acting as a major distribution point for the west Midlands. Less grand, but serving the same purpose, the village of Shardlow expanded greatly where the Grand Trunk Canal entered the Trent (Fig. 7.2). In 1786 the Birmingham Canal was authorised which linked the town to Liverpool, Hull and Bristol, while fifteen years later the Thames and the Severn were linked. Of less economic significance, but somehow more grand in their conception, were those canals which linked the North and the Irish Seas, across the Pennines. The Leeds and

Fig 7.2 Shardlow Canal Basin. The junction of the Grand Trunk Canal and the Trent, which has recently been renovated to form a pleasant marina and touring centre

Liverpool Canal, begun in 1770, cut a 200 km course across the north of England and along the Aire gap. The Rochdale Canal, completed in 1804, linked Manchester to the Yorkshire Calder, and most spectacular of all the Huddersfield Canal pierced the Pennines in a 5 km tunnel.

Although many canals were not profitable from their earliest days there is no doubt that the canal network gave England a prodigious step forward. They encouraged trade, but more importantly they anticipated a fuel crisis and made the more widespread adoption of coal and steam power a practical proposition. Lastly, the building of the canals, cuttings and tunnels offered considerable experience in civil engineering, as well as in the co-ordination of large numbers of labourers, and in the raising of capital. This experience was to be put to further test and very good use during the period of railway construction which superseded the canal network during the Victorian period. The canals remaining open to the present are shown in Fig. 11.3 on page 135.

Railways

In 1825 the *Durham County Advertiser* proudly reported that on the 27th September:

> "About eight o'clock, thirteen waggons, twelve of them laden with two tons of coal each, and the other with sacks of flour, the whole of them covered with people, were drawn up the inclined plane at Brusselton in admirable style, amidst the cheers of assembled thousands."

Thus the Stockton and Darlington Railway was inaugurated, linking the coalfield in south-west Durham, near Bishop Auckland, with the navigable Tees at Stockton, and passing through Darlington on the way. Although railway lines, or waggonways had been in use in the north-east and elsewhere for two hundred years, and although a steam engine had been mounted on wheels by Trevithick more than twenty years before, this

81

event marks the opening of the railway age. The surprising element about the railway was the prodigious speed at which the rail network was extended across the country. Within twenty-five years of the opening of the Stockton and Darlington Railway, the main skeleton of the railway network was to all intents and purposes complete. First to follow was the line between Liverpool and Manchester, along part of which the celebrated Rainhill trials were held in 1829. In September 1830 the line was officially opened by the Duke of Wellington, and within a month half of the stage coaches operating between the two towns had

been taken off the road. As with the canals before them, the transport of coal had been one of the main aims of the early railways; but soon the wider benefits of speedy communications became obvious to most people, and the major goal of linking London to the provinces was set in hand. Birmingham was reached in 1838, Southampton by 1840 and Bristol by 1841. By 1845 most of provincial England was linked to London, and by the 1850s 'Celtic' Britain was being assailed both in the south-west and in Scotland (Fig. 7.3). Railways into more remote areas, whether in the mountains of Scotland or the remote valleys of the west country, were never so successful as the earlier lines linking obvious sources of traffic, but nevertheless new lines continued to be built well into the second half of the nineteenth century. At first they competed with the canals, but soon railway rates were much cheaper for many goods over longer distances. More importantly the railways diverted investment away from the canals, some of which were deliberately run down by railway companies who acquired control of them. The result was an arresting of the development of the canal network which even at this late stage we can regret.

The impact of the railway was manifest in so many ways. As a feature in the landscape it astounded all contemporary writers, and indeed until the motorway system was established in recent years, the railways still provided the most dramatic feats of civil engineering in the country. Cuttings, tunnels, viaducts, as well as massive goods yards, were the obvious features. Of rather more subtle effect was the way railway lines so often conditioned the growth of towns, dividing social areas, and inhibiting road construction beyond the line. As with the canals, new towns grew up to service the system – Crewe in the north, Ashford and Swindon in the south – while some long established and dignified provincial cities like Derby, Peterborough and York were changed beyond recognition by the establishment of railway works. On a wider scale the railways encouraged the general movement of goods initiated by the canals. In particular, Hoskins points to how local building styles were broken down as slate from Welsh quarries and brick from the east Midlands were used across the length and breadth of the country, although in fact much local diversity even in the terrace cottage persisted until the twentieth century. Of equal importance was

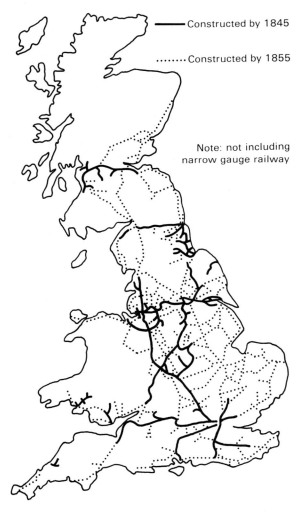

Constructed by 1845

Constructed by 1855

Note: not including narrow gauge railway

Fig 7.3 Early expansion of the railway network in Great Britain

the impetus the railways gave to population movement. Large-scale migration, whether over long or short distances, permanent or temporary, now became possible (Fig. 7.4). The result was in particular the continued growth of London, and the decay of smaller market centres, while on the coasts new resorts came into being in the latter half of the nineteenth century. These catered not for the gentle sea bather and drinker of spa water, but for the industrial workers who by way of the day excursion were able to walk along the promenade at Blackpool and Clacton, Bridlington and Weston-super-Mare.

Fig 7.4 New mobility for all. The railways not only promoted working class trips and holidays, but also promoted the growing tourist trade to the Highlands, patronised by the middle and upper classes. (Crown Copyright reserved)

Without doubt the railways were the most dramatic symbol of the revolutionary changes that were overtaking the landscape and the environment in the British Isles. Yet the most revolutionary changes of all were those that affected the way of life of the majority of the population. Over the course of the nineteenth century the British people ceased to live in the countryside, but instead became townspeople. Instead of the seasonal labour of the land, they found themselves working in the comparative monotony of the factory.

INDUSTRIAL CHANGE

Of all the changes which took place in the British environment, it is those in industry which characterise this period in everyone's mind. There were revolutionary changes in the scale of production, and in the methods and location of production. It is not possible to do justice to the whole range of industry here, so we will first sketch in some of the major features of this period of change, and then look in rather more detail at the iron and steel industry and the wool textile industry.

We have already noticed how the seeds of change in industry, just as in agriculture, were sown in the sixteenth and seventeenth centuries. We can regard the period until 1780 as a period of gestation, and then in the last two decades of the eighteenth century came the birth of our modern economic growth. The economic historian Rostow, has called this period the 'take off', when output in most branches of industry began a period of sustained growth that was to last for four generations. Although there were fluctuations in industrial production during the nineteenth century, often engendering periods of acute distress to the mass of the population, the general curve was resolutely upwards (Fig. 7.5). The end result of this expansion was an entirely new way for man to interact with his environment. In the British Isles most families were supported by processing raw materials, and distributing new products among a mass market, rather than by producing food from the land. The market was no longer local but often global, and the raw materials were similarly drawn from an intercontinental area. Specialization of activity was increased and industry became concentrated into small areas, leading to the creation of entirely new environments.

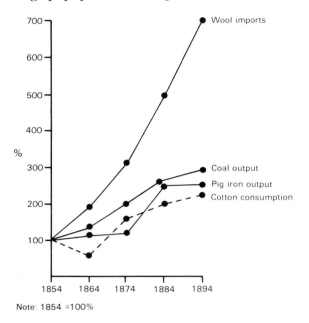

Note: 1854 =100%

Fig 7.5 Industrial expansion, 1854–94

Characteristics of the New Industry

Industry at this period was marked out from earlier developments by three characteristics. First, it was a mechanised rather than handicraft industry, with the operative being a machine-minder rather than a craftsman. This was important for it meant that the skills of production were simplified and industrial expansion could take place faster because the training of labour took less time. Secondly, this was a powered industry. The water wheel had been linked to corn grinding, cloth fulling and bellows blowing for centuries, but during the later eighteenth and early nineteenth centuries it was harnessed to a wide range of other processes in the textile, mining and iron industries. More importantly the steam engine was adopted and later superseded the water wheel as a source of motive power. Initially the steam engine was less reliable than the water wheel and the motion it produced was suited to pumping rather than rotary motion. Accordingly it was first applied in manufacturing, for pumping water into a reservoir for use on a water wheel. Rotary motion was eventually provided by Boulton and Watts in 1784, and the steam engine then began to be adopted by industry in general.

Nevertheless, it took two generations before steam was producing more power than water, and new water wheels continued to be set up well into the nineteenth century. The use of steam power, though, had profound effects upon the location of industry. The earliest steam engines were very inefficient and required such large amounts of fuel that their use was only practical on the coalfields. Advances in mechanisation were concentrated on the coalfields therefore, and this early lead proved to be crucial. From Fig. 7.5 it can be seen that the real build up of industrial production came in the latter half of the nineteenth century, by which time the railways had ensured that coal was available and cheap in almost every part of the country. By this time the coalfields had so secured the earliest advances, that as we shall see, other industrial areas were left far behind.

The third characteristic of the new industry was that it was based on relatively large operating units. The new engines whether driven by steam or by water offered power to many machines. This led directly to two quite new elements in the British environment. The first was the large, purpose-built 'manufactory', still called a mill in the Pennines where they were first of all powered by water wheels like the ancient mills. The new factories themselves generated new developments in building techniques, and some soon came to rival the medieval cathedrals and eighteenth century country houses for sheer size. They also demanded a local pool of labour and so led to the development of factory towns. The second new element was the appearance of the capitalist entrepreneur who was willing to invest and re-invest his profits in his business, a vital personal figure in British industrial development in these early phases.

Iron and Steel

The melting point of iron is about 1500° C. Consequently the need for fuel has always been an important factor in the manufacture of iron and steel goods. It would be true to say that the search for fuel, and a more efficient way of using it, was the most important factor in the development of the industry over this period. The search for efficiency led to the development of new techniques of smelting which in turn favoured ores of particular chemical composition. Thus, as the industry progressed we can see the ores of particular parts of the country coming into prominence and a number of metal-working regions established.

The one major factor which distinguishes the iron and steel industry of the industrial revolution from that of earlier periods is in the use of coal for smelting. Previously charcoal had been the predominant fuel and the search for timber had even driven the industry into the Western Highlands of Scotland during the eighteenth century. Many 'iron masters' attempted to use coal for smelting, but the first successful attempt seems to have been made by Abraham Darby at Coalbrookdale in Shropshire in 1709. Darby's secret was to expel the sulphur and phosphorus from the coal, thus forming coke, and to use the coke in the blast furnace in place of the raw coal. The idea was not taken up quickly, partly because of the increased blast needed to raise the coke to the required temperature, partly because coal suitable for coking was not to be found everywhere.

Having discovered that coke could be used instead of charcoal to produce pig and cast iron, the next steps were to discover how coke could be used in the forges to make wrought iron, and how to use less fuel in the whole process. The first was accomplished by a number of iron masters, but notably by Henry Cort in 1784, who introduced the 'puddling' process. By this method the pig iron was remelted on hot clinkers, and by stirring the resulting mixture, the carbon in the metal combined with oxygen in the clinker, leaving pure metal behind. The second was to be a much longer search, but was helped on its way by the discovery of the hot blast process by James Neilson of Glasgow in 1828. Previously it had been thought that the best metal was produced by blowing cold air through the furnace, but Neilson demonstrated the the hotter the incoming air, the hotter the furnace itself became. He heated the air using heat coming off the furnace and by this means more and better iron was produced from less fuel. The use of coal for both smelting and forging drew the iron industry out of the forests and onto the coalfields, and the process was encouraged by the increasing use of coal-powered steam engines to produce the blast needed. By this means bigger and more productive furnaces could be built, enhancing the economic attractiveness of the coalfield areas of the English Midlands and the North-East (Fig. 7.6).

Fig 7.6 St. Hilda Colliery, Co. Durham, 1884. Colliers and chaldrons, engine house and winding gear complete this photograph of a famous north-eastern coal mine, sunk through the Magnesian Limestone at South Shields

Wrought or cast iron lacked tensile strength. Steel is an alloy of iron which contains a very small proportion of carbon, and has considerable tensile strength. Until the mid nineteenth century steel could only be produced by successively reheating the iron to expel impurities, and then carefully controlling the proportion of carbon. The process was mainly reserved for the making of blades and required a great deal of fuel. In 1856, however, Henry Bessemer introduced into County Durham a new method of making steel which did not require the successive reheating of pig iron. Instead he ran the molten pig into a large vessel, a converter, and blasted a powerful jet of air through the molten metal. The oxygen in the air combined with the carbon in the metal, while the required amount of carbon was then put back in the form of *spiegel,* an alloy of iron and manganese. This process worked well with haematites, but not with the phosphoric ore found in the coal measures and the Jurassic series. As a result, the Carboniferous limestone ores of Weardale and more importantly the haematite of Cumberland became specially significant, while steel making on Teesside had to rely for a time on imported Spanish ore. The iron and steel industry of Teesside, however, received its greatest boost through the introduction of the Gilchrist and Thomas process in 1879. By this method the phosphoric ores of the Jurassic series could be used if the converter or the 'hearth' was lined with magnesian limestone. Imagine how the Quaker iron masters of Teesside rejoiced in 'God's Providence', for within ten miles of each other was to be found good coking coal, Magnesian limestone and Cleveland ore. The early lead taken by British industry during the nineteenth century owed much to happy accidents such as this. It was a lead that was already lost by the last quarter of the nineteenth century, although the effects of this were not to become apparent until much later.

Wool Textiles

Innovations in the iron and steel industry tended to promote particular regions, but did not necessarily mean the total eclipse of older areas of production. Developments in the wool textile industry, however, led to the progressive concentration of the industry into one major and one minor area. Formerly wool textiles had been widely dispersed and there was a domestic industry to be found from the north of Scotland to the south-west of England. By the mid nineteenth century wool textiles were almost exclusively concentrated into a small area of the West Riding (within which there were even smaller and tighter local specialisations) and in the area around Hawick and Galashiels in the Scottish borders. It will be sufficient for us to examine the woollen industry in Yorkshire, where we can see a part-time, semi-rural domestic industry transformed into a highly mechanised, concentrated industry providing the basis for an urban way of life. It is often alleged that supplies of local wool, soft water and coal were the factors which gave the West Riding its lead over other wool textile areas in the industrial revolution. In reality none of these were especially significant. Yorkshire wool merchants had scorned the fleece from their local flocks by the Middle Ages, and instead used wool brought from Lincolnshire or the limestone pastures of Craven. The expansion of the wool textile industry after the Napoleonic Wars was largely fed by Australia. While the softness of the water was certainly useful, it was the presence of many swift-flowing streams which was more formative, for it enabled processes to be mechanised at an early date. The steam engine was a relative latecomer to the woollen industry, and while it was useful to have supplies of coal nearby, in contrast to Norfolk or the West Country which were far removed from the coalfields, the fact is that Yorkshire manufacturers had secured the edge over their competitors *before* the steam engine was at all common in the woollen industry. The most important influence on the woollen industry at this time, without a single doubt, was the proximity of the West Yorkshire industry to the Lancashire cotton trade. Almost all the mechanical innovations in the textile industries as a whole at this period emerged in the cotton rather than the woollen sector. They were *subsequently adapted* for use in the woollen industry. Yorkshire benefited because it was next door to Lancashire.

This illustrates a most important phenomenon, namely that all innovations have a point of origin, not only in time, but in space, and they are most likely to be adopted by people who are nearer them, than by people who are far distant. Powered spinning was introduced into the Lancashire cotton trade in the 1770s, into the Yorkshire worsted industry in the 1790s, but it was not until the 1830s that powered spinning was introduced into the worsted industry of East Anglia. Similarly, innovations in weaving originated in Lancashire, and were delayed in reaching other textile areas. Kay's *flying shuttle*, which enabled one man instead of two to weave broadcloth, was introduced in the cotton industry in the 1730s, was widely used in Yorkshire by the 1760s, but was not introduced into the West Country until the 1790s, and into East Anglia until the early 1800s. It should be noted that this delay in the adoption of the various processes was not just a matter of distance, but of adapting a machine designed for one purpose to another. In a general sense the cotton yarn was stronger than woollen yarns, and thus inventions that were satisfactory for the cotton industry tended to snap the finer woollen yarn, and thus had to be modified – but it is significant that it was the Yorkshire manufacturers who made the necessary modifications, and not their competitors elsewhere.

The use of the steam engine ensured that the lead that the Yorkshire manufacturers had already secured by the early years of the nineteenth century was maintained. During the early phases of steam generation, the engines were relatively inefficient, and large amounts of fuel were required to raise the necessary horsepower. Thus proximity to coal supplies was more important in the earlier decades of the nineteenth century, than later on, when the engines were more efficient, and when the expansion of the railway network had reduced the cost of coal at places off the coalfields. By this time, though, it was too late for the woollen manufacturers of the West Country and East Anglia to catch up. By the late 1830s over 70 per cent of the total horsepower at work in the woollen and worsted industry in Yorkshire was generated by steam, and within twenty years steam had become entirely dominant. By the 1850s competition from East Anglia and the West Country was reduced to a shadow of its former self, producing only a very few specialist lines.

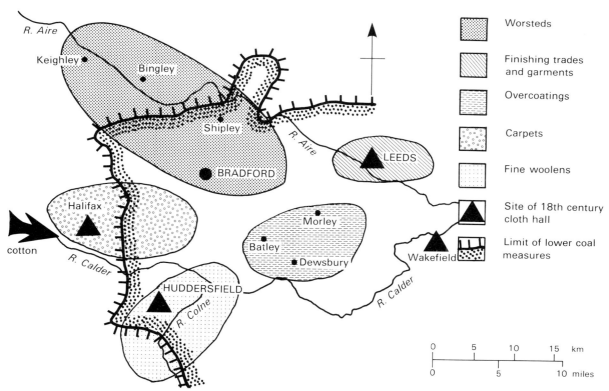

Fig 7.7 West Yorkshire textiles, 1760–1890

The adoption of steam power also had important effects upon the location of the woollen industry within Yorkshire. Up to the 1820s the wool textile industry had expanded most in the gritstone uplands west of the coal measures, where water-powered spinning mills had been established along the upper reaches of the Aire, Calder, Colne and Holme. With the adoption of steam power, the main locus of development shifted eastwards to the exposed coalfield (Fig. 7.7). It was here that steam power was applied to weaving, with the result that by the middle years of the nineteenth century, the Yorkshire woollen industry underwent a marked shift to the east leaving a relic landscape of handweavers' cottages and small water-powered spinning mills in the western hills.

Lastly, we should note the development of very marked local speciality trades, a very significant feature of nineteenth century industry. In the Staffordshire potteries, particular towns specialised on the production of a few types of pottery goods. In the West Riding, the structural changes in the wool textile industry, which we have discussed above, produced similar specialisations. The worsted trade became concentrated around Bradford, the fine woollen trade became centred on Huddersfield and the Colne valley, while the heavy woollen trade – lower quality blankets and overcoatings, once the mainstay of the Yorkshire trade – centred on Batley and Dewsbury, and used recycled fibres derived from rags. There was also the development of the carpet industry associated with the Halifax and Brighouse areas, a development which saved Halifax from severe economic difficulty, for the woollen trade had by the mid-nineteenth century been almost totally drawn out from the upper Calder valley.

After such a long chapter, in which so many threads have been spun, we ought to make a few concluding points. The first is that the changes we have seen were all fuelled by the expansion of coal mining. We can see the value of having a plentiful supply of fuel today, with the changing significance of oil and natural gas reserves around our shores. In the last half of the nineteenth century the total British output of coal quadrupled, and Britain was a net exporter of energy. Despite the terrible toll of manpower that was taken by this expansion, and the scars that are left on Britain today, self-sufficiency of fuel requirements was an important factor in British economic progress up to the beginning of the twentieth century. The coal industry was very significant in other directions, however. The introduction of coal-gas production first for lighting and then heating transformed not only the streets of the newly expanding towns, but enabled the working of night shifts and the more rapid expansion of industrial production. Coal also became an important raw material in its own right, forming the basis of the British chemicals industry, providing fuel, oils, dyestuffs, weatherproofing for wearing apparel and railway sleepers alike, and industrial acids.

Secondly, we have to bear in mind that the changes that occurred in Britain at this time were not isolated events, but were closely shadowed and in some respects anticipated in other west European countries and North America. Also overseas there was an opening up of new sources of raw materials and the creation of new markets in the Americas and in what we now refer to as the Third World. When we look back to the imperial past we can see that much of the strength of the European powers in the nineteenth century was drawn from lands far from the coalfields of the North and the newly enclosed fields of the English midlands. It is easy to see the action of the European manufacturers and merchants as wilful exploitation of the uncomprehending and unsophisticated natives of Africa and the Far East. The men who built the empires, though, saw things very differently.

Thirdly, all these changes combined to produce an entirely new environment for the majority of people, who now found themselves part of an economic system that was global rather than local and in a habitat which was almost entirely man-made. Put at its simplest, mankind had come inside. No longer subject to the vagaries of the seasons and the weather, most workers found themselves labouring inside factories, shops and offices. No longer part of a small closely related community, many found themselves in the teeming maelstrom of rapidly expanding towns. No longer working with a team of a dozen or so field labourers or craftsmen, the factory workers numbered their colleagues sometimes in thousands. The perceived world of the Victorian man-in-the-street was far removed from his peasant forbears. The rapid advance of western Europe over the rest of the world produced the great cleavage between the Developed and the Developing

Countries, that is perhaps the greatest world issue of today. In Britain we can see that many of the problems of regional imbalance, population agglomeration and environmental degradation which we shall be examining later in this book, have their origins in the changes of the nineteenth century.

References

Chambers, J.D., & Mingay, G.E., *The Agricultural Revolution, 1750–1880* (Batsford, 1966).

Kerridge, E., The Agricultural Revolution, (Kelley, U.S.A., 1977).

Hoskins, W.G., *The Making of the English Landscape,* (Hodder & Stoughton, 1955).

Rostow, W.W., *The Stages of Economic Growth,* (Cambridge University Press, 1966).

Smith, W., *An Historical Introduction to the Economic Geography of Great Britain,* (Routledge & Kegan Paul, 1968).

Wild, M.T., 'The Yorkshire Wool Textile Industry', in *The Wool Textile Industry in Great Britain*, ed. J.G. Jenkins, (Routledge, 1972).

Open University, *Coal: the Basis of 19th Century Technology,* (Milton Keynes, 1975).

8

Population Changes and Patterns

In our last chapter we outlined some of the changes which led to the growing prosperity of Britain, and transformed a small off-shore island into one of the most potent centres of influence the world has ever known. Since the late nineteenth century, however, Britain's paramount influence has declined, and there has been astonishingly rapid technological change. Both these factors have affected the lives of the people enormously, and in this chapter we shall examine the changing structure and distribution of the population over the last three or four generations, as a prologue to the structural and regional problems that form the content of Parts Three and Four of this book.

The study of population depends upon the availability of reliable statistics. Because of the lack of anything approaching a serious census our knowledge of pre-industrial population, for instance, is very tentative. Students of British historical demography have used a variety of sources to make good this deficiency, including the Domesday Book, the poll tax returns of medieval kings and the Hearth Tax returns of the seventeenth century. In 1695, Gregory King made a serious attempt to estimate the population of England and Wales, but it was not until 1801 that the first of the decennial British censuses was undertaken. For a variety of reasons the earlier censuses are less valuable than their successors, and it was not until 1841 that the British census was conducted on modern lines.

THE BRITISH CENSUS

The first census of 1801 owed its origins to Government interest in population statistics in the

face of the French wars, and also to a general interest in population growth stimulated in part by T.R. Malthus's *Essay on Population,* published in 1798. Because the census is today such an important source of statistical information on a wide range of topics, it is worthwhile knowing a little about its background and its recent characteristics. Before the 1841 census the information that was collected related only to basic information on the occupancy of houses, the numbers and sex of the population, and their employment. While this

Fig 8.1a Specimen page from the Census form, 1981. (Crown Copyright reserved)

90

still forms the basis of census information, its detail is considerably more elaborate, so that in the 1971 census the head of household was asked more than 50 questions relating to himself and other residents (Fig. 8.1a). Before 1841, too, the census was undertaken by the Overseers of the Poor in each parish, which meant that unlike the modern system of asking the head of household to complete details on a particular night, there could be no simultaneous recording.

Under the Census Act of 1920, a census of population may be taken every five years, but a census is such an expensive and elaborate operation that decennial censuses are the rule. In the 1960s it was felt that the rate of population change was so rapid, particularly in highly urbanised areas, that public service decisions of all kinds were being taken on inaccurate information. It was therefore decided to undertake a 'sample census' based on a sampling frame provided by the 1961 census. Dealing with only ten per cent of the information normally available under a full census, it was expected that the results would be available much earlier and at a fraction of the cost. In the event the publication of the results was considerably delayed because of computer difficulties, but the case for more frequent sample censuses is still maintained in some quarters. Unfortunately, plans for a similar sample census to be taken in 1976 were abandoned because of the economic climate. Census publications have become steadily more elaborate, and those of 1971 are more than three times the length of the 1951 census, running to over 25,000 pages of tabulation, at various degrees of aggregation, from national totals to county districts. In addition, the Office of Population Censuses and Surveys is able to supply tables relating to areas as small as individual enumeration districts, that is the data collected by one particular census enumerator and consisting of between 50 and 150 households.

The manipulation of so much data clearly demands a very considerable effort, and even on the full 1971 census some information was processed on the basis of a ten per cent sample. The length of time needed to analyse the collection of so much data is a serious problem since detailed configurations of population can alter considerably over the space of a few years. Quick computer analysis is vital and the territorial matching of data from one year to another (for enumeration districts, wards and other local authority boundaries may change

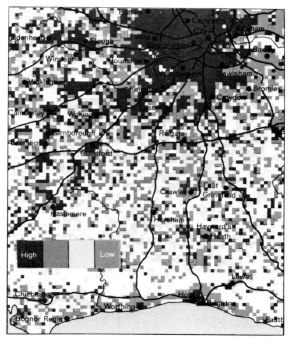

Fig 8.1b London and the South Coast—variations in people born abroad, at 1 km squares. New computer-assisted techniques allow data to be assimilated rapidly and transformed into maps. (Crown Copyright reserved)

between censuses) has been made possible since the 1971 census by the grid referencing of dwellings to the nearest 100 metres in towns and 1,000 metres in rural areas. Such information has been very beneficial in allowing spatial print-outs and manipulations of data, such as those accomplished by the University of Sheffield and Durham for the 1971 census (Fig. 8.1b).

CHANGING POPULATION STRUCTURE

The population of Britain increased very slowly over the pre-industrial period. From a base of about 3·7 millions immediately before the Black Death in 1348, population had only risen by about one third by the end of the seventeenth century (Fig. 8.2). During the eighteenth century, however, the population almost doubled, and then increased again by almost two and a half times in the course of the nineteenth century. During the twentieth century the rate of increase has again slowed down so that since 1900 the population has only increased by about one third to give a total population of 53,821,400 at the census in 1971.

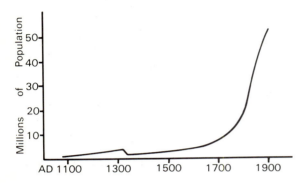

Fig 8.2 Population increase in Great Britain, 1100–1900

The Demographic Transition

These changes in the rate of population increase are largely due to a period of marked disparity between the birth and death rates in a phenomenon that is referred to as the *demographic transition,* illustrated in Fig. 8.3. The rise in population is largely attributed to a falling death rate, particularly of infants, as standards of nutrition rose, advances were made in preventive medicine, and improvements came in environmental hygiene (ranging from the use of easily washable cotton underwear to the more effective supply of fresh water to towns, and the provision of associated systems of drainage). Enhanced economic opportunities, due to the success of the industrial revolution, also contributed to a lowering of the age of marriage, and with it a tendency for birth rate to rise a little. However, the relative importance of these factors is open to considerable debate, particularly since reliable statistics are not available for most of the period of rapid population expansion.

Similarly there is considerable debate as to the exact mechanisms by which the rate of population increase slowed down. Undoubtedly a progressive fall in the birth rate is the reason, but our understanding of the long term decline in fertility which may have begun by the 1860s, but was certainly noticeable from the 1880s, is less than

complete. Tranter reviews the three factors that may have been responsible: a fall in fecundity, a fall in nuptiality and increased contraception. Of the first, the ability of the population to actually procreate, it would seem that the population was if anything of a higher rather than a lower fecundity over this period, so that factor may be discounted. In the later decades of the nineteenth century, and in the early twentieth century there does seem to have been a fall in nuptiality, that is the readiness of the population to marry. This may have been due to rather more uncertain economic conditions which led to the putting off of marriage, but more likely due to a high rate of emigration over this period. Single young men are the most likely section of any population to emigrate, and it does seem that there was a mild distortion of the sex ratio precisely in the marriage age-groups. Thus there was an increase in the proportion of unmarried women and consequently a fall in overall birth rate. By the second decade of the twentieth century, though, this was correcting itself as the tide of emigration slackened in the face of stricter control, particularly in North America. By this time, though, the third factor, that of birth control, had become the most important factor in reducing birth rate. Although it is known that contraception had been practised regularly by a significant part of the population since

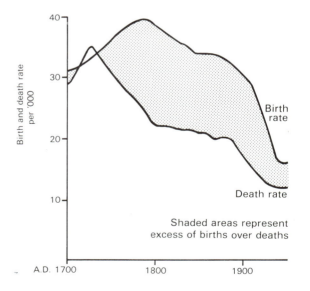

Fig 8.3 Demographic transition in Great Britain, 1700–1900

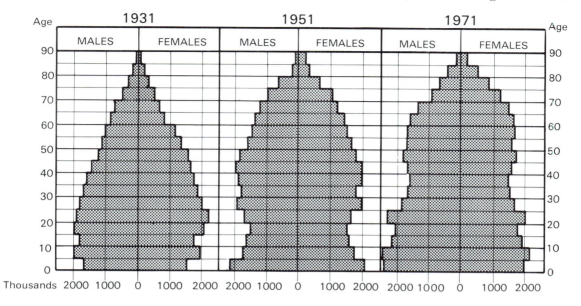

Fig 8.4 Age/Sex pyramids for Great Britain, 1931, 1951, and 1971

at least the seventeenth century, its growing popularity can be attributed to three factors. A decline in infant mortality, coupled with the increased cost of child raising, tended to discourage the large families of an earlier period. An enhancement of the woman's role, partly due to the movement towards female emancipation, played its part, along with the progressive erosion of the religious sanctions against contraception; but perhaps the most important of all was the greater appreciation of contraceptive methods following the Bradlaugh-Besant trial in the last century, and especially the development over the early years of the twentieth century of more acceptable contraceptive devices. The result was that by the 1930s there were considerable fears that Britain would experience serious population decline, and that the population would be composed more and more of the older and less vigorous age groups. In the event, of course, the population did not decline, and indeed experienced a marked increase after the Second World War.

Post-war Changes

Since 1945 the birth rate has undergone marked fluctuations. The period 1945–7 saw the celebrated post war bulge in live births, but this quickly fell away only to rise again for nine successive years between 1955 and 1964, since when there has been a progressive reduction in the numbers of live births.

The changes in the overall structure of the population between 1931 and 1971 are shown in Fig. 8.4. The fewer numbers of children is clearly shown in the 1931 pyramid which tapers towards the base covering the lowest three age groups. Above the age of 15, however, the pyramid is notably squat with a fairly rapid short-fall with each upward step of the pyramid. One interesting feature is the imbalance between males and females from the ages of 30 to 55 due to the male casualties of the First World War. By 1951 the pyramid has assumed quite a different shape. Better survival rates are reflected in the relatively equal numbers in age groups between 20 and 50, the small families of the 1930s are represented in the small numbers in the 10–20 age groups, but then the pyramid opens out markedly with the celebrated 'baby bulge' of 1945–7. By 1971 the pyramid has achieved a much more columnar characteristic indicative of a high level of general health and survival, the post 1945 bulge has transferred itself to the 20–25 age group, and the fewer numbers of children in the 0–5 age group is a reflection of the falling birth rate which was to characterise the 1970s. These overall characteristics, however, hide structural differences (as well as regional differences which will be discussed in the next section).

For many generations there has been a persistent tendency for fertility to vary with socio-economic groups, with family size being somewhat larger among manual workers than among non-manual workers. This has generally been attributed to different attitudes towards contraception and economic expectation. The difference between the groups has tended to be narrowed over recent years, and family size in general has been reduced, except among professional groups where a persistent tendency towards rather larger families has been maintained. Similarly socio-economic differences are reflected in the pattern of mortality, and despite an overall improvement in standard mortality rates, and a narrowing of the differences between the groups, mortality rates remain higher for lower socio-economic groups. Overall, however, the expectation of life has increased over the twentieth century, due in no small measure to better health care of the young, and of pregnant and nursing mothers, which has also considerably enhanced female life-expectancy rates.

The changing numbers and structure of a population has important repercussions in the demands placed by that population upon the resources available for its support. In particular we must highlight the changes that have been brought about in the size and nature of the dependent population, that is the section of the population, both young and old, who are not economically active (Table 4). With a declining birth rate between the wars, the numbers of dependent children (under the age of 15) fell, but with better survival rates the numbers of elderly people (above the age of 65) increased. The net effect until 1951 was actually to increase the proportion of the active population. Since 1951 the active proportion of the population has fallen slightly. The character of the dependent population meanwhile has changed quite dramatically. In 1901 there were more than six times as many children under 15 than there were people over 65. In 1971 the difference was reduced to about 2:1. Such changes are very important as they have a significant effect upon the nature of public service provision for education and health and welfare.

CHANGING POPULATION DISTRIBUTIONS

Whatever the aggregate changes in the composition of the population, changing economic conditions have had a profound effect upon the regional pattern of population in all its aspects. Lawton has shown how the main features of the changing geography of population in Britain – rural depopulation, selective urban growth, suburbanization and the drift to the south – all became apparent during the latter half of the nineteenth century. Net out-migration from the countryside became widespread from the 1840s and within ten years many country areas were experiencing a steady decrease in population. Many country market towns, robbed of their hinterland population, also declined as the new railways made the attractions of larger centres more readily accessible. As a result country areas entered into a period of decline or at best fossilisation from which they have

Table 4: Changes in the dependent population, Great Britain, 1901–1971

	AGE GROUP	1901	1911	1921	1931	1951	1961	1971
Population (millions)	Under 15	12.4	13.0	11.9	11.1	11.3	12.3	12.8
	15–64	24.0	26.9	26.7	31.4	33.4	34.1	35.7
	Over 65	1.8	2.2	3.1	3.4	5.5	6.1	7.4
% total	Under 15	32.4	30.9	28.5	24.2	22.5	23.4	23.0
	15–64	62.8	63.9	64.1	68.4	66.5	64.9	63.8
	Over 65	4.8	5.2	7.4	7.4	11.0	11.7	14.2

Note: There was no census in 1941

Source: *Abstract of British Historical Statistics*

only recently been rescued by the advent of commuters or second home owners; 'key village', or in-fill policies on the part of the local planning authority (see chapter 14) have also helped to arrest rural decline. In contrast a few areas in the nineteenth century experienced massive population increases, so that the population as a whole became rapidly urbanised. Law has calculated that at the beginning of the nineteenth century only 33·8 per cent of the population lived in urban settlements, while by 1911 that figure had increased to 78·9 per cent. While the industrialised urban areas had (persistently) high rates of natural increase during the nineteenth century, there were regional differences with rates being highest in coal mining and heavy industrial districts, and lowest in the textile districts, where high levels of female employment were maintained.

Migration

However, it was migration that gave the real dynamic to regional disparities in population change, and what is the more remarkable is the way these changes were funnelled into just a few areas – London and what were to be the provincial conurbations. The labour demands of the earlier magnets on the coalfields and textile areas of the north subsequently came to be met by the natural increase in population provided by the youthful migrants themselves, so that by the 1890s and 1900s these areas began losing population by migration, both overseas and to the towns of the East Midlands and the South-East. In contrast to this 'gain-loss' profile of migration, many Midlands and south-eastern towns experienced a 'loss-gain' pattern of migration, only London experiencing persistent migrational gain over the nineteenth century. Even, here, however, a centrifugal movement of population was evident with the growing suburbanisation of the metropolis, a pattern also being followed in the other major provincial centres.

Changes since the first decade of this century in the regional distribution of the population are shown in Fig. 8.5. It is important to remind ourselves in the following discussion of regional losses and gains by migration, that no region has actually experienced an absolute decline in population over the period. Even Scotland has had a 9·8 per cent increase in population between 1911 and 1971. The problem lies in the fact that over the same period gains by regions in the Midlands and the South have been four times as great. The origins of these different regional performances in population increases lay in the different economic and industrial structure of the regions. Industry on the coalfields, and of course mining itself, which had provided the staples of Victorian prosperity, found themselves particularly badly hit by the depression years after the First World War. During the 1930s, employment rates were almost consistently better in the Midlands and the South-East than they were in the northern regions, in Wales and in Scotland. This regional imbalance in the impact of the depression focused attention on population and migration, and in 1940 the Barlow Commission presented the results of its enquiry into "the present geographical distribution of the industrial population of Great Britain and the probable direction of any change in the future". The Barlow Report lies at the root of all subsequent regional policies for it proposed governmental intervention in the economy to restore regional imbalances by assisting and persuading firms to move into declining regions. In the event the declining regions are still declining, though hopefully not at the rate they would have done had there been no policy initiatives over the last forty years. Both the symptom and to some extent the cause of the varying regional economic performance has been population movements between the regions, of which the most pronounced has been the 'drift to the south'.

Although, as we have seen, a southward drift of the population in search of employment was evident in the later decades of the nineteenth century, becoming specially apparent in the 1920s, this is by no means a new phenomenon. London has been a magnet since medieval times, and if it was drawing then on areas closest to it, there is no reason to suppose that those areas were not similarly drawing from areas further out into the provinces. What characterises the present drift to the south, though, is that it is not centred exclusively upon London, but is a characteristic shared by the whole of the country, with a net effect of dividing Great Britain into a northerly region of net migration loss and a southern region of net migration gain. While in the 1950s the West Midlands and the South-Eastern regions were the major recipients of migrants, over the 1960s and into the 1970s the situation changed rather, so that

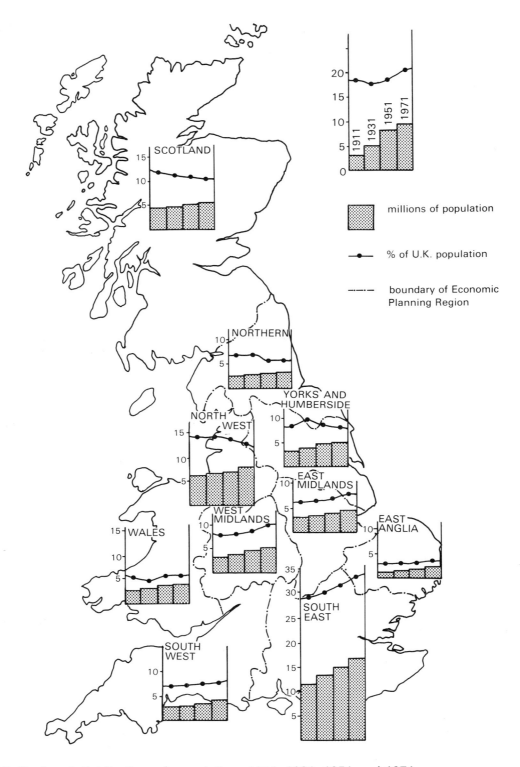

Fig 8.5 Regional distribution of population, 1911, 1931, 1951 and 1971

the South-Western region and East Anglia became the most popular destinations of migrants. In contrast, the greatest population losses were felt by Scotland and the Northern region. The implication is that this is truly a drift to the south, and not a drift to the metropolis.

Scottish Migration Patterns

The drift to the south is a more complex phenomenon than we might at first imagine, and we can best understand it by examining in rather closer detail the picture for particular regions. Of prime importance is the pattern of population movements in and from Scotland.

Within Scotland there has been pronounced migration inwards to the areas focusing upon Edinburgh and Dundee. These regions received migrants from all the peripheral areas of Scotland, with the greatest number emanating from the Glasgow region in the west. Unfortunately, in the whole of Scotland, the New Towns of East Kilbride and Cumbernauld were the only areas which had a net in-migration, whether from other regions of Scotland or from other parts of the U.K. Indeed over the period 1961–1966 there were only five National Health Executive areas in the whole of Scotland where out-migration to the rest of the U.K. (mainly England) was more than balanced by in-migration from the rest of Scotland, and this is really the root of the Scottish drain of population. Since 1951 Scotland has lost by migration more than half a million people. Losses on this scale have only been possible by high levels of fertility and also by much smaller inward flows of migrants than would normally be expected.

We must now direct our attention to the Scottish migrant in England. While every English conurbation is losing population by net out-migration, there was a net-inflow of Scots, except at Tyneside. Apart from flows to the conurbations, the largest numbers of migrants are to be found in the East and West Midlands, which is an element of surprise, for theory suggests that most Scots should be found in those regions closest to Scotland. On the other hand, recent Scottish migrants do not make up large numbers in the southern regions, and when these figures are examined more closely the reason for the Scots presence in the Midlands is at least partly detectable. Jones notes that between July 1962 and June 1968, Scotland provided almost 2,000 in-migrant families to Corby New Town. Similarly the N.C.B. inter-divisional transfer scheme was responsible for the movement of over 3,000 miners from Scotland to Yorkshire and the Midlands between 1962 and 1967.

Migration in the North-West and in Yorkshire and Humberside

As an example of the English net-losing regions, the North-West is very interesting because it contains within itself a microcosm of the whole British situation. In terms of social indicators, the former county of Cheshire shared with Surrey the highest levels of well-being, while in the remoter Pennine valleys, such as the Rossendale area, economic decline is accompanied by persistent out-migration on the part of the younger sections of the population, and a consequent decline in the level of fertility. Natural increase of population in the textile towns north of Manchester was barely 1 per cent between 1951–71, compared with a national average of 7 per cent. On the other hand, birth rate is remarkably high on Merseyside, in part at least, due to the presence of large numbers of Roman Catholics occupying low socio-economic status. Over the period 1951–71, natural increase stood at 10 per cent, but by migration Merseyside has been able to shed one third of its natural increase each year, especially into the zone of prosperity which stretches across most of Cheshire and into the southern fringes of Greater Manchester. The extensive middle-class dormitory areas between Altrincham, Macclesfield and Stockport are more reminiscent of leafy Surrey than the North, and the Macclesfield sub-region recorded population increases of 16·4 per cent over 1951–71. This combined pattern, then, of population loss in the north of the region, and population gain in the south gives a pronounced southerly direction to the overall current of movement on the west of the Pennines.

On the other side of the Pennines, the Yorkshire and Humberside region had a slightly lower rate of net out-migration than the North-West over the period 1951–71, and combined with a slightly higher rate of natural increase (due in some measure to significant numbers of new Commonwealth migrants) increased its total population by 6·7 per cent as opposed to the North-West's 5·2

Table 5:   Components of population change, 1951–71, by region (after Champion, 1976)

REGION	1951–61 CHANGE (PERCENTAGE)			1961–71 CHANGE (PERCENTAGE)		
	Natural change	Net migration	Total change	Natural change	Net migration	Total change
Northern	+6·2	−2·4	+3·8	+5·4	−3·3	+1·5
Yorkshire and Humberside	+4·3	−1·6	+2·7	+5·7	−1·5	+3·9
North West	+3·7	−1·7	+2·0	+5·2	−1·7	+3·1
East Midlands	+5·5	+1·8	+7·3	+7·1	+2·3	+9·1
West Midlands	+6·2	+1·4	+7·6	+8·4	−0·3	+7·6
East Anglia	+4·7	+2·6	+7·3	+5·6	+8·1	+13·2
South East	+4·4	+3·0	+7·4	+6·1	−0·2	+5·8
South West	+3·2	+2·6	+5·8	+4·4	+6·5	+10·4
Wales	+3·2	−1·4	+1·8	+3·7	−0·1	+3·4
England and Wales	+4·5	+0·9	+5·4	+5·9	+0·2	+5·8

Source: *Abstr. Reg. Statist.* No. 6, 1970, Table 7; *Abstr. reg. Statist.* No. 9, 1973, Table 10.

per cent. Over the 1960s Champion notes a change in the migration balances of the slow-growing regions (Table 5). Government strategies to reinvigorate the regional economies of both the Northern region and also of Wales seem to have met with some success for in both those regions there is a reduction in the numbers of young families leaving the region; whereas the North-West and Yorkshire and Humberside, which were not so strongly supported by government aid policies, continued to lose these younger age groups in great numbers.

Migration in Southern Britain

Turning now to the southerly regions there is a marked change in the distribution of growth over the post war period. In the 1950s the West Midlands and the South-East were the fastest growing regions in Britain, but over the 1960s both these regions experienced consistent net migration losses thus reducing their rate of expansion. Their place was taken at the head of the table by East Anglia and the South-West, with the East Midland region close behind. It is salutary to note the differences in the way such increases may be made up, however. Both the South-West and the East Midland regions experienced population increases of about 16 per cent over 1951–71, yet the rate of in-migration to the South-West has run at more than double that for the East Midlands, where

most of the increase must be reckoned to be due to the fertility of the population in a relatively economically buoyant region. In contrast, the increase in the South-West is largely made up of retirement migration, a phenomenon which has been persistently increasing over recent years.

The marked change in the rate of increase of population in the South-East region is worthy of note. By the 1960s the region was suffering a net loss by migration, although its rate of natural increase was still the third highest in Great Britain. But for the continued attraction of the region for the 15–24 age group (over 80,000 during the 1960s) it would have suffered a net loss of migrants in every age group. While the biggest losses are of those above the age of 60, significant numbers of young families have left the region, driven out by the high costs of housing, changing job opportunities, or government sponsored relocation policies.

This centrifugal movement of population is a feature which is largely masked at regional level, but is one which Champion considers to have taken on a noticeably new aspect over the 1960s. Over the nineteenth century there was a gravity effect on the part of the largest centres. During the 1960s, however, a process of centrifugalism had set in, by which a net outflow of migrants from the inner city and inner conurbation areas led to a more rapid growth of smaller centres on the peripheries of the major Standard Metropolitan Labour Areas.

Population Patterns

Overall, four major phases can be distinguished in the changing distribution of population in Great Britain since the advent of the Industrial Revolution.

(i) A marked rise in population numbers led to increased densities of population in both towns and country.

(ii) A strong current of migration, that set in towards London and the major industrial centres on the coalfields, led after 1840 to rural depopulation.

(iii) From the later nineteenth century there is some redistribution of population between the major agglomerations, as earlier centres of growth on the northern coalfields begin to lose population to the Midlands regions and to the South-East.

(iv) A dispersal of the population from the major agglomerations, heralded from the later nineteenth century by the process of suburbanisation, becomes particularly marked in the 1960s by centrifugalism into smaller peripheral centres, and by marked increases in the population of East Anglia, the South-West and the East Midlands.

Lastly, over this whole period we must note that some areas of Britain have seen a persistent loss of population and a progressive run down of the local community. Such regions are predominantly found in the marginal agricultural areas of the uplands and of the North and West of Britain where population decline has been even more severe than in more prosperous country areas in the agricultural lowlands. In these latter areas, out-migration of labour has been at least partly balanced by an in-flow of retirement migrants and long-distance commuters. These topics will be discussed in Chapter 14.

THE NEW IMMIGRANTS

As we noted in Chapter 4, with the exception of the Romanies very few new migrants have settled in Great Britain from the time of the Norman conquest to the Industrial Revolution. Since then, however, four significant groups of people have made their home in Britain and made a distinctive contribution to the national character.

Unfortunately, the British census is deficient in the recording of information associated with migration, particularly from overseas, and consequently our understanding of the structure and distribution of these new migrant populations is less than precise.

The most important single group is the Irish. Seasonal labour migration on the part of the Irish was commonplace during the eighteenth century. Equally industrialisation over the nineteenth century provided many job opportunities for a population that was anxious to improve its expectations. Irish labour was often casual, sometimes introduced by employers attempting to break strikes, and frequently occupied in the meanest sort of employment. In consequence much of the migration was temporary, both of men and of women. However, increasing numbers of Irish stayed, predominantly found in London, the conurbations, and close to the major ports of entry. Precise enumeration is difficult to obtain but by 1931 rather more than 360,000 people born in what was by then Eire were resident in the U.K., making up 0·8 per cent of the population. That figure has steadily increased to about three quarters of a million in the 1970s, approximately 1·4 per cent of the total population.

A second group is made up of migrants from a variety of European backgrounds, mainly coming to Britain as refugees. Anti-Semitism in eastern Europe, and especially in Russian Poland, stimulated extensive out-migration in the closing decades of the nineteenth century; and by 1911 upwards of 75,000 east European Jews were to be found in London, with additional significant colonies in Leeds, Manchester and Liverpool. Further anti-Semitism between the wars in Germany increased the flow of immigrants, and post-war migration and refugee settlements resulted in 101,000 Germans and 162,000 Poles being recorded in the 1951 census. Other small groups included Ukrainians, locally significant in London and the industrial cities of the North of England. Since 1951 the Polish-born community has steadily declined, but an interesting feature of migration of European origin is the large numbers of Italians who have settled in Britain since 1945. Over half the Italian-born migrants are to be found in the South-East, with strong concentrations in London, and in Bedfordshire where recruitment of labour for the brickfields drew heavily on Italian labour in the years succeeding the Second World War.

The most controversial aspect of post-war migration, however, has been the numbers of New Commonwealth citizens who have settled in Britain, mainly from the West Indies, India and Pakistan, but also including significant numbers of Singhalese and expatriated Indians from Uganda. This notable influx of British passport-holders from former colonies was drawn to Britain by the rising demand for labour in the late 1950s and early 1960s. Some of this demand was in highly skilled areas such as in the medical services, but most was in general industrial and service occupations, particularly in less attractive, low-wage sectors. In a study of West Indian migration, Peach has shown that the trend of migration over the 1950s was largely determined by the fluctuating demand for labour in Britain, while the degree of emigration from Jamaica and the Caribbean reflected home conditions. Once settled in Britain a quite distinct distribution of migrants occurred, with West Indians in general moving into areas from which British migrants were moving out. Thus there was a tendency for concentrations of West Indians to be found in the cores of the largest cities and the conurbations, within which, like immigrant communities before them, they tend to occupy relatively well defined districts. The precise enumeration of the West Indian community is difficult because the rate of migration in the 1950s was insufficiently monitored, and children born in this country are registered as British born, but the estimated population by the late 1970s was around 700,000.

Fertility amongst the West Indian population has tended to decline since the high rates associated with the earliest migrants, and Asian settlers have steadily grown proportionately more significant, so that they will probably total about 900,000 by the early 1980s. Their distribution largely follows that of the West Indians, being concentrated in London and the major English conurbations (except Tyneside). Because migration tends to be attractive to the young adult, fertility rates of migrant populations tend to be high, tempered only by the fact that migration is also sex-selective, and there is usually a preponderance of men over women. Although tighter restrictions have been placed on immigration since the 1961 and 1968 Commonwealth Immigration

Acts, there is still a flow of wives and other dependents, particularly of Asian migrants, so that the proportionate size of the immigrant population from New Commonwealth countries can be expected to continue rising for the medium-term future. Given the marked clustering of the immigrant population, this is likely to have a significant effect upon the structure of local populations and the public service provisions of some areas (see Chapter 16).

Lastly in our consideration of migration we ought to note that considerable numbers of British residents have moved overseas, mainly to North America, Australia and southern Africa. Since the beginning of the nineteenth century, more than twenty million people have left Britain, intending to start a new life overseas. This produced a net loss by migration of about 60,000 a year until the Second World War, after which there was a net gain until 1964 when a combination of tighter immigration controls and sustained emigration again produced a net loss of 60,000. Since then the pattern has generally been one of net loss, and it is estimated that for the United Kingdom as a whole there will be a net loss of 277,000 for the decade 1974–1984.

POPULATION PROJECTIONS

The projection of population numbers, structure and distribution is an important consideration in terms of planning. The numbers of children in future years will help determine the need for educational provision, for which building and training programmes have to be adapted well in advance. Similarly family composition will be an important factor in determining future housing provision, while fluctuations in the mortality rate will have important repercussions on the need for health and welfare facilities for the elderly. Equally the size of the labour force and changes in the market structure of the population will have significant economic implications. Even medium-term projections, however, are not easy as Fig. 8.6 shows. With an assumption of a fairly steady birth rate and continuing good health of the population, it is relatively simple to project the progressive ageing of the present population, and to predict the numbers and proportion of the existing population which will fall into the various age bands over the next twenty or thirty years. What

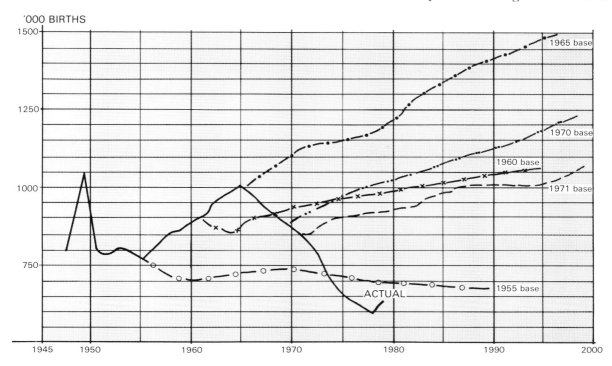

Fig 8.6 Projection of birth rates

leads to the greatest error, though, is the projection of births, since this is closely connected to prevailing social and economic conditions. Thus the widely varying projections shown in Fig. 8.6, are in large measure due to changing assumptions about the future size of families, based on the four marked shifts in the trend of birth rates since 1945. In addition it is not easy to predict the pattern of migration either within Britain or overseas, since changing economic and political conditions can have a marked effect upon both. Attempts to plan for the future, however, involve the making of assumptions about the population, and it is important that those assumptions are made on the best available data, and are progressively modified with the emergence of further trends.

References

Open University, *Statistical Sources, Unit 3, Population,* (Milton Keynes, 1975).

Coates, B.E. (director), *Census Atlas of South Yorkshire,* (Sheffield, 1974).

Tranter, N., *Population since the Industrial Revolution,* (Croom Helm, 1973).

Lawton, R., 'Population changes in England and Wales in the late 19th century: an analysis of trends by Registration Districts', *Trans. Inst. Brit. Geogrs.,* Vol. 44, 1968, pp. 55–74.

Law, C.M., 'The growth of urban population in England and Wales, 1801–1911', *Trans. Inst. Brit. Geogrs.,* Vol. 41, 1967, pp. 125–43.

Jones, H.R., 'Migration to and from Scotland since 1961', *Trans. Inst. Brit. Geogrs.,* Vol. 49, 1970, pp. 145–160.

Coates, B.E., & Rawstron, E.M., *Regional Variations in Britain,* (Batsford, 1971).

Champion, A.G., 'Evolving patterns of population distribution in England and Wales, 1951–1971', *Trans. Inst. Brit. Geogrs.,* New Series 1, 1976, pp. 401–420.

King, R., 'Bedford and the Italian connection', *Geographical Magazine,* Vol. XLIX, 1977, pp. 442–450.

Peach, G.C.K., 'Factors affecting the distribution of West Indians in Great Britain', *Trans. Inst. Brit. Geogrs.,* Vol. 38, 1966, pp. 151–164.

Part Three

Structural Problems

9

Agriculture, Forestry and Fishing

FARMING

Britain is looked upon as an essentially industrial and commercial country, and it comes as a surprise to many that agriculture is, as it has long been, a large and important activity. Over 19 out of a total of 24 million ha (47 out of 60 million acres) of the land are devoted to various types of farming which occupy around 230,000 full-time farm workers directly and perhaps as many indirectly. About 12 million ha are under crops and grass, with another 6·8 million ha of rough grazing. In 1975, agriculture (together with forestry and fishing) had an output of £2,116 million amounting to 2·8 per cent of the country's domestic output; this is greater than the equivalent figure for Canadian agriculture and equal to the equivalent figure for Australia and New Zealand combined. Below, we reproduce figures for a number of selected agricultural products which are characteristic of Britain, to show Britain's ranking among world producers and the relative importance of the agricultural sector considering her size. (See Table 6.)

Before the Second World War, British farms produced food for about 40 per cent of the population; today, they feed about two-thirds of an appreciably larger population – some 56 million as against 48 million in pre-war years. This greater output is achieved by far fewer farm workers, for the numbers have decreased from just under one million before the war to much less than one-third of this number. This greatly increased productivity has been due to a more mechanised, more efficient, and hence more pro-

ductive agriculture. During recent decades there have been dynamic changes within the agricultural industry and as Davidson and Wibberley (1977) have commented: "Although the agricultural scene has given an appearance of relative permanence in many of its physical characteristics, it is an industry of very real and rapid technical and economic change. In recent years the changes in, for example, the size of fields, the way in which crops are harvested, the size of farm buildings and the materials of which they are made, and techniques of livestock production, have been dramatic enough to convince even the layman travelling through the countryside that something dynamic is happening."

Table 6:   Britain's World Commodity Ranking, 1977

COMMODITY	'000 TONNES PRODUCED IN U.K.	WORLD RANKING 1977
Barley	10,738	4th
Potatoes	6,598	9th
Sugar-beet	6,382	12th
Apples	345	16th
Hops	7	5th
Hens' eggs	807	6th
Cow's milk	15,041	6th
Cheese	213	11th
Beef & Veal	987	10th
Mutton & Lamb	240	7th
Pork	906	10th

Source: *Geographical Digest 1979* (George Philip & Son)

The Second Agricultural Revolution

In an earlier chapter attention was drawn to the changes in farming – in its structure, methods and products – which occurred as a result of the Agrarian Revolution of the seventeenth and eighteenth centuries. But a revolution, just as far-reaching and perhaps of even greater significance, has taken place since the end of the Second World War – in a matter of some thirty years.

The chief changes in farming relate to the structure of the industry, the mechanisation of farming, the application of scientific techniques, to productivity and to specialisation. Let us, therefore, consider these very significant changes which have made it possible to speak of a Second Agricultural Revolution.

For many hundreds of years much of the land of Britain was in the hands of the landed gentry whose ample estates comprised farms of varying sizes let to tenant farmers. During the past fifty years social changes have altered completely the pattern of rural Britain. Estate duties have led to the break-up and sale of many large estates. The farms, which made them up, were often sold to the occupying tenants. Largely as a result of these changes, slightly more than 60 per cent of the present day farms, numbering some 300,000, are owner-occupied. The total number of holdings, as distinct from farms, is around 450,000. Half of these are small, averaging less than 6·5 ha (16 acres) and belong to small-holders who work them on a part-time basis. At the other end of the scale there are the 'large' farms (though these are small by, say, American or Australian standards) which average about 120 ha (300 acres). (See Fig. 9.1.) These farms form only about ten per cent of the total, but in general terms they are responsible for producing half of the total farm output, in contrast to the large number of small-holdings which account for only about one-tenth of the total output. However, it should be emphasised that the farm size/productivity relationship is also a function of the location and characteristics of the farm, as well as its size.

Fig 9.1 Manor Farm, Holbeach, Lincs. The rich agricultural lands of eastern England have proved ideal for the super-enlarged, capital-intensive farming of the 1980's

In more recent times there has been a trend towards a greater scale in all types of farming: the number of holdings has been contracting at the rate of two to three per cent per year and the smaller the size of the holding the faster has been the rate of its disappearance; on the other hand, holdings of around 160 ha (400 acres) or more have increased in number. Table 7 shows the changes in the size of agricultural holdings during the ten-year period 1961–71. There has also been a trend towards the amalgamation of small farm units into bigger units which can be worked more efficiently and are more economically viable, a trend encouraged by U.K. and E.E.C. grant aid.

Table 7: Changes in the Size of Agricultural Holdings

SIZE IN HECTARES	NUMBER OF HOLDINGS IN '000s	
	1961	1971
Under 2	70·1	23·4
2 and under 6	61·6	32·9
6 and under 8	14·0	10·3
8 and under 12	23·2	16·6
12 and under 20	36·7	25·9
20 and under 40	56·9	44·2
40 and under 60	29·1	24·5
60 and under 120	32·6	29·2
120 and under 200	9·6	10·6
200 and under 280	2·6	3·5
280 and under 400	1·2	1·9
400 and over	0·7	1·3

During this decade the area in holdings over 120 ha (300 acres) rose from 3 to 3·8 million ha, while the area in holdings below 120 ha fell from 6·8 to 5·6 million ha.

Source: Institute of Agricultural Economics (1972) *The State of British Agriculture 1971–1972* Oxford (converted to metric measurement).

A notable and important change has been the increasing *mechanisation* of agriculture; in fact, British farms are, in general, among the most mechanised in the world. Much capital has been invested in a wide range of machines now being deployed by the British farmer, though this investment has been made chiefly by the large and medium-sized farms. Small farms are much less mechanised since machinery is expensive and the small farmer seldom has the capital available for such investment. Associated with mechanisation has been the trend towards increased field size, especially in the more eastern arable parts of the country, such as East Anglia (Fig. 9.2). Thousands of miles of hedges have been uprooted in order to create larger fields which are more amenable to large-scale mechanised cultivation. While such action has brought economies of scale, it has had certain other effects of a deleterious nature not least of which has been to induce soil erosion; indeed, farmers are now beginning to have second thoughts about the wisdom of clearing field hedges. Another effect of the almost lavish use of machines on many farms is that it has enabled the labour force to be drastically reduced. But the point should be made that mechanisation itself has not necessarily led to agricultural unemployment; the drift from the land has been going on for a long time and, indeed, on such a scale that mechanisation would have had to be adopted to save the industry.

The role played by science in agriculture is hardly any less important than that in industry, though it is perhaps less obvious. We are all familiar with the use of artificial fertilisers, herbicides and pesticides, but added to these are a host of scientific developments affecting plants and animals, and farm management. To quote a few examples: experiments in plant breeding have produced new strains which may yield more heavily or be resistant to certain plant diseases; the use of artificial insemination has made it possible to breed better animals with specific qualities; the use of new drugs, vaccines, etc., has enabled the farmer to reduce disease in his animals; the use of hormone injections is giving the farmer greater control over livestock husbandry through regulating conception in animals or hastening growth; the feeding of animals and the fertilising of crops is also frequently scientifically controlled.

There has been a high and steady expansion in overall agricultural production at an average rate of about 7 per cent a year (compared with industrial growth which has rarely exceeded 3 per cent per year.) Output is well over double the pre-war level. Yields of wheat have improved by over 70 per cent and barley by about 50 per cent since the war. Total numbers of cattle, pigs and poultry have increased; sheep alone have decreased in numbers. The average milk yield per cow has risen from around 550 to 800 gallons a year, and the number of eggs laid per hen has doubled.

Fig 9.2 Amalgamation of fields north-west of Charsfield, Suffolk. Modern agricultural practice has reduced the former hedges to crop marks. Note the circular enclosures also marked by crop marks denoting ancient occupance

So-called 'factory farming' has appeared and is growing rapidly: this refers to intensive mass production indoors with highly regulated feeding; for instance, nearly all poultry are now reared in battery and broiler houses and the rearing of pigs, calves and cattle is beginning to follow suit. Such methods, though condemned by many, certainly effect great savings in production costs. All this increased productivity has been achieved by applying the arts of the biologist, the engineer, the scientist and the industrialist to farming.

Yet another factor in the situation has been *specialisation*. The traditional concept of the general or mixed farm has largely disappeared in the post-war period and most British farms, principally due to economic pressures, have switched to a measure of specialised production. Most farms are becoming simplified in their policy and operation, and are concentrating upon a few products which they are producing in quantity. Specialisation focuses not merely upon arable or pastoral farming or market-gardening, but upon commodities or crops, e.g. milk, beef, barley, fruit, or glasshouse produce. Large-scale specialised production of this kind is more economic, although the risks may be greater; for example, the outbreak of an animal disease, such as foot-and-mouth or swine fever, may lead to the farmer losing his entire herd, or the market price may suddenly drop, due perhaps to a glut, and place him in financial difficulties. Not even financial compensation or complicated farm price support systems can fully protect the farmer from disasters of this kind.

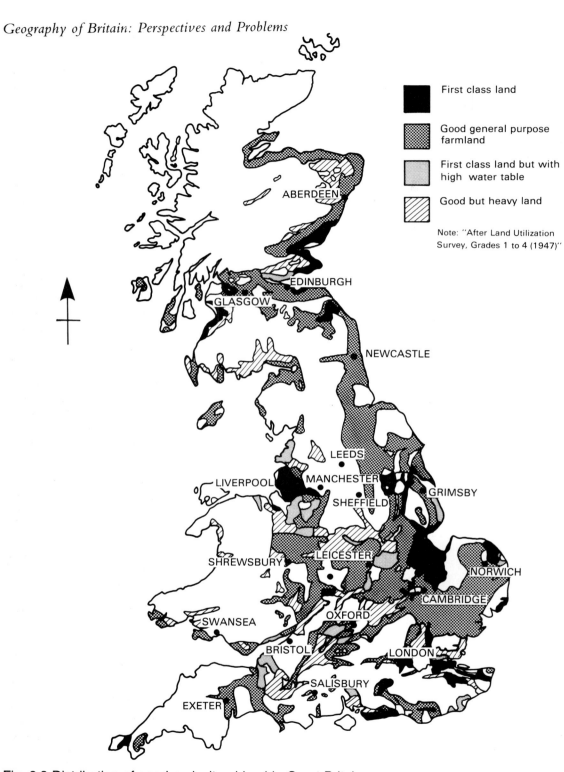

Fig. 9.3 Distribution of good agricultural land in Great Britain

Land and Labour

The problems of land and labour deserve some notice. As already mentioned some 12 million ha (30 million acres) or over half the area of Britain are under crops and grass, but pressure upon agricultural land is great. A gradually expanding population, the creation of new towns, and the construction of motorways are but three factors placing agricultural land under pressure. A growing population implies increased housing which frequently eats into the rural environs of towns. New towns, largely the result of recent town planning ideas, have been extravagant of space and eat up land. Modern motorway construction makes big demands upon land: e.g. it has been estimated that the motorway programme up to 1971 consumed land equivalent to the area of the county of Dorset, and that the programme for the period 1972 to 1980 has swallowed up a similar area!

Until quite recently it was generally assumed that Britain would require all the high-quality agricultural land there was available (Fig. 9.3). The country, it is true, can ill afford to be cavalier with good quality land but current trends in farming suggest that there is sufficient agricultural land available for present and future foreseeable needs. With greater technical efficiency, more intensive use of land, increasing crop yields and factory farming, it would seem possible that no further demands on land for agriculture will be required; indeed, it is even possible that a reduction could be made.

The numbers of the workforce engaged in agriculture have steadily declined, but this contraction is not a reflection of a declining activity; on the contrary, agriculture can show increasing productivity. Because farming is now a capital-intensive, highly mechanised and well-managed industry it has been able to adjust to a shrinking labour force. The reasons why people have left, and continue to leave, the countryside are many but among them are (i) the mechanisation of the industry which has enabled the farmer to cut back on his work force; (ii) the higher wages to be had in manufacturing industry and urban employment; (iii) prospects of promotion to positions of responsibility in farming have always been few; (iv) long and irregular working hours and the arduous nature of much of the farm work have not attracted people to the land; and (v) poor living conditions and the lack of social life have driven many, particularly the young, away from the land.

Factors Influencing Agriculture

The application of science and technology to agriculture has not been without very considerable effects upon the geographical controls which formerly exerted strong influences upon the types of farming practised.

Physiographical (altitude and terrain) and climatic conditions continue to exert a differential effect upon upland and lowland farming, and upon arable, pastoral and horticultural farming. Broadly, farms in England which are devoted primarily to arable crops occur in the eastern parts of the country, where there are greater areas of level or gently undulating land and where conditions are drier, sunnier and warmer during the growing season. Dairying and the rearing and fattening of cattle occur predominantly in the western and south-western parts of England, and in the same parts of Scotland. Potato and vegetable cultivation is concentrated very substantially in the lower lying, peaty and alluvial areas of the Humberhead region, the Fens and south Lancashire. Hence, the broad traditional pattern continues to exist.

In detail, however, this pattern has been considerably altered. The changes are of three kinds. First, the traditional rotations have been largely broken down; for example, long grass leys may be laid down in arable areas while, on the other hand, new fertilisers and soil conditioners are gradually making it possible for continuous cereal cultivation to be practised. Secondly, some areas have changed their agricultural economy; for instance, grain growing has replaced sheep on the South Downs, and market gardening in the Evesham area had spread onto the heavy Lias Clay. Thirdly, economic factors, such as market demand, have often over-ridden geographical factors as, for example, the development of milk production in Essex to serve the needs of London. As Coppock (1964) has commented: "while the ecological requirements of crops and livestock set ultimate limits on what is done, the choice . . . where farming is primarily an economic activity, will be determined chiefly by profitability." Technical

Fig 9.4 Irrigation lines on Italian rye grass, Boxgrove, Sussex

factors have sometimes been responsible for changes, e.g. the greater power and speed of the tractor has made it possible for certain heavy clays, which previously were under perennial grass, to be used for arable cropping. Again, the growing of crops by irrigation in the drier parts of the country is, without doubt, going to affect cropping in the future (Fig. 9.4).

While agriculture in the upland regions of Britain is more closely influenced and circumscribed by geographical controls (such as altitude, ruggedness of terraine, steepness of slope, shorter growing season, rain, mist and cloud, etc.), in the lowlands the growing use of machines, compound fertilisers and irrigation, together with advances in plant and animal breeding, have given the farmer a much greater measure of flexibility in rotations, and in cropping and stocking systems. Farming in lowland England is in a state of change and all the indications are that it will continue to remain so for a long time to come.

Political Influences

In the post-war period the planning of agriculture and the resultant changes in farming patterns have arisen from two important political developments: first, the Agriculture Act of 1947 by which the Government was able to exert a considerable influence upon price levels for the principal agricultural products; and, second, the acceptance, in 1972, of British membership of the European Economic Community, which entailed the country falling into line with the Community's Common Agricultural Policy (C.A.P.).

While the farming pattern within Britain is related to some extent to the physical environment and conditions within which the individual farmer operates, it also reflects the decisions and activities of the farmer. Nevertheless, government policy on prices and subsidy incentives almost inevitably exerts a strong influence, and may cause the farmer to modify or change his pattern of farming. One of the aims of the Agriculture Act was to encourage the production of those commodities considered to be in the national interest, e.g. grain, potatoes, sugar-beet, milk, eggs, beef cattle, pigs and wool. To this end, minimum national price levels were laid down, which were related to the quantities required and to the production costs incurred by efficient farmers. The minimum prices and cost levels were reviewed annually and, if necessary, adjusted. Thus the pattern and the output of British agriculture were largely geared to the Annual Review and Determination of Guarantees. Under the Act the Government was empowered to give grants and subsidies for such things as improvement of drainage, the laying on of water supplies, the provision of new farm buildings, fertilisers, the ploughing up of old pastures and hill farm improvements. As a result of this somewhat complex support system there gradually emerged a farming pattern strongly orientated towards arable cultivation, with a particular emphasis upon wheat, barley, potato and sugar-beet production. National agricultural advisory services were set up to provide free advice to farmers, while a Milk Marketing Board helped to stimulate a large home milk industry. All in all, "the planning of agricultural production in Britain since the end of World War II has been considerable and reasonably effective in terms of bringing forward the amounts and qualities of farm products thought by the Government to be desirable" (Davidson and Wibberley).

When Britain joined the E.E.C. in 1972, the system of agricultural planning which had prevailed for a quarter of a century underwent a change in order to accommodate itself to the Common Agricultural Policy. This was necessary since the underlying principles of the 1947 Agriculture Act were at variance with the C.A.P. The Community formed a large protected market in which home produced products of all the member countries were freely inter-changeable, while products imported from outside the Community had to face tariffs and sometimes quota restrictions. "The tariffs paid on products imported from outside are used to support the price levels decided upon for individual products produced within the Community and it is these tariffs which provide the large agricultural support funds used to pay farmers for their home produced products. Consumers within the Community pay for these protected agricultural prices directly in their food purchases and not through their taxes as was the case with the former British 'deficiency payment' system" (Davidson and Wibberley).

Regional Specialisation

Maps depicting agricultural regions no longer have any validity, although regional specialisations are still discernible. Formerly, the kind of farming practised in any area was very strongly influenced by geographical conditions such as accessibility, climate and soils, but such controls are much less operative today. Improvements in communications – such as speedier and more flexible transport, together with associated factors such as refrigeration and improved packaging – have transformed accessibility. Relatively remote and isolated areas are much less constrained in what they can produce and market: for instance, at one time milk produced in the Yorkshire Dales was mainly processed into cheese since liquid milk could not be despatched to urban markets. Also, soils nowadays can be treated and manipulated by mixing, fertilising, draining, using special shallow or deep ploughs etc., and so are much less of a determinant in farming: for example, the shallow, dry, chalky soils of the Yorkshire Wolds and the Downs, which once were given over almost entire-

ly to sheep rearing, are now frequently cultivated. Climatic controls are less easy to overcome and still to a very considerable extent determine the choice between arable and pastoral farming practice, although it may be noted that the increasing use of irrigation in the drier south-east of England is helping to overcome certain climatic constraints.

Farming nowadays is, as has already been said, principally a matter of economics. Market demand tends to outweigh almost every other factor. For instance, the presence of large urban markets almost invariably stimulates milk and horticultural production. At the same time British farming is becoming more versatile in its character with the farmer prepared to change from one type of production to another, e.g. beef to milk production or vice versa, according to the state of the market.

Pastoral farming is principally confined to the moister, hill country of Britain. High altitudes which cause low average temperatures and induce heavy relief rains, make cultivation impossible above about 800 feet; even at lower elevations a restricted range of hardy crops can only be grown and these are chiefly used for animal feedstuffs. While sheep and store cattle are grazed above the moorland edge and are to be found in the hilly parts of Scotland, the Pennines and Wales, the rearing and fattening of animals generally is carried on in the lowlands, valleys and foothills areas. Dairying is mostly confined to the wetter lowland areas in the western parts of Britain, but it is often important locally where large urban populations create a demand for milk. Dairying is frequently associated with pig and poultry rearing. The chief dairying areas are the Clyde valley, Galloway, the Lancashire-Cheshire plain, the middle Trent valley, the plain of Somerset and Devon. Only in the more equable parts of the British Isles, i.e. the South-west Peninsula, is it possible for cattle to be left out of doors throughout the year; elsewhere cattle have to be housed during the winter months and stall fed.

Along the Celtic fringe of Britain, relics of a more widespread system of farming linger on. This is crofting, found in the Scottish Isles and along the western coast of Scotland. The crofting system involves the cultivation of small patches of improved land to produce basic subsistence crops of oats, potatoes and other root vegetables, and the use of open land on hill slopes for stock grazing

111

together with, very often, supplementary fishing. Crofting is a self-supporting activity but it gives a bare subsistence economy; nevertheless, it continues to be of some significance in the Orkneys and Shetlands, and in the Highland Region of Scotland.

Arable farming is more demanding of climatic and edaphic conditions than pastoral farming. Crops fall broadly into two types: cash crops and fodder crops. Cereals – wheat, barley and oats – have an important place in crop rotation systems as, for instance, in the original Norfolk rotation of wheat, roots, barley and clover designed to maintain soil fertility and to combat soil exhaustion and erosion. Wheat is most extensively grown on the drier, warmer, sunnier plains and low plateaus of eastern Britain, especially in Fifeshire and the Lothians in Scotland, and between the Humber and the Thames in England. The wheat grown in Britain is of the soft kind and is unsuitable for bread-making. Barley is more tolerant of lower temperatures and poorer soil conditions than wheat and, accordingly, is more widely grown. Barley is chiefly grown as an animal feedstuff but much is cultivated for the brewing of beer and whisky distilling; when cultivated for the latter purposes, it is usually grown on heavier soils. Oats thrive in cooler and damper areas and are tolerant of poor soils, hence they are more particularly important in Scotland and Wales. Oats are useful as a fodder crop and are much used as a feed for dairy cattle and for pig-fattening.

Potatoes are an important crop and grown on a large scale in the Humberhead and Fen districts, in Lancashire and Cheshire, in Fifeshire, and in Ulster. Sugar-beet, which is rather demanding in its requirements, is mostly cultivated in the drier and warmer eastern parts of Britain, especially in Lincolnshire, the Fenlands and Norfolk. Hops require fertile soils and plentiful sunshine and need considerable skill and labour in their cultivation; production is largely concentrated in the vales of Kent and Sussex, in Essex, and in the lowlands of Herefordshire and Worcestershire.

Market gardening, which is concerned with the specialised production of fresh vegetables and glasshouse crops, is a highly capitalised, labour-intensive type of farming of wide occurrence. Important factors influencing the activity are light, stone-free soils which warm up quickly, sheltered sites, and proximity to markets. Most large towns have market gardens in their vicinity but there are some areas of special importance such as southern Essex, the Medway Valley, the area around Sandy in Bedfordshire, southern Cornwall, the Scilly Isles, the Vale of Evesham, the Fens, the Ormskirk areas of south Lancashire, the Fylde, the Upper Clyde Valley and the Carse of Gowrie. Fruit growing is often associated with market gardening, but of special note is the Vale of Kent for soft fruit, the Hampshire Basin for strawberries, Devon and Somerset for apples (cider), the Vale of Evesham for apples, pears and plums, the Fens for soft fruits, and the Carse of Gowrie for raspberries and strawberries.

FORESTRY

During the early centuries of the Christian era much of Britain was under forest and woodland, but with Anglo-Saxon invasion and colonisation, deliberate forest clearance (largely to provide land for agriculture) began to take place. The needs of timber for building purposes, for industrial processes, and for shipbuilding also laid a heavy toll on the forests. By the time of Elizabeth I most of the forests of England had been felled, and during the seventeenth century Scotland's forests also began rapidly to disappear as the hills began to be given over to sheep rearing. Thus, over a period of about a millennium, the natural landscape had been drastically transformed: the forests had largely disappeared and the chequered field landscape of the present day had taken their place.

By the beginning of the present century the total area of woodland in Britain had been reduced to a mere 1·13 million ha (2·8 million acres) or 5 per cent of the land surface. Domestic demands for timber were met by large imports of foreign (largely softwood) timber. During World War I imports were severely restricted and, in order to meet home needs, nearly half a million acres of British woodland had to be felled. The country's timber deficiencies led to a governmental enquiry and from this the Forestry Commission was set up (1919). Concern about the country's woodlands long antedated this development, for even in the late eighteenth century and during the nineteenth century some landowners had begun to take an interest in forestry and a number of private re-afforestation schemes were introduced. Such private planting, though well-intentioned and excellent, had, nevertheless, little impact on the total acreage of wooded land. However, during the inter-war period, the Forestry Commission undertook a programme of re-planting and some 148,000 ha (370,000 acres) of conifer plantations were established in England, Wales and Scotland. Concurrently, private planting added a further 81,000 ha (200,000 acres). Thus by 1939 the ravages of World War I had been made good.

World War II unfortunately brought a further devastation and some 151,000 ha (373,000 acres) of woodland had to be felled to help war-time needs. The basis of the post-war afforestation policy was a White Paper published in 1943. The aim of this policy was to ensure the rapid expansion of Britain's forests to 2 million ha (4·94 million acres), to reduce the country's dependence on imported timber, and to ensure as far as possible self-sufficiency in timber supplies in the contingency of any future war. An ambitious afforestation programme was outlined: this involved the replanting or upgrading of 800,000 ha of existing woodland and the afforestation of 1,200,000 ha of new land. This ambitious programme was never fulfilled, largely because of shortages of land but also because of some concern about the effects which such a vigorous policy of tree planting would have upon agriculture. Defence strategy was the primary objective of the White Paper's proposals and an attempt was made to build up a strategic reserve of timber which would enable the country to be self-sufficient for a limited period of up to three years. For this planting target to be achieved 120,000 ha were estimated to be necessary but, in fact, only about 20,000 ha were acquired and, in spite of regional surveys to identify plantable land in Scotland and Wales, little improvement in land supply was achieved. Nevertheless, there was considerable re-stocking and new planting up to 1955 when afforestation began to decline largely because of the scarcity of suitable land. Another factor militating against the proposed afforestation programme was the Hill Farming Act of 1946 which aimed to support production in marginal areas; as a result, the better hill areas remained in agricultural use, to the detriment of afforestation. This provides a good example of the conflicting land use claims of forestry and hill farming. Afforestation was also handicapped by the difficulties of procuring labour, especially in the remoter areas, while such workers as were attracted to forestry work were of poor quality and there was a high turn-over.

Changes in military technology, which reduced the likelihood of long naval blockades, led to forestry policy being questioned and in the late 1950s a review of forestry policy was undertaken. The growth in recreation, and the growing importance of social objectives, led to changed attitudes in the use and importance of forests. By 1957, afforestation rates had declined substantially, largely because of a scarcity of land but in the following year a policy statement was issued laying down the planting programme for the next decade. The programme for the period 1958 to 1963 was set at 120,000 ha and that for the ensuing five-year period, 1964–8, at 95,000 ha. This programme led to a reversal of the earlier downward trend, although only 80 per cent of the anticipated total planting was achieved. By 1972, the phase of accelerated planting initiated in the mid-1960s was more or less over, especially as hill sheep farming began to pick up and the sale of land for afforestation declined. It was decided to reduce the state planting programme to 22,000 ha per year largely because of land shortages (Fig. 9.5).

Private afforestation has also been strongly influenced by state forestry policies. Government grants-in-aid stimulated private investment in woodlands in the post-war years but since 1972 the rapid rates of afforestation in the private sector have declined rapidly. The reasons for this decline are complex but a reduced level of grant-aid, the introduction of Capital Transfer Tax, and the passing of the Finance Act (1975) are some of the factors leading to a loss of confidence in the private sector and to the reduction in private planting.

Interestingly enough, out of the total woodland area of 309,000 ha, some two-thirds is in private hands; the remaining third is under the direct control of the Forestry Commission. Whereas the forest under private ownership is predominantly of the broad-leaved type, over half that under State control is composed of coniferous species. The planting of conifers has produced criticism on aesthetic grounds: their massed character is apt to give rise to a drab and monotonous landscape, alien to traditional landscapes embellished by the variegated colouring of broad-leaved species. However, during more recent times there has been a greater mixing of species to produce an

Acres

• under 5,000

● 5,000 to 10,000

○ 10,000 to 20,000

⬤ over 20,000

BLACK ISLE
SPEYMOUTH
CLASHINDARROCH
ARD
GLEN TROOL
KIELDER
WARK
ALLERSTON
SHERWOOD
DOVEY
THETFORD CHASE
DEAN
COED MORGANNWG
NEW FOREST

Fig 9.5 Forestry Commission plantations, Great Britain

improved aesthetic appearance. Conifers, however, have the advantage of quicker growth over native hardwoods and, moreover, will tolerate climatic and soil conditions unsuited to broad-leaved species.

Mention should be made of the forests in relation to recreation. Since World War II the Forestry Commission has begun to provide amenities for the public and the forest parks provide camping sites, picnic areas, nature trails, car parks and various other facilities. Something of the order of 5 million visitors already make use of the forest parks and one can visualise their ever-growing popularity; indeed, some of the forests in the south-eastern parts of the country are already under considerable pressure at weekends and bank holidays (Fig. 9.6).

Table 8: Areas of Forest Ownership and Use, 1975

PRODUCTIVE	ENGLAND ('000ha)	SCOTLAND ('000ha)	WALES ('000ha)	GREAT BRITAIN ('000ha)
Forestry Commission	245	432	132	809
Private	479	297	62	838
Total	724	729	194	1,647
UNPRODUCTIVE				
Forestry Commission	9	11	3	23
Private	174	82	30	286
Total	183	93	33	309

Source: Forestry Commission, 1975.

FISHERIES

Since the British Isles lie on the continental shelf and are therefore surrounded by shallow waters rich in food for fish, fisheries occur and fishing has for many centuries been an important domestic activity. The presence of an embayed and estuarine coast has also provided many harbours for fishing vessels. The North Sea was originally the most important fishing area but changes in the habits of the herring, and over-fishing generally, have lessened its significance and forced fishermen to fishing grounds further afield. Ships now sail to Icelandic waters, to the Barents Sea and the Grand Banks for their catch. Although the world's landings of fish have increased very substantially during the past quarter of a century, largely resulting from new techniques of fishing, the British catch has declined. Over the period 1948 to 1970, land-

Fig 9.6 Hollands Wood Caravan Site, New Forest. A pleasure ground for Norman Kings, the New Forest is now an important recreation and holiday area. More recent afforestations are also being opened up for tourism and recreation pursuits

ings have dropped from around 1·25 to less than 1 million tons.

British fisheries are of three principal types: (a) *inshore* fishing for crustaceans such as lobsters, crabs, crawfish, prawns and shrimps, which takes place around almost all the coasts, although the North-east and East Anglian coasts and the coasts of the South-west Peninsula are more especially important; (b) *pelagic* or surface fishing by drifters for herring, mackerel and pilchard, mainly in Scottish waters and in the seas around Cornwall and south of Ireland; and (c) *demersal* or deep-sea fishing for such fish as cod, haddock and hake, caught by trawling and lining in the northern part of the North Sea around the Faroes and Iceland, and in the Barents Sea. Cod is the most important catch in both terms of quantity or weight landed and in value. Cod accounts for about 45 per cent of the total catch. Haddock comes second, accounting for about 20 per cent, and plaice third

at around 10 per cent. Herring, once important, are now of small consequence: between 1950 and 1970 their value dropped by half. A number of factors have been responsible for this decline: among them are a reduction in demand in the home market, a contraction in the export market but, above all, the serious depletion in the stocks of herring in the North Sea.

Grimsby, Hull and Aberdeen are the major fishing ports; each is principally concerned with demersal fishing. Grimsby, whose docks were first opened in 1854, was formerly one of the greatest fishing ports in the world. It is still significant within the U.K., but although it has largely absorbed Hull's trade, the fishing industry is so contracted that it is only a shadow of its former importance. Fleetwood, whose fishing interests are in the Irish Sea and in Icelandic waters and which is also primarily concerned with demersal species, ranks fourth in the U.K. During

115

the past twenty years Great Yarmouth and Lowestoft have seriously declined as the herring fishery has declined. Ullapool, in north-western Scotland, is now the chief herring port; Fraserburgh, Lossiemouth, Mallaig and Oban are also significant for herring and other pelagic species. Of rather minor importance as fishing ports are Scarborough, Eyemouth, Peterhead, Wick, Whitehaven, Milford Haven and Brixham.

The British fishing industry has been subject to many changes since World War II. The continuing depletion of stocks of fish in national waters has compelled fishermen to seek their catches in more distant waters; this has led to the introduction of factory ships which process the fish on board. New types of processed and packaged food have resulted in the growth of fish processing industries at the ports. A more recent development has been the experimental work in 'fish-farming', i.e. the hatching, rearing and artificial feeding of fish in enclosed waters; for example, in parts of western Scotland the activity is already well-established and salmon and other species are being produced in quantity – something of the order of 20,000 tons annually.

The world total catch of fish increases annually, and is already over 73 million tonnes. Catches of such magnitude imply that fishermen, with their modern techniques, are becoming too efficient for the industry to survive in its present form. Many authorities believe world fish stocks are now in a very delicate state of balance. The recent introductions of 200-mile exclusive economic zones (E.E.Z.s) by countries which have coasts, is an attempt to conserve fish stocks and to restrict catches by highly productive long-range fishing fleets who have been practising 'raid fishing', e.g. the U.S.S.R., Poland, East Germany, Japan. It is clear that the North Sea herring fishery has been overfished and recent warnings and pleadings to stop catching herring were ignored. So serious was the depletion that it was feared the stocks might not be able to recover. As a result, the government was constrained to place a ban upon fishing for herring in the U.K's 200-mile zone. Warnings were given that it might not be safe to resume fishing before 1979 at the earliest.

The vulnerability of sea fishing has proved particularly embarrassing for the economy of parts of western Scotland, the Humber ports, and the small ports of Devon and Cornwall. Although the total numbers employed in fishing are small (about 16,500 full-time and 4,800 part-time) their concentration in areas of poor alternative employment gives cause for concern. In 1976, landings of all types of fish totalled 1,063,00 tonnes.

References

Coppock, J.T., *An Agricultural Atlas of England and Wales* (Faber and Faber, 1964).

Davidson, J. & Wibberley, G.P., *Planning and the Rural Environment* (Pergamon, 1977).

Hanna, L.W., 'Environment and Land Use', Chapter III in *The U.K. Space*, edited by J.W. House, 2nd edition (Weidenfeld & Nicolson, 1977).

Thomas, D., 'The Changing Rural Scene', Chapter 3, pp. 69–88, in *An Advanced Geography of the British Isles* (Hulton, 1974).

Coppock, J.T., 'The challenge of change: rural land use in Great Britain', *Geography*, Vol. 62, 1977, pp. 75–85.

Forestry Commission, *British Forestry* (HMSO, 1974).

Mather, A.S., 'Patterns of Afforestation in Britain since 1945', *Geography*, Vol. 63, July 1978, pp. 157–66.

Hjul, P., 'World Fish Stocks on a Delicate Balance', *Geographical Magazine*, Vol. L, October 1977, pp. 27–40.

Duckham, A.N., 'The current agricultural revolution', *Geography*, Vol. 44, 1959, pp. 71–78.

10

Industry

PRINCIPLES OF MANUFACTURE

Until the Industrial Revolution all manufacturing was of the craft or domestic kind. Simply stated, manufacture may be defined as the processing and altering of materials to make products, sometimes to serve new ends. A principle of industrial manufacture is that the more processing and altering a material is subjected to, the more valuable it becomes: indeed, the processing of raw material to enhance its value might be one way of defining manufacture.

The Industrial Revolution introduced a new pattern of manufacturing which was to last for 150 years until the Great Depression of 1929–34. During this period two main factors exerted a powerful influence. First, was the powerful attraction of the coalfields since coal became the primary source of energy; this led to the new, growing industrial regions becoming co-terminous with the coalfields. Secondly, regional specialisation began to develop, e.g. cotton manufacturing in Lancashire, woollen textiles in the West Riding, and pottery on the North Staffordshire coalfield. Major industrial concentrations thus grew up on all the main coalfields, and the bonds remained firm until about fifty years ago when the spread of electrification and the development of motor transport helped to undermine and finally to break up this long-established pattern. Gradually a new pattern began to emerge: that of industrial dispersion, aided by new sources of energy, new forms of transport, and politico-economic factors.

Industrial production, like many other forms of production, has gone through an evolutionary development. Perhaps the most significant change in modern times has been the tremendous growth in the size and complexity of the industrial plants and the modern methods of mass production. Whereas in the past industrial growth was mostly effected by horizontal integration, now it is largely achieved by vertical integration. Large, integrated plants are more economic to run than smaller ones, for production can be streamlined, large-scale mechanisation can be applied, standardisation can be adopted, by-products can be used, and big firms can employ their own research and training staffs. The logical development of such major-scale mass production is automation. Automation may be defined as the use of machines to control machines; in other words, electronic devices supersede man in the supervision and control of machines. In automation, the bulk of the manufacture is done by automatic processes, and the need of human intervention and control is reduced to an absolute minimum. The future will see an increasing application of automative techniques associated in particular with micro-processors – already the British Steel Corporation has one large plant that is practically fully automated – but precisely how quickly and to what extent, as well as with what results, it is difficult to forecast. All that one can say is automation is bound to have far-reaching effects upon industrial production, organisation and employment.

Finally, it should be noted that it is the manufacturer's task to reduce manufacturing costs to as low a level as possible consistent with satisfactory workmanship. This can be effected in a variety of ways but chiefly by: (a) mass production: usually the greater the number of articles produced, the smaller is the unit cost of production; (b) mechanisation: the machine can increase the numbers and speed of output of articles; (c) the reduction of labour costs: the cost of labour is normally the largest single production cost; (d) selecting an economic factory site: a site which will give economies with respect to raw materials, fuel, transport costs, etc.

CHANGING LOCATION OF INDUSTRY

During the period of rapid and precocious industrialisation of the late eighteenth and the nineteenth centuries, perhaps the single most important influence was the presence of coal, the major source of power, especially when it was associated with ease of access to mineral ores, especially iron ores, or to other raw materials which were available locally or could be readily imported. Accordingly, major industrial concentrations grew up in the Central Lowlands of Scotland based upon coalmining, iron and later steel, with shipbuilding on Clydeside; on the north-east coast, founded on coalmining, iron and steel, and ship construction on Tyneside, at Wearmouth, and Teesside; on the north-west coast based on coalmining and the rich hematite ores of Furness which gave rise to iron and steel production at Workington, and the shipbuilding industry at Barrow; in South Lancashire, founded on coalmining, salt extraction and cotton manufacture, with shipbuilding on Merseyside; in the West Riding founded on coalmining, engineering and woollen manufacture; in the West Midlands based on coalmining, iron and steel and engineering; and in South Wales based on coalmining, iron and steel, and the smelting of non-ferrous ores. These various coal-based centres of heavy industry flourished until the coal seams began to show exhaustion, as in West Durham, or the iron ores began to fail causing re-location of some of the iron and steel works on the ironfields, as at Corby, or on the coast where they could conveniently import ore. The development of these regional specialisms served as a geographical counterbalance to London which was a major industrial centre in its own right, the country's largest port and the focus of its commercial activities. The growth of the above centres of heavy industry and textile manufacturing, with their associated burgeoning towns, led as we have already seen to a dramatic redistribution of population in Britain.

Since the First World War the pull of the coalfields for the establishment and expansion of manufacturing activity has steadily weakened and factors other than coal have become more important for economic activity. Thus, the spread of the electricity grid and the development of motor transport made industry much more footloose, while nearness to large consumer markets drew the new, rapidly developing light industries to new locations. The newer industries which began to grow up during the inter-war period, but which have expanded especially vigorously after 1945, showed different locational preferences from many of the older industries which were the foundation in the nineteenth century of the country's economy. Industries which are based upon a few heavy, bulky raw materials, such as iron-smelting, brick-making, and cement-manufacture, are frequently located near the supply of raw materials. But even in cases of this kind it should be recognised that indirectly the factor which is often involved is the deterrent effect of transport costs rather than the positive attraction of the raw material. Where raw materials are of the lighter kind, less bulky, and more valuable, the manufactured products are better able to stand transport costs. New light industries producing goods such as cookers, refrigerators, typewriters, electronic goods, cosmetics and pharmaceuticals, clothing and a host of modern consumer goods, which use varied, valuable, and relatively small amounts of raw material, are much more mobile and are readily attracted to large towns which at once afford a ready supply of labour and a big consumer market.

INDUSTRIAL EMPLOYMENT

The British workforce totals 25·25 million; of this total about 2 per cent are engaged in agriculture, forestry and fishing, 42 per cent are in industry, and 56 per cent in services of all kinds. The most striking change that has taken place in the postwar period is the transfer from a goods-producing to a service economy. If we look at civilian employment in detail we find that approximately 33 per cent are engaged in manufacturing industries, 16 per cent in professional and scientific services, 12 per cent in distributive trades, 7 per cent in transport and communications, 6 per cent in construction and 5 per cent in insurance, banking and financial services. Since the energy crisis of 1973, the number of unemployed has gradually risen: from around half a million in that year to 1,000,000 in 1975 and to about 1·5 million in early 1980.

About 41 per cent of Britain's gross domestic product is in the form of industrial production: manufacturing (29 per cent), construction (8 per cent), electricity, gas and water (3 per cent) and mining and quarrying (1 per cent). Table 9 lists the principal branches of industry with the approximate numbers of workers in each activity.

Table 9: Total Employment in Secondary Activities, 1976

Iron and steel	250,000
Shipbuilding and marine engineering	177,000
Mechanical engineering	929,000
Electrical engineering	739,000
Motor vehicles	457,000
Aerospace	200,000
Chemical and allied industries	423,000
Textiles	180,000
Clothing manufacture	310,000
Bricks, pottery, glass & cement	264,000
Construction	1,200,000
Timber and furniture	264,000
Paper, printing and publishing	542,000
Food, drink and tobacco	714,000

Some of the above industries are contracting in importance, notably textiles, which for half a century has been running down as a result of acute foreign competition; shipbuilding, largely through foreign competition, especially Japanese, and over-production; the iron and steel industry partly as a result of over-capacity and reduced demand; and the motor vehicle industry because of foreign competition and internal structural and industrial relations problems. On the other hand, some industries, especially the engineering, chemical and food and drink industries, are expanding.

INDUSTRIAL PROFILES

The Iron and Steel Industry

Until about a decade ago, the Open-hearth process was the method of steel production most widely used in Britain. Great strides, however,

have been made in recent years in using the Basic Oxygen process (see Fig. 10.1). In these new pneumatic or converter processes, use is made of an oxygen/steam blast in bottom-blown converters, or oxygen is injected at high speed onto the surface of the liquid iron, i.e. from above instead of from below. In the U.K. the use of oxygen in the steel-making process has increased greatly during the past fifteen years and by 1975 more than two-thirds of all the British Steel Corporation's production of steel came from oxygen converters compared with under one-third in 1969.

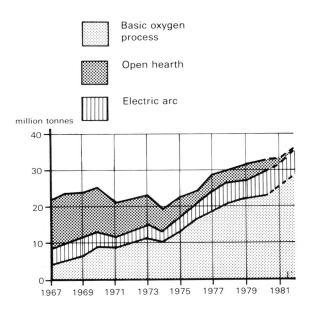

Fig 10.1 Growth in the use of Basic Oxygen process by British Steel Corporation

The Iron and Steel Act 1967 brought most of the industry into public ownership, although it had been subject to some form of public supervision since 1932. The British Steel Corporation (B.S.C.) produces about 75 per cent of Britain's crude steel and employs around 70 per cent of the workers in the industry. Remaining production is in the hands of numerous private companies operating in Sheffield, and scattered throughout the other traditional metal-working centres in the Midlands, South Wales and Central Scotland. Until 1974, when world steel output reached a peak of 705 million tonnes, the steel-making industry had been expanding and Britain had shared in this expansion. Nationalisation of the industry led to B.S.C.'s plans to rationalise and build up the industry so that it could compete in the world market. Unfortunately, the energy crisis (1973) and the subsequent economic recession led to a drop in consumer spending and in the demand for steel. Currently there is large-scale over-capacity and B.S.C. in the year 1975–6 suffered a loss of £255m, in 1976–7 £520m, and in 1977–8 £450m.

Major Works

● Expansion

○ Reductions

□ Closures

Fig 10.2 The rationalization of British Steel, 1979

As a result of these losses, many of the older and uneconomic plants had been closed down by the end of 1979, including such famous and historic centres as Ebbw Vale. Closures had also been announced at Corby, Shotton and Cleveland. Further retrenchment yet, however, was in hand, and plans were announced in December 1979 to cut the total labour force of 153,000 by one third and reduce productive capacity to 15 million

tonnes p.a. (instead of the 30–40 million tonnes predicted in the early 1970s). The effect of the cuts would be to close Hallside (near the new Ravenscraig plant in Scotland), Consett in Co. Durham, and drastically reduce the workforce at Port Talbot and Llanwern in S. Wales, and at Sheffield (Fig. 10.2).

Non-ferrous Metals

Some non-ferrous metals occur in Britain, but they are little worked now since they have largely become exhausted. Nevertheless, numerous other metals are required by modern industry including ferro-alloy metals such as manganese, nickel, chromium, tungsten, copper and selenium for electronic equipment; aluminium and niobium for the aircraft industry; tin for the tin-plate industry; and uranium, beryllium and zirconium for nuclear energy. Most of these must be imported since there are only small indigenous resources of tin, lead, copper and zinc, although ores are frequently imported, smelted and refined by processes very similar to those used in the reduction of iron ore; moreover, since coal is mainly used to fire the furnaces, the smelting works are usually on, or near to, the coalfields. Nearly half of Britain's non-ferrous metal industries are located in the Midlands because of the demands of the engineering industries, but they are also well represented in the London area, South Wales, at Avonmouth, on Tyneside, and in the Central Lowlands of Scotland.

The Black Country is the oldest and most important of the great engineering provinces but the present industrial character of the West Midlands is essentially based on the finishing trades which use a variety of metals in the making of aero-engines, machine tools, small arms, bicycles, motor cars, etc. Birmingham is especially noted for its non-ferrous metal industries. In South Wales early centres of metal working grew up at Pontypool, where tin-plate was made, and in the Neath and Swansea areas, where copper ores were imported from Cornwall. Lead and zinc ores were also smelted in the area. The non-ferrous industry has now become concentrated in a few large works, e.g. nickel processing at Landore, titanium at Waunarlwydd near Swansea, aluminium at Resolven in the Neath Valley and at Rogerstone near Newport. Avonmouth, the outport of Bristol, imports and smelts lead and zinc. Sheffield is noted for its steel industry, especially its alloy and special alloy steels, such as stainless, heat-resisting, manganese steel, steel for permanent magnets for the electrical industries, and various special steels for heavy machinery, guns, springs, and precision tools for engineering. Because of its 'silverware trade' Sheffield is also concerned with silver refining. Non-ferrous metallurgy is also located in Lanarkshire because of its relationship with shipbuilding. Burntisland, on the Firth of Forth, has an alumina plant which reduces bauxite while there are smelting works at Fort William and Kinlochleven, which make use of the hydro-electricity of the Scottish Highlands; and at Inver-gordon on Cromarty Firth is British Aluminium's large smelter which processes alumina imported directly from the Caribbean.

Shipbuilding

Steel and many non-ferrous metals are required in the shipbuilding industry. At one time the world's premier shipbuilding country, Britain had already lost this position by the time of the outbreak of World War II. She had already been elbowed out of her dominating position by the growing competition from the United States. After World War II, the industry underwent a period of resuscitation in the 1960s as a result of Government help and until 1973 there was a world shipbuilding boom largely because of the need for bulk carriers. By this time, however, Japan had become the world's greatest shipbuilding country and out of a world total production of 31,520 thousand gross registered tonnes, 53 per cent of which comprised tankers, Japan launched 15,673 thousand gross registered tonnes, 59 per cent of which were tankers. At this time Britain was responsible for only slightly more than 1,000 thousand gross registered tonnes and ranked seventh as a world producer – behind Sweden, West Germany, Spain, France and Norway. The energy crisis of that year, however, precipitated a ship-building crisis from which the industry has still not recovered; there is gross over-capacity and not only is a high proportion of the tanker fleet 'mothballed' but the Japanese shipbuilding indus-try is now in great difficulties.

In Britain, the shipbuilding yards were mostly concentrated in a few areas where conditions were favourable: on sheltered estuaries with deep water

for safe launchings, in close proximity to steel-works for girders, steel plates, etc., and for im-porting timber. The chief shipbuilding areas have been Clydeside, Tyneside, Barrow-in-Furness and Birkenhead, with Belfast in Northern Ireland; less important centres are Hull and Southampton, and Aberdeen and Dundee in Scotland.

The world market for shipbuilding is now so bad that even heavily subsidised orders (£300m to British Shipbuilders) have only a short-term benefit. In August 1979 it was announced that four shipyards were to be closed with a loss of 10,000 jobs. British shipbuilders have warned that thousands of jobs in shipbuilding and repair are at risk unless substantial new orders are won.

Britain now accounts for only 8 per cent of world shipping (i.e. carrying) whereas prior to World War II it had 40 per cent. Although its carrying role has greatly diminished, Britain's mer-cantile marine earns the country £1,000 m a year in invisible earnings. The fleet is a very modern one, half of it being under ten years old; the liner fleet, which carries mixed cargoes, is one of the most up to date in the world; Britain has also invested vast sums in building container ships and has pioneered world container services. Ninety-nine per cent of Britain's external trade is carried by ship, hence the mercantile marine is absolutely essential.

There is a growing threat to Britain's mercantile marine, first, from Third World countries such as Singapore, India, Brazil, Nigeria, who are rapidly building up their fleets and so beginning to com-pete with British vessels for the carrying trade and, secondly, from the Soviet merchant marine which has not only expanded greatly in recent years but by offering cut freight rates is touting for Western trade. Soviet merchant ships operate at rates which cannot be matched: they are able to do this because (i) the merchant navy is a strategic addition to the fighting navy, and (ii) it helps them to earn precious hard currency, which is very important to the Soviet Union.

The Engineering Industry

The importance of the engineering industry in the country's economy is indicated by the fact that it earns approximately £5,000 m a year in exports. The industry is not necessarily tied to the iron and steel producing areas for, so long as steel is available, machinery is frequently made where it is required as, for instance, in the case of agricultural machinery or sometimes textile machinery. Nowadays the general location of the industry is related to the presence of skilled labour and the position of the consuming markets.

It was the presence of coal and iron in the early days which gave rise to some of the leading engineering areas in Britain but since electricity is the main form of power now used the engineering industry has become more widely dispersed. The English Midlands is the principal area for the manufacture of machines and tools. Birmingham and the Black Country have highly developed engineering industries which are the outcome of centuries of tradition. The Derbyshire-Nottinghamshire area in the north-east Midlands has developed as another main area. In northern England, the two industrial areas on either side of the Pennines, south Lancashire and West Yorkshire, have grown into major engineering areas. Manchester, formerly much concerned with the making of textile machinery, has grown to be one of the world's greatest centres of engineering. Leeds, Bradford, Huddersfield, and particularly Sheffield are important centres, and the engineering industries of Sheffield are highly specialised: marine engineering, strangely enough, is especially important, and cutlery is a well-known speciality. In Scotland, the Central Lowlands has long formed a leading engineering area. The presence of a huge market requiring a wide variety of engineering products has largely contributed to the growth of the engineering industry in the greater London area.

There are other important branches of engineering: the making of agricultural machinery and implements has led to the scattered growth of engineering centres in the eastern counties. In the early days, when the railways were run by private companies, railway engineering was largely the concern of the companies and they established their building and repair shops on their own lines, in central positions, at important railway junctions where land was cheap, e.g. Ashford, Swindon, Crewe, Derby, Doncaster, York and Darlington. Aircraft engineering is often concentrated in the same areas as the automobile industry. Including aero-engine production and repairing, the aerospace industry employs about 200,000 people. It is one of the largest in the world and undertakes much research and development. Exports of air-

craft and parts are valued at over £300 m annually.

Another specialised branch of engineering is electrical engineering which has grown very rapidly. There are two branches; the *heavy* and the *light*. The great engineering towns (except Rugby) have become centres of the *heavy electrical industry*, i.e. the construction of electrical machinery and power plant. Electrical machinery and cable manufacture uses a variety of raw materials, especially imported non-ferrous metals, and a large part of the finished products goes for export. These factors encouraged the concentration of the industry in the non-ferrous metal district of south Lancashire and in the Thames estuary. Bradford became an important centre for the production of electrical transmission machinery. Glasgow is the chief centre of the industry in Scotland. The *electronics* or *light electrical engineering industry* is principally concerned with the production of small but valuable consumer goods which can be made anywhere and which employ mostly female labour. Transport facilities are of minor importance to these industries since neither the raw materials nor the finished products are very bulky. Exports of electrical machinery total around £1,530 m per annum.

The Motor Vehicle Industry

Table 10: Chief locations of the motor industry

TOWN	FIRM
Dagenham (London)	Ford Motor Co.
Halewood (Liverpool)	Ford Motor Co.
Birmingham	Talbot
Longbridge (Birmingham)	British Leyland
Oxford	British Leyland
Bathgate (West Lothian)	British Leyland
Leyland (Preston)	British Leyland (Buses, heavy trucks)
Speke (Liverpool)	British Leyland
Coventry	British Leyland
	Talbot
Linwood (Paisley)	Talbot
Ellesmere Port	Talbot
Luton	Talbot
	General Motors
Crewe	Rolls Royce
Slough	Citroen
Dunstable	Talbot

Table 11: The British Motor Industry, 1976

PRODUCTION		CARS IN USE	PERSONS PER CAR	EXPORTS	IMPORTS
CARS	COMMERCIAL VEHICLES				
1,333,449	372,057	14,354,766	3·9	683,899	485,665

The manufacture of motor cars and commercial vehicles, such as buses, lorries and vans, is largely dependent upon sheet steel and engineering products. Apart from a small number of small firms producing specialised motor cars, the motor industry is essentially one of assembly undertaken by a dozen or so large plants relying upon numerous components – engines, tyres, electrical equipment, windows, upholstery, etc. – supplied by specialist firms, sometimes from abroad.

The presence of an already well-established engineering industry in the English Midlands contributed to the rise (initially at Coventry) and

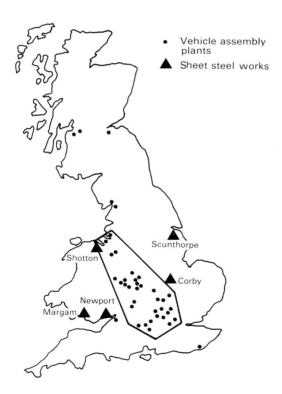

Vehicle assembly plants

Sheet steel works

Scunthorpe

Shotton

Corby

Newport

Margam

Fig 10.3 Motor vehicle industry in Great Britain and the Midland 'Coffin'

progress of motor manufacture in that region. Most of the industry is to be found in the Midlands and the South-East but since the early 1960s the most powerful locating factor has been the (former) Department of Trade and Industry which largely controlled the siting of new plants by directing their establishment to areas of high unemployment. For example, the Ford Motor Company opened their new works at Halewood, on Merseyside, in 1963 and Vauxhall (Talbot) commenced operations at Ellesmere Port in 1966; in both cased the companies were granted expansion permits on condition that they built their plants in areas designated by the government (Fig. 10.3).

The British motor car industry continued to expand until 1972 when production reached 2,329,000 cars and commercial vehicles. The oil crisis in 1973 brought a halt to this expansion and recently the industry has been plagued by strikes and internal difficulties. The proportion of British made vehicles sold in the home market has severely contracted in the face of German, French, Italian and Japanese competition. Table 11 gives some figures for the British motor industry in 1976.

The Chemical Industry

The chemical industry is a key industry since chemicals are required in a host of activities. It is greatly diversified and has many branches, the chief of which are: (i) the production of *heavy chemicals,* e.g. caustic soda, chlorine, acids and hydrogen; (ii) the production of *coal-tar chemicals,* e.g. dyes, disinfectants, fibres, explosives, etc.; (iii) the *petro-chemical* industry, e.g. petroleum distillates, sulphur, synthetic rubber and fibres; (iv) the *electro-chemical* industry, e.g. wood-pulp, calcium carbide, ammonia, fertilisers; (v) the production of *pharmaceuticals,* e.g. drugs, medicines, vitamins, lotions, etc.; (vi) the *derived chemical manufactures,* e.g. soap, paint, leather, paper and glass; and (vii) the *plastics* industry, which has been one of the fastest growing in the country.

Britain has a very highly developed chemical industry with almost all branches represented. The industry, which is capital intensive (it accounted for 17 per cent of manufacturing capital expenditure in 1975), is dominated by several large companies, largest of which is Imperial Chemical Industries (I.C.I.) with some 150 factories. The chemical industry as a whole employs around half a million people and exports goods to the value of £3,000 million or about 15 per cent of the total value of British exports.

Three areas are of special significance in relation to the chemical industry: Teesside, Merseyside and London, while Severnside is rapidly growing to become the fourth. On Teesside, one of the largest complexes in Europe has grown up based upon the local salt deposits, potash deposits, nearby coal, and chiefly imported petroleum. I.C.I. has huge plants at Billingham and Wilton producing heavy chemicals, plastics, synthetic fibre and many other products. The firm of Monsanto has a plant on the north bank to produce raw materials for its acrylic fibre, while the British Oxygen Company produces liquid oxygen and nitrogen. Along the Mersey estuary, using salt from the Weaver valley, coal from the South Lancashire and North Wales coalfields, together with lime from Derbyshire and imported vegetable oils, there is the second major chemical area – Northwich, Runcorn, Widnes and Warrington are the chief centres of production. In this area, too, there are derived chemical industries, such as soap at Port Sunlight and glass manufacture at St. Helens. The third principal area is London with its pharmaceuticals, paint and varnish industries and, further down the Thames, paper-making and heavy chemicals production based on oil refining. I.C.I., on a 1,000 acre site on Severnside, has built a great new plant using petro-chemicals piped from the Fawley refinery. Among the other important chemical centres are Bristol, Birmingham, Manchester, Huddersfield, Leeds, Hull, Newcastle, Glasgow and Grangemouth.

Textiles

Britain processes all the important textile fibres – cotton, wool, flax, jute, silk, as well as rayon and the truly synthetic fibres. Although the East Midlands and the Glasgow area developed *cotton* manufactures, these declined after the 1860s; Lancashire, however, continued to thrive and attained its peak between 1900 and 1914. Immediately prior to World War I, the Lancashire cotton industry had a workforce of around 600,000 men and women tending to no fewer than 60 million spindles and 700,000 looms. Nearly 60 per cent (7,000 million yards p.a.) of all cotton piece goods entering international trade at that time came from Lancashire, forming the country's leading export. Although both India and Japan had already started their own cotton textile industries the volume of their export trade was small, but during and after World War I cotton factories began to be built in China, Brazil, Mexico and elsewhere. The growth of foreign competitors together with the effects of the Great Depression (1929–34) accelerated the decline of the Lancashire industry. After World War II, other countries, notably Pakistan, Taiwan and South Korea, along with Hong Kong, joined the list of important producers. In 1959 an attempt was made to rationalise the Lancashire cotton industry but it came too late and after the mid-1960s the industry was in difficulties once again and factories, on average, were closing down at the rate of two a week. Today the cotton industry has fallen on very lean times: by 1974 the number of spindles had dropped to 2·6 million and the number of looms to 52,700. Although Lancashire still accounts for some 90 per cent of Britain's cotton industry, the number of workers now engaged in it, in Lancashire, has dropped to around 50,000.

The *wool* textile industry is more widely spread since it was the original domestic textile industry and has tended to linger on in some of the older centres, e.g. the West of England, in Leicestershire, noted for its knitwear, in the Tweed basin, and in the Outer Hebrides. With the Industrial Revolution the woollen industry came to be especially developed in the valleys of the Aire, Calder and Colne in the West Riding where there were supplies of local wool, soft water, coal and good transport links to nearby ports for importing raw wool and exporting the finished cloth. Something over 80 per cent of the woollen and worsteds are made in West Yorkshire. Although the wool textile industry has not suffered as seriously as the cotton industry, there has been a big contraction and, in 1974, there were only 1,981,900 spindles and 17,300 wool looms. In 1975 there were 93,000 workers in the woollen and worsted trades. Bradford, Halifax and Huddersfield tend to specialise in worsteds, Dewsbury, Batley, Morley and Wakefield in woollens, while Dewsbury and Batley are also centres of the 'shoddy' and 'mungo' trades and Halifax has one of the largest carpet firms in the world. Unlike the Lancashire cotton industry which was horizontally organised, the West Yorkshire woollen industry tended towards vertical organisation and there are numerous instances of mills undertaking all the processes of manufacture. Hosiery and knitwear are most important in the East Midlands and in Scotland. Although production increased by 7 per cent between 1968 and 1975, some firms in the East Midlands have recently run into difficulties.

Silk manufacture, never very important, has greatly declined but is still carried out, on a small scale, at Macclesfield, Congleton and Leek. Half a century or so ago there were about twenty silk mills in Brighouse, near Huddersfield; today there are none.

The rayon industry has grown very rapidly during the past fifty years and to it has now been added the even more important petroleum-based *synthetic fibre* industry. Among the more important centres are Bradford, Manchester, Derby, Spondon (near Nottingham), Lancaster, Flint, Wolverhampton, Coventry and Pontypool. Large firms characterise the synthetic fibre industry.

Jute processing is principally carried on at Dundee, which has the world's oldest jute industry, and Barnsley. The production of jute in the U.K. is no longer significant in terms of world production.

Pottery

The making of pots must have been widely spread in earlier times, but the pottery industry as we know it today had its origin in North Staffordshire. The development of the industry owed much to the initiative and inspiration of Josiah Wedgwood, who set up his own factory, the Etruria Works, in 1769. Wedgwood was a notable innovator and improver, introducing better designs and producing high quality china, and, as a result of the lead given by him, the foundations of the modern pottery industry may be said to have

been laid. At this time there were problems of transporting both the raw materials required by the growing industry and its fragile, and easily broken, finished products; these difficulties were largely solved by the cutting of the Trent and Mersey Canal for which Wedgwood was largely responsible. When it was completed in 1777, the raw materials (kaolin, ball clay and chalk flints) could be brought in cheaply and in quantity, while transport by water reduced breakages of the expensive china. Other important contributing factors at that time were the long-flame coal, mined locally, which was especially well-suited for burning in the kilns and Derbyshire lead needed in the glazing process.

A certain specialisation by product has gradually developed so that the pottery industry includes the preparation of the raw materials, known as *milling,* usually on the canal banks, the manufacture of high quality china at Longton, the making of electrical porcelain at Stone, and the production of sanitary-ware, drainpipes, bricks and roofing tiles from the local clays. The old bottle kilns, formerly such a distinctive feature of the Potteries, have disappeared in favour of electric furnaces. Much of the work in potting, especially in the finishing branches, is undertaken by female labour.

Outside the Potteries of Staffordshire, pottery is made at Derby, Burton-on-Trent, Worcester and Poole. Something of the order of £180 million worth of china is produced annually; much of it goes to the North American market.

The Construction Industry

Some one and three-quarter million workers are employed in the *construction* industry whose output ranges from power stations to private houses. The industry comprises more than 75,000 firms, over a quarter of which are one-man businesses. Public authorities often employ their own labour, mainly for maintenance, but about 85 per cent of the industry's output is from the private sector. In 1975, as well as building factories, office blocks, shops, schools, hospitals, roads, harbours, waterworks, etc., the industry built 364,000 houses and flats. Of these, 174,000 were for private owners and the remainder largely for local authorities; most of the privately-owned dwellings were houses rather than flats, but for local authorities the balance was slightly in favour of flats. After World War II the construction industry flourished, first due to the repairing of war damage, and subsequently through the construction of new towns, the rebuilding of town centres, the strong demand for additional office accommodation and the construction of the motorways. The recent economic crisis has led to a big cut-back in the industry.

Bricks and Cement

The most common house building material is brick and, for larger construction projects, concrete. Clay, from which *bricks* are made, is a very common raw material and its wide occurrence has resulted in a fairly well-dispersed brick-and-tile-making industry. This was especially the case in earlier times in areas lacking in building stone and when bulk transport was less easy. The building materials industry has tended to become concentrated during the past fifty years as a result of improved transport services and the advantages which accrue from large-scale operation. Since clay is a bulky raw material, brickworks are mostly attracted to the site of the deposit. In 1975, 4,405 million bricks were made in Britain and about one-half of this total came from the Oxford clay belt between Bletchley and Peterborough, with brickworks concentrated in the neighbourhood of these two towns and Bedford. The clay must be fired in kilns and fuel consumption is high, hence a coalfield location or a site where coal haulage costs are low is desirable. Since brick distribution costs are fairly high, brickworks tend to be situated as close as possible to the markets they serve. Apart from this remarkable concentration on the outcrop of the Oxford clay, brickmaking is mostly carried on in smaller works on the northern and Midland coalfields; for example, the Staffordshire blue bricks are manufactured from the Etruria marl in the vicinity of Fenton in the Potteries, while Accrington in Lancashire is known for its distinctive red bricks and tiles.

With modern methods of building of blocks of flats and offices, roads, bridges, etc., much use is made of cement and *concrete* (a mixture of gravel, sand and cement). Cement is made from chalk or other limestones, clay and small amounts of anhydrite or gypsum which are crushed and mixed to form a slurry. This is then poured into a rotary kiln and is subjected, for a time, to temperatures of between 1300° C and 1500° C to enable the lime and clay to combine. When the mixture has cooled, it is ground to a fine powder and bagged. A typical cement works consumes annually in the order of 750,000 tonnes of limestone, 175,000 tonnes of shale, 45,000 tonnes of gypsum, and 160,000 tonnes of coal in the production of 600,000 tonnes of cement. The cost of assembling the raw materials is lowest when the cement-making plants are near to supplies of limestones and clay or silt and can obtain coal either by rail or water transport. Cement works are usually sited close to large markets to ensure low distribution costs.

In 1975, Britain produced 16·9 million tonnes of cement. The single most important area of production is around the Thames and Medway estuaries at Grays, Northfleet, Gravesend and Rochester, where about one-third of the total British output originates. Most of the rest comes from or near the chalk and limestone outcrops south and east of the Tees-Exe line.

Office Occupations

Just as there has been a marked changeover in the post-war period from a goods-producing to a service economy so, too, the occupational structure has seen a substantial change; office-based professional, technical and clerical workers have come to occupy an ever-increasing proportion of the country's workforce. Daniels (1978) has commented: "Centrality exerts a strong pull on the location of office occupations and although the pull exerted by this factor may diminish in the longer term as the full impact of post-industrial technology begins to emerge, it seems reasonable to assume that it will continue to focus demand on major urban areas." In spite of the growing number of government incentives, government decentralisation, and the efforts of the Location of Offices Bureau (L.O.B.) since 1963, the regional imbalance in the distribution of office activities appears to be persisting.

Using data yielded by the 1971 Census returns, it has been possible to identify, in broad terms, the growth and structural change which occurred between 1961 and 1971. While office occupations made up some 20 per cent of the national work

Table 12: Growth of Office Occupations in Economic Planning Regions, England and Wales, 1966–71

REGION	REGIONAL SHARE (PER CENT)		PERCENTAGE CHANGE OF EMPLOYMENT
	1966	1971	1966–71
Northern	4·8	4·8	9·4
Yorkshire & Humberside	7·9	7·7	6·7
North-West	13·0	12·7	6·3
East Midlands	5·5	5·6	12·9
West Midlands	9·8	9·6	6·5
East Anglia	2·3	2·7	23·5
South-East	46·9	46·9	9·1
Greater London	30·6	28·8	2·4
Outer Metropolitan Area	9·6	10·5	19·4
Outer South-East	6·7	7·6	24·5
South-West	6·2	6·3	12·5
Wales	3·6	3·7	10·9
Total	100·0% (4,986,310)	100·0% (5,440,000)	9·1

Source: *Census of Population 1966*, 1969; *Census of Population 1971*, 1975.

force in 1961, a decade later it reached 25 per cent. The rate of increase, which had been of the order of 13 per cent between 1961–66, decelerated to 9 per cent during the period 1967–71 but, as Daniels pointed out, this deceleration concealed some interesting trends, notably the restructuring of the workforce away from clerical jobs towards administrative and professional occupations. It seems very probable that the reduced growth rate in clerical occupations will continue and will not be entirely compensated by the increased demand for administrative and professional workers. Just as automation has done much to change manufacturing industry and led to cutbacks in the workforce, so it is now having a growing impact on office work. Technological innovations, such as electric typewriters, photocopying machines and mini-computers in office work, are making it possible to dispense with some office staff; on the other hand, these innovations are creating a need for new, highly specialised, workers such as computer programmers and systems analysts.

Table 12 shows the regional inequalities in the growth of office occupations in the various Economic Planning Regions in England and Wales.

Careful study of the table makes it clear that national trends in office occupation change are by no means consistent. The South-East Region had the same share of office jobs in 1971 as it had in 1966, notwithstanding the attempt to control the location of office activities. Outside Greater London, growth in the Outer Metropolitan Area and in the Outer South-East proceeded at twice the national rate. East Anglia alone of the economic planning regions, with its low base total, achieved the rapid expansion of office employment attained in the Outer South-East. Elsewhere in the country the regional growth rates were much nearer the average, notably in the North-West, Yorkshire and Humberside, and the West Midlands which had a declining share of all office occupations. Daniels has commented: "Although almost all parts of the country have shared in the expansion of office occupations, significant inequalities remain at the regional level. Decentralisation has caused some downward transfer of office employment through the urban hierarchy but some areas such as those parts of the South-East Region outside London continue to attract a larger share of office jobs than they really require."

References

Jarrett, H.R., *A Geography of Manufacturing* (Macdonald & Evans Ltd., 1969).

Stamp, Sir L.D. and Beaver, S.H., *The British Isles,* 6th edition (Longman, 1971), Chapters 16 to 23.

Humphrys, G., 'Power and the Industrial Structure', in *The U.K.Space,* ed. J.W. House, 2nd edition (Weidenfeld & Nicolson, 1977).

Daniels, P.W., 'Post-Industrial Britain', *Geography,* Vol. 63, Part 3, July 1978.

Cooper, E.H., *Economic Geography,* 3rd edition (University Tutorial Press, 1975).

Carter, H., 'Developments in Manufacturing', in *An Advanced Geography of the British Isles* (Hulton Educational Publications Ltd., 1974) pp. 89–106.

11
Transport

PRINCIPLES AND PROBLEMS

The role of transport is to move people or goods for some particular purpose. In economic language, the demand for transport is a *derived* demand; in other words, the meaning of the word 'demand' in such a situation is that transport is required not for its own sake but because it is useful in satisfying some other want. Transport is a form of capital good but is economically useful in supplying a *service,* hence it is referred to by economists as a *factor of production.* The various forms which transport takes vary widely but there is, too, some specialisation of function depending upon the nature of the goods carried, e.g. whether solid or liquid, small or bulky, perishable or non-perishable; and accordingly a number of special types of transporting mechanisms have been devised.

Although it will become clear that marked variations exist in Britain's transport system, it shows a number of outstanding features:

(i) The remarkable density over most of the country of the various networks of roads, railways, airways, pipelines, electricity transmission lines, etc.

(ii) The large numbers of inter-connecting nodes, commonly in the form of purpose-built terminal facilities, which exist not only within each modal system but between the different types of system.

(iii) The large number of agencies involved in the operation and maintenance of the transport systems, whose roles are frequently regulated and even controlled by legislation.

(iv) The very substantial involvement by government, as a result of investment or nationalisation, in transport undertakings – e.g. the railways, waterways, ports and motorways.

(v) The major change, especially during the past fifty years, has been one of a switch from public to private transport, coupled with the tremendous growth of the latter.

(vi) The successive transport networks which have emerged – canal, railway and motorway – show remarkable similarities in orientation and pattern: a reflection chiefly of the great pull of London, and of geographical conditions.

Transport is essential to the lives of all but the most self-contained and self-sufficient of communities since it is impossible for people to concentrate all their activities in one small area. This becomes very clear in the case of an advanced and industrially highly developed country such as Britain, since its requirements are so great and multifarious that they can be satisfied only when goods and services are drawn from the world at large. Manufacturing nowadays has become technologically so complex and labour so specialised that even relatively simple products tend to be manufactured in stages, the various components finally being assembled to make the final product. The various component parts may be made in geographically dispersed centres, with each using the factors of production – natural resources, labour and capital – in differing amounts and differing ways. Thus transport is a prerequisite for industrial manufacture, its function being to link the various stages of production from the exploitation of the raw materials to the finished article, and then to distribute the product to as wide a market as possible. Transport, then, provides a vital role in production and circulation.

TRANSPORT COSTS

Transport is demanded because it is useful, but anything which is useful normally commands a price and hence (in the case of a service) usually involves a charge to the user, and transport is no exception to this economic principle. Where the means of transport is owned by the user, this cost comes in the form of an *operating cost* of the vehicle but where public or hired transport is used then the cost to the user is the *charge* he has to pay for the service. The cost of using a given form of transport really reflects the quality of the service which is provided: this can be measured in terms of speed (and hence time), comfort (in the case of personal travel), and the level and reliability of the service provided. A further consideration to be included is safety since, in both person and goods movement, transport is used on the assumption of a safe arrival. Thus, in a study of transport, cost is a complex phenomenon reflecting all other aspects of the service provided.

The total costs to any carrier of moving a consignment of goods from one place to another involve more than just movement costs; they may, and usually do, involve the following:

(i) The cost of loading into the transporting vehicle.
(ii) Movement costs between point of origin and final destination.
(iii) Trans-shipment costs if break of bulk is involved en route.
(iv) The cost of unloading at the ultimate destination.
(v) Insurance charges.

It should be noted that the loading cost, which is primarily determined by the ease with which the goods can be handled, bears no relationship to the distance over which the goods are to be moved, neither does it vary with it. Actual haulage costs may vary according to the nature of the route which is used for transport; otherwise the movement costs normally increase directly in relation to the distance over which the goods are carried. If trans-shipment has to be resorted to, involving the transference of freight from one vehicle to another, then an additional cost will be entailed at the break of bulk point for extra handling will be necessary. At the final destination the goods will have to be unloaded and this will involve a further cost. Finally, there will be insurance charges to cover such eventualities as spoilation of goods, breakages, theft and perhaps even delay in delivery. Overall, the haulage cost is likely to be the greatest element in the total costs, but it should be appreciated that it is not the only factor to be considered in transport costs. In the physical distribution process there may be further additional costs over and above the five referred to, for there may be charges for documentation, for storage and warehousing, for inventory management, etc., all of which are functions in physical distribution. The percentage of distribution costs for the average firm are given in Table 13.

Table 13: Distribution costs as a percentage of total cost for an average firm

Transport	$5\frac{1}{2}$
Inventory	3
Packaging	2
Warehousing	$2\frac{1}{2}$
Administration	3
Total	16%

Source: Murphy, *Transport and Distribution* (Business Books, 1972).

The transport costs levied by carriers do not always reflect the true costs of providing a particular service. There are several reasons for this: preferential rates may be granted to firms who can guarantee regular shipments of goods; special rates may be allowed at times on commodities carried as a 'return cargo' thereby avoiding a vehicle having to return empty; seasonal under-utilisation of transport may cause a transporting company to reduce its rates to keep its fleet of vehicles in operation; the existence of competing transport services may affect freight rates; and cross-subsidisation may allow profitable services to support uneconomic services, as is often the case in public transport undertakings.

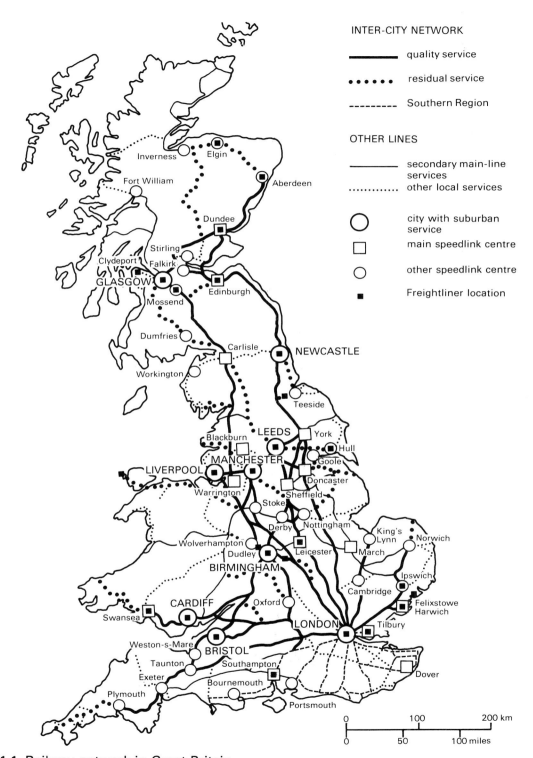

INTER-CITY NETWORK

― quality service

•••••• residual service

------- Southern Region

OTHER LINES

― secondary main-line services

.... other local services

◯ city with suburban service

▢ main speedlink centre

◦ other speedlink centre

■ Freightliner location

Inverness Elgin
Fort William Aberdeen
Dundee
Stirling
Clydeport Falkirk
GLASGOW Edinburgh
Mossend
Dumfries
Carlisle NEWCASTLE
Workington
Teeside
Blackburn LEEDS York
MANCHESTER Hull
LIVERPOOL Goole
Warrington Doncaster
Stoke Sheffield
Derby Nottingham
Wolverhampton King's Lynn Norwich
Dudley Leicester March
BIRMINGHAM Ipswich
Cambridge
CARDIFF Oxford Felixstowe
Swansea Harwich
Weston-s-Mare LONDON Tilbury
BRISTOL
Taunton Southampton Dover
Exeter Bournemouth
Plymouth Portsmouth

0   100   200 km
0   50   100 miles

Fig 11.1 Railway network in Great Britain

131

Traditionally, the function of the railway has been that of a carrier over medium to long distances, although in earlier days some lines were short in length and others provided local services in urban and rural areas. The railway dominated overland transport until World War II and it was not until about 1950 that motor transport became a serious competitor. As Tables 14 and 15 show, the decline of the railway has been rapid since 1955. The railway system felt the shock of contemporary economic facts of life with the Beeching proposals of 1963 which led to a drastic pruning of the British railway network. There have been threats of further rationalisation, but perhaps the network has now been cut back to its basic skeletal structure (Fig. 11.1).

Table 14: Passenger transport in Great Britain (thousand million passenger-km)

	ROAD			AIR (INCLUDING
	BUSES AND COACHES	PRIVATE TRANSPORT	RAIL	N. IRELAND AND CHANNEL ISLANDS)
1954	80	76	39	0·3
1955	80	87	38	0·3
1960	71	144	40	0·8
1965	63	233	35	1·7
1970	56	306	36	2·0
1975	54	357	35	2·2
AVERAGE ANNUAL % CHANGE				
1955–65	−2·4	10·4	−0·8	16·5
1965–75	−1·5	4·4	—	2·5

Source: *Annual Abstract of Statistics,* Transport Statistics, Great Britain, 1965–75, H.M.S.O.

The railway's main contemporary advantage lies as a provider of *inter-urban* travel, the role envisaged by Beeching and reflected in the demand for speedy rail travel from the provinces to London in particular. For domestic journeys of around 250 km the railway can even compete favourably with air transport. While air transport has less elapsed travelling time, it suffers from problems of access to and from airports and of wasted time spent at the terminal. Road transport by private car is rail's principal competitor but railways are able to achieve higher speeds and also

Table 15: Goods transport in Great Britain (thousand million tonne-km)

	ROAD	RAIL	COASTAL SHIPPING	INLAND WATERWAYS	PIPELINE
1955	37·0	34·4	20·4	0·3	0·2
1960	48·4	30·1	15·3	0·3	0·3
1965	68·8	25·2	25·0	0·2	1·3
1970	85·0	26·8	23·2	0·1	2·9
1975	91·8	23·5	18·3	0·1	3·3
AVERAGE ANNUAL % CHANGE					
1965–75	2·9	−0·7	−3·1	−10·2	9·6

Source: *Annual Abstract of Statistics,* Transport Statistics, Great Britain, 1965–75, H.M.S.O.

have easier access into the hearts of cities. Rail's chief disadvantage lies in its being tied to a fixed track and a scheduled service, so that for some journeys the car's greater flexibility may be the overriding factor determining the choice of transport.

Rail also plays a significant role in travel over shorter distances, especially for commuting into the larger cities such as London, Birmingham, Manchester and Glasgow; in the case of the big cities the use of the private car creates congestion and becomes self-defeating, and workers and shoppers are compelled to make greater use of the trains. Rail also has advantages for travelling within cities, as large volumes of passengers can be transported efficiently over short distances; London has its underground railway system to serve this end, as do many capital and large cities in various parts of the world. It now seems likely that rail travel will become more widely used for *intra-urban* movement in smaller cities, and plans have been approved for such circulatory systems in Liverpool and Newcastle-upon-Tyne, while similar schemes have been proposed for Manchester and Nottingham.

New railway technology has helped the railways to develop the above main functions and to improve rail travel. Steam traction has now disappeared in Britain and been replaced by diesel oil or electric power. Although the old Southern Region pioneered electrification before World War II, it was a relatively late innovation in Britain; however, in more recent years there has been electrification of some high-volume, main-line routes. In order to permit increased speeds of travel, the traditional rail has been replaced by a continuous welded track while changes to automatic signalling are gradually taking place. Finally, train speeds of up to 200 k.p.h. are now being achieved by the High Speed Train which was brought into service on the non-electrified route to Bristol in 1976, while future plans involve the development of the 250 k.p.h. Advanced Passenger Train. For goods transport by rail, changes have been less significant; perhaps the most important development was the introduction and expansion of the Freightliner services in the 1960s, a service necessitated by the growth in *containerisation*. On the other hand the greater part of goods traffic is bulk transportation of mineral products, which has not necessitated much innovation.

ROADS

Since World War II the private car, vans and lorries have come to play an important and ever-increasing role in the transportation of passengers and goods (see Tables 14 and 15). For a period, 1945–65, buses played an active part in passenger transport, but the growth in ownership of the private car has severely undermined bus transport. Since 1945 the rapidly increasing numbers and more varied use of motor vehicles drew attention to the fact that Britain's road system was far from adequate to meet modern needs. After a long period of patchy development and piecemeal improvement, Britain's road system is at long last beginning to take the shape of a national road network which is capable of carrying the vastly increased volume of motor traffic at high speeds.

Road transport has the decided advantages of flexibility of service, greater speed over short distances, and directness of communication over other forms of land transport. For long-haul traffic and for the transport of heavy bulk loads, railways are still required and, usually, to be preferred; although, with the development of the large, heavy lorry and bulk transport vehicles there has been an accelerating growth of long-distance motor traffic. The situation today is that 85 per cent of Britain's freight, measured by ton-mileage, and 90 per cent of the passenger traffic is carried by road. The idea of *motorways*, drawing on the model of the German *autobahnen*, really goes back to the immediate post-war years,

for the official road programme for 1946 included plans for a modest beginning. The motorway construction programme in Britain really started in the 1950s – the first motorway being completed in 1958 – gained momentum in the 1960s, but began to slow down in the 1970s, especially after the economic crisis of 1973–5. Today, Britain has 2176 km of motorway. The publication of the Government's White Paper on Transport Policy (1977) indicates that modifications to the strategic highways are very likely to take place. For north-south travel in Britain the motorway backbone has almost been completed, but apart from the M4 and the M62 there are fewer major arterial highways crossing the country. As might well be expected London is the great hub of the motorway system (Fig. 11.2).

Apart from Britain's trunk motorways, there are some *urban motorways*. In the late 1960s, following recommendations put forward in Buchanan's *Traffic in Towns* (1963), the urban motorway was adopted by many large cities in their transport planning programmes. Urban motorways were then looked upon as the answer to urban traffic congestion, but now their prohibitive cost and the implications they have for the environment have caused a change in strategy. As Turton (1978) has commented: "Manchester and Newcastle-upon-Tyne had already embarked upon motorway building but are modifying their original plans and no other major British city is now prepared to commit itself to the construction of super-highways on the scale of a decade ago. A workable compromise between public transport and private mobility has still to be achieved but in our inner cities the motorway has been virtually abandoned as a remedy for urban traffic problems."

INLAND WATERWAYS

Faced with the competition from first the railway and then road transport, the British canal system became obsolete; many, especially the narrow canals, were allowed to decay and became silted and choked with weed while some, like the former Bradford Canal, were filled in. The canal network is little used today and, in 1975, although there were 569 km still being used, there were only 354 vessels in service carrying 4,200,000 tonnes (Fig. 11.3).

Although the canals were intended to serve the

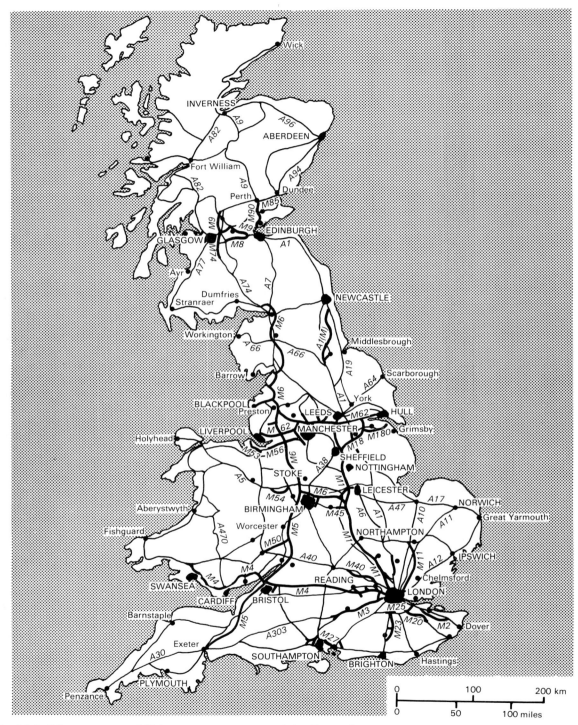

Fig 11.2 Motorway and Primary route network in Great Britain

growing industrial towns of a couple of centuries or so ago, they nevertheless traverse wide areas of pleasant rural country. Since they would appear to have only a very minor role to play in the future transport system, the time has come to use them for other purposes, particularly for recreation activities such as boating, angling, walking, natural history and industrial archaeology. The movement to realise the recreational assets of the waterway network is already well under way. The Inland Waterways Association fosters public interest in the waterway network, while many local societies and clubs work to restore the canals or try to prevent others from falling into decay. For example, in Huddersfield, a private venture has turned Aspley Basin, the old canal wharf almost in the centre of the town, into a small, pleasant marina. Obviously to keep the commercially un-used canals clear, clean and navigable for pleasure craft entails a heavy financial burden: it has been estimated that something of the order of £1 million annually would be needed to keep the canals open for recreation and amenity. However, as Buchanan concludes: "There cannot be the slightest doubt that Britain will eventually need every mile of this . . . pattern of waterways to assist in the provision of worthwhile recreational outlets . . . Further decay of this invaluable national asset must be halted by any means possible."

AIR TRANSPORT

Internal air transport, if we ignore the early experimental flights in the 1920s, goes back nearly fifty years, for almost all the routes in operation at the present time had been established in the early 1930s, though the traffic was then small. Just prior to World War II the number of passengers carried by air was around 160,000 but today over 10 million passengers are carried on domestic flights. Internal domestic traffic is, perhaps, not as large as one might expect, but the size of the country should be borne in mind. This tends to restrict the average length of flight to around 260 km; "this distance", says Fullerton, "is less than the most economic flying sector of most medium-range modern aircraft, and contributes to the problems of air passenger transport in competition with land transport in Great Britain". Thus with the development of motorways and speedy inter-city rail services, the air routes have less advantage than formerly.

All the larger cities have their own airports and there are regular scheduled flights. Most of the traffic is to the London airports (Heathrow, Gatwick and Luton) and the greatest flows are between London and Belfast, Glasgow, Edinburgh and the Channel Islands. The growing volume of air traffic approaching London led to proposals in 1965 for an additional airport and exhaustive investigation took place which considered sites at, chiefly, Stansted, Cublington and Maplin. The Government rejected the Roskill Commission's majority decision in favour of Cublington and started negotiations for the building of an airport (Maplin) on Foulness Island, together with a new seaport. This scheme, which was likely to be

_____ Canals with locks 7 feet wide

_____ Canals and rivers with locks 14 feet or wider

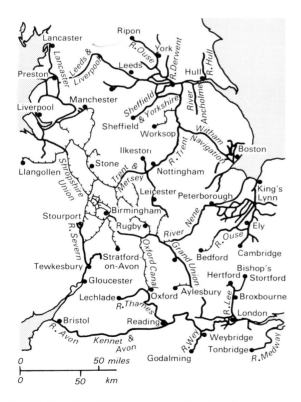

Fig 11.3 Inland Waterways, England

Fig 11.4 Heathrow Airport from 15,000 ft. The complex of runways, hangers, terminal buildings, warehouses and container stores indicates the multifaceted importance of air transport, and its massive impact on the local environment

extremely costly, was shelved following the economic crisis which set in after 1974. In 1979 the search for alternative sites was resumed and Stansted was decided upon.

Commercial airports are usually built, owned and maintained by municipal or state authorities, and not by the airlines which use them. The building of a modern airport of international standards involves enormous capital investment, not merely for its construction but also for its operation. Aircraft using airports must pay for that use, but the airlines are at least relieved of the prohibitive cost of building their own airports. The growth in the size of modern aircraft and the fact that they fly faster has meant that longer runways are needed (about 3,500 to 5,000 metres) and more elaborate terminal facilities are required.

Because of these demands many of the older airports are becoming obsolete and so there is a tendency for airports to be located further and further away from the urban centres they are intended to serve. As an example of the problems facing airport authorities, let us take Heathrow (Fig. 11.4): in the late 1960s the airport was already handling around 10 million passengers, in the mid-seventies around 15 million, and it is anticipated that in the early 1980s the number may well be around 30 million. During peak periods aircraft movements at the rate of one per minute may take place. Such congestion could lead to the airspace near the airport becoming dangerously overcrowded, or air traffic control being unable to cope with the constant stream of aircraft movements.

SEA TRANSPORT

As mentioned earlier, there has always been a considerable amount of coastal carriage by small ships, but with the development of overseas colonies the volume of trade between the colonies and the mother country began to grow. At about the same time the Industrial Revolution led to a growing demand for industrial raw materials and foodstuffs for the expanding population of Britain. Accordingly, Britain was constrained to develop shipping services and by the end of the nineteenth century she had built up a large mercantile marine which was carrying trade in every ocean. Until quite recent times shipping services had a virtual monopoly of all freight and passenger movements over the seas. But now the rapid developments in air transport, especially in terms of speed and carrying capacity, has stolen most of the overseas passenger traffic and one by one the great passenger liners – *Isle de France, Normandie, Queen Mary,* and *Queen Elizabeth* – were withdrawn from the North Atlantic crossing. Although most of the passenger liner traffic has disappeared, the ship remains the only vehicle capable of transporting most cargoes, especially bulk cargoes, across the oceans. Until some new revolutionary method of water transport is devised, the ship will remain unchallenged as a carrier of freight across the world's seas. In July 1975, the maritime fleets of the world totalled 63,724 ships with a gross tonnage of 342,162,000 tons; Britain possessed 3,622 vessels having a gross tonnage of 33,157,000 tons or 9·7 per cent of the world total.

From the very earliest times ships have been specialised in function: at first, they were built for military purposes or for trade, but during more recent times sea-going ships have developed a much greater specialisation and several distinct types of commercial vessel have been developed. Today, about half a dozen main types of merchant ship are recognised: passenger and cargo liners, specialised carriers, tramps, container ships, coastal craft, and short-sea and cross-channel ferries. The function of the *cargo-liner* is gradually being undermined through the development of specialised carriers, the most important of which is the *oil tanker*. Britain, for example, has 560 oil tankers totalling rather more than 16 million tons gross,

half her mercantile marine tonnage. Certain other commodities which hitherto were carried in general cargo vessels are now transported in bulk and special ships have been designed for their carriage. Mineral ores, liquefied natural gas, grain and sugar are now increasingly being transported in bulk carriers since they give economies in scale.

As ocean carriers, *tramps* are becoming less important, though they continue to transport commodities in bulk, such as coal, ores, lumber and fertilisers. Freight rates are negotiated between tramp owners and those chartering the vessel.

Recent years have seen a spectacular growth in *containerisation,* a new form of transport technology, which has answered the need for reducing handling costs. Containers are simply unit loads in, usually, metal packing cases of standard sizes which fit motor vehicles, rail cars and ships' holds and so can be moved easily from one kind of transporting agent to another. But the stage has now been reached where vessels – *container ships* – are being purpose-built to carry the maximum number of containers. Containerisation has reduced the cost, the delay, and the pilfering of goods in transit.

Coastal craft are mainly used for transporting heavy, bulky commodities such as coal, ore, gravel or china clay from point to point along the coast. Britain, from the medieval era at least, has made much use of coasters; commonly they are small vessels of shallow draught to enable them to penetrate rivers and coastal creeks. Finally, there are the *ferries* which link Britain with Ireland and with the continent. Separated as we are from our European neighbours by narrow seas, there has long been a need for ferry links and numerous packet stations developed. Our closer links with the E.E.C. countries and the recent explosive growth in tourism have led to more and better ferry services, including car ferries, while during the past few years hydrofoil and hovercraft services have come into operation.

PORTS

The principal function of a port is to provide facilities, sometimes of a highly specialised nature, for the transference of freight and passengers from land to sea transport, and the reverse. Since Britain is an island, a fundamental modal change of transport is necessitated when external relations, other than by air, are developed. In early medieval times when ships were small in size and of shallow draught, ports could be located up navigable rivers as well as on the coast where there were sheltered harbours. Generally speaking, the cost of carriage by water is low and, until the increase in ship size became a constraint, ports tended to become established as near the head of navigation on a river or estuary as was possible to reduce the distance that commodities had to be carried overland – especially since land transport was slow, limited, costly and difficult until the revolution in transport associated with the Industrial Revolution. As vessels grew in size, ports had either to migrate downstream, as happened in the case of London where many of the older docks upstream have been closed, or *outports* had to be developed in order to accommodate those vessels incapable of reaching the main ports – for example, Tilbury for London and Avonmouth for Bristol.

In more recent times two important developments have had major effects upon many ports: these developments are the building of bulk carriers of vast size and the growth of containerisation. The greatly increased size of vessels, especially tankers, which have been built in more recent years has meant that most of the traditional ports are incapable of handling them and this has meant that new deep-water terminals, such as Milford Haven and Finnart, have had to be made. Thus, although on the one hand modern technology has made possible the use of greatly increased transporting units and thereby effected economies of scale, on the other hand, such large vessels have rendered some ports largely obsolescent and greatly reduced the volume of their trade. Containerisation has also adversely affected many ports since much of the handling of goods which formerly was done at the dock-side is now undertaken at inland depots and the introduction of roll-on-roll-off operations has further limited the function of ports.

There are about 250 port authorities in Britain and they are of four main types: nationalised undertakings, public trusts, local authorities and statutory companies. The ports handle about 350 million tonnes of cargo a year, including coastal traffic.

London

London grew up at the lowest fordable point on the Thames and where a gravel terrace provided firm land for a bridge to be built. Partly because it was the capital and the largest populous city, London developed as an important port. The lower Thames was tidal and today has a 6-metre rise in tide which permits ocean-going vessels to reach the city. The soft rocks of the floodplain made the excavation of docks a relatively easy matter, while the drained marshlands provided ample space for warehouses and factories. The fact that London lay opposite the mouth of the Rhine and the Scheldt stimulated its trade with one of the busiest parts of the continent. In modern times the port of London has tended to move downstream and since 1967 some of the older docks have been closed and their sites redeveloped. Tilbury docks, which lie 25 km downstream from the Royal Docks, have been extensively developed but it has become primarily concerned with container traffic (especially to the continent) and is Britain's largest container port, handling well in excess of quarter of a million containers a year. The port of London handles some 55 million tonnes of imports and exports annually, or 17·5 per cent of the total national trade. London is noteworthy, also, as a great entrepot.

Table 16:   The Major Ports of Britain

	% TOTAL TRADE HANDLED BY PORTS
London	17·5
Southampton	8·2
Liverpool	8·1
Dover	6·0
Harwich	5·1
Felixstowe	4·9
Hull	4·5
Manchester	3·3
Immingham	2·5
Tees	2·2
Milford Haven	1·3
Clyde	1·3
Bristol	1·2
Forth	0·7

Liverpool

Liverpool vies with Southampton for second position in importance after London. It lies on the eastern bank of the bottle-shaped estuary of the tidal Mersey with 10 km of waterfront and docks. The medieval port grew up around 'the Pool' and began to flourish through its links with Ireland. Later, it developed links with tropical America and during the heyday of the Lancashire cotton industry it imported large amounts of raw cotton and exported cotton piece goods. Liverpool currently handles around 25 million tonnes of goods a year, although its import trade is very much greater than its export trade. Imports comprise principally petroleum, ores and scrap metal, grain, animal feedstuffs, and a variety of industrial raw materials such as cotton and rubber. Exports are mainly manufactured goods, chemicals and machinery. At one time, Liverpool had an appreciable passenger traffic, chiefly to the Americas but this has disappeared. Many of Liverpool's industries have grown up because it is a port and its activities in flour milling, sugar refining, rubber and chemical production are characteristically port industries.

Southampton

Southampton's history as a port goes back to medieval times when it was a walled town. Located at the head of Southampton Water, a sheltered estuary with double tides, Southampton now has a 10 km long waterfront. Traditionally a passenger port, its function in this respect has declined with the increase in air travel, although it still deals with over 300,000 ocean-going passengers a year. As a result of its improved road and rail communications and the fact that it now has container and freightliner terminals, Southampton has increasingly become concerned with shipping cargoes. It imports a great variety of foodstuffs (grain, fruit, vegetables and wine), wool and motors, while crude oil comes to the Hamble depot. Its principal exports are machinery, motor vehicles of various kinds, chemicals and chemical derivatives such as fertilisers. Southampton has widened considerably its manufacturing base which includes flour milling, the manufacture of car components, telecommunications, light and electrical engineering, chemicals, boat building and rope making.

Hull

Kingston-upon-Hull, to give the port its proper name, was a medieval 'new' town established by royal authority. It grew up as a small port where the little River Hull entered the Humber and in its early days functioned mainly as a trans-shipment point from river craft to larger ships. Its later development was mainly associated with the industrial growth of West Yorkshire, the improvement of inland waterways and the arrival of the railway. Very recently it has gained increased accessibility as a result of its links with the M1 and the M62 trans-Pennine motorway; this accessibility has been improved even further with the completion of the Humber Bridge. Hull serves much of northern England, but more particularly West and South Yorkshire and the East Midlands; its hinterland, however, overlaps with that of Liverpool and Manchester. Traditionally its overseas links have been especially with the Scandinavian and Baltic countries but more recently it has strengthened its links with the E.E.C. Hull's principal imports are petroleum, timber, woodpulp, wool, cereals and oilseeds; its exports, machinery, vehicles, chemicals and fertilisers. Hull has a wide variety of port industries including the traditional activities of flour milling, oil-seed crushing, and animal feedstuff manufacture, together with the ancillary industries associated with its declining fishing industry. It has newer manufactures such as central heating equipment, chemicals (including paint and varnish and soap products), toilet hardware, caravans and confectionery.

Bristol

Bristol on the Avon became an important river port – it is 11 km upstream – in medieval and early modern times, but its inland location, limited depth of water and circuitous approach limited its expansion and today it handles a mere 5 million or so tonnes. Bristol's medieval trade was with Ireland, Aquitaine and Spain from whence it imported fish, hides, wines, salt and iron ore. Later, it became involved in the 'triangular trade' shipping slaves to the Americas and bringing sugar back to England. Many of its imports, e.g. grain, sugar and molasses, tea, coffee and cocoa, fruit and timber, and tobacco, have given rise to the city's specialised industries as, for example, the manufacture of cigarettes, chocolate, furniture, and flour milling and sugar refining. More modern industries are engineering and aircraft manufacture, chemicals, fertilisers and paper making. It seems likely that the City Docks will eventually be closed down as more and more port activity shifts to Bristol's outports at Avonmouth, Portishead and the new port of Portbury.

There is not space to discuss all the main ports of Britain but we should perhaps make special mention of *Felixstowe* which not so long ago was a small, run-down port. When containerisation began to be developed, the port authority was quick to realise its potential and commenced to develop Felixstowe as a container terminal, with the result that the port provides an excellent example of the impact which the new transport technology in cargo-handling may have. Its trade has increased from around 60,000 tonnes in the 1950s to around 2·5 million tonnes at the present day.

PIPELINES

Pipes have been used for thousands of years but, until little more than a century ago, the chief purpose of a pipeline was to carry water from reservoirs to consuming areas; piping was, in fact, the only satisfactory means of carrying water over long distances since it is a commodity of low value consumed in large quantities.

The discovery and use of petroleum ushered in a new era in pipeline use. The first oil pipeline was a wooden one laid down in the United States in 1861 but four years later an iron pipeline had been introduced. Although at first pipelines served only local purposes, carrying the crude oil to railheads or to local refineries, the value of transporting crude or refined oil in bulk by pipeline came to be appreciated; and by the end of the nineteenth century a number of trunk lines had been constructed. Today, around half a million kilometres of oil pipeline, together with a similar amount of natural gas pipeline, exist in the world. The spectacular growth in pipeline systems is, as Manners commented, "one of the most notable revolutions in the history of transport, especially in the transport of energy."

In Britain, pipeline development has increased greatly over the past fifteen years, more especially in relation to energy. There can be little doubt that the role of the pipeline will continue to increase as a transporting medium, although the size and shape of the country tend to place limits on its use. It should be borne in mind that pipelines are most economic when they are concerned with bulk movement over long distances as in Europe, the Soviet Union and in North America. Since, in Britain, water transport is readily available and tankers can provide cheap movement of oil, there is no great need for crude oil pipelines.

Leaving aside natural gas pipelines for the moment, pipelines mostly distribute oil from the oil terminals and refineries to petro-chemical plants, industrial areas and airports. The pipelines fall into three main groups: those carrying crude oil, those carrying oil products, and petro-chemical feedstock. The first crude oil pipeline was that running from the deep-water terminal at Finnart on Loch Long to the refinery at Grangemouth in 1951. Subsequently, other crude oil pipelines carried oil from Angle Bay in Pembrokeshire to Llandarcy, and from Ellesmere Port to the Stanlow refinery and further north to Heysham. The oil-products pipelines run from the refineries of the Thames estuary to London airport and across the Midlands to Merseyside; others run from Fawley to London airport, from Stanlow to Severnside, and from Humberside to West Yorkshire. Finally, petro-chemical feedstock pipelines run from Fawley to Severnside, from Stanlow to Carrington near Manchester, and from Teesside to Fleetwood and South Lancashire.

In 1959 a very large natural gas deposit was discovered in the north of the Netherlands and this was followed by the search for, and discovery of, gas in the North Sea. The West Sole gasfield was located in 1965 and since then about half a dozen other fields have been found off the east coast of England. In 1979 a new gasfield was discovered in Morecambe Bay. In 1976 Britain produced over 37 thousand million cubic metres from the West Sole, Leman Bank, Hewett, Indefatigable and Viking fields. The natural gas is carried by submarine pipelines to three terminals: Easington in Holderness, Bacton in Norfolk, and Theddlethorpe in Lincolnshire. From these east coast terminals the gas is distributed to the Southeast, the Southwest Peninsula, Wales and to Glasgow in Scotland.

140

TRANSPORT POLICY

There is no all-embracing policy towards transport in Britain, unlike the case of other sectors of the economy involving widespread public interest and participation. The reasons for this are largely historical and arise from the complex nature of the transport industry. A rationally controlled transport policy would seem to be sensible and desirable, yet the fact is that both public and private sectors have substantial transport interests. But, even in the public sector, it is only recently that efforts have been made to co-ordinate policies: the Transport Act of 1968 was a significant move in this direction and the impetus it provided has been further strengthened by the White Paper on Transport Policy issued in 1977.

Any discussion of transport policy involves two largely conflicting principles: that of *co-ordination* and *competition*. A policy of *co-ordination* has been seen as an ideal for public sector activities but where transport is concerned co-ordination involves the relationship between two or more different modes of transport. Ideally, under a co-ordinated transport system, a particular type of traffic is carried by the mode for which it is best suited but in practice, largely for historical reasons, such an ideal cannot always be attained. For example, the role of railways within the British transport system has always been seen as that of a middle to long distance carrier for passengers and for transporting bulk loads of freight. Its more local passenger functions have largely been taken over by public service vehicle operation while local freight services have become monopolised by road hauliers. "Co-ordination on the basis described (above) ought to result in a more efficient transport system, but such a process is a long one in terms of time and also a difficult one in terms of policy formulation and implementation" (Robinson & Bamford, 1978).

Competition implies the opposite to co-ordination since it means that two or more modes of transport are in direct competition for a specific transport need. Such competition has usually occurred as a result of the public/private sector interaction, although there may even be competition within the public sector. The most obvious illustration of competition is that between the private car and public transport within urban areas. For longer distance public transport demands, there may be competition between bus and rail or rail and air. Moreover, they are all likely to be in competition with private road transport. The individual, in a free market, makes his choice on the basis of such factors as the cost, speed, safety and quality of the service offered. It is true that in some cases competition may promote efficiency, but in transport it almost always leads to a duplication of effort and a sub-optimal allocation of resources.

Co-ordination and competition tend to be conflicting issues in transport policy although, in general, a mixture of the two may be said to characterise British transport policy.

A Labour government's views on transport policy were enunciated in a series of Command Papers published in 1966 and 1967. Four main principles were laid down: (i) the transport infrastructure and services needed modernisation; (ii) the problem of traffic conditions in towns demanded priority consideration; (iii) the transport system should take account of the social as well as the economic needs of the country; and (iv) public transport should play a key role in solving the transport problems. These principles were central to the Transport Act which followed in 1968.

A White Paper on Transport Policy was published in June 1977. The Paper favoured maintaining expenditure on public transport services, although less money would be available for new road construction. It argued that more responsibility for the planning of transport services should be handed over to local government, and that in all decisions there should be a more systematic and open involvement of all interested parties in the decision-making process. The particular effects of this policy would be: (i) no major cuts in the railway network, and continued financial support for commuter fares; (ii) improved co-ordination of local bus services, with support for rural services; (iii) a reduction of expenditure on roads but with priority being given to schemes assisting regional development and the relieving of heavy congestion in built-up areas; (iv) more traffic management powers to be given to local authorities to regulate urban transport; (v) increased revenue support for bus services, with new legislation to facilitate community mini-bus schemes and car sharing; and (vi) new standards regulating noise, braking and pollution in connection with freight transport.

The overall transport policy in Britain is likely to continue to remain one of co-ordination through competition, and the competition between public and private transport, inherent in the country's transport system, will remain.

References

Buchanan, C.D., *Traffic in Towns* (HMSO, 1963).

Buchanan, C.D., 'Wide world of the Narrow Way', *Drive Magazine,* Autumn 1967, pp. 69–71.

Williams, A.F., 'Policy for mobility', *Geographical Magazine,* Vol. L, No. 6, March 1978, pp. 386–392.

Turton, B.J., 'The road that started at Preston', *Geographical Magazine,* Vol. L, No. 7, April 1978, pp. 452–456.

Manners, G., 'The Pipeline Revolution', *Geography,* Vol. 47, pp. 154–63.

Masefield, P.G., 'The challenge of change in transport', *Geography,* Vol. 61, 1976, pp. 232–245.

Beaver, S.H., 'Ships and Shipping: the Geographical Consequences of Technological Progress', *Geography,* 1967, pp. 132–56.

Robinson, H. & Bamford, C.G., *Geography of Transport* (Macdonald & Evans, Ltd., 1978) pp. 401–2.

12
Administration

Public administration is one of the most significant sources of employment in the United Kingdom. It disposes of a steadily increasing proportion of our national income, and yet in the past geographers have paid very little attention to it as a specific area of study. However, land use planning regulations and regional policy innovations have always been of interest because of their locational and landscape implications. In the 1960s and early 1970s local government reorganisation attracted a great deal of comment from geographers. Political geographers have been taking an increasing interest in voting patterns and the importance of electoral districting, while the work of social geographers in studying spatial inequalities in social and economic well-being has involved a consideration of systems of administration and social welfare structures. In 1974 the Institute of British Geographers recognised the significance of public policy-making by devoting its annual conference to the theme of 'Geography and Public Policy'.

THE SCOPE OF PUBLIC ADMINISTRATION

Public administration in the United Kingdom operates at two levels – central government and local government. These two levels represent the twin origins of the system in the pre-industrial era. On the one hand the Crown was responsible for the administration of justice, and the defence of the realm, and to that end levied taxes on the whole country for the support of the armed services, and the maintenance of the judiciary and associated services. On the other hand the need to regulate community life, both in the co-operating agricultural systems of the countryside and the mercantile life of towns, led to a variety of local assemblies making regulations under the authority of lords of the manor or municipal charters of incorporation. In the last years of Elizabeth I's reign a universal system of local government based upon the ecclesiastical parish was instituted. Such a system was unable to cope with the radical structural changes that were engendered during the nineteenth century, and consequently the last hundred years has seen an astonishing increase in both the size and the scope of public administration, with its extension into virtually every part of our lives.

Since the period of the post-war government the range of publicly controlled services and industries has also increased dramatically, with the progressive nationalisation of energy provision, transportation, water supply, the iron and steel industry and shipbuilding. Today the defence of the realm and local community regulation are all but submerged under an array of functions which can be rather arbitrarily divided into two groups. First there are those associated with the provision of capital infrastructure (what we could call environmental hardware) such as highways and transportation, water supply and drainage, energy provision and of course housing (almost half the population lives in 'council' housing of one sort or another). Secondly there are the services which rest more on the provision of skilled personnel than on hardware, in the provision of social and welfare support to the deprived, delinquent and maladjusted. In between are the really big spenders of the education and health services, which require not only expensively trained specialist staff

143

but also large and elaborate facilities, ranging from the local welfare centre and primary school to the regional hospital and university.

The significance of public administration can be appreciated by reference to Fig. 12.1. At the centre of control is 'the government'. We are all familiar with the government and perhaps identify it with one or two political personalities, but in reality *central government* is an immensely wide ranging and far reaching institution that does not have an easily defined formal structure. At its core, certainly, is the Prime Minister and his or her ministerial colleagues, who are officially the Queen's government; but of course they preside over what can only be called an army of civil servants (738,000 in 1978) arranged into ministries and departments, whose composition changes from time to time. In the early 1970s, for instance a number of departments were amalgamated to form complex departments, such as the Department of the Environment with responsibility for almost all the environmental services referred to above. Although some departments are almost exclusively London-based, such as the Treasury,

most spread their tentacles across the length and breadth of the country, in what is termed *field administration*. Thus we find that most departments divide England into regions – by no means the same regions incidentally – and have offices and sometimes quite substantial numbers of staff in each region. In addition some aspects of central government have been deliberately moved to provincial centres as part of regional policy – Post Office Savings Certificates Division to Durham City, for instance, or part of the Department of Health and Social Security to Newcastle upon Tyne.

Around the periphery of the identifiable ministries and their field staff, however, is ranged a great variety of public agencies and corporations. Some of these represent very significant areas of interest such as the Regional Water Authorities, the Energy Boards, the Regional Health Authorities, British Rail, British Waterways, National Bus Company, National Coal Board, all of which relate directly to central government policy, even though they may operate as semi-autonomous undertakings. Simply in terms of employment

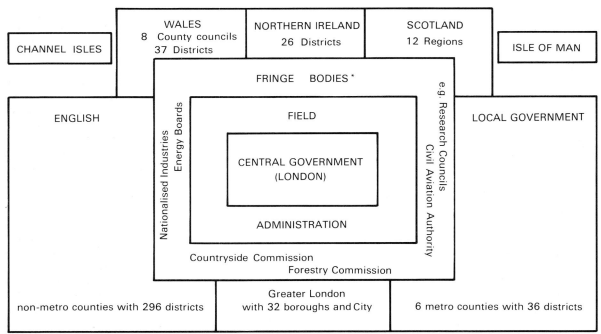

*Note: The alternative title for Quangos (Quasi-Autonomous Non-Government Organisations)

Fig 12.1 Structure of public administration in the UK

Fig 12.2 Whitehall and Westminster: 'corridors of power'

structure this vast array of public servants is geographically significant: the structural implications of their decisions and policy implementation, of course, are fundamental.

Central government and its peripheral institutions does not act in a vacuum. Since the accession of the U.K. to the European Economic Community, an increasing area of our general life has fallen under Community Regulations which have the force of law in this country; and while the public may resent commodity imbalances popularly reported as the 'butter mountain' or the 'wine lake', it is perhaps not always aware of the significant subsidies afforded to the farming community and the regional support grants that aid the peripheral regions. These are among a range of benefits channelled towards Britain by this supra-national administration, even though the overall balance of advantage is contentious.

Of more immediate impact, however, is the system of *local administration* which we shall examine in more detail later in this chapter. As an introduction, though, it is worth pointing out that local government in England operates in three distinct systems. The majority of the country is divided up into 39 *non-metropolitan counties,* each of which is divided into districts – most have around seven districts, although Lancashire has fourteen

and Bedfordshire only four. These counties are more or less identifiable with the old shire counties. The second system is that of the *metropolitan counties* which broadly conforms to the conurbation areas, and are entirely new creations of the 1972 Local Government Act. They, too, have districts, but the distribution of functions between county and district are rather different. The third system operates in *Greater London*, which was constituted as one area under the London Government Act of 1963 and is divided into 32 London boroughs, plus the City of London, which is in a category on its own. Local government in Wales follows the English pattern for non-metropolitan counties, but in Scotland (and N. Ireland) quite different patterns have been produced, while the Channel Islands and the Isle of Man retain their autonomy under the crown.

We have, then, a huge array of services and functions that play an important part in the ordering of space and resources in Great Britain. They are all in some measure susceptible to a geographic analysis, and many deal with problems that have a specifically geographical aspect as will be apparent in other chapters. Before passing on to look in more detail at some of these issues we ought to note that the system operates under the general principle of *public accountability*. This is provided

145

by a system of public representation at both central and local levels, which also has an important spatial component, for the arrangement of constituencies has a considerable impact not only on the result of elections but on the effective operation of the principle in its fullest spirit.

CENTRAL GOVERNMENT

The influence of central government permeates into every sector of national life, and it would not be possible in the space we have available to discuss the total effect this has – a contentious enough subject anyway. We can, however, point to those effects which have a particularly geographical component of which the most obvious is the role of central government in *land use* and *regional planning*. Land use planning is a parti-

cularly interesting example because it illustrates the control central government exercises over what is in the first instance a responsibility of local government.

Land Use Planning

The fundamental way in which central government regulates land use planning is by providing the initial legislative framework under which the system operates. This is by no means a simple process as Fig. 12.3 shows. The core legislation is provided by the various Town and Country Planning Acts, but there is an array of associated legislation which has significant land use planning implications. The present principles of planning were first enunciated in the 1968 Town and Country Planning Act, which laid down that planning should be conducted at two levels. County plan-

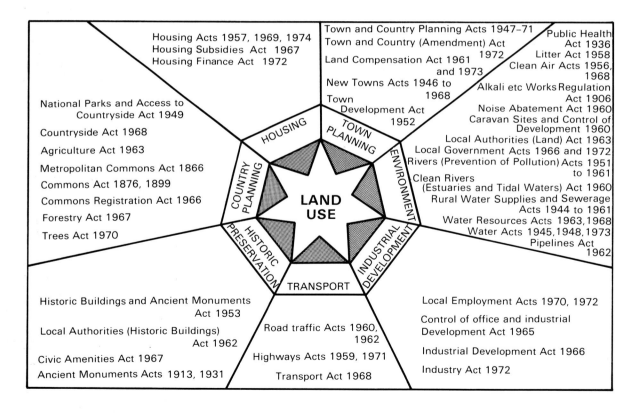

Fig 12.3 Legislation and Land Use in England and Wales

ning departments were to prepare what came to be called Structure Plans, which mapped out the general strategy of development within the county, taking into account social and economic trends, not only within the county but in relation to neighbouring authorities. These plans are quite different from the old Development Plans prepared under the 1947 Town and Country Planning Act, in that they express intentions only in diagrammatic form, and not in terms of detailed land use allocations. The working out of the general strategy on the ground was to be undertaken at district level by a series of Local Plans of various kinds, from detailed land use allocations for whole districts to specialist plans for conservation or housing redevelopment. After the 1972 Local Government Act these two levels of planning were allocated to the county and district authorities. In the event the separation of powers in this way has not always been successful, particularly in the metropolitan counties.

Legislation also allows for the direct intervention of the Secretary of State for the Environment. All Structure Plans have to be approved by him, and he can stipulate changes as seem appropriate. The influence of the Secretary of State is also manifested by the system of 'calling in' planning applications in certain circumstances. If the Secretary feels that a certain application is specially contentious, or deals with an important point of principle, he can call in the application and set up a public inquiry. The inquiry is held under the auspices of an Inspector from the Department of the Environment, who then advises the Secretary of State who himself makes the decision on the application, confirming, modifying or rejecting the Inspector's report. The same process is followed when an appeal is made against a decision made by a local authority on a planning application. By this system the government, acting as the central planning machine, is able to guide the evolution of planning policy, within the framework provided by planning law. In addition it issues circulars, bulletins and memoranda which help the local planning authority to interpret the law under changing circumstances. Cherry goes so far as to say that by these means, "the central planning machine operates as the key to land planning".

Land use is also affected of course by other central government decisions. Amongst the most spectacular, if localised, are decisions to set up New Towns under the New Towns legislation of 1946 and 1965 (1968 for Scotland), which is discussed in Chapter 13. Less apparent, but perhaps more important, are the land use interests of the Ministry of Agriculture, Fisheries and Food, which within the context of E.E.C. regulations has a responsibility for farming policies. Policy changes here, as we have seen in Chapter 9, can have very widespread land use implications. As well as subsidies for individual foodstuffs which may encourage particular cropping patterns, special provisions for hill farming and for reclamation schemes have been locally significant. The Ministry is also responsible for the Forestry Commission, whose woodlands are being increasingly seen as a multi-function resource. The designation of National Parks, Areas of Outstanding Natural Beauty, and the allocation of land for Defence purposes, are among other major central government decisions that have a direct impact upon land use. The investment and development programmes of the energy boards, the water authorities and the transportation boards have significant ramifications upon both urban and rural developments. It is important that we appreciate that changes in all these sectors do not just happen haphazardly, but are part of a more or less co-ordinated evolution of public policy.

Regional Policy

The evolution of government policy in response to changing circumstances and shifts in political power is particularly well shown in the development of regional policy, an outline of which is given in Part Four. For our purposes we can pick out three features. Of prime importance has been government reaction against the spectre of unemployment. It was high rates of unemployment particularly on the coalfields that prompted the earliest regional policy measures in the Special Areas Act 1934, and ever since, rising rates of unemployment have sounded alarm bells for government policy-makers.

Secondly, it is clearly apparent that Labour governments are much more susceptible to regional policy initiatives than Conservative governments. It was Labour governments that introduced the 1945 Distribution of Industry Act which laid the groundwork of industrial controls and inducements for all future legislation; the 1966 Industrial Development

Act, which re-introduced a system of development areas which had been relaxed by the intervening Conservative governments; the 1965 Selective Employment Tax, which had differential application between regions, followed by the Regional Employment Premium in 1967 – all pieces of legislation which contributed directly towards labour rather than investment costs. Labour also set up the Hunt Commission on Intermediate Areas, which reported in 1969. On the other hand the development of growth zone strategies (for the North-East and Scotland), and the setting up of the Location of Offices Bureau were important initiatives of a Conservative government in 1963.

Thirdly, regional aid programmes have become steadily more complex (so that by 1972 the country was divided into no fewer than five categories for development purposes) and also more extensive – so that the great majority of Great Britain fell within an assisted area of one sort or another (see Fig. 18.3, on page 226). The 1979 Conservative government, however, proposed to apply regional policy much more selectively, as is outlined in Chapter 18. The regional aid programme is also now seen in much broader terms than simply the provision of extra jobs. While the stimulation of further economic activity remains the prime goal, it has been increasingly realised that that will only be achieved by an all-round improvement in the physical and social environment as well as in the direct provision of employment. However, regional aid programmes are themselves little more than cosmetic measures against the vicissitudes of national economic policies and the fortunes of the nation at large.

LOCAL GOVERNMENT

It could be argued that the most important spatial allocation in Britain is the division of the country into local authority areas for the provision of local government services. The pattern of counties and their constituent districts provides the structure for the provision of our public services, and the basis for most of our statistical knowledge of the fabric of our society. This is a spatial matter *par excellence* and demands the attention of geographers.

The main features of the pattern of local government are very ancient. Both the system of counties, constituted of townships and parishes, themselves arranged into districts (termed

'wapentakes' in the north of England and 'hundreds' in the south of England) and the separation of town and country local government, extends back into the medieval period. Although there have been two major re-castings of the system of local government in England and Wales, and also in Scotland, these twin features have persisted.

Until the re-organisation of local government during the 1970s the system of administration was based in England and Wales upon the provisions

Fig 12.4 Town Hall, Leeds. Built in 1868 as an explicit symbol of municipal pride, Leeds Town Hall is shown here in its uncleaned state. It was built to house a concert hall, magistrates' courts, and municipal offices

of the 1888 Local Government Act. This was itself a thorough-going reform that provided a contiguous system of comparable local government stretching across the whole country. It replaced a complicated amalgam of municipal corporations, shire counties, sanitary authorities and parish vestries with a broadly uniform system based upon the old counties, but also creating new ones. From the 40 old shire counties were created 50 administrative counties by dividing Yorkshire into three Ridings, Lincolnshire into three parts, Suffolk and Sussex into two divisions, and separating the Soke of Peterborough from Northamptonshire, and the Isle of Ely from Cambridgeshire. In 1890 the Isle of Wight was also separated from Hampshire. Most radical of all, however, was the creation of the County of London from the closely built up parts of the adjacent counties of Kent, Surrey, Middlesex and Essex. In some senses this was the forerunner of the metropolitan counties of 1972. The counties were subsequently divided up into districts, urban or rural, based upon the former Sanitary Districts of the 1875 Public Health Act. Into this uniform spatial system, however, were punched a number of 'holes'. Towns with a population of at least 50,000, and thirteen ancient 'cities', were designated as county boroughs, having all the powers and responsibilities of the counties. This perpetuated the medieval split between town and country areas, and in some counties seriously weakened the effectiveness of local government. Thus in the large industrialised counties of the north of England, local government was most fragmented where it should have been most co-ordinated. The West Riding, for instance, had ten county borough 'islands' within the administrative county. Despite modest boundary adjustments in succeeding years, the spill-over of urbanisation from the county boroughs into adjacent county districts was considerable in some areas, and provided for a great deal of inter-authority conflict and an unco-ordinated approach to problem-solving, particularly in the conurbations. With a rapidly growing population, particularly in urban areas, and the pattern of population redistribution that we saw in Chapter 8, it is not surprising that modifications and amendments continued to be made to the 1888 arrangements. A further 24 county boroughs were created, and there were successive attempts to tidy up and rationalise boundaries, particularly in the Midland counties.

More serious attempts to re-arrange boundaries were made with the setting up of the Local Government Commission in 1958, which was charged with "reviewing the organisation of local government in England (outside the metropolitan area) and of making such changes as appear to be desirable". The Commission were also given the special task of reviewing the areas that had been defined as conurbations at the time of the 1951 census. By 1966 when the Commission was wound up after the creation of a full scale Royal Commission on Local Government, a number of locally significant changes had been made. Amalgamations of neighbouring districts produced new county boroughs for Teesside and Torbay, the West Midlands conurbation was given a new structure of county boroughs, and there were some modifications in rural areas. By the mid 1960s though, it was clear that the whole system needed a comprehensive review, and the Redcliffe-Maud Commission set in train a series of events which led to the 1972 Local Government Act.

Deficiencies of the pre-1972 System

The deficiencies in the pre-1972 system of local government can be seen as threefold: democratic, administrative and geographic, without assigning any order of priority. We can refer to the first objection as democratic, because an important political aspect of the problem was the growing feeling that nobody really cared about local government. Local residents appeared to take little interest in the democratic process, rarely turning out to vote at anything approaching the level for a general election. Many councillors were returned unopposed, particularly in country districts. This apparent apathy helped to persuade politicians that the system needed an overhaul.

The administrative objection stems from the incoherencies and complexities of the system. Both counties and county boroughs varied greatly in geographical extent, rateable value and population. In consequence the quality and quantity of services inevitably varied, as indeed did the range of problems that had to be tackled. In many of the smaller county boroughs, for instance, land use planning, which may have been extremely necessary, was something the Borough Architect or the Borough Engineer did in his spare time. Within

149

the system, relationships between the county districts, the municipal boroughs and the county councils were far from simple, while the role of central government in local affairs was a subject of considerable disquiet. In addition, most counties divided their areas into divisions for the purposes of their own field administration. These divisions rarely coincided with individual county districts, and often not with each other. Thus, Redcliffe-Maud and Wood (1974) cite the example of Cheshire County Council, where the citizens of Stalybridge had to attend four different towns for education matters, health, child care and planning.

The geographical objection was one which the general public was least aware of. It had several facets. First, the boundaries that marked the civil parishes, wards, districts and counties themselves, were often over a thousand years old, and in many cases bore little relationship to modern conditions. Secondly, even the most recent boundaries of the larger towns and cities, some of which were county boroughs, were very anachronistic. The contiguous built-up areas spread irregularly into neighbouring districts, while existing administrative divisions did not take into account important factors such as travel to work areas or regional spheres of influence. The result of this disjunction between administrative areas and patterns of activity often resulted in very bad relationships between the county boroughs and the shire counties in which they were set. This was particularly acute in matters such as land use planning. Strategic planning as such was rendered very difficult especially in the conurbations. Even if joint consultative committees were established it often proved extremely difficult to secure agreement between neighbouring but rival authorities.

The Royal Commission, 1969

The Royal Commission reported in 1969, and because the great deal of research it commissioned provided the groundwork for all the subsequent proposals, it is worth noting its main features.

(i) The existing system should be replaced by 58 unitary authorities, responsible for all local government services, and embracing towns and neighbouring countryside. Because these authorities should pay regard to the facts of social geography, they were to be of very uneven size. In Greater Manchester, Merseyside and the West Midlands, a two-tier system was proposed, similar to that which had been established for Greater London in 1963.

(ii) Local interest and participation should be encouraged by the formation of a system of parish or local councils within the unitary authorities and the metropolitan districts if it seemed appropriate.

(iii) Above the unitary authorities a system of provincial councils should be established, coinciding with the existing Economic Planning Council regions, to encourage broader strategic thinking and to act as a sort of referee between the authorities in each region.

However, controversy was fanned by the submission of a Memorandum of Dissent by Derek Senior, one of the members of the Commission. He proposed a drastic re-ordering of boundaries and the creation of thirty-five city regions, divided into districts as appropriate, with a top tier of five provincial authorities. These proposals appeared a little too radical, however, and the Labour government accepted the general principles of the Majority Report, adding S. Hampshire and W. Yorkshire to the list of Metropolitan counties. In the event, though, a change of government in 1970 meant that it was the Conservatives who introduced the 1972 Local Government Act, which set up the present system of local administration from April 1974.

Local Government Act, 1972

Metropolitan counties were indeed created for the conurbations – S. Hampshire being deleted, but S. Yorkshire and Tyneside being added. A two-tier system (county and district) was favoured rather than a unitary system, although the allocation of functions between the two differed in the metropolitan counties from the majority, as can be seen in Table 17. Provincial councils were not created, although local or parish councils are permitted where communities wish to have them set up. The impact of the new system varied greatly. In some rural counties such as Cornwall or Wiltshire there was really very little change beyond the adjustment of district boundaries, although the combination of Herefordshire and Worcestershire

Table 17:   Local Government Functions

	COUNTY	DISTRICT
Responsibility	*POLICE, FIRE, AMBULANCE*	Not responsible
Limited reserve powers	*HOUSING*	Provision, management, slum clearance, house and area improvement
Construction and improvement, traffic control, maintenance of main roads	*ROADS*	Minor road maintenance, car parking
Structure planning, development plan scheme and major development control (according to local conventions)	*PLANNING*	Local Plans, most development control
Consumer protection, refuse disposal	*PUBLIC HEALTH*	Hygiene, slaughterhouses, smoke control, refuse collection
Responsibility in non-metropolitan counties	*EDUCATION, SOCIAL SERVICES, LIBRARIES*	Responsibility in metropolitan counties and some large former county boroughs in non-metropolitan counties
Metropolitan counties are Passenger Transport Authorities (P.T.A.s)	*TRANSPORT*	Retain bus fleets in non-metropolitan counties according to local policy
Co-responsibility	*PARKS, MUSEUMS, BATHS*	Co-responsibility

and the disappearance of Huntingdonshire, the Isle of Ely and Rutland created local storms. The biggest jolts were in the county boroughs and the conurbations. The loss of status that was involved from the reducing of a county borough to a county district, particularly if the county town was elsewhere (as with Plymouth and Southampton) has created some obvious difficulties. Similarly, in the conurbations, entirely new administrative units have been created that relate neither to ancient counties, nor to simple extensions of the former county boroughs.

While it may well be many years before the new system of local government can be adequately assessed, two major points need to be made. The first is that a generation after the idea of the city-region was developed, the concept did not find its way into what was intended to be a thorough-going reform of local government. Boundaries around the metropolitan counties – the conurbations – were drawn very tightly indeed,

perpetuating the difficulties some of the county boroughs had faced earlier. As Chisholm points out, it seems almost by accident that the interdependence of town and country was acknowledged in some largely rural counties – most often in the case of towns with populations of less than 60–70,000, which found themselves in the same district as their local service area.

The second point is that the functions of local government before reorganisation were deliberately not tampered with. In consequence, the relationship between local and central government was never really properly debated. The *ad hoc* system that had developed over the preceding eight decades or so was adopted uncritically as the one appropriate for the immediate future. Had that not been the case it may well be that a quite different local government map would have emerged. One reason that was given for not tampering with the relationship between central and local government was that another Royal

151

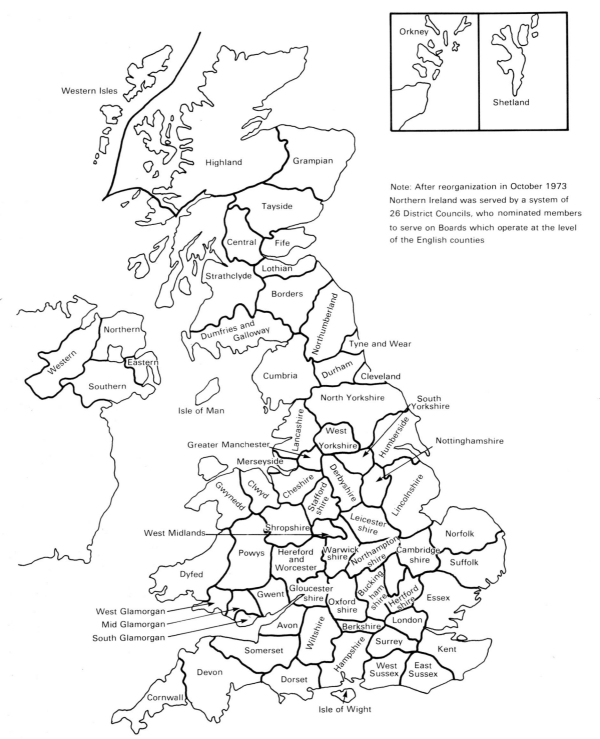

Western Isles

Highland

Grampian

Tayside

Central

Fife

Strathclyde

Lothian

Borders

Dumfries and Galloway

Northumberland

Tyne and Wear

Northern

Western

Eastern

Southern

Cumbria

Durham

Cleveland

Isle of Man

North Yorkshire

South Yorkshire

Lancashire

West Yorkshire

Humberside

Nottinghamshire

Greater Manchester

Merseyside

Derbyshire

Gwynedd

Clwyd

Cheshire

Stafford shire

Lincolnshire

Leicester shire

Norfolk

West Midlands

Shropshire

Powys

Hereford and Worcester

Warwick shire

Northampton shire

Cambridge shire

Suffolk

Dyfed

Gwent

Gloucester shire

Oxford shire

Bucking ham shire

Hertford shire

Essex

West Glamorgan

Mid Glamorgan

South Glamorgan

Avon

Wiltshire

Berkshire

London

Surrey

Kent

Somerset

Hampshire

West Sussex

East Sussex

Devon

Dorset

Isle of Wight

Cornwall

Orkney

Shetland

Note: After reorganization in October 1973
Northern Ireland was served by a system of
26 District Councils, who nominated members
to serve on Boards which operate at the level
of the English counties

Fig 12.5a Local government structure after re-organisation in 1971–74: showing English and
Welsh Counties, Scottish Regions, and Boards of Health and Social Security in Northern Ireland

Commission had been set up in 1969 to consider this very problem, particularly in regard to agitation for the devolution of power to Scotland and to Wales.

Before we pass on to the important topic of regional government, however, let us note that the system of local government for *Scotland* was also reorganised at this time, into a system of regions, some of which had a second tier of districts. In *Northern Ireland,* local government, which was a major bone of contention, has also been reformed. The former county councils were replaced in 1973 by a system of 26 district councils, elected on a single transferable vote (unique in the United Kingdom). While the transferable vote system was adopted to safeguard minority interests, there is no doubt that there exists in the region a strong feeling that power has been removed from local government, for important local functions such as Education, Health and Social Services, are now administered by a series of *nominated boards,* upon which the district councils merely have representatives. These boards operate at the approximate level of English counties.

The new local government structures for England and Wales, for Scotland, and for Northern Ireland, are summarised in Figs. 12.5(a) & (b).

REGIONAL GOVERNMENT

The sustained campaign for the *devolution* of some degree of administrative and political power from Whitehall to Scotland and to Wales dates from the late nineteenth century. The idea of a 'Federal United Kingdom' was subsequently floated at a Speaker's Conference in 1919, but in the event, it was only Ireland which achieved Home Rule. The Scottish National Party was formed in 1926, and in 1931 gained thirteen per cent of the popular vote, as a result of which a 'little Whitehall' was

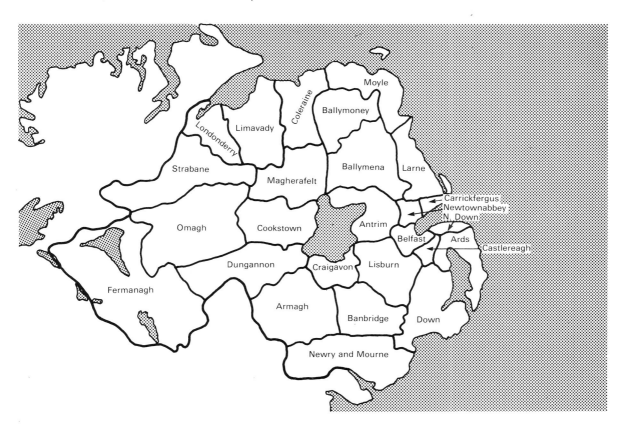

Fig 12.5b Districts of Northern Ireland

153

set up at St. Andrew's House in Edinburgh to house the Scottish departments. Since that time the responsibilities of the Scottish Office have been progressively increased so that much central government administration for Scotland was carried out from Edinburgh before the setting up of the Royal Commission on the Constitution. This has been by no means insignificant. J.C. Banks, for instance, points out that the creation of the Scottish Development Department in 1962 played a critical part in "putting the brake on the economic decline that characterised the decade preceding its creation". In contrast, the Welsh Office has played a much less significant role, and indeed was only created in 1964, although Welsh language enthusiasts secured much more publicity in the 1960s than their Scottish counterparts. The rising tide of nationalism was encouraged in Scotland by the North Sea Oil discoveries in the 1970s, but it was also given momentum by a set of other factors which are at work throughout Europe, which we could call the regional groundswell. Notwithstanding the referendum defeat on the Scotland Bill and the Wales Bills in 1979, this groundswell remains.

To geographers it may appear strange that the regional dimension enters so little into public administration. The reason for this of course is because of the twin points of origin of our system of government – either local or central. Over the last fifty years, however, there has been an increasing tendency to turn to the intermediate tier of the *region,* and we can see that this has, perhaps, three roots. The first is that, with the general increase in mobility consequent upon wider car-ownership, the general scale of patterns of activity has become enlarged beyond that of the purely local community. Consequently some system of government is desirable to take account of this trend, not least because many services would appear to be best provided for at that level, from the ubiquitous need for water supply and drainage to the specialist facilities of high level health care and education. Secondly, because economic growth is reflected in these new regional activity systems, so differential growth between regions has highlighted the need to approach structural problems at the regional level, whether they are problems of overgrowth, stagnation or decline. The identity of the North-East of England, for instance, is closely bound up with its regional difficulties. Thirdly, there seems to be, particularly

in the more peripheral regions, a growing alienation from the concept of central government, and a wish to locate a greater proportion of decision-making closer to the people and the areas that are affected. This often builds upon a pride in the region which has deep cultural and sociological roots. (It is noteworthy that such a situation was outlined with prophetic accuracy by Halford Mackinder as far back as 1919.)

In much of Europe the difficulty has been in defining the region and of fixing a regional dimension into the existing mesh of decision making. In Great Britain, the problem of definition for both Scotland and Wales does not arise, simply because both countries have preserved their distinctiveness to a greater or lesser degree. In Scotland institutional distinctiveness has been maintained by the legal system, by the Presbyterian church (influential not just through its 'Parliament of Morals', the General Assembly, but also through its early provision of universal education in every parish) and by the universities. In Wales the distinctiveness has been mainly cultural, particularly focusing upon the Welsh language, out of which grew the Welsh universities and the Welsh National Library. The distinctiveness of Northern Ireland hardly needs remarking upon here. The events which led to its formation and the difficulties associated with its present identity are outlined in Chapter 20.

Scotland and Wales form identifiable units, but arguments have been advanced that equivalent regional units can be discerned within England. Much field administration of central government has a regional basis. During World War II civil defence regions were established within England, subsequently forming the basis of the Standard Regions. These regions were modified in 1964 to form Economic Planning Regions, each of which was equivalent in status to the Scottish E.P.R., and the Welsh E.P.R. Subsequent reform of the National Health Service and water resources was based upon a regional principle, as are the energy boards, British Rail, the B.B.C. and commercial television. In addition, the E.E.C. regards the region as the appropriate level for spatial, as opposed to commodity, intervention. As both the Royal Commission on Local Government, and that on the Constitution, favoured some system of regional administration, it is not unlikely that some such system will be devised in the foreseeable future.

References

Cherry, G.E., *The Evolution of British Town Planning* (Leonard Hill 1974).

House, J.W., (ed), *The U.K. Space: Resources Environment and the Future,* 2nd edition (Weidenfeld & Nicolson, 1977).

Freeman, T.W., *Geography and Regional Administration: England and Wales 1830–1968* (Hutchinson, 1968).

Redcliffe–Maud, J.P., & Wood, B., *English Local Government Reformed* (O.U.P., 1974).

Royal Commission on Local Government in England, 1966–69, (HMSO, 1969).

Chisholm, M., 'The reformation of local government in England', in *Processes in Physical and Human Geography,* R. Peel, (ed) (Heinemann, 1975).

Banks, J.C., *Federal Britain?* (Harrap, 1971).

Hall, A.P., 'Mackinder and the course of events', *Annals of the Association of American Geographers,* Vol. XLV, 1955, pp. 109–26.

13

The Built Environment

Great Britain was the first country in the world to become almost fully urbanised. Even by 1851 over half the population of England and Wales lived in urban environments and by the end of the century that proportion had risen to over three-quarters, giving a total urban population of over twenty-five millions. In consequence, much of the pattern and a great deal of the fabric of our built environment was already realised two generations ago. In this chapter we shall review how both the pattern and the fabric have changed over the intervening period, and examine some of the interrelated problems that have characterised the urban scene in recent years.

URBAN PATTERN

The process of population agglomeration, arising from the rapid movement towards industrialisation, has been described in Part Two. The result was a marked change from the distribution of population which had characterised Britain before the nineteenth century. For the first time there were significantly large concentrations of population outside London, representing a marked switch in the balance of major built-up areas towards the north and north-west. The pattern at the outbreak of World War I was described by Patrick Geddes, who coined for us the now familiar name of *conurbation*. He identified eight areas which he felt were distinctively agglomerated urban areas: *Greater London, Lancaston* (southern Lancashire and northern Cheshire) *West Riding* (the annulus of towns now making up the West Yorkshire conurbation) *South Riding* (the Sheffield/Barnsley/Rotherham area) *Midlandton* (the

Black Country and surrounding areas) *Waleston* (the industrial zone of South Wales) *Tyne-Wear-Tees* (the discontinuous urbanisation of the three Durham estuaries) and *Clyde-Forth* which Geddes envisaged as a bi-polar city region extending between Edinburgh and Glasgow. Clearly, Geddes's areas extend beyond our notion of a more or less continuously built-up area, and it was the

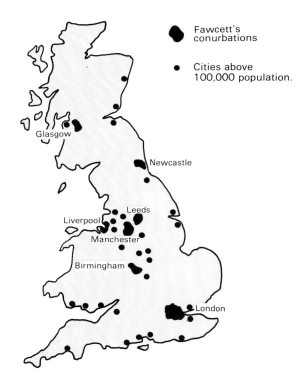

Fig 13.1 Major urban areas, 1931

geographer Fawcett who gave the term its conventional definition, when in 1931 he identified seven conurbations with more than one million inhabitants – London, Birmingham, West Yorkshire, Manchester, Liverpool, Tyneside and Glasgow. The distribution of these conurbations, along with intervening centres of population above 100,000, had given urban Britain enduring characteristics by the late 1920s. Two markedly urbanised areas stood out – Greater London, and the core area which stretched from the West Midlands to industrialised Lancashire and Yorkshire. Peripheral, and without exception on the coast, were the industrial centres of the North-East and Glasgow, and the ancient centres of Bristol, Portsmouth-Southampton, Hull and Edinburgh (Fig. 13.1).

Rank Order of Cities

Changes in the pattern of urbanisation to a large extent mirror the population changes which were described in Chapter 8, and consequently the years since World War I have witnessed a more rapid enlargement of towns in the southern half of Britain, than in the northern regions. The changing fortunes of the major cities in the various regions of Britain are shown in Fig. 13.2. The overwhelming and ancient dominance of London in the hierarchy of British cities is well known, and it is clear that this has been emphasised even further between 1901–1976. In that period, London has increased its size from 5·2 times the second city (Manchester/Salford in 1901) to 7·5 times the second city in 1976 (Birmingham). In contrast there has been no such change in Scotland, and Glasgow in 1976 was less dominant in population size than it was in 1901. Most cities have changed their place in the rank order. Most significant of all is the decline of the northern cities and the ascendancy of those in the Midlands. By 1976 Birmingham had long been Britain's second city, displacing Liverpool and Manchester/Salford by one position. The northern textile towns of Oldham, Blackburn, Bolton and Preston all suffer considerable relegation, with only Bolton retaining a place in the table at all in 1976. In contrast, accompanying Birmingham's rise, the major Midland cities of Leicester, Nottingham and Derby have increased their position, while Walsall and Wolverhampton, which failed to signify in the top

thirty in 1901 now occupy middle-tier positions, with Luton and Southend edging their way into the 1976 table.

Suburbanisation

The extension of the built-up area until 1939 was almost entirely due to the progressive enlargement of already existing settlements. Large towns extended their suburbs, while peripheral villages and smaller towns around the main centres experienced exurban growth, the two frequently coalescing in a web of mature suburbs. The very rapid extension of towns in the more prosperous regions of Britain between the wars provoked considerable alarm in some quarters, although the real scale of expansion was quite compact when compared with North America. Few provincial cities experienced suburbanisation more than seven miles from the centre, and even London was largely contained within a fifteen mile radius. The rate of suburbanisation, though, considerably exceeded the rate of population change, and owes far more to another range of factors.

The dispersal of population from urban centres, especially if the centre is also the prime source of employment, demands an effective public transport system. The development of the tramcar had encouraged the development of Victorian suburbs, and the electrification of much of the peripheral rail network around London was an enabling factor for metropolitan extension in the inter-war period. There were other transport factors at work, however, with the development of a near ubiquitous bus service which offered a much more flexible suburban transport system than the tracks associated with tram and railway alike. Another important set of factors in the inter-war period was the low price of agricultural land, the low cost of building materials and the cheap labour consequent upon the depressed state of world trade. As a result housing could be built cheaply: with no municipal development controls, private housing could be undertaken wherever there was a demand – and sometimes ahead of demand – and council housing schemes put under way at surprisingly low cost. For the private individual buying his own house, the cheap credit available through the various building societies was the key factor. Initially the new suburbs were almost entirely residential, with only the neigh-

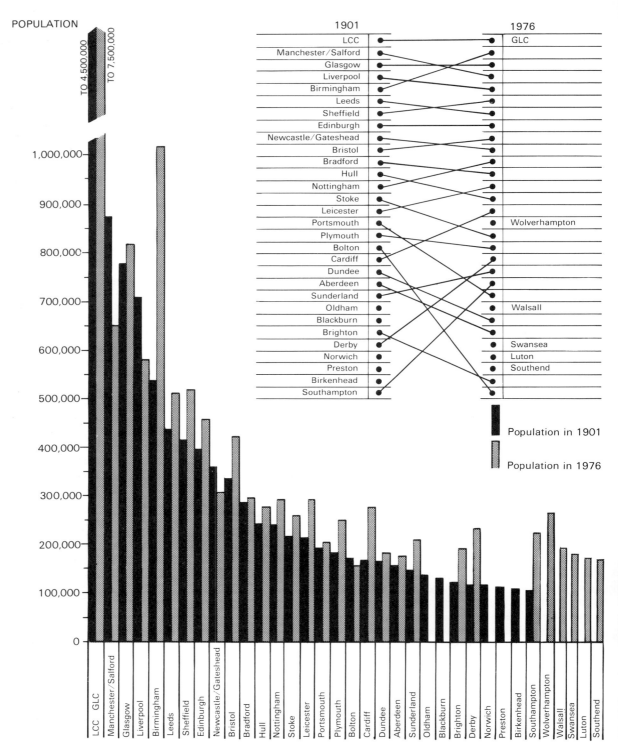

Fig 13.2 Changes in the Rank Order of Major British Cities, 1901–1976

158

bourhood shops, pubs, churches and other communal facilities that the pattern of local demand generated; but increasingly industry was attracted by the pool of labour, especially of women on low-income council estates. In addition the new industries particularly associated with the electrical and automobile trades demanded new types of plant which could best be established on 'greenfield', peripheral locations. In the case of the automobile industries the demand for space could be very considerable, and have a marked effect upon the local built-up area.

Regional Inequality

Not all these factors were at work nationally, however, and in the inter-war years there was marked regional disparity in the rates of urban expansion. The old-established industrial regions of Scotland, Wales and the north of England not only suffered high rates of unemployment, they also suffered from municipal poverty which inhibited the rate of council house building. More importantly, they had relatively fewer salaried workers, as opposed to weekly wage earners, who alone could attract a building society mortgage. This disparity in earnings and employment structure contributed towards the increasingly acute problems attendant on a too vigorous expansion of the built-up area in southern regions, especially around London, and problems attendant upon urban decay in the industrial regions of the north. The whole situation was too obvious to be ignored, and provoked a remarkable burst of public policy decisions which have radically affected the urban pattern since 1945. What was ignored, however, was the slow decay and inexorable decline of the smaller rural market towns and villages, which had been going on for two generations. While the result of this ossification was to preserve rural Britain from some of the worst excesses of inter-war development, it also created problems which we shall note in the next chapter.

The election of a Labour government after the war ended in 1945 was a sign that the British public were anxious for a fresh start, with new policies to combat the difficulties that were inevitable in a period of post-war re-construction. For a country whose almost total energies had been directed to the war effort, it is remarkable how much constructive thinking was being undertaken at the same time on public planning to combat the menace of urban sprawl and regional inequality. The period 1940–45 saw publication of a series of reports which were to be the context for the new 1945 Distribution of Industry Act, the 1946 New Towns Act and the 1947 Town and Country Planning Act. The latter gave local authorities the ability to contain the further spread of settlement and obliged them for the first time to draw up plans of designated land use for their areas. The New Towns Act, although more limited in its application, had a more novel impact.

New Towns

The idea of building entirely new communities has a long and distinguished history. In the mid-nineteenth century the idea was taken up in several industrial districts, especially in the West Riding, as a reaction to the appalling conditions of the mushrooming factory towns. Several manufacturers constructed 'model' villages to house their workforce, the most famous example of which is Saltaire near Bradford, begun in 1854. Several other developments followed, among them Port Sunlight in Cheshire and Bournville in the Midlands. The new towns of the 1946 Act however, owed their direct inspiration to Ebenezer Howard's *Garden Cities of Tomorrow,* published in 1902. In this book Howard advocated catering for urban growth by the creation of satellite communities which would be separated from the parent city by a stretch of open country and would offer a completely new 'town-country' environment. The quality of the environment in the new satellites would be assured by the careful disposition of land uses and the maintenance of abundant open grassy spaces. Not content with mere publications, though, Howard helped to found and develop a new town at Letchworth 30 miles north of London, and in 1920 a further town was established as Welwyn Garden City (Fig. 13.3).

The 1946 New Towns Act, then, added another variation to the pattern of urban expansion. Although some municipal housing estates had been on the grand scale, and developed on the edge of city boundaries – Wythenshawe in Manchester and Seacroft in Leeds are good examples – none had in any sense been conceived as fully-functioning new towns in their own right, detached from existing settlements. The Labour

159

Fig 13.3 Letchworth Garden City. The neat villas in their garden plots approach close to the town centre, in accordance with Howard's ideals

movement saw the new towns as fulfilling two functions. On the one hand they could be established peripheral to the expanding metropolis, while on the other they could be located in depressed areas like the North-East where they would act as a catalyst and confidence booster to new economic development. Eight new towns were established around London in pursuance of the 1946 Act – some, like Hemel Hempstead and Basildon, already functioning as small towns with populations of over 20,000. In Scotland, East Kilbride was founded outside Glasgow to fulfil both objectives above while, in the North-East, Newton Aycliffe (north of Darlington) and Peterlee (between Sunderland and Hartlepool) were to be regional catalysts. A further sixteen new towns have been designated since the initial batch in the 1940s (Fig. 13.4).

In 1952 a further mechanism of population dispersal was created with the Town Development Act. Under this scheme small towns could be expanded in conjunction with slum clearance schemes in big cities, and twelve Expanded Town agreements were made by London with towns as far distant as Swindon and Kings Lynn. Birmingham, Liverpool, Manchester and Newcastle upon Tyne also entered upon similar schemes, although involving fewer towns. The net effect of these new town and expanded town proposals, though, was only to confirm the overall pattern of urbanisation in Britain, changing only the detail in those areas involved.

The Built Environment

▲ 1947 to 1955

△ 1961 to 1968

□ After 1968 (and not now being
   further developed)

◆ Settlements designated as New
   Towns in Northern Ireland

Glenrothes
Cumbernauld
Livingston
East Kilbride
Irvine

Ballymena
Londonderry
Antrim
Craigavon

Washington
Peterlee
Aycliffe

Central Lancashire
Skelmersdale
Warrington
Runcorn

Telford

Newtown
Corby
Peterborough
Redditch
Northampton
Stevenage
Cwmbran
Milton Keynes
Welwyn Garden City
Llantrisant
Harlow
Hemel Hempstead
Hatfield
Basildon
Bracknell
Crawley

Fig 13.4 Designation of New Towns in the UK, 1947–72

161

URBAN SYSTEMS

The net result of expansion since Geddes's review of 1915 has been to more than double the urban area in Britain. The most rapid period of expansion occured during the inter-war years when, in the 1930s for instance, there was an annual loss of land to urban development of about 24,000 ha. per year. Since the enactment of stricter controls on development in 1947, the rate of loss has been only two-thirds of that figure, although development has proceeded at higher densities. The most rapid expansion between the wars was in London and the South-East, but over the last two decades faster rates of expansion have occured in northern regions. During the mid 1960s, for instance, the greatest conversions of land to urban development were occuring in Lancashire, Cheshire and County Durham. This appears paradoxical in view of the slow rate of population growth in these areas over the same period, and is rather, a reflection of the great need for urban improvements in northern England. It also reflects the fact that some parts of the South-East had already reached urban saturation point well before the 1960s, so that in the 1970s there was a premium on the re-use of existing urban land at higher densities.

Metropolitan Labour Areas

The dynamism of urban systems is shown not just in the growth of individual towns, but also in the relationships among them and between urban places and their urban fields, or spheres of influence. Journey to work is now regarded as one of the most significant indicators of the urban system, although we must remember that indust-

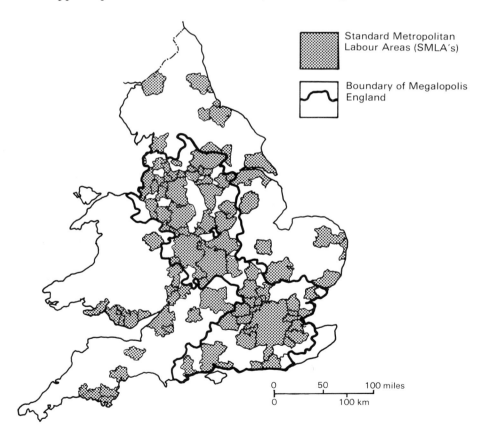

Standard Metropolitan Labour Areas (SMLA's)

Boundary of Megalopolis England

Fig 13.5 Journey to work areas

rial linkages, administrative patterns and cultural functions are also important. Fig. 13.5 shows the pattern of journey to work in England and Wales in terms of *Standard Metropolitan Labour Areas.* First derived by Hall on the basis of density of employment, population size and journey to work, *S.M.L.A.*s were centred upon towns which had either an average employment level of five persons per acre, or a total employment of 20,000 persons. The degree to which this core of employment spilled over into surrounding areas was indicated by the extent of a ring of contiguous administrative areas that sent at least fifteen per cent of their resident employed population to work in the core. To be regarded as a *S.M.L.A.,* the whole group should have an enumerated population greater than 70,000. Surrounding this core and ring Hall envisaged a further zone or *Metropolitan Economic Labour Area,* which took in all the administrative areas not included in the core or ring, but adjacent and sending more of their resident employed population to the *S.M.L.A.* core than to any other. Put simply, Hall devised a measure by which city regions could be identified that had a core of employment, a surrounding zone of commuting and a wider hinterland where the influence of the core was stronger than the influence of any other core in terms of labour demand.

These *S.M.L.A.*s reflect the distribution of the population, and do not cover the whole country. Indeed, Hall showed that 63 contiguous *Metropolitan Economic Labour Areas* contained around 69% of the population in a dumb-bell shaped zone stretching from the industrial districts of Lancashire and Yorkshire to the coasts of Hampshire and Essex. He termed this 'Megalopolis England'. Within this zone not only was the majority of the population and employment to be found, but over two-thirds of all postal, freight and passenger rail flows, reflecting other aspects of the urban system. The important fact, of course, is that this is not a continuously built-up area, and indeed only twenty per cent of the zone can be regarded as urbanised as such. Megalopolis England is therefore a functional rather than a physical reality. In this sense, then, the urban pattern is seen not just as a rash of settlement, but as a less apparent, but by no means less real, system of relationships. In such a system journeys to work, as well as other linkages, make complex patterns, particularly within the conurbations, or between

neighbouring large towns such as Derby, Nottingham and Leicester. Lawton has shown the predominant influence of the major provincial centres. The influence of the largest of these centres has in fact tended to grow fastest over recent years, even though their cores may have been declining in both population and employment. Nevertheless, the impact of commuting has spread further so that around cities such as Leeds, Manchester and Birmingham, the area from which significant numbers of commuters travel to the centre is over 100 km across. The equivalent area which focusses upon the City of London covers 150,000 km^2, stretching from the environs of Oxford and Cambridge to the Sussex coast.

Many other criteria have been used to investigate the working of urban systems. Formative work on the relationship between town and hinterland was undertaken in 1950 by F.H. Green by means of an examination of bus services. Bus transport was more widely available than today, and was used for all types of journey in addition to those for work. The growth in car ownership has largely invalidated such an approach. Weekly shopping trips, secondary school catchments and the availability of banking and other professional services have all been used to determine urban fields, often as composite maps. A very convenient expression of the community of interest which exists around a centre is provided by the circulation of local newspapers. Not all regions of Britain are served with provincial morning newspapers such as the *Yorkshire Post* (Leeds) or the *Northern Echo* (Darlington), but most have daily evening papers, and at a lower tier in the hierarchy, weekly newspapers which serve a smaller area (Fig. 13.6). In all of this, though, it is important to remember that the extent of the influence of any town is an expression of the effect of neighbouring centres, as well as its own centrality.

URBAN STRUCTURE

As British towns have spread outwards, it is possible to see, if only at the level of broad generalisation, aspects of the various models of urban structure developed in American contexts (Fig. 13.7). The concentric *zones* suggested by Burgess (1925) are now largely discredited, either

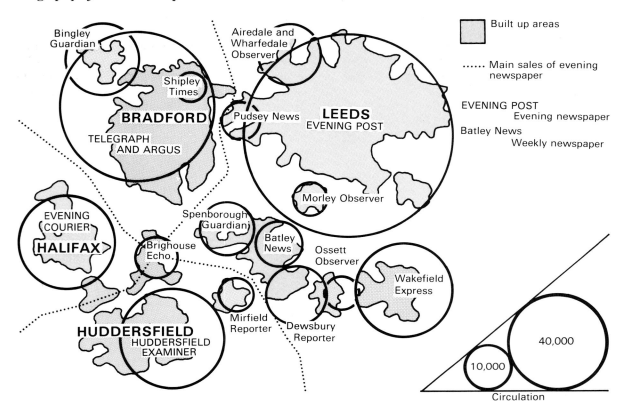

Fig 13.6 Evening and weekly newspaper circulation in West Yorkshire

because they were applicable only to the changing city of the American mid-west, or because zones as Burgess envisaged are to be found only infrequently. Nevertheless, the inhabitant of almost any British city would admit that inner areas generally contrast in social desirability with the outer residential areas and commuting zone. As Davies suggested, then, we can detect gradients of change, although reality often frustrates the model. Peripheral housing estates on the city boundaries of Leeds or Sunderland, for instance, lie beyond high status residential districts. It could be argued, of course, that Burgess did not formulate his model to take account of such public policy decisions, which work against the free play of market forces.

Similarly the *sectoral* approach suggested by Hoyt (1939) continues to have some attraction. Hoyt suggested that as the city expands, social

areas extend outwards as a series of sectors. Such a pattern is distinguishable in a general way around London, for instance, or in Belfast, but it must be emphasised that such patterns often rest upon the level of aggregation, and in finer detail would not appear so clearly. Nevertheless as heavy industry or manufacturing extends along a railway line or major arterial road, then so residential land use will be pushed into alternative sectors. Topography, too, has an important role to play, as is demonstrated in the hilly city of Sheffield. Harris and Ullman (1945) suggested that cities developed in a *poly-nuclear* manner. Such an idea is very applicable to the conurbation, of course, although the writers had a single city in mind. Many suburbs, however, crystallised around outlying hamlets, route intersections or peripheral industrial concerns, so the model does have some relevance. None of these models was ever intended to be universally applicable. Aspects of each can be seen in any one city, but they do remain as a useful starting point for our understanding of the structure of the city. As we look in more detail at changes in the fabric of British towns and cities, it is worthwhile bearing these simple patterns in mind.

Residential

We noted at the beginning of this chapter that much of the fabric of our towns was created by 1914. The principal legacy of the Victorian period was the *row house* – terraces of dwellings varying in size from one room upstairs and one room

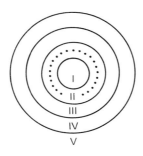

ZONAL (Burgess)

I C.B.D.

II Zones in transition (dots mark factory area)

III Workingmen's housing

IV Residential zone

V Commuters' zone

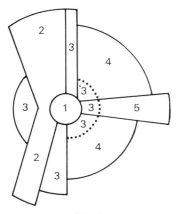

SECTORAL (Hoyt)

1. C.B.D.
2. Wholesaling/light manufacture
3. Low class residence
4. Middle class residence
5. High class residence

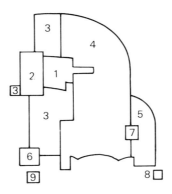

POLY-NUCLEAR (Harris and Ullman)

6. Heavy manufacturers
7. Outlying business district
8. Residential suburb
9. Industrial suburb

Fig 13.7 Models of Urban Structure

downstairs, to the grandiose mansions close to the centre of the biggest cities. The worst city centre slums, which had provoked the righteous indignation of the sanitary reformers of the mid-nineteenth century, had in general been cleared away in the generation before 1914. In their place was often now found the new department stores, grand premises for banks, insurance companies, and civic and ecclesiastical buildings that characterised the inner areas of the larger urban centres. The terraces of 'industrial dwellings for artisans' that had been built during the last third of the nineteenth century, though, even while they had been built in accordance with local bye-laws, were still inadequate by the improving standards of the twentieth century. While every house may have had running water laid on, that usually only meant one cold tap. While every street may have been provided with a water-carriage sewage disposal system, in practice that often meant that between two and four families shared an outside w.c. Back-to-back houses which had been condemned by the mid-century reformers had continued to be built in some towns, notably in the West Riding,

Fig 13.8 Industrial dwellings for artisans, Leeds. The layout of these streets hints at the former pattern of fields. The breaks in the terraces are occupied by outside lavatories for the use of the back-to-back houses

until the turn of the century. Even better-quality bye-law housing, with two or three rooms both upstairs and downstairs, was likely to have had only an outside lavatory positioned conveniently outside the kitchen door. The row house was a response to the need to provide high density housing close to sources of employment, and the emergence of a patchwork quilt of terraces close to town centres was chronicled by several writers during the 1860s (Fig. 13.8). A marked feature of the industrial towns was the close juxtaposition of contrasting land uses. In the textile towns of Lancashire and Yorkshire, terraces and mills were laid out cheek by jowl, and interspersed with other industrial works such as engineering shops and various communal facilities such as churches and chapels, corner shops and public houses – the whole overlain with a pall of smoke from cottage hearth and factory furnace alike. The same held true of the Black Country, the Potteries and the engineering centres in Scotland and the North-East. Most dismal of all were the grimy mining villages, where often was to be found the worst housing conditions, unrelieved by any municipal dignity, except perhaps in South Wales by a monumental chapel.

Out of sight of the workers' houses, manufacturers and the wealthier members of the professions had built substantial villas for themselves, often with an architectural flourish that was more reminiscent of Tuscany than of Coketown. In the larger centres, collections of these villas made up significant enclaves, which by 1915 were reaching their apogee as their leafy gardens reached maturity. Today many of these enclaves have been designated Conservation Areas, although the fine houses may have been subdivided many times into smaller flats. In between the two extremes of small cottage and manufacturer's mansion the better-off white-collar workers lived in more substantial terraced houses, perhaps with gardens front and rear. The railway excursion, the increasingly popular cycling clubs and a rash of guide books to 'picturesque Britain', combined to give their inhabitants an aspiration for the country life and for a certain cottage privacy that was to be met after 1918 by the 'semi'.

In Scotland, however, the picture was rather different. In spite of the fact that the first quarter of the nineteenth century had seen the development of some of the most distinguished residential accommodation in Western Europe (in the extensions to the Edinburgh New Town, whose grandiloquent terraces matched and in many cases surpassed those of the metropolis) residential development took a quite different turn. A distinctive system of landholding, combined with an architectural tradition that owed more to the continent than to England, gave a pattern of high density tenements for most sections of the population. At best these tenements offered spacious accommodation with a very efficient land use. At worst, and unfortunately it was often worse rather than better, tenements in the larger cities of Glasgow, Edinburgh and Dundee, as well as the manufacturing towns of the Central Valley, were little better than a squalid series of rabbit warrens.

World War I brought a period of uninterrupted urban expansion to an abrupt end. The factors that stimulated its renewal after the war was over have been described in the previous section. Its dominant characteristic was the *semi-detached house,* a singularly English contribution to the cultural landscape, and as important an addition to the urban fabric of Britain as the row house had been in the previous century. Although much early council housing took the form of the attenuated row, a good proportion of it was made up of the semi, while private development was overwhelmingly semi-detached. If the unit of housing was distinctive, so also was the arrangement. The *ribbon development* of a string of semi-detached houses alongside the roads leading out of towns was simply carrying further the earliest traditions of suburbanisation. Where more compact developments were undertaken, especially around London and the other major cities, a more novel form was introduced. Crescentic or other geometrical arrangements were its hallmark, punctuated with occasional culs de sac to fill in corner plots. As with the development of the pattern of rows in the nineteenth century, private developments often gave rise to discontinuous arrangements, and breaks in undertakings can be identified today by small variations of house detail and the former estate boundaries running around the site.

The most extensive single schemes were those associated with council developments, and this of itself represents a new agency in forming the fabric of our towns. The closing years of the war had brought considerable agitation that there should be 'Homes for Heroes', and the *Tudor Walters Report* in 1918 laid the foundation for a house building programme on the part of local authorities. The cramped two or three roomed terrace cottage was to be replaced with estates of houses at 30 to the hectare, each with their own lavatory and bathroom, large living room and separate kitchen. The report was implemented by the Housing and Town Planning Act 1919, and the 1924 Housing Act. By 1939 over 2·5 million council houses had been built, perhaps accommodating more than a quarter of the population. It was an astonishing achievement in view of the economic difficulties of the times, and made a massive impact not just upon the urban fabric but upon the way of life of the whole country. Even then, though, much more remained to be accomplished. By the end of the 1930s there were still a million houses that were either unfit for habitation or with a very short life expectancy. Although

some cities had already embarked on quite adventurous slum clearance programmes, much remained to be done, especially in the smaller industrial towns where the scale of the problem was less dramatic, and municipal energy not so dynamic.

The outbreak of war in 1939 inevitably called a halt to house-building and slum clearance programmes, during which time the quality of the urban fabric continued to decline. The concentration of bomb damage in a few centres both eased and aggravated the situation. Blitzed areas such as the East End of London, and inner Liverpool experienced a ghastly and rapid clearance, but peripheral damage severely affected about half a million other houses, while the shortage of materials for repair, renewal and improvement had

Fig 13.9a Failures in rehousing: In an attempt to rehouse large numbers of families quickly, Sheffield City Council, in common with many other local authorities, used industrial building techniques to produce extensive blocks of flats—municipal vandalism?

Fig 13.9b Only a few years after completion, this part of Kirkby (Liverpool) was ruined by vandals. The simple act of rehousing population does not necessarily cure social ills

implications for the whole country. In short, the built environment became steadily shabbier throughout the 1940s. The poor quality of the nation's housing stock was revealed by the 1951 census, the first for twenty years. While the years following the end of the war had been occupied by the provision of housing for those displaced by wartime damage, including the rapid construction of prefabricated bungalows, the twenty years following the Housing Repairs and Rents Act of 1954 was to be occupied by a sustained series of slum clearance programmes which provided over three million new council dwellings, affecting almost a quarter of the population. At first the new council houses followed the old pattern of short terraces and semi-detached houses, but increasingly as building costs rose the provision of flats became more common, so that by the 1960s the pre-war concept of the huge peripheral council estate had been replaced by high rise tower blocks and 'streets in the sky' (Fig. 13.9a and b).

While private building has never attained the levels of completions that were seen in the later 1930s, the freer availability of building materials, and the easing of building restrictions that followed on the change to a Conservative government in 1951, saw a steady growth in speculative building for the private home buyer. By 1959 more private houses were being built than council dwellings, most of which were following on from the semi-detached and detached traditions of the pre-war period. Similarly the planning and layout of the new private estates remained very traditional, and while local authority developments were often adopting policies of traffic segregation. The provision of a garage or garage space adjacent to every house, coupled with a low level of imagination on the part of the developers, has led to a country-wide mediocrity that has none of the architectural panache of the speculators of the early nineteenth century. It is also worth bearing in mind that the nationwide spread of many

169

property developers has led more effectively to a national house type, and the breakdown of regional housing characteristics, than the bye-law housing of the late nineteenth century ever did.

Industrial

Industry can today be found in every part of a city, from central business district to suburb. This is due to the great range of activities subsumed under industry. In a study of London, Hamilton noted four sorts of location, occupied by certain types of industry. In the *central area* need for high accessibility offset high land costs for industries such as printing or instrument making (access to skilled labour), clothing and office machinery (access to CBD), certain services and newspapers

(access to the whole urban market for distribution). The centre is typified by clustering of small enterprises gaining external economies of scale, e.g. industries associated with garment making, or printing. Other locations relate to transportation, either to specialised *port* facilities or to *radial or ring-road* locations. Here industries such as food manufactures, electrical and engineering light industries require larger amounts of less expensive land, access to suburban labour, and the market beyond the city. A fourth location, on the *periphery* is characterised by assembly-line plants such as motor vehicles, or dangerous or obnoxious industries such as oil refining.

In the sub-metropolitan case, such as the industrial cities of northern England, rather different locational characteristics apply. In Leeds, or Manchester, for instance, the rapid growth of industry

Fig 13.10 Team Valley Trading Estate, Tyne and Wear. Located on former marshland, reclaimed with colliery spoil, Team Valley was one of the pioneer developments of the English Trading Estates Corporation. The main east coast rail link crosses the top of the photograph, while in the foreground lies the Tyneside Western By-pass to the A1(M)

during the nineteenth century meant that it took up a location around the pre-industrial kernel, and so produced a discontinuous zone of manufacturing and artisan housing reminiscent of Burgess's Zone III. In Newcastle-upon-Tyne, heavy industry was concentrated along the river front on either side of the ancient city waterfront. Among the textile towns of West Yorkshire, Huddersfield is characterised by a sectoral development of industry along the canal and railway, but in nearby Bradford, the building of steam-powered mills at peripheral hamlets encouraged a more dispersed, poly-nuclear pattern.

A common feature of recent years, since the success of inter-war experimental projects, has been the development of the trading estate. The Team Valley Industrial Estate, south of Gateshead, was inaugurated in 1946. It now accommodates about 100 firms in small-to-medium sized factories, and has proved the model for a rash of similar developments on the fringes of many cities, or in areas of inner-city redevelopment (Fig. 13.10).

Central Business Districts

Lastly, before examining three specific problems of the built environment, we should note the changes that have taken place in the central areas of British towns and cities. Although we do not yet know enough about the processes and chronology of change in the centre of our major towns and cities, the central business district as we know it today, with its retail stores, commercial and municipal offices, public buildings and transport terminuses only began to emerge about a century ago. Apparently small technical changes have had enormous cumulative effects, apart from the macro-scale forces tending towards the centralisation of systems of control. The telephone, the typewriter and the word-processor are the basic tools of the city-centre worker, along with the telex and the computer. From the basic office skills of communication and co-ordination to the sophisticated systems of control needed to service a large department store, these small devices are critical.

City centres are today characterised by an array of large buildings, yet in 1875 very few of them were in existence. The railway stations were the first, followed by the municipal chambers and the concert halls. Large departmental stores were foreshadowed, particularly in the industrial towns by large covered retail markets, few of which unfortunately now remain. The new department stores catered for the growing middle classes, and their earliest premises tend to date from the last decades of the nineteenth century. The most remarkable changes though have occurred between about 1955 and 1975, a period not without significance in terms of the former date of 1875, for 99-year leases negotiated in the first flush of city-centre development began to expire, giving unparalleled opportunities for development. At the same time recovery after the post war years of austerity released a rapidly expanding flood tide of consumer goods of all kinds onto the market, while considerable sums of money raised by insurance companies and pensions schemes became available for investment. By the later 1950s a property boom was well under way as property companies developed individual sites, largely for offices, or in joint ventures with local authorities, undertook comprehensive redevelopment of significant portions of town centres. Here a mixed development of shops and offices, with perhaps a hotel or bowling alley thrown in for good measure, was the order of the day. These new developments were usually characterised by a segregation of pedestrian and vehicular traffic, taking as their direct inspiration the redevelopment of the Coventry city centre in the late 1950s. Many have proved remarkably successful, and by the 1970s such shopping precincts were being entirely enclosed so that the effect was of a greatly enlarged Victorian shopping arcade (Fig. 13.11).

While almost every medium and large sized town in the country has experienced a comprehensive redevelopment scheme of some sort, London, later followed by a few other major provincial cities such as Leeds, experienced a massive increase in office accommodation. London almost doubled its office accommodation in the twenty years after the end of World War II, with satellite booms in office building at suburban centres such as Croydon. In addition a most important addition to the urban fabric was provided by the rapid expansion of university campuses after the Robbins Report of 1963. Sometimes undertaken with a little more architectural flair than the commercial office developments, city-centre sites such as Newcastle and Leeds were radically changed, while the foundation of new Universities at towns such as York and Norwich provided new almost

171

Fig. 13.11 Silbury Arcade, Central Milton Keynes Shopping Building. Although in a New Town, this integrated shopping centre is typical of several city-centre redevelopments in the 1970s

self-contained accretions at the edge of town. A similar but smaller scale expansion followed on the designation of 30 Polytechnics in the late 1960s and early 1970s.

Attempts to give an overall theoretical framework to developments in the central business district have to contain problems of accessibility, availability and linkages between businesses within the technological and social framework we have just outlined. A convenient approach has been found to be that of *land value,* expressed either as rateable value, or as bid rent – that is the amount of rent a user is prepared to pay for a particular property. Competition among users who need a location that has maximum accessibility, therefore, leads to peaks in land value at city centres and in the vicinity of main route intersections, and it is at such locations that multi-storey developments are most profitable. In a sense, then, building elevation becomes a surrogate for land value, although this cannot be applied directly in the field, as building patterns are a function of past development as well as present value. Urban geographers have found that the concept of bid-rent is a useful tool, and helps to explain the segregation of functions within urban areas. Rent structure goes some way towards separating those functions which require access to a population that will generate a high income, from high order goods and services, and those which need to be accessible to smaller populations making more frequent trips for goods and services of a lower order. The concept thus helps in the explanation not only of city centre functions, but also in the distribution of peripheral and suburban shopping centres.

INTER-RELATED PROBLEMS

Conservation

Even as some towns were seeing their redevelopment schemes come to fruition, it became clear that many towns, and particularly the larger ones, were running into a series of difficulties. The first alarm bell to be sounded seemed initially to be of marginal importance. The pressure of development was changing the character of towns so rapidly that familiar, often historic buildings were either being lost, or their setting was being changed so radically that they themselves were threatened. New buildings specifically designed for the new technology of the 1960s and 1970s pointed to the inefficiency of older buildings, while the increasing densities of road traffic simply overwhelmed the road pattern that had evolved under quite different conditions. The problem was how to reconcile the old with the demands of the new. The problem was most acutely faced in the historic towns, and to probe the situation more deeply, and suggest possible solutions, the government commissioned pilot studies to be made of four historic centres, York, Chester, Bath and Chichester. The studies were an undoubted help to the towns concerned, which would probably never have received such detailed and expert investigation. A review of progress in Chester remarks, though, that the local government machine often works too slowly for effective conservation, and any success at Chester is due in large measure to personal initiative, and a sufficient determination on the part of elected officers to levy an additional rate charge for conservation. It is difficult to assess the impact the findings of the four investigations had on other historic centres, but the mechanism of the *Conservation Area,* introduced under the 1968 Civic Amenities Act (in Scotland the 1974 Town and Country Amenities Act) has been widely used to effect a closer control on development in fairly compact areas of special historic or visual importance. The areas concerned have differed widely, from village centres to canal-side industrial sites of the Victorian period, and although designation does not preserve the areas from either demolition or change, it does afford some protection, and draws attention to their particular qualities.

Edinburgh is a fine example of a major city which has had to cope with severe pressures for office development in particular, yet contains townscape of outstanding quality and importance. Edinburgh's principal difficulty lay in the fact that the main office district lay in the 'New Town', 2 km² of brilliant neo-classical architecture, forming one of Europe's most impressive monuments. While on the one hand there was strong pressure from developers to maximise the profit potential of the site, on the other much of the property had fallen into a poor state of repair. One answer would have been to demolish the old property and rebuild on strictly modern lines to higher elevations, but that would have been unacceptable. In consequence, office development has either had to adapt existing property, or move to locations on the edge of the city – a move to be applauded in terms of city-centre traffic congestion. In addition a multi-authority New Town Conservation Committee was set up in 1970 to restore the external appearance of New Town buildings, by the awarding of grants according to the value of the property. The New Town is only one of five important areas for conservation in Edinburgh, and the high cost of sponsoring and encouraging conservation on this scale places a heavy burden upon any one local authority.

The conservation of historic or other special areas is only part of the general problem of environmental improvement. Air and water pollution, housing and visual factors are all important, to which may be added the pervading problem of the later 1960s, that of traffic in towns.

Housing

Of all these aspects, however, housing is perhaps the one that most affects the inhabitants of our towns and cities, and despite the massive housing programmes, both private and public, that we have noted, by the mid 1970s considerable numbers of people were either inadequately housed, or in housing that was unsuited to their needs. Part of the problem was a continuation of the old story, as the least advantaged members of society were to be found occupying the poorest accommodation. The problem was particularly severe in the inner city areas, where shortage of council houses put pressure on the privately rented accommodation, which in turn had been severely reduced in quantity after 1957 when Rent Control was eased and tenancies were sold off in increasing numbers. Not only in the largest towns, though, but also in rural areas, almost two million homes were reported to be below standard in 1965. By the early 1970s that figure had been reduced to about 1·25 millions, but the problem will never be eradicated simply because with increasing age more buildings are going to become less satisfactory year by year. A neat example is provided by the council housing of the 1920s and 30s which was in the process of being improved and brought up to date during the 1970s. Indeed, improvement rather than clearance has increasingly become a keynote for housing since the Housing Act of 1964 which introduced the concept of improving whole areas rather than bestowing grants just for individual properties, a system which with variations had been in existence for 15 years.

In the event it was the Housing Act of 1969 which was to be the foundation for the new policy of *General Improvement Areas,* under which the local authority should designate appropriate areas to be generally upgraded, by helping and encouraging property owners to take advantage of existing grant schemes. In addition, the authorities themselves would remodel the street setting by closing certain areas to through traffic, planting trees and introducing other public amenities such as seating, play apparatus for children, improved lighting, etc. Such policies have proved acceptable in that they enable existing communities to stay together, result in an extension of the life expectancy of old property, and provide upgraded accommodation at a lower cost than would have been the case under a policy of clearance and rebuilding. They also help to maintain the traditional fabric of our towns. Improvement policies have been citicised, however, for the fact that they simply put off the evil day when the property really will have to be replaced, and in the second half of the 1970s an unexpected controversy arose, particularly in some inner city areas. The problem was exemplified by the Islington district of London. In that area medium-sized middle class houses of the nineteenth century had progressively declined in quality and been either sub-divided into flats or let at modest rentals to low wage earners. Taking advantage of improvement grants, however, many of the properties were being bought up by young middle class families who were restoring the property to something approaching its former use, but in the process inevitably driving out the present generation of tenants who could not afford the initial costs of such a project. *'Gentrification'* as the process was unkindly called, while improving the fabric of such areas, has had the effect of changing the social structure of some parts of some cities.

High social costs have also been encountered by the positive rehousing of families over the last twenty years. Extensive new housing developments, whether public or private, have inevitably promoted a dislocation of relationships as families have been scattered and old contacts severed. 'New Town Blues' is recognisable on nearly every suburban housing estate, an ironic result since architect-planners have deliberately tried to create a 'neighbourbood' effect in very many developments. The problems have often appeared to be particularly aggravated when high rise housing policies were undertaken. Construction faults in some tower blocks apart, the forced juxtaposition of families with quite different attitudes towards public open spaces has often tended to lower rather than raise environmental quality, while the concrete wastelands in which many high rise schemes have been set have done little to enhance the life style of their inhabitants.

Inner Urban Areas

Despite the comprehensive redevelopment of many city centres, and real moves to clear away slum property and replace it with modern housing facilities, many problems remain and seem to have been aggravated over the 1970s. The two processes of city centre redevelopment and suburbanisation appear to have been counter-productive in very many cases. In London, Birmingham, Manchester and many other large centres, the brand new city centres seem almost dehumanised, particularly at night since there are now very few residents, while around the inner-most core lies a ring of blighted industrial property, high rise housing accommodating the least advantaged members of the community, and a barren wasteland criss-crossed by urban motorways. Most inner city areas have lost both people and jobs. Census comparisons are alarming, when we can see that employment in manufacturing in inner London fell by twenty per cent between the 1966 and 1971 censuses. Housing and employment go together and a decline in both has meant on the one hand a fall in rateable value – and thus a reduction in the ability of the local authority to maintain its services – while on the other the social and economic decline of a neighbourhood places greater demands upon local authority services, particularly in the education and social service departments.

The spiral of decline has been remarkably rapid. Rehousing schemes have resulted in a loss of labour to suburban housing estates. This has led to labour shortage in the inner city, and the closure of some firms. Others are tempted out to new suburban sites, either to follow their labour, or to the facilities provided on new industrial estates close to improved communications. In any case, inner city employment is reduced and the residual population has difficulty finding jobs. As employment opportunities decline so also does the amount of locally expendable capital, so that the quality of shopping is reduced and the neighbourhood becomes less attractive. The residual population, by now either rehoused in multi-storey blocks of flats, or left in poor quality old houses, is thus largely made up of the old and the deprived, and the area becomes a drain on local authority finance rather than a source of revenue. However, policy makers are now much more aware of this situation and, as we note in Chapter 15, initiatives are now being made to attempt to reverse the trend.

These three problems of *conservation, housing* and the *inner-city,* are all pointers to the dynamism of the built environment. The changes in both pattern and fabric that we have noted in this chapter have become greater in scale over the last hundred years, but are nonetheless continuations of a long process of change, natural decay and rebuilding. The fact that we can recognise problems and seek to remedy them is of itself grounds for optimism, but we should be less than realistic if we think we shall ever create Utopia with bricks and mortar, or even with pre-cast concrete.

References

Geddes, P., *Cities in Evolution* (Benn, 1915).

Clawson, M., & Hall, P., *Planning and Urban Growth: an Anglo-American Comparison* (Johns Hopkins University Press, Baltimore, 1973).

Creese, W., *The Search for Environment: the Garden City Before and After* (Yale University Press, New Haven, 1966).

Best, R.H., & Champion, A.G., 'Regional conversions of agricultural land to urban use in England and Wales, 1945–67', *Trans. Inst. Brit. Geogrs.*, Vol. 49, 1970, pp. 15–32.

Ward, D., 'The pre-urban cadaster and the urban pattern of Leeds', *Ann. Ass. Am. Geogrs.*, Vol. 52, 1962, pp. 150–66.

Lowenthal, D., & Prince, H., 'English landscape tastes', *Geogr. Rev.*, Vol. 55, 1966, pp. 186–222.

Cherry, G,E., *Urban Change and Planning: a History of Urban Development in Britain since 1750* (G.T. Foulis & Co. Ltd., 1972).

Esher, V., *York, A Study in Conservation* (H.M.S.O., 1968).

Tilley, R., 'Conservation in action at Chester', *Built Environment*, 2, 1973, pp. 287–9.

Carter, H., *The Study of Urban Geography*, 2nd Ed. (Edward Arnold, 1975).

Chorley, R.J., & Haggett, P., *Models in Geography* (Edward Arnold, 1967).

14

The Rural Environment

Because such a large proportion of the population live in towns and cities, and so many of our structural and economic problems relate to the built environment, it is very easy for us to neglect the four-fifths of Great Britain that are neither urbanised nor even suburbanised. Yet to many, if not most of the population, the countryside *is* Britain, for as Lowenthal and Prince have pointed out, the predominant image the English in particular have of their landscape is rustic rather than civic. Although the proportion of the population that is directly dependent upon the land for its living is very small, between a quarter and one-third of the total population actually live in the country, if we include the smaller market towns. The environment in which they live, therefore, and the problems that they have to contend with are of some significance and merit examination.

LANDSCAPE CLASSIFICATION

To use terms like town and countryside, urban and rural, however, is at once to invite an unnecessary dichotomy. While there is a clear difference between, say, the Vale of Blackmoor and central Liverpool, town and country represent points on a spectrum, rather than neatly defined opposites. Gwyn Jones (1973) puts the point succinctly when he refers to the meaningful question not as "is this place or is this community, or are these people rural or urban, but rather to what extent is this place or people relatively rural or urban in character?". Similarly the Countryside Review Committee in a recent Discussion Paper point to the complication of an "increasingly blurred distinction between town and country in personal and social terms" as well as the fact that the "generic term 'the Countryside' conceals wide regional and local variations – each with its own mix of priorities and problems". How, then, are we to approach such a rich area of study that contains both regions of population decline, and expansion; regions of almost nil productivity and regions of almost cornucopean plenty? One useful framework was provided by Alice Coleman with her 'scape' and 'fringe' classification. *Townscape* (with which we are not concerned here) was separated from *Farmscape* by the *Rurban fringe*; the *Marginal fringe* represents regions where the activities of the farmer are beset with natural rather than human difficulties, while *Wildscape* represents the largely unimproved or abandoned moorlands and heaths. Even this, though, is no simple zoning, for *wildscape* and *townscape* can be juxtaposed in parts of South Wales, or the Pennines, with almost brutal effect.

Farmscape (Fig. 14.1)

The general pattern of agriculture itself was outlined in Chapter 9, but that pattern has social, structural and resource implications that are very significant for the future of the whole country. For most townsfolk the most important aspect of the countryside is its amenity value, principally expressed in the way it looks, and increasingly in the facilities it provides for recreation and enjoyment. The 1968 Countryside Act insists that both the Government and other public bodies are to "have regard to the desirability of conserving the natural beauty and amenity of the countryside", and over one-quarter of England and Wales comes under

Fig 14.1 Farmscape: Sutton in Derwent (excerpt from Land-use map 699, Crown Copyright reserved)

some form of designation for landscape protection (by no means all of which are the wilderness areas of the Lake District and the Welsh mountains). Such designation and protection, however, is largely cosmetic and the real influence upon the countryside are the people who own it and live in it, and the powerful resource policies under which they operate. British governments have traditionally been interested in agricultural productivity, but particularly since 1945 there has been a deliberate attempt to foster an increase in the output of British farming. One of the major parts of that policy has been (since the 1947 Agriculture Act) the annual farm price review. This fixed minimum national price levels for agricultural products, any difference between market price and production costs being met by a government subsidy. The result is that cropping patterns relate as much to government policies as to natural conditions, and since accession to the E.E.C. in 1972, to the Common Agricultural Policy of the Community. The result of this has been that the cultivation of wheat, barley, potatoes and beet has been encouraged so that in farmscape areas of lowland Britain, because arable cultivation has also been the subject of considerable technical change, there have been significant social as well as landscape adjustments.

The landscape effects of highly mechanised arable farming are well known, and there have been many who have expressed misgivings on the super-enlargement of fields, the heavy applications of artificial fertilisers and the massive extensions to farm buildings that look more like industrial warehouses than rustic barns. Such changes are a matter of profit and loss to farmer and landowner, though, and of equal significance to them are the social changes that accompany this technical transformation. The obvious result of mechanisation is the reduction of the agricultural labour force. This in turn has implications for the general densities of population in such rural areas, and their ability to support a sufficient range of educational, welfare and social services, as well as the traditional service industries such as retailing and public houses, along with the maintenance of public institutions like the church. As a result what we could refer to as 'deep rural areas' have suffered severe community deprivation, which in turn encourages out-migration. This then feeds back into farming by encouraging family enterprise rather than the employment of scarce labour,

so that almost paradoxically, the mechanised farming of the late twentieth century is encouraging a return to a peasant-like social structure of family farming.

There is no doubt at all that family farming now predominates in British agriculture, and very few farms employ labour other than that of the immediate family. A further trend during the 1950s and 1960s was for more and more farmers to own their farms, rather than rent from landlords, a situation which was encouraged at least partly by the break up of large estates in the face of large death duties or a wish to find alternative sources of investment. This in turn has implications for the capital structure of British farming, for the whole burden of both stocking the farm and maintaining and improving plant now falls upon the farmer, rather than being shared between landlord and tenant. During the 1970s, though, this trend was reversed in some measure as productive farmland was seen to be a good investment by both wealthy individuals and, particularly, by investment institutions such as insurance companies and pension funds. The majority of farms, however, remain as family concerns.

Marginal Fringe and Wildscape

In *farmscape* areas the concept of resource management is largely equated with what the general public would refer to as 'farming', the traditional activity of the countryside. In the areas of *marginal fringe* and *wildscape,* resource management has much wider implications, involving forestry, water catchment, keepering for shooting sports, and other forms of recreation as well as the raising of agricultural products (Fig. 14.2). Social implications from adjustments in the relative importance of these sectors are therefore complicated, but as in *farmscape* areas generally characterised by population decline. Marginal areas are inevitably more responsive to changes in the relative profitability of particular activities and consequently often exhibit the result of change quite dramatically. The flooding of upland valleys for water catchment is an obvious example, bringing with it immediate population evacuation, not just because the valley land is flooded, but because the loss of improved pasture renders the unimproved moorland unusable, although peripheral settlement may benefit slightly from the development of re-

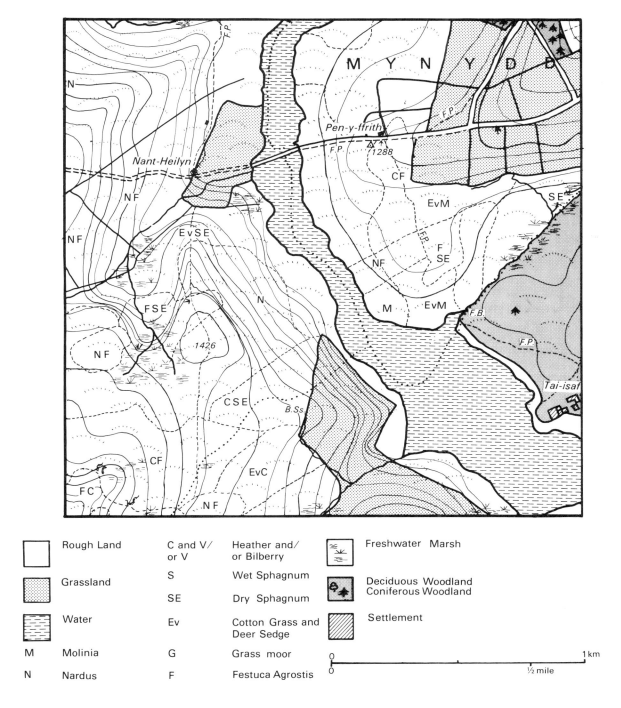

Fig 14.2 Wildscape and marginal fringe: Mynydd Hiraethog (excerpt from Land-use map 572, Crown Copyright reserved)

creational activities. A major resource planning agency which has been active in wildscape areas is the Forestry Commission. Rather more than six per cent of Great Britain is forested, about half of which is managed by the Forestry Commission. About 24,000 ha (60,000 acres) of new woodland is established every year, needing about seven men per thousand acres for their management. As these are generally new jobs, the role of afforestation can be significant in thinly populated rural areas. Thus, many parts of Wales, Scotland and Northumberland have forestry to thank for the maintenance of viable rural communities. Although in the years immediately following World War II there was a tendency to establish special 'forest villages', the policy has now been for some years to establish forest workers' housing in existing communities, where it has played a life-saving role. Recently the recreational use of forests both in the public and private sector has become increasingly significant, in places perhaps of more economic return than the pursuit of forestry itself. Although income from recreation tends to be seasonal and susceptible to changing demands, there is no doubt that it is an important input to a local economy, and the multiple use of forests is an encouraging development in a countryside which has too often been the victim of sectoral rather than integrated planning initiatives.

The use of *marginal fringe* and *wildscape* for farming is mainly for stock rearing. Indeed, one definition of hill land is land that is only suited to stock rearing and not fattening, and this may perhaps account for as much as twenty-five per cent of the area of Great Britain. For many years hill farming has only been maintained at the cost of considerable public subsidy. The 1946 Hill Farming Act and the 1951 Livestock Rearing Act have now been supplemented by aid from the E.E.C., which offers special aid to those farmers who live in uncongenial areas with a growing season of less than six months and a harsh topography, and where average income is less than two-thirds the national farming average. With persistent losses of population from such areas it is quite clear that the system of subsidies is offering only a holding operation, and the severe problems of such areas are by no means being solved. Davidson and Wibberley point out that it is not just a matter of physical marginality – i.e. that agricultural production just fails to be possible – but that there is an economic margin

and a social margin beyond which either individuals or families refuse to live permanently. As the general level of aspirations for both public and private goods continues to rise, then so this problem can be expected to become progressively more acute, for it just does not seem possible in many marginal areas, particularly in peripheral regions of Britain, to provide all the community services that most people come to expect. On the other hand family sentiment and a real love of the place and the life it offers encourages some to remain in their traditional activities.

Rurban fringe (Fig. 14.3)

This fringe area, between the built-up area and *farmscape* zones, represents those areas where town and country meet and mingle to such a degree that the 'normal' pattern of farming is adjusted to the pressures of urban neighbours. *Part-time farming,* which is increasing nationally, is particularly important in such areas, not least because the opportunity for other employments is so much greater than in other parts of the country. This can take many forms. Where farms remain family ventures, the total family income is important, and the contribution made by a member of the family working in the town may represent a form of part-time farming. Other activities compatible with farming are operating a riding school, or providing kennel accommodation for cats and dogs, both of which activities make use of the local demand for 'rural' services. The letting of fields for rallies, fairs or motor-cycle scrambling can also provide extra income. A reverse sort of part-time farming is to be seen especially in the more prosperous parts of the country, where successful businessmen engage in hobby farming, running small farms not necessarily at a profit, but as a source of interest and sometimes status. Life in the *rurban fringe* is often more a matter of urban than rural life, and its problems stem from the close proximity of urban occupations. Wilful damage and trespass represent one end of a spectrum of urban pressures, which may also include a closer interest taken by the local planning authority, perhaps under pressure from local amenity societies, in such things as tree preservation

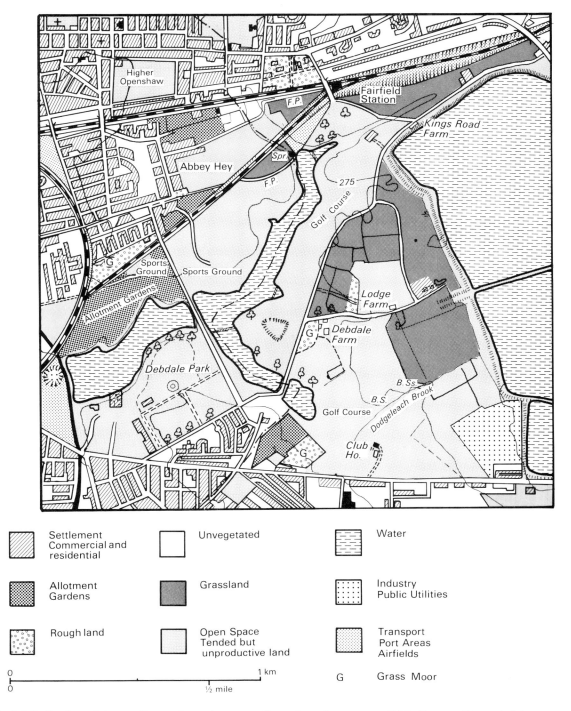

Fig 14.3 Rurban fringe: Openshaw (excerpt from Land-use map 640, Crown Copyright reserved)

orders, permission to demolish or erect new buildings, rights of way, etc. In a survey of the Slough/Hillingdon area, sixty per cent of the farms were damaged by trespass, mainly through destruction and pilfering of crops, and rubbish dumping. In the Tyne/Wear area, over eighty per cent of the farmers complained of trespass and almost half complained about livestock worrying by dogs. One of the major penalties of farming in the rurban fringe is often the fragmented nature of the agricultural land, which may be interspersed with settlement or perhaps other semi-open areas like golf courses, cemeteries and public parks. This renders farming difficult, while the transfer of stock or other produce (and manure) along busy roads is often hazardous and time-consuming. On the other hand it may be possible to engage in direct sales of foodstuffs to the public, a practice which has become more popular with the increase in domestic freezer ownership.

Considerable stretches of the *rurban fringe* are now designated as Green Belt, covering almost 6,000 square miles in England and Wales. Such designations recognise the pressures placed upon the countryside by nearby urban areas. There is a growing tide of opinion which is pressing for not only more comprehensive planning, but also more comprehensive management of such areas so that a sense of rurality is maintained. Experiments in this direction were developed over the late 1970s with the Bollin Valley in Greater Manchester an important pointer. In this scheme, county and district authorities have co-operated with the Civic Trust for the North-West and with local farmers, in developing and managing a system of footpaths and access to a stretch of countryside that is within easy reach of a considerable urban population, whose movements through the area could be very damaging if they were not carefully directed.

Fig 14.4 The Market Cross and Square, Alfriston, Sussex. Formerly a market town, Alfriston is now a picturesque Sussex village. This quiet view belies its popularity with visitors, who help maintain its retail outlets

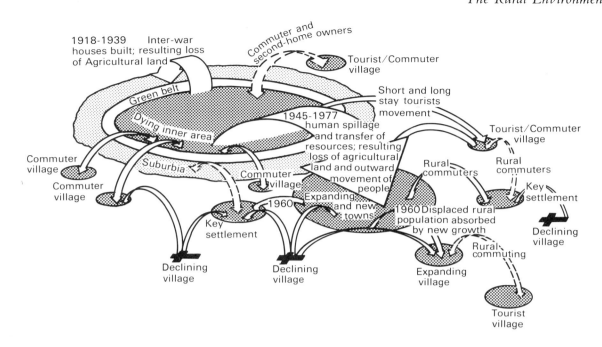

Fig 14.5 Generalised model of population movements between town and countryside, Great Britain 1918–1977 (after G Moss)

THE VILLAGE

Our view of the rural environment would be incomplete without some examination of the village, considered by many as the very symbol of rural life, yet very often the locus where rural problems are played out on the ground. Once again there is the problem of definition, for villages take many forms and come in many sizes. In the general mind the village is little more than an identifiable grouping of houses set in the midst of the countryside and containing one or two significant buildings like a church, a public house or a shop (Fig. 14.4). But of course the reality is much more complex. Villages vary in size from a few hundred inhabitants to several thousands; they may have an array of retail and community services, or none at all; they may be visually discrete, or now form only extensions of neighbouring towns, preserving their identity only in the minds of older inhabitants. In a recent study of the village, Graham Moss suggests that villages can be defined on the basis of three related factors – a population size of between 200 and 5,000, an

ability to support a parish council or its equivalent, and visual identity. On this basis he suggests that there may be as many as 10,000 villages in England, 1,000 in Scotland and 800 in Wales. There are almost as many problems as there are villages, but at the risk of oversimplifying, they can be grouped into those associated with satisfying the needs of established residents and those associated with the short or long term demands of outsiders. (Fig. 14.5).

External Pressures

Pressures on the village from outside take many forms and are most acute in those villages which are either close to large centres of population, or which have a special value associated with their visual appearance, landscape setting, or cultural association. The strongest development pressure comes where attractive villages lie within easy *commuting distance* of large towns and cities. In many cases green belt villages, for instance, have become refuges for the wealthy. Older houses are

183

snapped up at high prices and renovated at great cost. The result is that while the traditional heart of the village may be visually enhanced, the indigenous inhabitants are unable to compete in the housing market and so are forced onto council house waiting lists. Unfortunately most rural council housing is as bland, if not identical to, its urban counterpart and so the visual quality of the village may be seriously impaired by a peripheral council estate, perhaps larger than the pre-1919 core of the village. Meanwhile development pressure may become such that additional farmland is released for up-market housing. As the social make-up of the village changes, so the demand for local retailing changes its character – and its price – and the original residents are once more forced out. Paradoxically, the newcomers are often most vociferous in defending the village against additional development, particularly if it may generate employment, and so local life is destroyed and the countryside becomes merely a tableau against which the rural fantasies of the commuter are played out.

Villages which have a particular attraction, but which are not necessarily close to major urban areas, suffer from rather different pressures. Demand for residential accommodation may indeed rise, but this may well take the form of *second homes*. It is difficult to estimate the total number of second homes. Demand seemed to be rising rapidly before the oil crisis made regular weekend travel to distant cottages very expensive, but the figure may well exceed 300,000. The majority of these are to be found in coastal areas, their owners being normally resident in the nearest conurbation. It has been suggested that the level of local ill-feeling towards second-homers may be exaggerated, yet their impact upon a village may be important. House prices, for instance, may be forced up, local demand for retailing and other public services will be reduced, which may pull the total demand below the threshold needed to maintain an acceptable level of services for full-time residents. An alternative demand for residential accommodation in such localities comes from the *retired*. Where large numbers of such people are involved, the pattern of public service requirement shifts in favour of welfare and medical provision at the expense of education, and once again this may push demand below the viable threshold. This then becomes a push factor for young families who prefer villages with schools, and the age

structure of the village shifts markedly upwards.

A recurrent pressure in attractive villages, however, is for development to cater for the *visitor* or *tourist*. Clearly this can bring both benefits and disadvantages. On the positive side, visitor-generated income helps make the village a more viable settlement. The seasonal trade in ice cream and soft drinks, for instance may subsidise the year-long sale of bread, while catering for bed and breakfast helps make up for restricted employment opportunities for married women. On the other hand an over-emphasis on provision for the visitor can completely alter the character of the village, and indeed destroy the very quality that the visitor is seeking.

Village Decay

Problems which are associated with the satisfaction of needs arising from existing village populations are predominantly not problems of growth and development pressure, but problems of *decline* and *contraction*. The spiral of decline is most acute in the most remote villages in peripheral regions. There a combination of factors interact and lead to a progressive decline in the community; these factors include out-migration (leading to an ageing population) contracting job opportunities and the difficulties of maintaining an adequate provision of social and educational services. In fishing villages along the coast from Cornwall to Cromarty, for instance, the story is everywhere the same as inshore fishing declines, and the life of the communities is maintained only by a sharing of employments and the widespread receipt of welfare benefits. Similarly, in *farmscape* areas we have seen that community decline has followed technical change in agriculture. Villages that have not been able to attract either commuters, second homers or retirement migrants have often suffered sustained decline. This is manifested by the closure of traditional meeting places such as the public house and village hall, the withdrawal of resident clergy at the parish church and perhaps the abandonment of regular Sunday services. With very often the lack also of a village school, the village is deprived of any focus and community life evaporates, property declines in value and the village fabric literally crumbles away. Few villages in fact nowadays have a population large enough to support a reasonable variety of services. A two-form entry primary school needs a population of 5,000, and the catchment for a secondary school needs to be at least 10,000. In the vast majority of villages, health care is non-existent with neither optician, dentist, chemist nor doctor's surgery. This does not mean to say that inhabitants of the countryside are denied such services. They obtain all manner of services by travelling for them – sometimes over fifty miles – and this therefore raises the important points of the relationships that exist between rural settlements (and between rural settlement and nearby town) and the transport by which such relationships are achieved.

First of all it must be stressed that very few villages have ever really been self-sufficient communities in terms of the range of services that are provided for their inhabitants. Village self-sufficiency, if it ever really existed, vanished before the last century in the majority of cases, and villages have looked not only to the nearest market town or regional centre, *but to one another* for the mutual provision of services. Dependency is therefore not just a matter of up and down the tiers of an hierarchy of settlement, but within the tier. One village may have a post office, another a garage; a Nonconformist chapel may be in one village, an. Anglican church in another. By this means, most wants were supplied, but equally the closure of any one of these facilities may deprive not only the host village but also neighbouring communities, and trigger off a subtle series of readjustments in the spatial relationships that exist within a set of rural communities.

The answer most commonly followed by county planners in these circumstances has been the development of some variation of a *'key village' policy*. By this means certain villages are selected on the basis of infrastructure and accessibility as the principal local bases for public sector investment and general development. Surrounding villages are then subjected to containment or holding policies. There is considerable attraction in this procedure: the building of council homes, for instance, needs to be done in units of around 40 to be economically feasible, yet this is far more than any one village is likely to need. Similarly there is the argument that, as development may well alter the character of villages, there is merit in altering the character of only a few rather than many settlements. The counter argument is that key village policy can be seen to imply the death of

non-key settlements, so that development is not so much directed to one place, but discouraged everywhere except in one location.

THE RURAL TRANSPORT PROBLEM

The crux of these problems of decline lies in the low population densities which characterise rural areas. Consequently the need is for considerable movement of the population across a wide area, to support services which in a big city could be provided very often within walking distance. The problem therefore is chiefly that of *transport*. With the exception of mountainous areas in northern and western Britain the countryside is provided with a close-textured network of well-surfaced roads. Movement in the countryside is therefore no significant problem, unlike the rural areas of some other countries. The problem is not so much a matter of *potential* accessibility but of *actual* accessibility given the existing system of transportation. The railway system ceased to be an effective part of rural transportation in all but a few areas, such as the Highlands of Scotland, long before the Beeching Inquiry resulted in extensive closures of lines after 1963. By this time the vast majority of rural journeys were made either by car or by bus. Unfortunately the population changes to which we have already referred have meant that the demand for bus services has been considerably reduced, along with the demand for other services, while the drastic rise in fuel costs has had a particularly punitive effect upon the rural car-owner.

The demand for rural bus services has declined, first as a result of rural depopulation and a shifting of the distribution of population away from remoter areas, and secondly because of a rise in car ownership. As a result the residual demand is often insufficient to maintain a profitable service, which is in any case rendered less viable than an urban service because of its 'point to area' nature. In previous years it was generally accepted by the major bus companies that unprofitable services should be maintained, partly as a social service, cross-subsidised from profitable routes, but partly also because they acted as feeders to other routes whose own profitability would be reduced if the feeders were removed. This is no longer generally accepted policy, however, partly because of the extent to which rural demand has declined and partly because of the high costs of fuel since the rapid rise in oil prices. Since the 1968 Transport Act the burden of subsidy has generally been passed directly to the public. Under that Act, local authorities may now subsidise specific routes if they so determine, being able to claim back half of that subsidy from central government. Not all local authorities have taken advantage of the subsidy scheme to the same extent, with the result that rural bus services in some areas have been considerably cut back. This has implications both for the non car-owning family, and also for members of a car-owning family who do not have access to the car when it is in other use. Mothers, children and the elderly suffer particularly in this regard. On the other hand, the level of car ownership is higher in rural areas than in urban centres. This reflects necessity rather than affluence, however, and often contributes to rural deprivation, because income spent on a motor car is not available for other uses.

The rural transportation problem has become so critical that alternative ways of meeting demand are being developed. Licensing restrictions have been relaxed to allow the use of minibuses in areas where no other service operates. The combining of general carrying with passengers services has been developed by a few enthusiastic entrepreneurs, but most successful of all has been the 'postbus' service, which has been particularly well developed in Scotland (Fig. 14.6). Once again, however, the responsibility for promoting a postbus scheme rests with the local authority whose members inevitably weigh the cost of such a scheme to the ratepayers against the benefits to a few residents.

Because there have been so many important structural changes in the way the rural environment is occupied and utilised, it has become increasingly clear that the planning and the management of the countryside needs to be much more carefully thought out. Since the development of Town and Country planning legislation, the main thrust of research and policy has been towards the solving of urban problems, and many observers now agree that the countryside cannot be left as the passive recipient of planning procedures designed in an urban context. New and distinctive measures are called for if the rural environment is to be preserved from the mistakes that have characterised planning in the city.

Fig 14.6 Post Bus, Strathconon, Highland Region. Not only in northern Scotland, but in many other rural areas, the post bus has proved a helpful means of maintaining a limited public transport service

References

Lowenthal, D., & Prince, H., 'English Landscape Tastes', *Geographic Review,* Vol. 55, 1965, pp. 186–222.

Jones, G., *Rural Life* (Longman, 1973).

Countryside Review Committee, *The Countryside – Problems and Policies* (H.M.S.O., 1976).

Coleman, A., 'Is planning really necessary?', *Geographic Journal,* Vol. 142, 1976, pp. 411–437.

Davidson, J., & Wibberley, G., *Planning and the Rural Environment* (Pergamon, 1977).

Mathews, J.D., Philips, M.S., & Cumming, D.G., 'Forestry and Forest Industries', in *The Remoter Rural Areas of Britain*, ed. J. Ashton & W.H. Long, (Oliver & Boyd, 1972).

Moss, G., 'The Village: a matter of life and death', *Architects Journal,* 167, Pt. 3, 1978, pp. 100–139.

Bielckus, C.L., Rogers, A.W., & Wibberley, G., *Second Homes in England and Wales* (Wye College, Ashford, 1972).

15

Recreation and Tourism

In earlier times, when work was characteristically a group activity, work and play were inseparably interwoven and individuals secured most of their recreational satisfactions incidentally. Later on, when an elaborate division of labour came into being, the relations of those who came together for work purposes began to be depersonalised and their contacts became increasingly utilitarian. Thus, for many workers today work is a means to an end – their weekly wage or monthly salary – and they seek their recreational satisfactions elsewhere and usually away from their work colleagues. This separation of work and play led, on the one hand, to a reduction in the length of the working day and, on the other hand, to the growth of breaks from work, i.e. holidays.

Modern man's recreational activities are not only separated from his work both in time and place but have become specialised, and the individual increasingly has come to seek his recreational satisfaction through media such as the press, television, theatre, or through clubs or watching sporting events, etc. Although participant forms of recreation exist and there has been a recent active growth in new types of recreational activity, e.g. horse-riding, climbing, pot-holing, water-skiing, gliding, sailing and the like (Fig. 15.1), it is generally true to say that the modern individual secures his recreation in non-participant ways; he does not so much entertain himself, rather is he entertained.

This chapter examines the problem of increasing leisure at the disposal of the individual, his recreational involvement and activities, and the annual holiday which has become such an important feature of modern social life in the West.

Fig 15.1 Poole Harbour, looking south towards Studland

THE GROWTH OF LEISURE

During the past one hundred years, but especially since about 1950, there has been a spectacular growth of leisure activity – a development aptly termed by Dower 'the Fourth Wave'. There are many reasons behind this growth of leisure and leisure activities, but four are particularly important. First, increases in income and higher standards of living, including shorter working hours and longer holidays with pay, have resulted in people having more time and money to spend on leisure. The development of leisure activities is part of the process of economic and social development. Secondly, as incomes increase, the amount of surplus income at the disposal of the individual – i.e. that not spent on the essentials of life such as rent, rates, food, clothes, heating – increases, the pattern of the consumer's expenditure changes, and more money is spent on leisure activities, including holidays. Thirdly, improvements in communications technology, such as the growth in private car ownership in particular but also in air transport, and the decreased cost of air travel, especially through 'package tours', have created a boom in both leisure activities generally and in holidaying. And, fourthly, there has also developed a new philosophy of leisure activity and holidaymaking (partly stemming from changing social conditions, better education, and the influence of the mass media) which has stimulated active participation in leisure pursuits and promoted a desire to engage in sightseeing and adventurous activities.

Patmore has pointed out that the last decade or so has seen a greatly increased interest in, and concern for, leisure and its use. This arises from deeper roots than merely a greater amount of leisure time at the individual's disposal, stemming from shorter working hours, longer holidays or even from the growing rejection of the protestant work ethic. It comes as much from the increasing recognition that "Leisure is as much a part of life as work and it plays an equally important part in a man's development and the quality of his life. Every individual requires opportunities for the constructive use of his leisure time", to quote the words of the House of Lords Select Committee on Sport and Leisure. Sadly, the quality of life is becoming increasingly equated with the quantity of leisure rather than with pride in, and satisfaction from, work; nevertheless, it remains a truism that, for many, leisure pursuits provide the greatest opportunity they have to achieve, whether consciously or unconsciously, a natural inborn sense of fulfilment.

RECREATION

It is not easy to define *leisure*. "We are at leisure when we have time free from the necessity to work", is one modern definition. *Work* in this context means the daily activity for which we are paid remuneration, for it will be clear that many leisure activities or hobbies – e.g. gardening – involve work or physical effort.

Recreational activities fall into two broad contrasting groups: (a) passive, (b) active. Passive recreation includes such activities as reading, listening to music, watching television, playing cards or other indoor games, dining and drinking out, etc. All are relaxing, and usually pleasurable, activities. Active recreation almost always involves some physical effort – walking, gardening, or playing outdoor games. Active recreation usually occurs out-of-doors, and yet passive recreation is the most important form of outdoor recreation. Large numbers watch sporting events, but the greatest demand for passive recreation comes from the car-borne family on a whole-day or half-day outing.

In times when the average length of the working week is steadily falling, holidays with pay are increasing in length, and people are retiring earlier, Britons generally have more leisure time on their hands than ever before. In view of this and the fact that recreational activities and patterns reflect, to a very considerable extent, the supply of facilities, it is becoming increasingly important that authorities should start to plan and to create the facilities, in both urban and rural areas, to satisfy what certainly will be an increased demand for recreational activities in the future.

Recreation in south-west Yorkshire

At this point it may be useful to take a regional example to highlight the range and some of the problems of recreation. In the loosely-structured conurbation comprised of Leeds, Bradford, Halifax, Huddersfield, Dewsbury and Wakefield live some two and a half million people. Like other large urban areas, it possesses a wealth of sporting, amusement and cultural facilities which provide recreation outlets for its people. But with the growth in car ownership and increased mobility, the marginal rural areas have felt the pressures generated by the conurbation. Before World War II, neighbouring upper Airedale, Wharfedale and Nidderdale were virtually deserted except for hikers and the occasional car; nowadays, in summer and on fine week-ends, a constant stream of traffic

Fig 15.2 Main street in Heptonstall, West Yorkshire

renders walking well-nigh impossible. Former tranquil spots such as Malham, Burnsall, and Kettlewell are bursting at the seams and have had to provide car-parks for the many short-stay visitors.

Associated attractions are monastic foundations such as Bolton Abbey, Kirkstall, Selby and Fountains, castles such as Skipton, Ripley, Knaresborough and Conisbrough, and the fine mansions of Nostell Priory, Wentworth Woodhouse, Temple Newsam and Harewood House, all readily accessible. There are dozens of small market towns and villages – among them Ilkley, Skipton, Ripon, Appletreewick, Heptonstall (Fig. 15.2) and Aldborough – with rich historical associations, and physiographical features such as Hardcastle Crags, Brimham Rocks, the Cow and Calf Rocks at Ilkley, and the Strid near Bolton Abbey, all of which on fine days have their many visitors. Haworth, the home of the Brontë family, has developed a thriving tourist trade and the visitors have become so numerous that a by-pass road and large car park have had to be built to accommodate the hundreds of cars that descend upon it on a fine week-end. The 'Brontë' industry has recently been supplemented by the picturesque

steam railway between Keighley and Oxenhope. In 1978 it carried its millionth passenger since it was re-opened by the Keighley and Worth Valley Railway Preservation Society.

An important aspect of recreation is the flourishing literary, dramatic and musical societies. Almost every town has its Thespians and Amateur Operatic Society, and many possess brass bands. In the past almost every chapel in the Huddersfield area had its local 'sing', while the Huddersfield Choral Society has more than a national reputation. Within the region most of the larger towns have their own sports centres and civic playing fields while Huddersfield has developed its own marina. Facilities for most activities are provided and well supported. One could extend the list of attractions in the region but perhaps enough has been said to indicate how rich the area is topographically and culturally. The recreative demand, already strong, is likely to grow and such growth necessitates careful planning and management; if not, the attractions which draw people will be progressively spoiled, damaged and ultimately destroyed. This threat is common to many areas outside south-west Yorkshire.

189

TOURISM

Modern tourism is distinguishable by its mass character from the travel undertaken in the past. The mass movement of people annually from their home location to some other temporary location for a few days or weeks, is a product very largely, if not entirely, of the period following World War II. The annual migration of large numbers of people began rather more than one hundred years ago, as a result of the coming of the railway which for the first time provided easy mobility; but the present-day exodus, especially in relation to international tourism, is a post-war (really post-1950) phenomenon.

Over the period since that date there has been an astonishing growth in both domestic and international tourism, but more especially in the latter. While domestic tourism in all the developed countries has grown, in some countries more than others, the expansion in foreign tourism has been truly remarkable. The United Nations reported that in the ten-year period 1955–65 the number of tourist arrivals (in some 67 countries) trebled from around 51 million to over 157 million. By 1975 it was around 200 million. Although since 1973, as a result of the energy crisis and world economic difficulties generally, there has been a slackening off in the rate of expansion, prior to that date international tourism had been growing at a rate not lower than 9 per cent annually. In recent years the average annual increase has been about 6 per cent in terms of international tourist numbers. In 1974 this global trend was checked, but it recovered in 1975.

The nature of modern tourism differs from that of pre-war days not only through its mass character but in other ways too, for a number of changes have taken place which have radically changed its character. Three are especially significant. First, the whole *concept* of pleasure travel has changed since World War II: prior to that time foreign travel was largely for the affluent and leisured classes, who enjoyed travel for its own sake. The present-day traveller is typically from a wider social background, his tastes and desires are more varied and his leisure time and his stay abroad is much more restricted. Secondly, there has developed what has been described as the *democratisation* of leisure pursuits; for example, winter sports, which not so long ago were almost exclusively confined to the wealthy, are now enjoyed by many. The commercialisation of many hobbies or leisure-time activities such as riding, boating, water-skiing, gliding, etc., formerly rather exclusive pursuits, has made them available to the ordinary man who is interested. Large numbers of people are now also going abroad to participate in the more exciting and exotic activities of mountaineering, scuba diving and safari touring. Thirdly, there has been the development of what is generally called *social tourism*. This kind of tourism, epitomised in the British holiday camp, not only by-passes the usual facilities provided by the traditional tourist resorts but is responsible for the opening and development of new areas. Organisations such as the *Club Méditeranée* cater for large groups of people and offer specially designed low-price accommodation, catering facilities and entertainment. There has also been a big growth in camping and caravanning, and many camp and caravan sites provide varied amenities for the motorised tourist.

The Tourist Industry: Components, Organisation and Character

Although there are many factors predisposing towards the development of tourist areas or centres (e.g. good weather, scenic attractions, cultural features, or the sea), three elements – *transport, accommodation* and *amenities* – are fundamental.

Strictly speaking, tourism, like recreation, is not an industry: it is an activity; but in economic terms, it creates a demand or provides a market for a number of quite separate and varied industries. In some areas tourism represents the major part of the market, in others a complementary, but frequently highly profitable, demand for accommodation, catering, transport, entertainment and other services designed largely, perhaps even primarily, for a residential or industrial community.

Considering tourism in economic terms, i.e. demand (or production) and supply, we can divide tourism into two sectors, the *dynamic* and the *static*. Within the dynamic sector fall the economic activities of (i) the formation of the commodity, (ii) the motivation of demand, and (iii) the provision of transport; and, translated into practical terms, the dynamic aspects embrace the activities of travel agents, tour operators, transport undertakers and ancillary agencies. The static sector looks after the 'sojourn' part of tourism – the demand for accommodation, food and refreshment in the main – the chief provider of which is the hotel and catering industry, although there are also other ancillary services involved.

The organisation and administration of tourism varies widely. In some countries it is closely controlled by the state; in others, it is less rigidly regulated and the private sector is important. In Britain, it is organised in a rather loose way by the Tourist Boards set up by the British Tourist Authority (B.T.A.) under the terms of the Development of Tourism Act, 1969. Nearly all countries, however, have some sort of National Tourist Office (N.T.O.).

The industry is primarily a service industry and a large proportion of those actively engaged in it find employment in tertiary occupations, e.g. catering, transport or entertainment. The industry is normally marked by a fairly distinct seasonal rhythm; there are few places enjoying an all-year-round trade. The seasonal character implies that casual and seasonal employment are usually distinguishing features of the industry. In season the industry is labour-intensive; out of season, much of the tourism plant lies idle and this, of course, is uneconomic. Hence the attempts which are made to extend the season through the staggering of holidays, out-of-season holidays at reduced prices, special celebrations, conference organising, etc. Anything which will help to lengthen the tourist season will help the industry generally.

Tourism in Britain

So far we have been discussing tourism in rather general terms. Let us now focus our attention more particularly upon tourism in Britain. British people took 48,750,000 holidays of four or more consecutive nights away from home in 1979. Only once before, in 1973, was this peak reached.

Over the years the volume of domestic tourism has not changed to any significant degree. Although there has been some growth, the principal changes have been in the growth of second holidays and in the nature of the holidays taken. In pre-war days it was customary for a large proportion of families to holiday at a nearby resort with almost unfailing regularity (Fig. 15.3). Nowadays, largely no doubt because of the motor car, which makes them more mobile and allows them

Fig 15.3 Blackpool: The only UK resort to have a motorway (M55) built specifically to carry its traffic. Blackpool is within two hours motoring of most of the populous industrial centres of northern England and the west Midlands

to be more venturesome, people tend to travel farther afield and to vary their destination. The British Tourist Authority's National Travel Survey for 1979 revealed that the British people took a total of 38,500,000 holidays in Britain in that year, slightly fewer than in 1978 when some 39 million were taken. 10,250,000 holidays were taken abroad (including Northern Ireland and the Republic of Eire), compared with 9 million in 1978, which itself was a record year.

Expenditure on holidays over the past decade has substantially increased. The expenditure on domestic holidays in Britain increased by 40 per cent over the previous year, to £2,380 million in 1979. Spending on holidays abroad rose by 38 per cent over 1978, to £2,570 million in 1979. These increases in expenditure may be accounted for in part by inflation, and in part by the previous weakness of the pound in relation to foreign currencies. The greatly increased strength of the pound in 1980 is reducing the cost of foreign holidays.

191

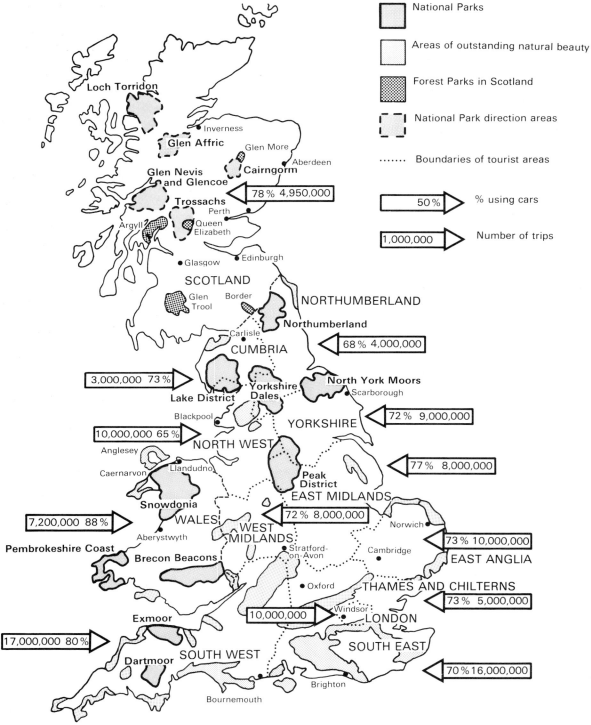

Fig 15.4 English Tourist Board regions, National parks and AONBs of England and Wales, and Scottish Forestry Parks

Fig. 15.4 shows the English Tourist Board's regions in 1975 (the regional divisions of the Scottish and Welsh Boards are not shown) and it gives figures relating to the number of trips to each region by British residents, and the percentage travelling by motor car. Table 18 indicates the relative popularity of the Tourist Board regions within Britain, for British holidaymakers in 1978. (In 1976 the Southern region was formed by taking eastern Dorset from the South-West T.B. region, and Hampshire and the Isle of Wight from the South-East T.B. region.)

Average total *domestic* holiday expenditure per person in Britain, on holidays of four nights or more in 1979, was £62 (compared with £44 in 1978). This represented an increase of £18 (27·4 per cent) over the previous year. As in previous years, cars were by far the most popular form of transport and were used on 71 per cent of holidays in 1979. Rail transport was used on 13 per cent, and scheduled bus or coach transport on 7 per cent. Seventeen per cent of holidaymakers stayed at licensed hotels, 9 per cent at unlicensed hotels or guest houses, 12 per cent used static caravans, 13 per cent used rented accommodation, but 26 per cent stayed at the homes of relatives or friends.

Ten and a quarter million people went *abroad* for a holiday, 81 per cent of whom stayed in Europe. Just over half (56 per cent) of all holidays abroad in 1979 were inclusive packages: 42 per cent of these were arranged independently and 2 per cent were cruises. The majority of those holidaying abroad (71 per cent) used air travel to get to their destination. Average total expenditure per person in 1979 was £246 (22 per cent higher than the average £201 spent in 1978). The principal European destinations were mainland Spain, 14 per cent; the Balearic Islands (Majorca, Minorca, Ibiza) 11 per cent; France, 13 per cent; Italy, 7 per cent, and Greece, 7 per cent. The proportion of holidays taken in the United States was 6 per cent (an increase from 4 per cent in 1978).

Hotel accommodation was used on 58 per cent of all holidays abroad in 1979. The homes of friends or relatives (23 per cent) were the next most popular form of accommodation, followed by rented accommodation (10 per cent) and camping (5 per cent).

Summing up the domestic situation, it may be said that home tourism survived the difficulties of

Table 18: Regions stayed in for one night or more on holidays in Great Britain lasting four nights or more, in 1978

TOURIST BOARD REGION	TOTAL HOLIDAYS %	MAIN HOLIDAYS %	ADDITIONAL HOLIDAYS %
Great Britain	100	100	100
South-West	20	23	16
Southern	10	11	7
South-East	8	7	9
East Anglia	8	8	8
North-West	7	6	7
Yorkshire and Humberside	7	6	9
East Midlands	4	4	5
Heart of England	3	2	5
Cumbria	3	3	3
Greater London	3	2	3
Northumbria	2	2	2
Thames and Chilterns	2	1	3
England	74	74	75
Wales	14	15	13
Scotland	11	11	10

NB The percentages for individual regions amount to more than 100 because a holiday may involve staying in more than one region.

Source: B.T.A.'s British National Travel Survey

193

the period 1974–76, helped no doubt by the two splendid summers of 1975 and 1976, and the numbers in 1977, despite its rather dismal summer, were marginally up. The economic stringencies of the present time (1980) have had very adverse effects upon the home market. The current recession is likely to threaten the existence of many operators, especially hotels in remote areas, and may weaken the viability of the entire industry. The resultant cutback in capacity would reduce Britain's ability to cater successfully for a still fairly buoyant overseas demand.

International Tourism

While the domestic tourist industry appears to be in the doldrums, it is otherwise with respect to foreign tourism. To come through the difficulties of the past few years with annual increases both in the volume of, and in the earnings from, foreign tourism is a remarkable achievement. The growth of the overseas tourist trade to the U.K. was steady but rather slow: in the early 1950s only about 20,000 came a year, but by 1960 the flow had begun significantly to improve and by 1965 three and a half million visitors were coming to Britain. By 1968 the figure had reached nearly five million, by 1970 six and three-quarter million, and in 1973 in excess of eight million. In 1976 around ten million visitors came to Britain and tourism earnings increased by 45 per cent in that year to yield £2,100 million, including £500 million from payment of fares. By 1978 the number of visitors was over twelve million, and earnings were over £2,500 million.

Of foreign tourists to Britain, about 60 per cent come from Western Europe, while a further 15 per cent originate in the United States (Table 19). The sense of identification that Americans feel they have with British culture and history, as well as ties of kinship, together with the common language are important contributing factors influencing them to visit Britain.

Table 19:   U.K.'s Tourist Trade 1978

COUNTRY OF RESIDENCE	THOUSAND VISITS	EXPENDITURE £M
France	1,435	125·1
Germany F.R.	1,507	189·5
Irish Republic	873	85·6
Italy	358	54·8
Belgium/Luxembourg	740	74·1
Netherlands	1,003	124·0
Scandinavia	937	154·2
Spain	256	51·1
Switzerland	316	67·5
Other West European Countries	396	94·1
All Western Europe	7,822	1,019·9
United States	1,964	406·0
Canada	511	100·5
Japan	132	32·9
Australia and New Zealand	442	157·9
South Africa	155	45·9
Latin America	179	53·7
Middle East	638	387·9
Other Countries	763	269·3
All Other Countries	4,784	1,454·1
Total Countries	12,607	2,502·0

Source: Dept of Trade, International Passenger Survey.

The Benefits and Costs of Tourism

Tourism offers a wide range of economic and social benefits to the community. Not only does tourism bring wealth to Britain as one of its leading invisible exports, thereby helping the balance of payments, but it also leads to the circulation of money in local economies. In general, a high proportion of tourist spending occurs in areas which are – or would otherwise be – less economically developed. Tourism has an important contribution to make in the growing service economy. "Total employment in the tourism-related industries of transport, hotels and catering, sport and entertainment and retail distribution, approaches three million or almost one in eight of the total employed population. Of this about a third may be said to be directly attributable to tourism. Among the particular advantages of tourism employment is the fact that it is often quickly created in small units and is less dependent upon those economies of scale which make the dispersal of some industries less economic" (Young, 1973). In many rural and marginal areas tourism is valuable since it offers almost the only alternative employment to such primary activities as farming and fishing. Specific areas relying heavily upon tourism are South-west England,

North Wales, the Lake District and the Highlands of Scotland.

Overseas earnings from tourism are highly significant: in 1978, for instance, the total grossed was the huge sum of £2,502 million if earnings by British carriers are included. Furthermore, an approximately similar sum of foreign exchange is saved through the use of tourist facilities in Britain by British holidaymakers who might have gone abroad but who are persuaded to take their holidays at home. Yet again, spending by foreign visitors on meals, drink and tobacco brings in sizeable amounts of tax revenue; it is estimated that the Exchequer benefits to the tune of £200 million annually from tourist spending.

In addition to its important contribution to the standard of living, tourism also contributes quite substantially to the quality of life. For example, the revenue accruing from fee-paying visitors to historic monuments and properties helps to maintain these assets of our national heritage. This is also true of the theatre, concerts and festivals; for instance, the theatre, which is so crucial to the cultural life of London, could not survive if it was left purely to the patronage of Londoners. Good public services in the form of transport, shopping and restaurants are maintained to meet tourists demands. These and many other amenities and services bring advantages to local communities who would most probably not be able to support them were it not for the demands of the tourist industry.

It is said that every industry operates at some cost to the environment and its people, and against the above mentioned advantages must be set certain disadvantages. There may be social problems: the greater the influx of tourists, the greater the risk of inconvenience and loss of amenity and facilities for those resident in tourist areas. There may well be conflict with local interests: for instance, where the land is devoted to agriculture, tourism development (and, for that matter, recreational development too) may make unacceptable demands upon the countryside, in terms of space and public access. Undesirable attitudes, modes of behaviour and social intrusions may be introduced which undermine and upset traditional local life.

Economic implications of a different order are also involved: in Canterbury, for example, the loss to shopkeepers from pilfering and stealing runs into thousands of pound's worth per year in each large shop, and this must be set against the fact that 60 per cent of the trade done in the city of Canterbury is tourist trade.

In conclusion, however, it may be said that the advantages greatly out-weigh the disadvantages. Already tourism has become one of the major activities in the British economy but if we wish to maintain and expand our tourist trade then we must jealously guard our standards, make the optimum use of our tourism resources, invest in market research, and try to develop year-round tourism. These things are all of great importance for tourism is subject to the whims of fashion and there is increasing competition from an everwidening range of tourist destinations in the world.

References

Dower, M., *The Challenge of Leisure* (Civic Trust, 1965).

Patmore, J.A., *Land and Leisure* (David & Charles, 1970).

Patmore, J.A. Review of 'Man, Land and Leisure' a unit of the Schools Council 'Geography for the Young School Leaver' Project, *Teaching Geography,* April 1975, p. 39.

Cosgrove, I. and Jackson, R., *The Geography of Recreation and Leisure* (Hutchinson, 1972) p. 13.

Robinson, H., *Geography of Tourism* (Macdonald and Evans, 1976).

News from the British Tourist Authority, B.T.A., 1980

Young, Sir G., *Tourism: Blessing or Blight* (Penguin Books, 1973).

16

Social Patterns and Welfare Issues

When we realise that on average people living in the South-East region have to pay nearly twice as much for a second hand house as do people in Yorkshire and Humberside, yet the average level of wages for men is only eleven per cent higher in the South-East, we begin to appreciate that the subject of prosperity and well-being is a complex matter. Since the late 1960s there has been a growing interest in spatial disparities of this kind. While geographers have long been aware of regional variations in economic prosperity and economic activity, and that these variations make an impact upon living conditions generally, it is only recently that attempts have been made to measure these variations and relate them to local needs. This is partly because the statistical base for such comparisons has been lacking, but also because until recently it was thought sufficient to measure well-being simply in terms of economic activity. Thus the peripheral regions were 'backward' because of their poor employment prospects, and could only be 'rescued' by the provision of additional jobs. But of course, poor employment prospects are only a part of a chain of deprivation. Equally, the fact that even economically buoyant regions have high crime rates, pockets of bad housing and social unrest points to the fact that jobs alone are not the answer to promoting improvements in the quality of life.

The difficulty, however, is that the quality of life is not only hard to define, but difficult to measure. In one sense it is true that 'life is what you make it', and that human happiness and self-fulfilment springs from an individual view of things. In another sense, however, we can see that individuals live in an environment that is partly conditioned by the sort of job they have, house

they live in, health they enjoy and education they possess. These are measurable phenomena that show marked variation and which combine to provide at least a context for degrees of well-being. Several writers have explored the concept of well-being in an attempt to simplify and systematise a phenomenon that has many facets. In an American context, Smith drew out seven aspects of social well-being – Income, Wealth and Employment, the Living Environment (housing and neighbourhood conditions), Health, Education, Social Order, Social Belonging, and Recreation and Leisure. The difficulty comes in trying to put these various aspects into some combined measure, for different people regard each aspect as having a varying importance; some might consider housing to be more important than education, while for others personal wealth and recreation are the chief determinants of their well-being. The achievement of a single index of social well-being, then, is almost impossible, and the best that can be achieved is a comparison of areas under particular headings.

Fig. 16.1 shows the regions of Britain ranked in order for a number of indicators. Such rankings only offer the basis for crude comparisons, but the comparative advantage of the south of England is quite clear, while the three northerly regions of England stand out as rather worse than either Wales or Scotland. These indications, crude as they are, point to the fact that people may be disadvantaged simply because of the place in which they live, and it therefore become important that government policy in particular should aim to counter such regional inequalities.

Knox prefers the concept of *level of living* as "an integrated approach to well-being". Using no less

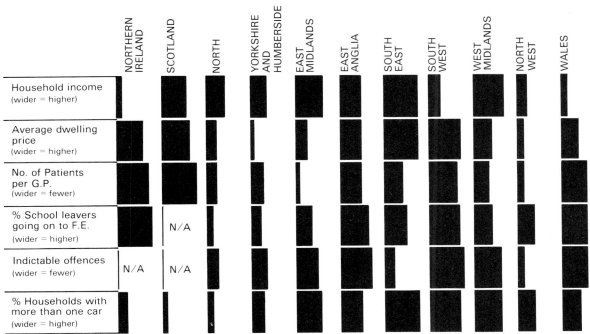

Note: The width of the bar for each indicator shows the ranking of that region in order of well-being for the U.K.

Fig 16.1 Regional variations in social well-being, 1976

than 53 variables, grouped into 20 'aspects', in turn grouped into 12 'constituents', he surveyed a wealth of material ranging from access to restaurants to mortality from bronchitis, in an attempt to get a rounded approach to the very elusive measure of level of living. Eventually he found that four diagnostic variables could be used:

(i) the average number of persons per room
(ii) percentage of households without exclusive use of a fixed bath
(iii) percentage of economically active persons out of employment
(iv) percentage of persons aged 60 or more

After the 1971 census it was found that the addition of two further variables, measuring the rates of divorce and illegitimacy, were needed to give a truly representative indication of level of living. His conclusions are broadly similar to those tendencies which were observable in Fig. 16.1. Higher levels of living were to be found, in 1971, in the Home Counties and the Midlands, with lower levels in the peripheral regions. Using

local authority data the results are at a lower level of aggregation, and so permit a finer grain of analysis. As the 1971 census was taken under pre-reformed local government, the county boroughs in particular stand out from the surrounding administrative counties, and tended to have lower levels of living, with the poorest conditions being found in the northern industrial county boroughs and inner London.

REGIONAL INDICATORS

The pattern of regional variation can be examined in closer detail by taking selected indicators of well being.

Incomes

In 1971, Coates and Rawstron in their seminal study of regional disparities made the point that it was very difficult to obtain accurate statistics regarding net personal income. Data was either

197

not of a fine enough level of aggregation, or else was not realistic because the differing tax burdens on individuals makes assessment of real net incomes virtually impossible. However, their studies of 1964–5 showed that total net income was lowest in peripheral regions and highest in a belt stretching from Essex along the Thames valley into the Cotswolds, and from there spilling over into Gloucestershire and northwards into Staffordshire and Leicestershire. Such a distribution should not afford any real surprise, for the highest incomes are likely to be in those places which offer the greatest concentrations of well-paid jobs. In a survey relating to the Board of Inland Revenue returns for 1975 a rather similar pattern was observed. Greater London and the South-East had above average proportions of the working population in higher income groups. Wales, Scotland,

the South-West and the three northerly regions had concentrations in the lower income groups, while the Midlands and East Anglia showed less deviation from the national income distribution.

Table 20 shows the distribution of weekly earnings for full-time men in Great Britain in April 1978. One surprise in the table is that Scotland has a similar proportion of men earning more than £100 to the average for Great Britain as a whole, and indeed more than any English region, with the exception of the South-East where the proportion is significantly greater than anywhere else. Indeed in Greater London the proportion of the population earning more than £100 was almost twice that of the lowest metropolitan county. At the other end of the spectrum it is interesting to note that the two predominantly agricultural regions, East Anglia and the South-West, had significantly larger proportions of their population earning less than £75 per week – in East Anglia almost half of the male labour force, whereas in the industrialised conurbations, West Yorkshire excepted, the figure was only approaching one third. These differences are not just related to different employment structures, although clearly that is important. An additional factor is that rates for the same job differ from one part of the country to another, a factor relating to local employment levels and general wage rates in other local industries.

Household Expenditure

Obviously the value of any income is directly related to the cost of living in a particular area, and we have already noticed the different costs of housing between Yorkshire and Humberside and the South-East region. It has been suggested that such differences are mainly a reflection of the higher cost of land, rather than building costs, and that such a factor would account for the higher value of houses in rapidly expanding urban areas. Equally, where housing is in demand but in short supply because of land-use planning controls (e.g. in attractive retirement regions such as the South-West) land values are likely to be high. Differences in household expenditure do not relate purely to the cost of housing. In conurbations, and especially in Greater London, the costs of commuting can add significantly to the cost of living. Regional variations in the cost of food is also important,

Table 20: Distribution of weekly earnings, for full-time men aged over 21 in Great Britain, April 1978

	% LESS THAN £50	% LESS THAN £75	% LESS THAN £100
Great Britain (average)	5·6	39·0	72·6
North	5·2	36·3	72·3
Tyne & Wear	4·9	38·2	75·6
Yorkshire & Humberside	5·9	42·0	75·6
South Yorkshire	3·5	33·3	69·8
West Yorkshire	6·5	45·7	78·9
East Midlands	6·1	42·8	76·5
East Anglia	7·2	48·8	80·0
South-East	4·5	33·8	66·4
Greater London	3·6	29·2	60·9
South-West	8·3	48·5	79·6
West Midlands	5·0	38·7	77·0
West Midlands	3·9	33·8	75·4
North-West	5·5	40·2	74·3
Greater Manchester	6·0	41·4	75·8
Merseyside	4·9	34·8	69·6
England	5·4	38·8	72·5
Wales	6·7	40·1	76·1
Scotland	6·1	40·9	72·2
Northern Ireland	12·4	50·8	78·9

Note: *Italic type shows metropolitan counties and Greater London*

Source: Regional Statistics 1979.

Table 21:   Household expenditure on commodities and services, 1977–78([1])

	Average weekly expenditure per person([3])	Average weekly household expenditure, in £										
		Total	Housing	Fuel, light and power	Food	Alcoholic drink	Tobacco	Clothing and footwear	Durable household goods	Other goods	Transport and vehicles	Services and miscellaneous([3])
United Kingdom	27·73	75·99	11·08	4·57	18·51	3·71	2·66	6·27	5·32	5·65		18·21
North	25·45	71·74	9·02	4·42	18·10	4·13	3·16	6·37	4·79	5·12		16·64
Yorkshire and Humberside	25·76	71·20	8·92	4·23	18·17	3·98	3·09	6·17	5·10	5·38		16·16
East Midlands	26·21	71·35	10·47	4·42	17·44	3·82	2·53	5·09	5·27	5·14		17·18
East Anglia	26·63	68·48	10·84	4·88	16·90	2·81	2·10	4·97	4·89	5·28		15·80
South East	31·57	84·11	14·11	4·43	19·28	3·59	2·32	6·59	6·34	6·52		20·93
South West	26·34	70·43	10·81	4·86	17·20	3·14	2·20	4·96	4·86	5·43		16·96
West Midlands	27·27	76·56	11·55	4·54	18·81	4·09	2·70	6·42	5·15	5·64		17·66
North West	26·06	72·21	10·35	4·41	17·95	3·71	2·81	6·11	4·61	5·23		17·04
England	28·07	76·36	11·62	4·47	18·40	3·69	2·57	6·11	5·43	5·75		18·31
Wales	26·19	74·55	9·32	4·86	19·02	3·60	2·59	6·85	4·39	5·51		18·41
Scotland	26·44	74·49	8·09	4·67	19·14	4·23	3·45	6·97	5·21	5·09		17·63
Northern Ireland	24·09	71·31	6·86	7·40	19·18	2·32	2·81	8·49	3·32	4·57		16·35

([1]) Averages for figures for the two calendar years taken together. The figures are subject to sampling variation.
([2]) The results for East Anglia and Northern Ireland are based on relatively small numbers of households and, although included in the United Kingdom figures, are considered to be too unreliable for separate publication.
([3]) Includes expenditure not assignable elsewhere.

Source: Department of Employment, (Family Expenditure Surveys), *Regional Statistics*, 1979

although price levels may relate to what the market will stand as much as to the cost of production and transportation. As the general price levels for many foodstuffs are set by national supermarket combines regional differentials are more apparent in meat and vegetables, which may be locally produced. Table 21 shows Household Expenditure for 1977–8. The figure should be seen in terms of disposable income, rather than in terms of cost of living as such. Regional preferences in terms of household budgeting should also be borne in mind.

Housing

Differences in housing stock can be listed under many headings. We referred in Chapter 13 to the large numbers of council or 'New Town' rented houses which had been built in Britain since 1945, but their distribution is by no means uniform. The proportion of such houses in Scotland has always been high and in 1978 reached 54 per cent (compared to 1966, 47 per cent). In the South-West, on the other hand, the proportion has always been low, 22 per cent in 1978 (1966, 24 per cent), with lower than the national average in the East Midlands, East Anglia, the South-East, and perhaps surprisingly, the North-West. In so far as owner-occupation is an indication of prosperity, and is generally regarded as a sign of social well-being, the South-West (63 per cent), Wales (59 per cent) and the North-West (58 per cent) top the league, with a U.K. average of 54 per cent. The lowest figures relate to Scotland (35 per cent) and the Northern region (46 per cent).

The age of dwellings in the housing stock is also regarded as an indication of well-being. In 1978, 30 per cent of the U.K. housing stock was built before 1919. In Wales the figure was 43 per cent, but in the West Midlands 25 per cent. Overall, 48 per cent of the national housing stock had been

199

built since 1945, but in Scotland the equivalent figure was 52 per cent – a figure which probably relates to the rate of council house building and the need for massive public sector investment in housing to counter poor conditions existing previously. An even greater proportion in East Anglia (51 per cent) can be seen as an indication of that region's remarkable growth referred to in Chapter 8. With these exceptions, however, the general quality of housing under these headings does not deviate greatly between regions. The greatest range of housing conditions are to be found *within* regions, especially in those regions which contain conurbations, and a regional level of aggregation does not do full justice to the scale of the problem, particularly with regard to the inner city, which was referred to in Chaper 13.

Education

The provision of education for all children between the ages of five and sixteen is mandatory upon all local authorities in the country. Further education is available for those who wish to pursue their studies beyond sixteen, and Higher Education is provided through universities, polytechnics and similar institutions for those who are able to attain the necessary educational entry requirements. Some provision is also made for nursery education below the mandatory age requirement. These various provisions are not uniformly made, however, and there are differences between education authorities and between regions in the take-up of these services, and the pattern of spending on the part of authorities. A

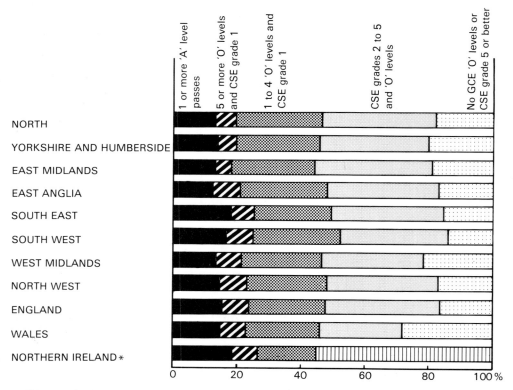

* CSE grades 2 to 5 and 'O' level grades D and E combined with no G.C.E. 'O' levels or CSE grades

Fig 16.2 **Percentage distribution of examination achievement by school leavers, academic year 1975–76**

survey of spending per pupil in 1973–4 noted that spending on primary education varied from £125·30 per pupil in Blackpool, to £206·84 in Cardiganshire, while secondary school pupil/teacher ratios ranged from 12:1 in Bradford to 20:1 in Wigan.

What appears to be even more surprising is the variation in achievement that exists across the country. Fig. 16.2 relates to the examination achievement of school leavers for 1975–6. A higher proportion of children achieve one or more 'A' level passes at G.C.E. in the South-East and also in the South-West than in any other regions, and indeed do better overall in the G.C.E. ratings. On the other hand although Wales comes close to the English average for 'A' level passes, it has far more children leaving school without qualifications than any English region. The interpretation of statistics such as these is not easy. Do these figures really represent differing levels of ability between the regions, or do they represent the socio-economic make-up of the regions and their regional attitudes towards education, or do they represent the measure of success of the education service? Certainly there are serious questions to be asked when the percentage of school leavers going on to full time education in the Northern region is only 15·0 per cent compared with 27·4 per cent for the South-West, and an average for England of 21·7 per cent (figures for 1978).

Medical Care

There is no doubt at all that some parts of the country are healthier than others. The environmental causes of many kinds of illness were established in the last century, and it remains true today that the countryside is generally healthier than the town, and that the biggest urban agglomerations are the locus of the highest incidences of respiratory disease, cancer and stress diseases such as heart complaints and psychological disorder. Equally some types of disease are more prevalent among certain socio-economic groups and so their distributions are parallel. The diseases caused by high concentrations of atmospheric dust, such as silicosis and pneumoconiosis, are not likely to be found in middle class residential districts, for instance. The need for medical care is therefore unevenly spread. Unfortunately the provision of medical care comes nowhere near matching the distribution of need, with the result that people in some parts of the country are not being provided with the facilities for health, and even survival, that are available to their more fortunate fellow citizens in another district.

So we find that in the run-down areas of the inner cities, particularly in the industrial conurbations of northern England, the list sizes of general practitioners are the longest, while in more attractive areas they tend to be shorter – although lists need to be shorter in rural areas because of the additional time spent in visiting the dispersed pattern of patients. Fig. 16.3 shows the size of practice for doctors and dentists, by region. The relative advantage of the South-East and the South-West is plainly obvious, while the list size for Scotland is also relatively advantageous. Coates and Rawstron pointed out that the distribution of dentists not only relates to socio-economic attitudes towards dental treatment, but also to the presence of dental schools, and it may be that a similar trend is discernible for doctors. Medical schools and teaching hospitals are heavily weighted towards the south of England and Scotland, and in both areas the ratio of doctors to the size of their list is favourable. This last factor is also of significance to the quality of medical care, for without wishing to enter a contentious area, it seems reasonable to assume that the greatest skill is likely to be found at and in the vicinity of the major teaching hospitals.

Unemployment

To all of these aspects must be added the pattern of unemployment. Regional variations in income were discussed earlier, but in some regions unemployment benefits make up a significant proportion of local income. The pattern of unemployment in April 1977 is shown in Fig. 16.4, and it will cause little surprise. The black spots of fifty years ago are still generally the worst areas today. Much of Scotland (particularly Strathclyde) Wales, the West Country, and the North-East and Merseyside have the highest proportions of unemployed. Deep rural counties in eastern England also have high levels of unemployment, and only in the axial belt stretching from the Thames to the Trent is there a continuous area of low unemployment (at less than 5·0 per cent). However, by August 1980, unemployment over the whole

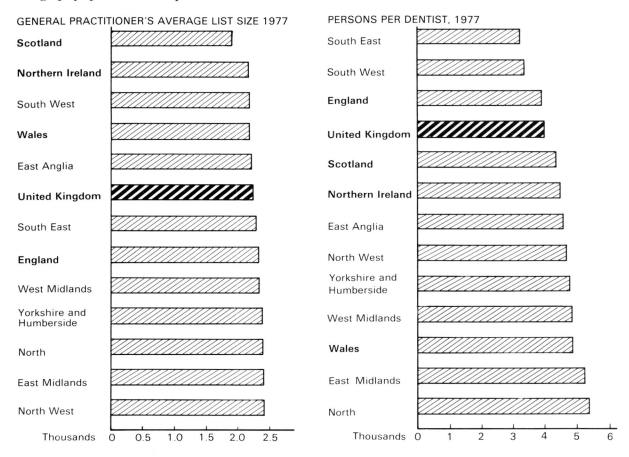

GENERAL PRACTITIONER'S AVERAGE LIST SIZE 1977

Scotland
Northern Ireland
South West
Wales
East Anglia
United Kingdom
South East
England
West Midlands
Yorkshire and Humberside
North
East Midlands
North West

Thousands 0   0.5   1.0   1.5   2.0   2.5

PERSONS PER DENTIST, 1977

South East
South West
England
United Kingdom
Scotland
Northern Ireland
East Anglia
North West
Yorkshire and Humberside
West Midlands
Wales
East Midlands
North

Thousands 0   1   2   3   4   5   6

Fig 16.3 General practitioners' and dentists' average list sizes, by region, 1977

country had risen to 2 million (8·3 per cent). Although this is a reflection of economic recession, there is also a demographic component, as the proportion of the active population has increased over the previous decade.

Percentage figures such as these, however, should not blind us to the absolute numbers involved, for this rather changes the spatial pattern of the problem. In 1980, for instance, there were more people unemployed in the South-East than in the whole of Wales and Scotland together. The West Midlands, too, is a black spot in terms of numbers unemployed, though not as bad as some other regions in terms of unemployment *rates*.

INTRA-REGIONAL DISPARITIES

While regional variations point to differences in public service provision and social needs in the country as a whole, they mask the considerable and often more dramatic differences that are shown up from data of a finer level of aggregation. Thus, while Scotland has been shown to fall behind in many indicators, and the South-East to be generally well endowed, an examination of census data reveals not only the depth of deprivation in parts of Scotland, but also many similarities between Clydeside and Inner London. In 1975, Holtermann examined the worst 5 per cent

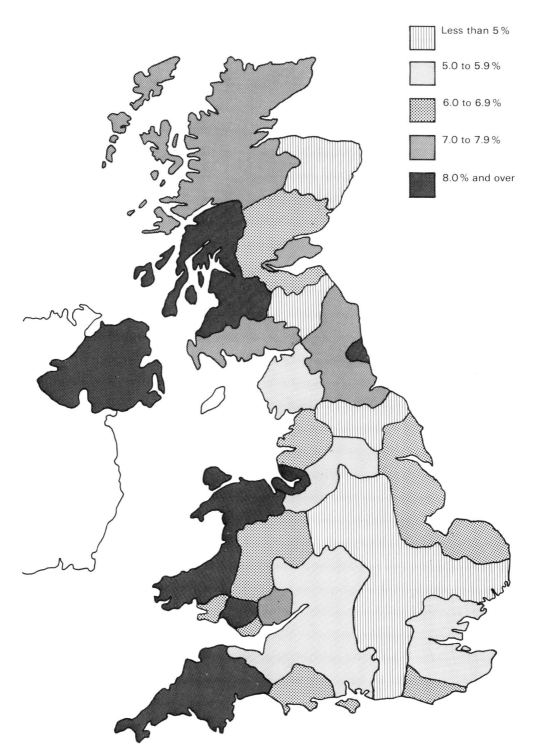

Fig 16.4 Unemployment in Great Britain, April 1977

enumeration districts (the smallest census unit of about 200 households) in the urban areas of Great Britain, in terms of housing and unemployment. From her study, Clydeside in particular stood out as the most deprived area in Great Britain on nearly every measure. Inner London stood out as having a more than proportionate share of housing deprivation, while the core of each of the English conurbations while not as bad, was poor. Holtermann showed that 18·9 per cent of Glasgow's population lived in enumeration districts which suffered from multiple deprivation, as compared with 7·2 per cent for Birmingham, 7·9 per cent for Manchester, 5·6 per cent for Newcastle and only 2·9 per cent in Leeds.

Variation can also be very marked even within one county district, as anyone familiar with his own surroundings will appreciate. In a study of census data for Kirklees, one of the districts of the metropolitan county of West Yorkshire, Barrowclough was able to distinguish five types of area in terms of social well-being, illustrated in Fig. 16.5. *Group A* represents the most deprived areas, mainly in inner urban areas, and often with increasing populations of New Commonwealth immigrants; *Group B* is made up of wards on the fringe of inner areas, with rather a mixed profile. They may be said to represent 'average' conditions in predominantly working class areas. *Group C* takes in the old cores of the small mill towns on the Pennine fringe, where remoteness, poor living conditions and limited employment opportunities has contributed to persistent loss of population. *Group D* are predominantly rural wards which are neither particularly run down, but nor are they particularly suburbanised, except by high income commuters converting country properties. *Group E* represent the most advantaged wards which have experienced considerable growth in population since the 1961 census, mainly living in new owner-occupied housing.

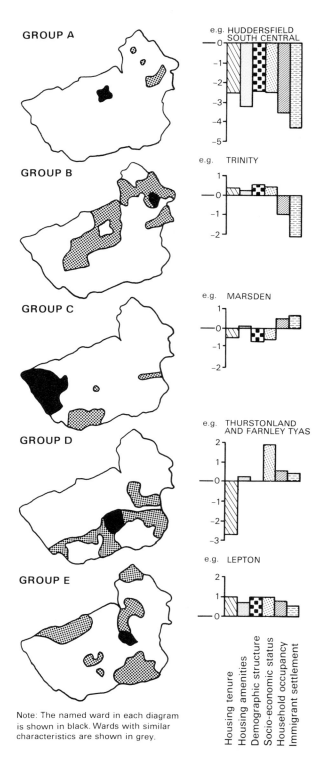

Note: The named ward in each diagram is shown in black. Wards with similar characteristics are shown in grey.

Fig 16.5 Variations in social well-being between wards in Kirklees, West Yorkshire, 1971 (after Barrowclough)

AREA APPROACHES

From all that has gone before in this chapter, we could be forgiven for assuming that there are widespread spatial inequalities within Great Britain, which require a massive re-evaluation of policy both in the public and private sectors. While some may believe this to be true, the fact remains that the general level of well-being across the whole country is relatively high, especially in world terms, and most variations between regions are fairly small. However, the real difficulties occur in sometimes quite small and localised areas. As we have seen in West Yorkshire, there can be areas of considerable affluence and areas of deep poverty within a few miles of each other, and so increasingly the government has turned to the use of specific small *area policies,* in addition to blanket measures relating to whole regions. Education, and housing have been two sectors which have been treated in this way, along with social service provision.

Education

The role that a 'good' school can play in enhancing the subsequent life chances of its pupils is generally accepted, and the converse is deplored. As Herbert reminds us, "Low levels of attainment, high drop out rates and truancy are often closely associated with other indicators of deprivation". In 1967 the Plowden Report took up an American principle of positive discrimination in favour of deprived areas. Although all its recommendations were not taken up, especially as regards the provision of nursery education, some important steps were taken. A special building programme was set up to replace old and unsatisfactory school buildings, particularly in urban areas. In 1968 special allowances were introduced for teachers in schools which were considered to be particularly difficult. Part of the problem lay in deciding which were the schools and the areas which came in this category. *Educational Priority Areas* proved difficult to define, and local authorities adopted differing criteria. A method adopted by the Inner London Education Authority is widely regarded as being particularly good, and it is based upon the characteristics of the area in which particular schools are found, e.g. occupations of parents, public amenities, etc., and characteristics of the schools such as absenteeism and teacher turnover.

Social Services

A similar emphasis on positive discrimination was also adopted in the report of the Seebohm Committee in 1968, which felt that social service departments should be organised on the basis of area teams, concentrating their effort towards those parts of their district where there was evidently very special need. At much the same time, the Home Office sponsored the 1969 Local Government Grants (Social Need) Act which sought to help fund special projects which local authorities felt would particularly benefit small local areas. Between 1969 and 1978 approximately £140 million has been spent on this form of *Urban Aid*. In addition the *Community Development Project* was set up as twelve separate units in deprived areas all over the country to undertake 'action research' "to identify needs and possible solutions which are beyond immediate local action, but merit feeding back to wherever policy is formed". The last of the units was closed in 1978 after a stormy life, although much useful research was undertaken.

Housing

Housing policies in the inner city were referred to in Chapter 13. The 1969 Housing Act introduced specific area policies designed to improve particular localities, with the concept of General Improvement Areas – although in a sense area-based approaches have characterised the housing programme since its very beginning with selected demolition and clearance. The Housing Act of 1974, however, was specifically designed to impinge upon the social problems associated with inadequate housing. Improvement grants of up to 90 per cent were payable in Housing Action Areas, compared with 60 per cent in General Improvement Areas and 50 per cent elsewhere. It has been suggested that even such high levels of grants have not resulted in very high levels of take-up, largely because of the high costs of building repairs and the low incomes of owner occupiers and landlords. Housing associations have played an important role in such areas by acquiring and converting old property, and then renting the improved houses back to tenants in association with the local authority. Unfortunately the period since the 1974 Housing Act has seen severe curbs on local authority spending, and although Housing Action Areas have been very effective in improving selected areas, perhaps as little as 10 per cent of the suitable property has been treated in this way, and there are growing fears that the end result will be little islands of improvement in the midst of a sea of dereliction and decay.

These fears are increased when set against other policies which seem to be working in the opposite direction. Considerable controversy, for instance, has surrounded the policies of building societies in some inner urban areas. The societies have been naturally unwilling to lend money for house purchase in areas which appear to be deteriorating, and which are consequently a bad risk. As a result the sale of property is made difficult, prices fall and the values of neighbouring properties decline further. In the end property is bought by means other than a building society mortgage – perhaps through rental purchase or high interest bank loans. As Williams has pointed out, West Indian and Asian migrants make greater use of these alternative methods of house purchase, so that it almost becomes inevitable that they buy properties in such areas. As such methods of purchase are very expensive, a smaller proportion of the household budget is available for other expenditure, and further deprivation ensues.

Multiple Deprivation

While some areas may suffer deprivation on only one or two counts, it will be clear that in many cases many of the factors we have mentioned come together to make for multiple deprivation. In such areas a 'climate of despair' is engendered on the part of residents that renders specific improvements difficult if not impossible. Many studies have revealed the operation of a 'neighbourhood effect' which disposes the inhabitants towards particular attitudes. In deprived areas these attitudes may well condone delinquency, vandalism, and truancy which do little to enhance the lifestyle of residents. The need for a compre-

hensive approach to such problems was highlighted by the *Shelter Neighbourhood Action Project* (SNAP) undertaken in Liverpool between 1969–72. Both Conservative and Labour governments responded to this initiative, and there is currently a series of *Comprehensive Community Programmes* being undertaken of which the metropolitan district of Gateshead is something of a spearhead.

In the space we have available we are only able to touch upon some of these major issues, but it is increasingly apparent that the geographical dimension has in the past been neglected, and that the spatial implications of private and public policy decisions need much more careful evaluation. For, in spite of the evening out of living standards over recent years, the South-East, as the richest region, was still almost 40 per cent better off than the poorest regions (Wales and Northern Ireland) in terms of personal disposable income in 1976.

References

Smith, D.M., *The Geography of Social Well-Being in the U.S.A.* (McGraw Hill, New York, 1973).

Knox, P.L., *Social Well-Being: a Spatial Perspective* (O.U.P., 1974).

Coates, B.E., Johnston, R.J., & Knox, P.L., *Geography and Inequality* (O.U.P., 1977).

Coates, B.E., & Rawstron, E.M., *Regional Variations in Britain* (Batsford, 1971).

Manners, G., 'Regional policy rethink', *Town and Country Planning*, 44, 4, 1976, pp. 208–14.

Holtermann, S., 'Areas of urban deprivation in Great Britain: an analysis of 1971 Census data', *Social Trends*, 6, 1975, pp. 33–47.

Barrowclough, R., 'A Social Atlas of Kirklees', *Huddersfield Polytechnic, Department of Geography, Occasional Paper No. 3, 1975*.

Herbert, D.T., & Johnston, R.J., *Social Areas in Cities, Vol 2: Spatial Perspectives on Problems and Policies* (Wiley, 1976).

Hambleton, R., *Policy, Planning and Local Government* (Hutchinson, 1978).

Short, J.R., & Bassett, K., 'Housing action areas: an evaluation', *Area*, 10, 2, 1978, pp. 153–157.

Williams, P., 'Building societies and the inner city', *Trans. Inst. Brit. Geogrs.*, N.S., 3, 1, 1978, pp. 23–34.

17

Economic Policy

The post-war years in Britain have been dominated by the growing interest and intervention of successive governments in the affairs of the economy. A mixed economy, of which Britain is typically a good example, is the characteristic form of economic organisation in the modern industrial world. It is a reflection both of the need to avoid the trauma of the inter-war years, when there was mass unemployment and almost total economic collapse, and of the growing complexity and manageability of the modern economy. Consequently, the government is responsible (i) for the general performance of the economy, (ii) for the operation of a range of public sector activities and (iii) for a series of other policies which directly affect the private sector. The first two aspects of this policy emerged almost simultaneously in the immediate post-war years from 1945 to 1950, while the third aspect has come much more to the fore over the 1970s.

An understanding of such events has considerable relevance in a geographical review. Firstly, it enhances the geographer's appreciation of how the economy works so that he may more fully understand its spatial make-up. Secondly, it is an important contribution to the emergence of structural problems which almost inevitably have their roots in the growth and development of the British economy. Finally, economic policy has an important bearing on regional prosperity. Regional problems are the spatial by-product of structural change and, through its regional and industrial policies, government economic policy is striving to protect the well-being of less favoured regions like north-eastern England and Scotland.

MANAGEMENT OF THE ECONOMY

The immediate post-war years saw the birth of a new approach to British economic policy through the application of ideas and methods suggested by John Maynard Keynes. Basically, Keynes was critical of the prevailing attitude that the unfettered market mechanism could solve problems like that of mass unemployment unaided. Instead he advocated that the government should regulate the economy through its own actions by controlling the level of demand (i.e. total demand for goods and services). The broad outline of such a policy was originally conceived by Keynes in response to the Depression of the 1930s and his ideas formed the basis of Roosevelt's New Deal in the U.S.A. The principles of this policy were adopted by the British government's White Paper on Employment Policy issued in 1944. This stated, "We can make a fresh approach . . . to the task of maintaining a high and stable level of employment without sacrificing the essential liberties of a free society". The execution of this policy was to be undertaken annually through the use of Budget measures. At the same time, the White Paper contained a warning that high levels of employment could endanger price stability. This conflict has become clearer over the post-war years and is a continual source of difficulty. A further complication, which became a source of worry during the late 1950s and 1960s, was the danger which a high level of employment posed for the Balance of Payments. So economic policy has developed largely as an attempt to stabilise the

Table 22: Annual Percentage Changes in Gross Domestic Product (G.D.P.), Consumers' Expenditure and Fixed Investment, 1951–75

	1951–2	1952–5	1955–9	1959–61	1961–3	1963–5	1965–72	1972–3	1973–5
Gross Domestic Product	−0·2	3·9	1·7	4·1	2·5	4·3	2·1	5·3	−1·0
Consumers' Expenditure on goods & services	−0·5	4·3	2·5	3·2	3·2	2·3	2·5	4·8	−0·6
Fixed Investment	0·8	8·5	4·6	9·5	0·8	10·0	2·6	4·3	−1·0

Source: A.R. Prest & J. T. Coppock (1976).

need for a high level of employment with that of price and external stability (Fig. 17.1). As a package, this is referred to as *Stabilisation Policy*. It is beyond the scope of this text to examine the mechanics of demand management in detail. It is sufficient to say that (for much of the post-war period) due to the basic conflict referred to above, the level of demand in the British economy has followed a cyclical or 'stop-go' pattern with distinct phases of expansion and contraction. An examination of Table 22 reveals these trends.

Gross Domestic Product (G.D.P.) is the total value in monetary terms of all goods and services produced in the economy and is a good approximation of the overall level of demand. As Table 22 shows, the annual percentage changes in G.D.P. follow a detectable cyclical pattern, popularly referred to as the business cycle. In the 'go' phases, these changes are significantly higher than during the deflationary 'stop' phases. Fluctuations in consumers' expenditure are less marked than changes in G.D.P., although the opposite is true for changes in fixed investment. This overall cycle was regular up to 1965, but this was followed by a period of economic uncertainty, with two years or so of 'false' boom in G.D.P. Over the last few years G.D.P. has actually fallen and in 1979 was just showing signs of recovery. In spite of these problems, however, the intensity of the fluctuations has been much less severe than in the past. The business cycle has presented its own problems. Some industries, e.g. motor vehicle manufacture and the domestic appliance industries, are more vulnerable than others since the demand for their products closely follows G.D.P. prospects. In addition, parts of the service sector, e.g. activities tied up with leisure and tourism, face similar problems. Geographically this linkage can present certain problems for those regions in which the activities are concentrated. The West Midlands was particularly hard hit in 1974–8. Other peripheral regions, e.g. the South-West and Scotland, relying heavily on tourist activities, have also been affected by national circumstances.

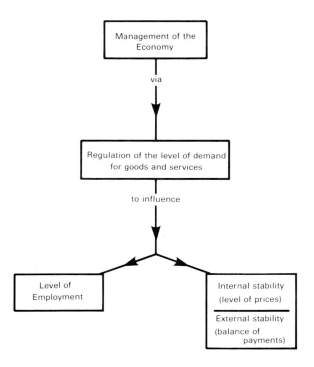

Fig 17.1 The mechanics of stabilisation policy

Employment

The success of stabilisation policy should also be viewed in terms of its stated objectives. The maintenance of a high level of employment as laid down in the 1944 White Paper has been achieved for most of the post-war period. In spite of fluctuations, the average unemployment rate varied only between 1·0 per cent and 2·5 per cent until 1970. This of course in direct contrast to the experience of the inter-war years, when the average percentage rate reached double figures in most years. There has been a worrying upward trend since 1970, largely brought about through problems associated with the two other stabilisation variables (see Table 22). The statistics in this table do hide an important geographical issue – regional unemployment variations. Some regions, e.g. Scotland, the North and North-West, have persistently had unemployment rates well above the averge shown. Others, notably the South-East, have been below this average. The 'regional problem' tends to be less severe in times of growth in the national economy, but more severe in problem periods. There is, therefore, a strong link between the regions and the national economy. It remains a fact that the problem regions are always the first to suffer in times of cut-back and the last to benefit in terms of prosperity. Their future prospects are inextricably tied up with those of the national economy.

Table 23: Key Indicators of the U.K. Economy, 1965–79

	AVERAGE % UNEMPLOYMENT RATE	% CHANGE RETAIL PRICES	BALANCE OF PAYMENTS (£M)	
			VISIBLE BALANCE	CURRENT BALANCE
1965	1·3	4·8	−237	− 49
1966	1·4	3·9	− 66	+104
1967	2·2	2·5	−555	−300
1968	2·3	4·7	−667	−287
1969	2·3	5·4	−156	+440
1970	2·5	6·4	− 25	+695
1971	3·3	9·4	+280	+1058
1972	3·7	7·1	−702	+105
1973	2·6	9·2	−2353	−922
1974	2·6	16·1	−5194	−3565
1975	4·0	24·2	−3203	−1701
1976	5·8	16·5	−3571	−1405
1977	6·2	15·8	−1709	+289
1978	5·3	8·4	−1176	+443
1979	5·4	13·4	−3312	−2436

Source: *Annual Abstract of Statistics*, 1980.

Price Stability

The employment objective of demand management has been in a continual and increasing conflict with the need for price stability. Until 1970, the level of inflation was contained, but from 1970–76 it averaged 13 per cent per annum (Table 23). The largest increases were recorded between 1973 and 1975, with much of this increase being the consequence of rocketing oil, food and raw material prices. Control of this 'new' imported inflation is outside the scope of normal demand management policies and requires more direct methods. These rising charges have also been reflected in a critical balance of payments position. In 1976, payment for petroleum imports was over £5500 m, compared with less than £1700 m in 1973. By 1979, the rate of increase of the Retail Prices Index again moved upwards, to a peak annual increase of 20 per cent in 1980. Although North Sea oil has reduced the balance of payments burden, there has been an increased flow of other imported goods.

Domestic inflation and the balance of payments also have geographical implications. If the British rate of inflation is in excess of that of trading rivals, there is a danger that Britain's products will be forced out of certain export markets. Alternatively, home produced goods may become less attractive than lower cost imports. This has been particularly true in the vehicle, textile, clothing and electronics industries, which have faced strong competition from Eastern Europe and South-East Asia. The maintenance of an internationally competitive position is crucial for both the balance of payments and those regions producing goods in the categories listed above. The changing fortunes of the British coal industry are largely a consequence of the balance of payments strain. At a regional level, East Midlands, and Yorkshire and Humberside seem most likely to gain in terms of employment and output, while in other mining regions, the run-down of the industry may have been delayed a little. Due to the same balance of payments trends, the future prospects of North Sea oil are now far in excess of predictions made in the early 1970s, and this has undoubtedly brought increased prosperity to certain parts of Scotland.

In conclusion, Keynsian methods have been generally successful in achieving their stated objectives. There is nevertheless a growing awareness of their limitations, particularly in dealing with problems of price stability. A more fundamental criticism is that demand management is a short-sighted approach, not taking into full consideration the longer-term growth of the economy. The problem of economic growth will be discussed in the next section.

PROBLEMS OF ECONOMIC GROWTH

Policies of demand management are concerned with the stabilisation of the economy around a particular level of demand. As such they are short-term policies. The ultimate long-term objective of economic management, however, is for economic growth, and this is achieved through a persistent increase in G.D.P. over time, so raising the productive potential of the economy. Unlike some other types of economic system, growth is not the predominantly overriding objective of economic policy in Great Britain. It remains an objective, but only when stabilisation success has been achieved.

Economic growth is desirable since it leads to an increase in living standards. To the man in the street, it means that he is better off through being able to purchase a greater volume of goods and services in real as distinct from monetary terms. The consumer society, common to developed industrial economies, is very much a consequence of real G.D.P. growth. Nevertheless, although the growth performance of the post-war British economy compares quite favourably with that of earlier periods in this century, it suffers in comparison with most other industrial countries (see Table 24). From a position of second behind the U.S.A. in 1938, the level of G.D.P. per head in the U.K. has slumped to nineteenth overall in the world economy. Within the E.E.C., Italy alone of the major states stands below the U.K. and the gap is gradually being closed.

Level of Investment

The causes of economic growth and the reasons for the poor U.K. performance have been widely debated. Although there is no simple concensus, economists see an increase in the quantity and quality of factors of production as being the key to G.D.P. growth. Of particular importance is the rate of increase of a nation's stock of capital since this has an important bearing upon labour productivity. Consequently, increasing investment, particularly in manufacturing industry, has long been a concern of government economic policy. Various incentives to encourage investment have been tried, usually involving some generous system of tax allowances. From a geographical angle, these have been strongly linked with regional policy, the main argument being that national growth should be stimulated through a vigorous regional economy. Following the 1972 Industry Act, investment incentives currently take the form of accelerated depreciation allowances throughout the U.K., with regional development grants being paid in the Areas of Expansion (Assisted Areas).

Table 25 compares the levels of fixed investment in the U.K. with that of five other industrial economies. Although it has risen since the early

Table 24: Rates of Growth of Selected Industrial Economies, 1951–1976

	AVERAGE % GROWTH OF REAL G.D.P.	G.D.P IN 1976 AS A MULTIPLE OF G.D.P. IN 1951
U.K.	2·5	1·9
France	4·8	3·2
W. Germany	5·5	3·8
Italy	4·9	3·3
U.S.A.	3·1	2·2
Japan★	8·5	7·1
★ 1952–1976		

Source: *Economic Progress Report*, C.S.O., July 1978.

Table 25: Fixed Investment as a Percentage of G.D.P.

	1950–1954	1970–1975
U.K.	14	19
France	18	24
W. Germany	20	24
Italy	19	21
U.S.A.	17·5	17·5
Japan	21·5★	33·5
★ 1952–1954		

Source: *Economic Progress Report*, C.S.O., July 1978.

1950s, compared with other nations, the investment/G.D.P. ratio of the U.K. is still a low one in spite of a progressively vigorous system of incentives. The level of investment is a key determinant of productivity, and British investment has either not been enough or its quality has been inferior, because international productivity comparisons are equally disappointing. The average rate of increase in output per employee in the U.K. is by far the lowest in the E.E.C. Britain's poor growth record in short is attributable to a failure to break out of this vicious cycle of low investment and low productivity.

Government Economic Planning

Frustration over the poor growth record of the U.K. economy was especially strong in the early 1960s, when other western European economies were forging ahead. The National Economic Development Council (known as 'Neddy') was established in 1962, one of its objectives being to consider the obstacles to economic growth and to make recommendations on how the growth record could be improved. The Council set a growth target for G.D.P. of 4 per cent per annum for the period to 1966 and set up 'little Neddies' in seventeen industries to try and enhance growth. In spite of this open-minded approach to economic growth, the actual rise in G.D.P. was only about 3 per cent per annum. With the change of government in 1964, the Labour administration was much more strongly inclined towards the idea of state planning of the economy and in order to have better machinery to create growth, created two important new government departments, the Department of Economic Affairs and the Ministry of Technology. One of the early tasks of the former was to draw up the now ill-fated National Plan. In terms of economic planning, this remains by far the most comprehensive document ever produced on the British economy. The various little Neddies were retained, and along with the new Regional Economic Planning Councils, were seen as key instruments in the operation of the Plan. The National Plan itself was based upon a target for economic growth of a 25 per cent increase in G.D.P. over the period 1964–70. This amounted to an annual average increase of 3·8 per cent, half as much again as the normal post-war

average. The Plan outlined in some detail the growth requirements of certain industries. If its full target were to be met then an estimated 200,000 new jobs would have to be created in the widened Development Areas and a similar equivalent number of jobs made good through increased productivity. In the event, a G.D.P. increase of 2·4 per cent per annum was achieved over the given period. The shortfall was due almost entirely, as had been past expectations, to problems associated with other economic variables. The need for a period of severe deflation from 1966 in order to attempt to stave off balance of payments worries killed hopes of increasing the level of investment. Business expectations were far from good at a time when they needed to be rosy. So, once again, other economic priorities had impaired the prospect of enhanced economic growth.

The early 1970s provided false hopes. For the first two years or so, the rate of increase of G.D.P. was at an unprecedently high level of around 4 per cent, with investment booming. The Industry Act of 1972 had provided nationwide investment allowances and, with E.E.C. membership on the horizon, the economy was buoyant. There was, however, an abrupt ending to growth prospects with the tremendous rise in world oil prices in 1973–4 and their crippling impact on the British economy. In 1975, G.D.P. actually fell below its 1974 level and there was little or no growth in 1976 and 1977. A slow recovery began in 1978, but within a year the U.K. economy, along with other developed economies, was again experiencing negative growth.

Structural Changes

Looking at the overall post-war growth performance, two further points should be noted since both have geographical significance and implications. Firstly, the structure of the economy changes as a consequence of growth – some industries experience an increase in demand for their products, while others are adversely affected. This impact, however, varies across the country throughout the economy. Some regions, particularly those which are peripheral or contain staple industries, experience more decline for their products than others. The 'regional problem', whereby some regions lack job opportunities and have unemployment levels in excess of the national average, is very much a product of economic growth and can be directly related to a region's industrial structure.

One of the first investigations of this much tested hypothesis was by M.F. Hemmings. For the period 1952–62, each Standard Industrial Classification (S.I.C.) grouping was ranked on the basis of employment change. Some groupings, e.g. Agriculture, Forestry and Fishing, Mining and Quarrying, Shipbuilding and Marine Engineering, and Textiles experienced decreasing employment. Conversely, other industrial groupings notably in the service sector and engineering/electrical goods, were expanding employment. Using this basic analysis, Hemmings defined a depressed region as "one where the number of employees grows more slowly than in the U.K. as a whole", noting that such regions have a higher proportion of industries in which there has been a large decline in employment. This so-called 'composition factor' would particularly apply to British problem regions such as the North, the North-West and Scotland. Regional imbalance is only partly explained by industrial structure. Hemmings further identified a 'growth factor', in so far as employment in a *given* industry has grown faster or declined less in certain regions than others. This is particularly important in the case of service activities. The impetus for their growth is contained in prosperous and core regions like the South-East. Service sector employment has grown in all regions, but not at the rate experienced in the South-East in particular. Between them therefore, the composition and growth factors explain how regional prosperity is related to economic growth. Government regional policy aims to create new job opportunities in problem regions and to disperse service sector employment, thereby counteracting natural forces in the economic and spatial system.

Labour Supply

A second geographical consequence of growth is related to the labour supply in the economy. The change in demand for the products of a region referred to above can have a bearing upon labour migration over the longer term period. As we saw in Chapter 8, it has been shown that certain regions experience a net loss of population through migration, while others experience a net gain. Although not all migrants move for employment purposes, a breakdown of migration by age shows that the more prosperous regions (especially the South-East) attract inflows of migrants in the younger economically active age-group categories. Such migrants of course move from less prosperous regions like the Northern, the North-West, and Yorkshire and Humberside economic planning regions. Economic growth also requires some degree of occupational mobility. The quality of labour in a region thus depends upon the facilities available for the education and training of labour. This aspect of the labour supply has been an integral element of government policy over the last twenty years or so. Taken together geographical and occupational mobility reflect the degree to which the labour supply can adjust to economic change. The quantity and quality of labour is undoubtedly an investment for future growth. If labour is not properly utilised then this represents a wastage of valuable resources. In fact, it has been argued that the relatively higher growth rate of certain other European economies can be attributed to the ease of movement of labour from the agricultural to industrial sectors. This has been particularly true in the case of Italy, the 'economic miracle' of Western Europe, where agricultural employment has been more than halved since 1958.

Economic growth, therefore, is desirable and remains an objective of economic policy in Britain. Growth can have a beneficial impact upon the space-economy of Britain by providing a suitable environment for reducing regional imbalance. On the other hand, as has been pointed out above, if the consequences of growth are not anticipated, regional variations may be widened. It is likely, however, that the meagre growth rates of the past thirty years may well be in excess of those to be expected in the 1980s.

PUBLIC ENTERPRISE IN THE BRITISH ECONOMY

We noticed in Chapter 12 that government involvement through the public services and nationalised industries was very important. In

Table 26: Nationalisation of major industries in Britain

	INDUSTRY		LEGISLATION
FUEL AND POWER	Coal	1946	Coal Industry Nationalisation Act
	Electricity Supply	1947	Electricity Act
	Gas Supply	1948	Gas Act
TRANSPORT	Railways	1947	Transport Act
	Long distance road haulage[1]	1947	Transport Act
	Some bus services	1947	Transport Act
	Some docks	1947	Transport Act
	Inland Waterways	1947	Transport Act
	Some air services	1949	Air Corporation Act
OTHERS AND LATER ADDITIONS	Bank of England	1946	Bank of England Act
	Iron and Steel	1949[2]	
	UK Atomic Energy Authority	1954	Atomic Energy Authority Act
	Post Office	1969	
	National Water Council	1973	Water Act
	National Enterprise Board[3]	1975	Industry Act
	British National Oil Corp.	1976	Petroleum and Submarine Pipeline Act
	British Aerospace	1977	
	British Shipbuilders	1977	

Notes: [1] part returned to private ownership in 1958.

[2] denationalised in 1952; large firms re-nationalised in 1967.

[3] The National Enterprise Board has major holdings in the following companies: British Leyland; Fairey Holdings; Rolls Royce (engineering); Herbert Ltd (machine tools); Inmos Ltd; Nexos Office Systems Ltd (micro-electronics).

economic terms the nationalised industries and government involvement in the private sector have ramifications beyond those of public administration which we noted earlier, and it is appropriate that we consider them here.

The late 1940s saw the nationalisation of a number of important activities (Table 26). Since then, it has only been over the last ten years or so that there has been further expansion. Most of the steel industry was renationalised in 1967, and in 1977, British Aerospace and British Shipbuilders were set up. Those industries which have been publicly owned for most of the post-war period fall into two groups, the first of which is concerned with the provision of fuel and power, and the second involving the provision of various transport services. The only obvious exceptions from Table 26 are the Post Office, which was a government department until 1969, the steel industry which has not consistently been a part of the public sector, and the industries associated with the N.E.B.

Nationalisation has always been a controversial issue, being based upon the dual criteria of political philosophy and economic necessity. Socialist thinking as developed by the Fabians in the late nineteenth century envisaged a gradual takeover of certain industries. These views were echoed in the depressed 1920s, when Sidney and Beatrice Webb in particular were preoccupied with ways of creating a more socially just and at the same time promoting industrial efficiency. Common ownership was also a cornerstone of the Labour Party Constitution drawn up in 1918. There was, therefore, a strong motivation from various sources for the first Labour government to carry out a nationalisation programme.

There were also sound economic grounds for nationalisation. Cases could be made for all the first crop of industries, coal and railways in particular. Both were undercapitalised and physically drained from the strain of supporting the war effort. Coal had suffered a continuing secular decline since World War I, and in general, there were too many mines and miners. Technical deficiencies were most glaring at the smaller pits, where the return in terms of profitability were not capable of promoting improvements. For rail, in spite of the 1921 rationalisation of ownership, the inter-war period had been one of almost continual

213

disinvestment at a time when their market was falling. There were many uneconomic lines and railway services being provided and there was a desperate need to replace outmoded rolling stock. Huge amounts of capital were needed to modernise both the coal industry and railways, but in neither case could this be provided by their private owners. Strategically, both were natural monopolies and vitally important in the post-war recovery programme. Similar cases could be made for the gas, electricity and steel industries. In short, nationalisation seemed logical and desirable.

These arguments and factual details of organisation have been widely discussed. Taken together, the nationalised industries currently make up about 11 per cent of G.D.P. In 1977 they employed about 1·7 million people (7 per cent of the total labour force), and they accounted for 14 per cent of total fixed investment in the economy and for 10 per cent of output. So, in terms of economic importance, the nationalised industries represent an immense concentration of resources in activities vital to the general well-being of the British economy. They also provide a special example of greater governmental control in the affairs of the economy.

Given the present scale of nationalisation, it has been argued that a further wholesale transfer of productive resources to public enterprise is unnecessary. Nevertheless, the trend in the 1970s has been for a greater control over the private sector, with the government providing financial help in certain instances. Under the 1972 Industry Act, the government were willing to provide financial help to private sector firms where:

(i) This help was likely to benefit the economy or any part of any region in the U.K.
(ii) Such help was in the national interest.
(iii) Financial assistance could not be appropriately provided from elsewhere.

The first of these provisions has marked geographical significance. Early examples of firms to benefit were Upper Clyde Shipbuilders, Harland and Wolff, Rolls-Royce and International Computers Ltd. Although criticised as 'lame ducks' such businesses may be vitally important in the regions in which they operate. Their downfall would have had serious employment repercussions, particularly in problem regions. This policy of greater state involvement was widened under the National Enterprise Board. In structure, the N.E.B. was envisaged as a type of industrial holding company. It was seen as a new source of investment capital for private industry, providing such help in return for a share of equity capital. Three important beneficiaries to date have been Ferranti, Burmah Oil and British Leyland. This latter example has turned out to be the biggest lame duck of all in terms of government help. The activities of the N.E.B. were, however, subsequently curtailed by the new Conservative Government in 1979.

In all cases, such financial help as has been provided was given on national and regional grounds. To allow such businesses to close down would place an added strain on our balance of payments and increase unemployment. The closure of British Leyland would be catastrophic to the regional economy of the West Midlands and those regions providing component parts. The West Midlands has already been heavily affected by industrial recession since 1974, so that it has been transformed from a prosperous to a problem region in a very short space of time. Even so, in spite of the scale of government assistance, certain employment blackspots remain, e.g. Merseyside, Clydeside and Tyneside.

TRADE AND THE E.E.C.

The British economy has traditionally depended heavily upon overseas trade. In 1977, for example, exports amounted to about 28 per cent of G.N.P., with imports providing a slightly higher percentage. Countries like Britain find it desirable to trade for two fundamental reasons. Firstly, international trade provides a *greater variety* of goods for the importing nation, so widening the geographical resource base of that country. History is littered with many examples of this type of interaction, from potatoes and tobacco from central America in Elizabethan times to tropical fruits and other crops at the present day. Through trade, a country is not restricted to its natural resource base. The second principle underlying trade is less obvious and involves the concept of *comparative advantage*. Instead of a country producing for all its needs, trade allows the development of specialisation and enables a country to concentrate resources on those commodities and products in which it has a relative superiority. This explains in simple terms why a country like Britain imports many goods she could produce for herself (Table 27).

Table 27: British Export and Imports by Commodity Grouping, E.E.C., 1977

COMODITY	EXPORTS (£M)	IMPORTS (£M)
Food and live animals	823·4	2,266·5
Beverages and tobacco	183·0	258·7
Crude materials, inedible	460·1	476·1
Mineral fuels, lubricants	1,217·5	1,099·3
Animal and vegetable oils and fats	33·3	63·1
Chemicals	1,396·6	1,506·2
Manufactured goods	2,683·8	2,520·8
Machinery and transport equipment	3,977·8	4,608·0
Miscellaneous manufactured goods	1,154·1	1,202·0
Others	222·0	169·6
Total	12,151·6	14,171·2

Source: *Annual Abstract of Statistics*, 1979.

Table 28: British Exports and Imports by Geographical Area, 1977

	EXPORTS (£M)	IMPORTS (£M)
Total	33,330·9	36,978·2
E.E.C.	12,151·6	14,171·0
Rest of W. Europe	5,605·6	5,576·2
N. America	3,820·8	4,947·7
Other developed countries	2,110·2	2,697·6
Oil exporting countries	4,374·4	3,800·4
Other developing countries	4,261·6	4,361·5
Centrally planned economies	910·7	1,371·2
(Low value trade)	96·5	52·5

Source: *Annual Abstract of Statistics*, 1979.

Patterns of Trade

Tables 27 and 28 show the pattern of Britain's trade with the E.E.C. With the exception of food items, there is a substantial cross-exchange of most processed and manufactured goods, although Britain has overall an unfavourable visible balance with its European partners. In 1976,

Britain's trade with all other parts of the world was also in deficit, the greatest relative deficit being with oil exporting countries. Traditionally Britain has relied upon invisible items such as tourism, shipping insurance and banking to make up the deficit on visible goods trade, but as the first section of this chapter has indicated, the overall balance of payments position has shown signs of considerable improvement. One of the most dramatic economic changes of the 1970s was the accession of Britain to the E.E.C.

Trade has been a central pinnacle of discussion for Britain's economic relationship with the E.E.C. As the Treaty of Rome has developed in practice, the E.E.C. is first and foremost a customs union, i.e. there is free trade between member states and a common external tariff on trade with third parties. Of particular concern to Britain for over twenty years has been the impact of this trading structure on the Commonwealth. In 1956, it was the reason for Britain's declining to join the Community and opting instead to help set up E.F.T.A. In the 1960s, Britain's stand weakened, but in the terms of accession agreed in 1972 and later modified, special concessions were agreed for some Commonwealth producers. Britain was allowed to import dairy products from New Zealand without their being subject to the external tariff and there was also a separate Commonwealth sugar agreement negotiated. The experience of the initial members of the Nine has been that the breaking down of trade barriers has fostered the growth of intra-Community trade. As Taber remarks, "Throughout a decade and a half of crisis, the Community's one consistently brilliant prodigy has been intra-Common Market trade". Trade between member states has grown far beyond the most optimistic predictions and Taber estimates that from 1958 to 1972, it grew at 15 per cent per annum. During the same period, world trade grew by 8·4 per cent per annum. New trade links have been created within the E.E.C., but what is perhaps more important, is that there has been a major geographical shift in E.E.C. trade. In 1974 about half the total export trade of the Community was between member states, compared with no more than a third in 1958. The Benelux nations and Eire in particular are greatly dependent upon this type of trade.

Britain's trading pattern is in contrast to that of all other E.E.C. members. At the present time, only around 30 per cent of Britain's total trade is with the rest of the Community, by far the lowest of any member. In order to benefit from this important aspect of membership, trade between Britain and the rest of the E.E.C. has to be increased both absolutely and relatively. The trading benefits of membership can be split into two elements, trade creation and trade diversion. The first aspect involves an increase in trade due to Britain being part of a much larger tariff-free market. New opportunities for trade are presented to British firms, and for the economy to benefit, more has to be sold to the rest of the E.E.C. Britain may also benefit through trade diversion, with British goods replacing products previously imported by the rest from outside the E.E.C. These processes, of course, equally apply to imports into Britain and this adds to the uncertain benefits of membership, for it is the overall impact which must be assessed. Trade is one area where Britain must gain in order to offset the costs of membership.

The most talked-about of the costs of membership is the agricultural burden. The E.E.C.'s Common Agricultural Policy is a 'dear food policy' and heavy food importers like Britain are forced to pay higher food prices in order to support the major producers, notably France. Although some British farmers have gained, it is once again the total impact which is important and the agricultural burden is clearly significant. The overall impact of the E.E.C. membership is very difficult to quantify. The two major areas of trade and agriculture have to be assessed, along with other factors such as payments received from the Regional and Social Funds.

Spatial Structure

The dynamic, as distinct from the financial, impact of membership is of particular interest to geographers. Economic integration has resulted in significant changes in the spatial structure of the Western European economy and these have taken on a greater importance with Britain's accession. Since 1958, the core area (particularly the Rhine Valley) has exerted a pull effect on the space-economy of the E.E.C. It acts as a magnet of attraction for labour and capital flows. The level of migration is being closely related to the state of the European economy. In good years, labour moves from poorer regions to more prosperous

regions, even though the workers concerned inevitably have to accept jobs at the bottom of the occupational hierarchy. In Britain's case, the Channel presents a formidable obstacle, so the impact of migration should not be over-stated. Similarly, in boom years, there is a greater movement of industrial capital within the Community and, of course, the core-areas provide the major attraction. The South-East, Britain's major core region, already houses many European companies and British firms have sought to expand in other parts of the Community. As the E.E.C. has prospered, the gap between the core and its periphery has widened. This is no comfort to the problem regions especially those of Britain which are peripheral not just to Britain but to the Community as a whole.

It can be expected that as integration is furthered and the idea of economic and monetary union moves to attainment, the space-economy of the E.E.C. will change in the way described. The accession of new, poorer nations will do little to offset the general pull of existing core regions. For Britain's problem regions the prospects can only add to the intense disappointment of the current size and importance of the Community's Regional Fund and Policy.

References

Gill, R.T., *Economies: a text with included readings* (Prentice-Hall, 1974) Chapter 7.

Employment Policy, Cmnd. 6527, 1944.

Prest, A.R., & Coppock, J.T., (eds), *The U.K. Economy: A Manual of Applied Economics,* sixth edition (Weidenfeld and Nicolson, 1976).

Economic Progress Report, No. 95, February 1978, HMSO.

Cmnd 2765, Department of Economic Affairs, 1965.

National Institute Economic Review, Vol. 25, 1963.

A.G. Champion, *Evolving Patterns of Population Distribution: England and Wales,* Trans. Inst. Brit. Geogrs., New Series 1, 1976, pp. 401–20.

A. Maddison, *Economic Growth in the West* (Allen & Unwin, 1964).

P.J. Curwen & A.H. Fowler, *Economic Policy* (Macmillan, 1976) Chapter 2.

G.M. Taber, *Patterns and Prospects of Common Market Trade* (Peter Owen, 1974).

Part Four

Regional Problems

18

Regional Themes and Variations

REGIONAL VARIATION

Part One of this book focused attention upon the physical conditions of the human habitat. The land – its location and its spatial relationships, its structure and relief features, its resource endowment, its climate and water supplies, its biotic and edaphic resources – is fundamentally the outcome of a unique set of geological events and processes aided by a prolonged period of climatic changes. This physical evolution initially created a rough-hewn and harsh environment for human occupation. Since men of Palaeolithic culture first entered Britain after the retreat of the ice, the physical landscape changed significantly: large areas under melt-water dried out, marsh and fen began to disappear, new species of plants colonised wide areas, and forests and woodlands covered much of the country. No matter what superficial physical changes occurred, the fundamental physiographical conditions (those of old rocks and uplands in the north and west and young rocks and lowlands in the east and south) did not; and many years ago Sir Cyril Fox drew attention to the Tees-Exe line which served as a useful dividing line separating these two major physiographical regions.

Within this general physical framework, and in spite of the small size of Britain, there are considerable, and sometimes quite marked, regional differences and it is important that these should be emphasised. For example, the coalfields occur in the Coal Measures of the Carboniferous rocks which are exposed in the Central Lowlands of Scotland, and intermittently in a belt stretching from Northumberland to South Wales. Although some of the coalfields have suffered

exhaustion others, including new hidden fields, such as those of Selby and the Vale of Belvoir, offer abundant reserves. Overall, water reserves are plentiful, especially in the northern and western parts of the country, but there is a relative shortage in the south-eastern portion of England. Finally, the quality of soils, a reflection of rocks, altitude and climate, varies widely regionally, some areas having good fertile soils, others infertile, poverty-stricken soils. Such regional differences of relief, climate, soil and mineral resources can either help or hinder regional development and prosperity.

Part Two concerned itself with the environmental history of Britain: the colonisation of the country, the establishment of settlement, the clearing of woodland and heath, the draining of marshes, the development of agriculture, the mining of minerals and the beginnings of simple manufacture. The agricultural and industrial revolutions wrought relatively sudden changes in the landscape and brought very significant changes in population growth and distribution patterns. Scientific and technological developments changed farming, mining, manufacture and transport. This study of the environmental history of Britain in Chapters 5–7, brings out quite clearly that Britain did not develop equally, due partly to physiographic and climatic differences, and partly to cultural influences. Up to the time of the Norman Conquest the north of England was very thinly populated and economically backward. The Domesday Survey of 1086 pointed to the relative poverty of northern and north-western England and its low level of urbanisation. Four hundred years later, in late medieval times, the most prosperous and most populated part of the country was East Anglia. Four hundred years later still, while London and its environs maintained their significance, the seat of prosperity and populousness had migrated to South Wales, the West Midlands, South Lancashire, the West Riding of Yorkshire, the north-east coast and the Central Lowlands of Scotland. Subsequently, the pre-industrial pattern of prosperity, largely located in lowland areas, has been reasserted.

Resource Imbalance

These regional variations imply differences in regional resources. Geographical conditions and natural resources, whether they be cultivable lowlands, fertile soils, water supplies, mineral deposits, or power resources are unevenly distributed throughout the world, and Britain is no different in this respect. We have seen that lowlands are fairly restricted in their occurrence, that fertile soils are limited in their extent, that water supplies are short in some areas, that mineral deposits are somewhat erratically located and have frequently become exhausted, and fuel supplies have become depleted. Areas which were once well-endowed are now largely exhausted of their resources (and sometimes their people) and regional imbalances consequently become inevitable.

Thus the differences between one part of Britain and another have long been making themselves apparent, manifesting themselves in some areas in declining agriculture, in the decline in fishing, the exhaustion of minerals, declining industry, cutbacks in communications and in the migration of people. In contrast, there have been positive developments in some areas towards improved and more intensive agriculture, the development of afforestation, and the exploitation of new oil resources; the growth of new types of industry, and the development of tertiary activities; improved communications, and the growth of recreation and tourism; and the creation of new towns.

Perhaps the greatest economic and social problem facing the governments of the developed world at the present time is how to correct these regional imbalances, and to regenerate decaying and decayed areas which have lost their economic vigour, are suffering out-migration, and have become depressed socially and psychologically.

We saw in Chapter 16 that certain factors can be used as indicators of regional economic imbalance: (i) *incomes* – whether they are above or below the national average; they are an indicator of the health and of the type of industry; (ii) *population* – out-migration into areas of attraction balanced against natural increases or decreases; (iii) *unemployment* – above or below national average, is an indicator of the health of regional industry in response to economic conditions; (iv) *employment growth* – which monitors expansion or decline of industries.

In any country, therefore, there are likely to be areas or regions which are flourishing and economically prosperous, and others which are declining and suffering economic stagnation. Such regional variations are not necessarily constant and may change during the historical period as we have already noted.

Regional Imbalance

Gunnar Myrdal interpreted this differential growth process in terms of what he called the process of *cumulative causation*. By this he implied that if a region gained some initial advantage, further new growth would tend to occur in this already expanding region, as a result of its inherent or derived advantages, rather than in other regions. Myrdal also explained the inequalities between regions as resulting from the spatial interaction which occurred between the thriving and expanding regions and the rest; for example, once economic development has commenced in a region, flows of capital, labour and goods are attracted to that region at the expense of the neighbouring regions. Furthermore, as a consequence of the higher returns accruing in a growth region, many of the factors of production – capital, skilled labour, entrepreneurial ability – are drawn there at the expense of the stagnating regions, which may lose some of their locally generated capital and some of their most skilled workers. Along with the *inflow of production factors* to the growth region(s), there is a reciprocal *outflow of goods and services* to the other lagging regions which compete to the disadvantage of the latter's secondary and tertiary activities. At the same time, the growth regions enjoy the *multiplier effects* and feedback advantages which are likely to manifest themselves in improved education facili-

219

ties, health services, recreation facilities and other specialised activities, although this is likely to result in the other regions being penalised and having to put up with poorer services.

Significant, too, are what Myrdal termed, "certain centrifugal 'spread effects' of expansionary momentum from the centres of economic expansion to other regions". In other words, as a result of creating a demand for food, minerals and other natural resources in spatially adjacent regions, development in one region may help to stimulate growth in others. Where the influence of such demands is strong enough to overcome economic stagnation, a process of *cumulative growth* may be initiated which eventually could result in the emergence of another area of self-sustained economic growth. Effects of this nature are most likely to happen in lagging regions which already display a reasonable level of economic activity, since they are likely to possess the necessary infrastructure of communications, transport, and educational facilities.

In his model, Myrdal assumes that self-sustaining growth takes place without the need of government intervention, although he does suggest that more powerful spread effects are likely to happen when government policies are directed at encouraging growth in stagnant regions. Many have questioned Myrdal's process of cumulative causation and are not convinced that it provides an altogether satisfying explanation of regional backwardness. But, when we come to discuss the Metropolitan Core area of England we shall find that it appears to reflect, fairly accurately, Myrdal's model.

REGIONAL SYSTEMS

Regional planning implies planning at a level somewhere between the national and the local level. But, it may be asked, what is meant by the term 'region'? Several geographers have remarked that regions are often conceptual – i.e. creations of the geographer's mind – rather than evident realities of the landscape.

Regional Concepts

Almost a century ago that father of modern English geography, Sir Halford Mackinder, asserted that, "it is especially the character of geography that it traces the influence of locality, that is, of environment varying locally", thereby focusing attention upon an area-specific or regional approach. Both objective and subjective paths have been followed in regional delimitation, and both have value today. A subjective approach, which has as its aim the revelation of the personality of an area, has its origins in the work of the French school of regional geographers, typified by Paul Vidal de la Blache, whose *Tableaux* evoked a literary art. In such works regional units were identified on the basis of distinctive landscape and land-use characteristics, and their success depended upon the sensitivity and skill of the observer. In many ways such an approach seemed more appropriate to pre-industrial settings where the links between society and nature were more direct. With a growing interest in perceptual and behavioural studies over the 1970s, however, such an approach is once more being valued, and studies of a sense of place and regional identity are gaining in popularity.

Objective views of regions have proved more fruitful than subjective approaches, however. The American geographer, Richard Hartsthorne, identified two sorts of region: the *formal region,* homogenous in terms of a specific phenomenon – farming for instance – or alternatively *nodal* or *functional regions* in which regional coherence is imparted by organisation around a particular centre. This latter approach in particular has proved a useful tool for analysis and examination of economic regions, and is typified by the Metropolitan Economic Labour Areas discussed in Chapter 13. Ideas of regions as systems can be traced back to the time of Patrick Geddes, biologist and planner, and to C.B. Fawcett, geographer, who suggested principles upon which England could be divided up into *Provinces* as early as 1919 (Fig. 18.1a). Over the next twenty years, ideas of the city-region received attention from Christaller in Germany and Dickinson in Britain, and their work laid the foundation for a new view of geography as a spatial science.

Theoretical systems of regionalisation were overtaken by events, however, with the outbreak of war in 1939. By that time central government

Fig 18.1 Regionalisation in the UK, 1919–1974

a) Fawcett's original provinces

Legend: Boundary of Province; Boundary of Administrative County

NORTH ENGLAND
YORKSHIRE
LANCASHIRE
PEAKDON
TRENT
SEVERN
WALES
CENTRAL ENGLAND
EAST ANGLIA
BRISTOL
WESSEX
LONDON
DEVON

b) standard region (1946) and conurbations (1951)

Legend: Boundaries of standard regions; County boundaries; Major conurbations

NORTHERN
NORTH WESTERN
EAST AND WEST RIDINGS
NORTH MIDLAND
WALES
WEST MIDLAND
EASTERN
SOUTH WESTERN
LONDON AND SOUTH
SOUTHERN

c) Economic planning region, 1965-74

Legend: Standard regions; Outer Metropolitan area conurbations

SCOTLAND
NORTHERN
NORTH WEST
YORKSHIRE AND HUMBERSIDE
EAST MIDLANDS
WALES AND MONMOUTHSHIRE
WEST MIDLANDS
EAST ANGLIA
SOUTH WEST
SOUTH EAST

d) Economic planning regions 1974

Legend: Offices of Regional Planning Councils and Boards

SCOTLAND
Edinburgh
Belfast
NORTHERN IRELAND
Newcastle
NORTHERN
YORKSHIRE and HUMBERSIDE
NORTH WEST
Leeds
Manchester
EAST MIDLANDS
WEST MIDLANDS
Nottingham
WALES
Birmingham
EAST ANGLIA
Norwich
Cardiff
London
Bristol
SOUTH WEST
SOUTH EAST

221

had used a variety of regions for purposes of field administration and a system of Civil Defence regions were established. These formed the basis of the *Standard Regions* adopted by the post-war Labour government in 1946 (Fig. 18.1b). The validity of these regions was often disputed by geographers, yet with minor modifications, adopted in 1956, these Standard Regions formed the backbone of regionalism for almost twenty years. In 1965, as part of its concept of a National Plan, the new Labour government set up a new regional framework to replace the former Standard Regions, within which physical and economic planning could be undertaken (Fig. 18.1c). The *Economic Planning Regions* so devised were subsequently modified after local government reform in 1972–4 (Fig. 18.1d), and these form the present Standard Regions.

Regional Planning

Given the regional variation we reviewed earlier in this chapter, a range of social and economic problems have arisen which have an area-specific or regional base. Glasson (1974) comments that though the problem regions are those which, characteristically, are materially worse off – reflected by indicators such as unemployment, low growth rates, poverty and a high level of out-migration – there may also be regions which, because of their accelerating growth rates, also suffer from particular problems such as land shortages, congestion, and rising prices. Regional variations are of wide occurrence, however, and a natural outcome of variable geographical conditions; hence the identification of problem regions does not necessarily call for intervention, although it may be advisable to investigate the case for intervention.

If intervention is deemed necessary, then aims and objectives should be formulated against which the effectiveness of any policy can be measured. More often than not the ends of inter-regional planning are geared to economic development as, for example, the more efficient use of resources or enhanced rates of growth. A number of broad strategies may be applied to effect inter-regional planning but, in general, two main approaches have usually been followed: either workers have been taken to the work, or work has been taken to the workers. As an illustration of the former we

could cite the inter-divisional transfer scheme of the N.C.B. whereby miners, as we noted in Chapter 8, have been transferred from a declining to an expanding coalfield; or the Durham County Council policy which is outlined in Chapter 20. The main thrust of policy, however, has been to attempt to introduce new industry into areas of acute unemployment.

Regional planning which rests upon the movement of industry, however, has to grapple with a host of problems. First of all is the important political question as to the degree of encouragement or coercion that can be applied to industry. The relative role of the public and private sector is obviously important here. While on the surface it may seem a simple matter for a government to re-direct its own employment to specific regions, there has been considerable resistance to the redeployment of civil service office jobs from central London, although some moves have been made as we noted in Chapter 12. The role of the public sector can be much wider than redeployment of civil service jobs. It can range from the stimulation of short-term employment through to the construction of public works – motorways, reservoirs, etc. It can include the provision of permanent employment through investment in education – universities and colleges – or the health service. In between lie a host of possibilities, including, the short-term programmes under the Manpower Services Commission, and job creation schemes.

Secondly there is the issue as to the mechanisms by which private industry can be stimulated in specific regions, discouraged from expanding in others, or encouraged to move between regions. What sort of employments should be encouraged to move – service or manufacturing, capital intensive or labour intensive? Equally important is the question as to what sort of area should the policy be applied – whole regions or only selected areas? Similarly should aid be applied where it is most needed, or where it has most potential for success, for the two are not necessarily the same as we shall see in Chapters 20 and 21?

REGIONAL POLICY

In Chapter 12 we noted that regional policy in the U.K. has been prompted above all by regional variations in the level of unemployment, and that although the type and characteristics of policy have varied according to the political complexion of the government of the day, policy has become steadily more complex. We cannot hope, here, to give a full account of regional policy over the last forty years, but in outline we can pick out four phases.

1. The Genesis of Regional Policy, 1928–1940

The impact of the inter-war Depression was most acutely felt on the coalfields and the heavy industrial regions of northern England. In the little coal mining villages in particular unemployment affected the majority of the workforce, and the first policy response was an attempt to transfer labour, rather than jobs. Under the *Industrial Transfer Act 1928* almost a quarter of a million workers were re-trained and encouraged to move to alternative employments between 1929 and 1938. Unfortunately the Depression was such that the results were largely ineffective. The reverse policy, of taking jobs to the unemployed was introduced under the *Special Areas (Development and Improvement Act) 1934*. Special areas for aid were designated in Clydeside, W. Cumberland, S. Wales and N.E. England (Fig. 18.2a), but there was little financial bite in the policy. Of more lasting impact during this period was the idea, based upon the munitions factories set up during the First World War, of creating special industrial estates, where new factories could be provided, supplied with all mains services, to be used by a variety of industrial concerns. This was the first 'advance factory'-type initiative and large estates were set up at Team valley in the North-East, at Treforest in South Wales, and at Hillingdon.

Although the onset of the Second World War revived the demand for armaments and uniforms, and so removed many of the symptoms of regional decline, the fundamental issues remained and in 1937 the government set up the Royal Commission on the Distribution of the Industrial Population, which produced the *Barlow Report* in 1940. This is generally regarded as the foundation of British regional policy, for it related the contraction of employment in the areas of Victorian industrialisation to the expansion of employment in the South-East. It advocated the decongestion of the largest urban centres, particularly London, by the shifting of both population and employment to those areas suffering contraction, and it pointed out that regional industrial policy and land-use planning generally were related issues.

2. Post-war reconstruction, 1945–1951

The spirit of the Barlow report was accepted by the post-war Government and given legislative effect by a number of Acts, some of which we have already noted in Chapter 13. As far as regional industrial policy was concerned, the *1945 Distribution of Industry Act* (supplemented in 1950) enlarged the Special Areas, renaming them Development Areas; to these were added smaller areas in 1946 and 1949 (Fig. 18.2b). Loans, grants and tax allowances were made to industries within these areas. The most important policy initiative during this period, though, was the introduction of the Industrial Development Certificate (I.D.C.). Wartime building licences had introduced the idea of control on specific developments. Since the *1947 Town and Country Planning Act,* an I.D.C. has been required for all developments in excess of government determined norms (generally 5,000 square feet). Thus the government produced a 'stick and carrot' policy whereby firms could be prevented from expanding in prosperous regions, and encouraged to expand, or move to, less prosperous regions.

The post-war period of prosperity in the 1950s tended to hide the regional problem, as coal-mining in particular benefitted from a rapid rise in demand for electricity generation. In addition a change of government had produced a less aggressive attitude towards the regional problem, and when the problem began to re-emerge again in the later 1950s the major policy response was the *1960 Local Employment Act*. This replaced the Development Areas with Development Districts, defined as any Local Employment Exchange area with an unemployment rate higher than $4\frac{1}{2}$ per cent (Fig. 18.2c).

3. Regional re-adjustments, 1963–1979

During the 1960s successive governments sought to grapple with the growing problem of regional imbalances. In 1963 special White Papers on Central Scotland and the North-East of England intro-

223

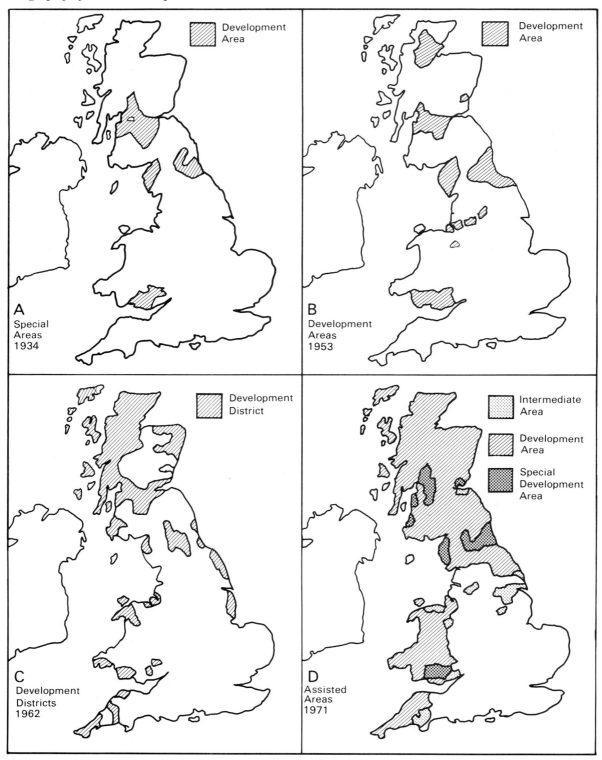

A
Special
Areas
1934

Development
Area

B
Development
Areas
1953

Development
Area

C
Development
Districts
1962

Development
District

D
Assisted
Areas
1971

Intermediate
Area

Development
Area

Special
Development
Area

duced special benefits to these two regions irrespective of unemployment levels. (The so-called Hailsham Report on N.E. England is reviewed in Chapter 21). A change of Government produced the *1966 Industrial Development Act* which once more widened not only the benefits available to industrialists but also the areas which could benefit, now including Scotland (excluding Edinburgh) the Northern Region, Furness, Merseyside, most of Wales, Cornwall and Devon. The following year *Special Development Area* status was introduced for selected parts of Central Scotland, the North-East, Wales and West Cumberland. This conferred additional benefits relating to employment rather than capital investment. In 1969 the *Report of the Committee on Intermediate Areas* (the Hunt Report) introduced the concept of 'Gray' or Intermediate Areas, where aid was required (though less than would apply in Development Areas). This array of legislation at least acknowledged that regional economic aid required different characteristics in different regions, though the end result was confusing to many industrialists (Fig. 18.2d).

All these varying levels of assistance were brought together in the *1972 Industry Act,* in what was described as the most comprehensive programme to stimulate industrial and regional regeneration ever undertaken in Britain. It extended the assisted areas, made provision for more re-training of labour, and rationalised the administrative framework within which the Act operated. Fig. 18.3 shows the *Special Development Areas* and the *Development Areas* which were already recognised before the Act was passed. The Act, however, gave *Intermediate Area* status to almost the whole of the north-west and the Yorkshire and Humberside planning regions which lay outside the Development Areas, and to those parts of Wales which were not already assisted areas. Two years later, in the summer of 1974, the Development

Areas of Merseyside and parts of north-west Wales became Special Development Areas, the Intermediate Areas at Cardiff and Edinburgh became Development Areas, and a new Intermediate Area was created in the Chesterfield area. Thus practically the whole of Britain outside what we term Metropolitan England fell within the Assisted Areas.

4. Changes in the 1980s

A new chapter in regional aid was undoubtedly opened with a further change of government in 1979. With a change of government policy the 'map of regional aid is being rolled back'. The changes, which are being progressively introduced over a transitional period ending in 1982–3, are intended to reduce the Assisted Areas and to make the impact of regional policy more selective. Fig. 18.4 should be compared with Fig. 18.2c, also the result of a more areally selective approach to aid.

Evaluation of Regional Policy

It is very difficult to evaluate the degree of success of over forty years of regional policies. As we noted in Chapter 16, the areas of highest unemployment remain in general where they always have been. On the other hand without the generation of alternative employment it is difficult to imagine what would have been the economic condition of those areas which have witnessed such a massive run-down of the coal, iron and steel, shipbuilding and textile industries. Manners (1976) has pointed out that the emphasis on providing manufacturing employment in the assisted areas seems a little contrary in the face of a structural shift in the economy towards office-based and service industries, and to that extent would suggest at least mismanagement. Equally, the fact that much of the assistance is in the form of capital investment has meant that capital intensive industries have been aided, at the expense of the labour intensive industries which may have been more appropriate to the regional situation. At best, then, U.K. regional policy can be said to have been only a holding operation.

Fig 18.2 Regional Industrial Policy, 1934–1971
a) Special Areas, 1934
b) Development Areas, 1953
c) Development Districts, 1962
d) Expanded Development Areas, 1971

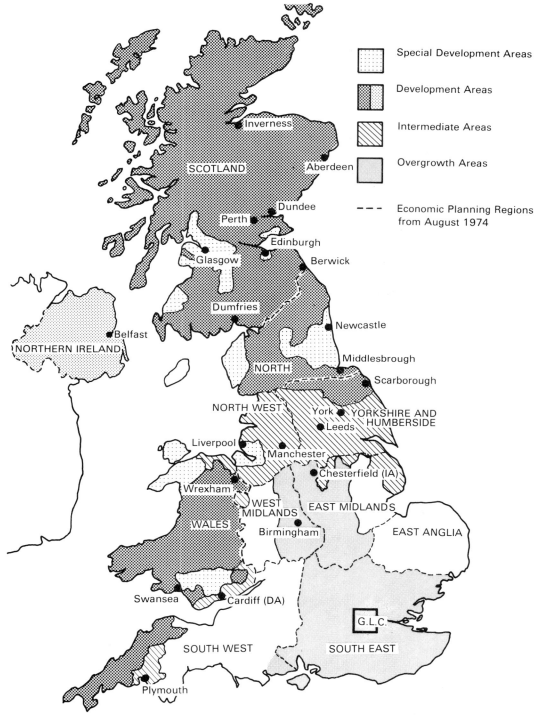

Fig 18.3 Assisted Areas, UK, 1975

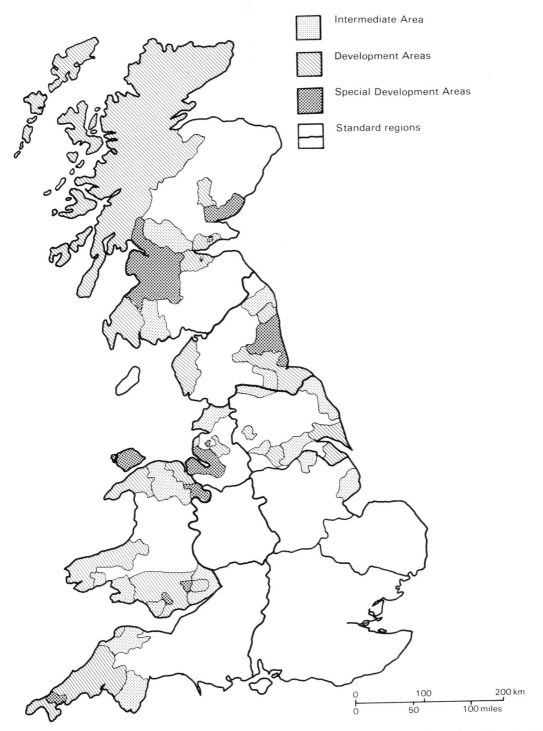

Intermediate Area

Development Areas

Special Development Areas

Standard regions

Fig 18.4 Assisted Areas, as proposed by The Department of Industry 1979 (to take effect in 1982)

THE REGIONS OF BRITAIN

We shall turn our attention in the last three chapters to Britain's regional problems: first, to the regions of expansion in the Metropolitan Core area; secondly, to the Peripheral Regions in the north and west; and, lastly, to the regions which occupy positions both economically and geographically intermediate between the two. Although this broad division is based essentially upon economic criteria, it will become apparent that there are other similarities between the regions in each chapter, which derive from the resource endowment, social development and spatial orientation of the areas concerned. We should not allow the current enthusiasm for employment statistics to cloud a broader, more geographical view of the regions, and our hope is also to give something of their personality. Equally it is important to realise that regional aggregations conceal many local variations, and so we have tried to include a few smaller-scale examples to show the complex cross-grain of reality which underpins the regional generalisation. Lastly, it is as well to note that not all the problems in the regions are problems of inequalities. While they may be measured in terms of economic advantage and disadvantage they are very often problems of location, resource endowment or social development, which we should try to see in their own context.

References

Myrdal, G., *Economic Theory and Underdeveloped Regions* (Methuen, 1957).

Minshull, R., *Regional Geography* (Hutchinson, 1967).

Glasson, J., *An Introduction to Regional Planning* (Hutchinson, 1974).

House, J.W. (ed.) *The U.K. Space,* second edition (Weidenfeld & Nicolson, 1977) Chapter 1.

Department of Trade and Industry, *Industrial and Regional Development,* Cmnd. 4942, 1972, HMSO.

Manners, G., 'Regional policy re-think', *Town and Country Planning,* 44 (4), 1976, pp. 208–14.

19

The Metropolitan Core Area: Regions of Expansion

To a greater or lesser extent, all the economic planning regions demarcated in the lowlands of England – the South-East itself, East Anglia, the East Midlands and the West Midlands – fall under the influence of Greater London and form a part of the 'region of expansion'. To a considerable extent the northern sub-region, i.e. the Bristol-Gloucester-Cheltenham area of the South-West economic planning region, also falls within this region of expansion but it will be dealt with in Chapter 20. This exemplifies the core-periphery situation with Metropolitan England functioning as the core, the London region as the inner core, and northern England, Scotland, Northern Ireland, Wales and south-west England as the periphery.

The rapid development of the core regions owed much to the growth and extension of the electricity grid on the one hand; and to the rapid growth in motor transport and the extension of the road highway system, including the motorways, on the other hand. Both of these made for greater flexibility and mobility. Industry became, in a sense, footloose, freed from the coalfields and the railway. This process rapidly gained momentum among the newer type of manufacturing industries, concerned with consumer durable goods. They were developing products such as electric heaters, electric and gas cookers, refrigerators, washing machines, vacuum cleaners, radio and television sets, along with typewriters (and more recently calculators and data processing equipment) cosmetics, pharmaceuticals and the like. Nearness to large or specialised consumer markets, resulting from increasing standards of living, also became a decisive factor in the location of many of the new-type manufacturing industries.

Other factors, too, as Manners has indicated, have played their part in the more recent location of industrial enterprise. For example, the availability of appropriately skilled labour and the role of innovation and enterprise should not be discounted. The importance of other changes in transport technology, such as liner train developments, oil and gas pipelines, container facilities and the growth in air transport have all made important contributions, especially through their concentration in southern England. As a result, the nodality and the relative attractiveness of the London-Midlands area for economic activity has steadily grown.

THE SOUTH-EAST

South-East England comprises geographically the London Basin framed within the encircling chalk hill country of the Chilterns in the north and the Downs in the south. The region comprises 3 million ha or 11 per cent of the country's total land area. Within it are concentrated some 17 million people or nearly one-third of the country's total population. One can discern a threefold zonal structure in the region: (i) *Greater London,* the built up area almost all of which is administered by the Greater London Council; (ii) the encircling *Outer Metropolitan Area* (O.M.A.), with a population of some 5·5 million, which makes up most of London's city region outside the metropolis; and (iii) the outermost zone, known as the *Outer South-East* (O.S.E.), which comprises the remainder of the South-East region, i.e. Essex, Bedfordshire, Buckinghamshire, Oxfordshire, Solent, Sussex Coast and Kent. The term *Metropolitan Region* is

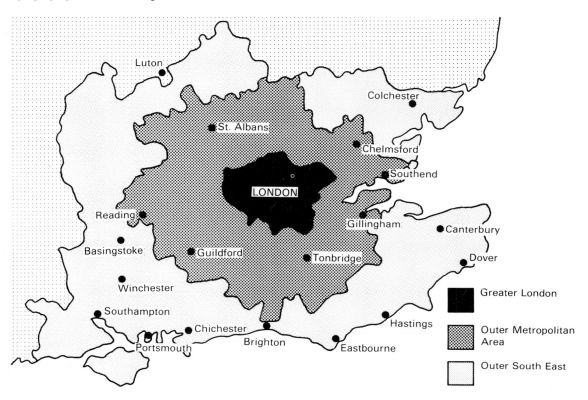

Fig 19.1 Planning zones in the South-East

used to embrace the Greater London area and the O.M.A. (Fig. 19.1).

South-East England is the largest, most populated, most economically important and most prosperous region in Britain. The huge concentration of people in the region is in part a response to, and in part a cause of, the largest concentration of economic activity and jobs in the country. Greater London and surrounding towns constitute the country's most important manufacturing area: some 2·5 million workers are engaged in a wide range of industries which include food, drink and tobacco, pharmaceuticals and toiletries, instruments of various kinds and electronic apparatus, clothing, printing and publishing, electrical goods, mechanical engineering, vehicles, etc. Notwithstanding the importance of the manufacturing industries, these are even surpassed by the service trades which employ over 5 million people or some 39 per cent of the British total service employment. These are absorbed by the national

government administration, local government, medical and hospital services, education, electricity, gas and water services, and the building industry. In addition, there are numerous other service activities grouped as professional, scientific, hotel and catering, and the entertainments industry.

The highly concentrated development of a very wide range of manufacturing industries and service activities in the South-East owes much to the demands of inner London itself, with its 7·3 million inhabitants enjoying relatively high incomes, and to the region's unrivalled nodality in terms of communications. Population growth in London and its region – from 10·5 million at the beginning of the century to 17·0 million today – and its remarkable economic developments during the past 50 years, have led to a host of problems relating to housing, land shortages, water supplies, transport, waste disposal, pollution, etc. We must now turn to these planning problems.

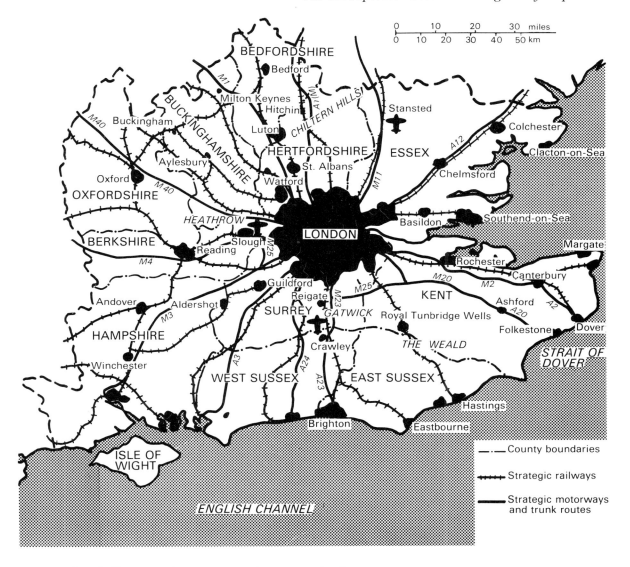

Fig 19.2 South-East—major towns and communications

The Necessity for Decentralisation

We noted in Chapter 18 that the *Barlow Report* drew attention to the need to reduce the rate of population expansion in the London area, and to direct industrial development elsewhere. At about the same time the *Abercrombie Report,* produced for the L.C.C., proposed the development of a 'green belt' around the capital. Decongestion and control were already in the mind of decision-makers during the Second World War, therefore, when bomb and fire damage in inner London made some measure of redevelopment and decentralisation not only desirable, but possible. The diversion of industrial development away from the attractions of the metropolis has not been easy, but decentralisation of people has been promoted in three different ways: (i) the building of 'out-country estates' on the borders of the Greater London area; (ii) the construction of New Towns, and (iii) the expansion of existing towns well away from London to house industries and people.

231

The New Towns Act of 1946 led to the establishment of eight new towns around London: Basildon, Bracknell, Crawley, Harlow, Hatfield, Hemel Hempstead, Stevenage and Welwyn, which ultimately came to have a total population of half a million. Some were not entirely new, for Basildon and Hemel Hempstead were already functioning as small towns with populations of over 20,000. The New Towns have, on the whole, proved to be successful. Each was planned as a self-contained community but they are not necessarily of the same pattern because of the geographical site factors. (See Fig. 13.4, page 161).

Other existing towns were selected for expansion, e.g. Ashford, Andover, Buckingham, Bedford, Luton, Hitchin and Bury St. Edmunds. It was intended that these 'expanded towns' would sprout new industries as well as absorb people; while this has frequently happened, many residents continue to commute over long distances to London. (Fig. 19.2).

Housing, Land Shortages and Land-use

Pressure on land resources for houses, offices, shops, industry and transport facilities is common to all great cities in the world. Competition for urban land, e.g. by large department stores, office blocks, markets, and factories, tends to sort itself out in economic terms because of differential land prices (explained in terms of bid rent in Chapter 12). For example, a large department store is prepared to pay a higher price than other users for the privilege of having an accessible and desirable city centre site, whereas a manufacturing firm which does not require accessibility to urban shoppers would be prepared to locate itself away from the town centre, where land prices or rents and rates are considerably lower. When it comes to housing, however, this is not nearly so true, for its provision must take into consideration social as well as economic factors; lower paid workers cannot, for instance, afford to live far from their

Fig. 19.3a Housing contrasts in London. North of Docklands, the 19th century row houses of Plaistow typify working class housing susceptible to redevelopment and rehabilitation

place of work because of high commuting costs. In a place like London many jobs are in or near the city centre where, of course, land values are high and, as a consequence it becomes almost impossible to provide reasonably priced housing without a large measure of public subsidy.

Pressure on land for new housing in London is acute, although it must be admitted that the magnitude of the housing problem is a matter of debate: the *South-East Study, 1961–81,* suggested a shortfall of around 150,000 houses but, on the other hand, the Greater London Council's Development Plan, 1969, estimated that there was sufficient vacant land in London to provide for over 200,000 new houses. If one takes into consideration slum clearance, the up-grading of decaying dwellings, and the decline in local authority house building, there is probably a need for at least 200,000 new dwellings. It is not likely that London's housing problem will be solved in even the medium term future (Figs. 19.3a and b).

The shortage of domestic dwellings, and perhaps more especially of building land, has had, Keeble (1972) points out, four main effects. First, up to the outbreak of World War II, was the extension of urban sprawl around the edge of the built-up area. Some 85,000 houses a year were built in the 1930s, often in huge estates, which devoured first class farmland. This flood of metropolitan expansion was effectively halted by post-war planning legislation which created a 'green belt'. Secondly, building upwards instead of outwards was initiated and this led to the construction of 'high-rise' blocks of flats and office skyscrapers, particularly in or near central London. Such tall blocks of flats have been shown to be socially undesirable but at least they provided much needed basic accommodation. Thirdly, land values have escalated in recent years, especially when compared with those in other parts of the country. The high cost of house building land in the Greater London Area is one

Fig 19.3b Housing contrasts in London. The Barbican, City of London: Office blocks and high class housing are juxtaposed in this controversial development in the very heart of London

reason why houses are so much more expensive than elsewhere. Another effect has been to stimulate high-rise building at the expense of horizontal unit building. Moreover, because of the scarcity and cost of land, developers, whether they be private or public, are compelled to plan in terms of minimum space requirements. Fourthly, the scarcity and high cost of land has also militated strongly against the provision of such socially desirable developments as schools, hospitals, public open spaces and improved roads (i.e. what is usually called social overhead capital). The result of these trends is that policies aimed at decentralisation now need to be reversed to aid the inner urban area.

London's Transport Systems

The provision and maintenance of transport facilities, in both the public and private sectors, has created another set of acute planning problems. London's public transport system – suburban railway lines, underground and bus services – has been faced with serious and growing problems especially over the past 15 years. There are, perhaps, two fundamental transport problems: the massive *growth in motor-car ownership* and the consequent congestion to which it has given rise. This development to a large extent has become self-defeating, since the vast amount of traffic clogging the highways has slowed down movement in central London, especially at peak periods; and in spite of the introduction of traffic management schemes, it must be admitted that the road network is inadequate to meet the growing volume of traffic. The second main problem relates to the *financial difficulties* facing London's public transport services: the services have to cope with a very marked peak demand between 07·00 and 10·00 hours in the morning and 16·30 and 19·00 hours in the evening, in connection with journeys to work. Accordingly, the public transport systems (rail, underground and buses) have to meet the costs of vehicles, track, equipment and staff which are economically used only during the two peak periods of the day. In order to be viable, constant increases in fares have been imposed, although this has merely encouraged the loss of off-peak traffic to private transport.

A number of attempts have been made to help solve the financial difficulties of London's public

transport system: these include raising fares which are strongly objected to by the travelling public; direct government subsidisation for the period 1968 to 1972, though the subsidy was withdrawn in the latter year; a massive investment in modern equipment in an effort to lure passengers back by providing better services; and a recent suggestion made by London Transport is to offer a 10 per cent discount deal on fares with firms and offices to persuade more employees to travel by bus and tube. It would seem that the fundamental financial problems of London's public transport system cannot be overcome other than by some form of massive subsidisation.

The problem raised by the growth of private road transport in London can, it would seem, be solved only by rapid and radical road improvements, which are far too costly in the present economic climate. Equally, environmentalist concerns can slow down road improvement schemes, as was shown by the opposition to the proposed motorway box round London. Efficient transportation, however, is the lifeblood of any modern economy and the planners must address themselves to this most serious problem regardless of cost and disruption; otherwise mobility will just grind to a halt.

London's airports

Another major transport problem relates to London's *airports*. They grew up in a somewhat haphazard way with, at first, Croydon, Hendon and Gatwick, all in the Greater London area, sharing the traffic. It was not until 1946, after the war, that Heathrow (an R.A.F. station) and Northolt were taken over for civil flying. In 1954 traffic was finally transferred to Heathrow which was re-named London Airport. Not only has its passenger traffic increased enormously – to more than 23 million annually – but it now ranks, in terms of the value of goods passing through, as the first 'port' in Britain, with a bulk trade of 3,500,000,000 tonnes in 1976–77. The problem of road traffic congestion, and the estimates that the volume of its passenger traffic may rise to 30–40 million a year, have focused attention upon the need for a third London airport. Several alternative possibilites were considered including Stansted, Cublington and Maplin (on the island of Foulness off the Essex Coast). The selection of

Fig 19.4 Tilbury container port. The spacious layout of the downstream site contrasts with the congested conditions of Dockland further west

Maplin was abandoned for financial reasons in 1974; in August 1979 the Government announced its decision that Stansted airport was to become the third London airport.

The Port of London

A brief reference to the Port of London has already been made in Chapter 11. As London grew in importance during the nineteenth century, increased facilities were required to overcome the growing congestion on the wharf-lined river, and a series of docks were built which were gradually extended further and further downstream, with a series of increasingly large dock basins. The docks tended to specialise in the types of cargo they handled. Since World War II great changes have taken place: the Older docks – the London, St. Katherine, Surrey Commercial, and East India docks – all of which were constructed in the early part of the nineteenth century, have now been closed while the Tilbury complex, 24 km downstream, has been greatly extended and has the largest container docks in the country (Fig. 19.4).

The amount of business that the Port of London is now doing has fallen severely and it now accounts for only 17·5 per cent of the total national trade. Once Britain's biggest port, it is now struggling for its life and is operating at a heavy financial loss – £16 m in 1978. Its problems and difficulties reflect in large measure the industrial decline of Britain in recent years. Without doubt many of its difficulties arise from changes in world trading conditions, but many more arise from conditions in the docks themselves and a bad record of industrial relations. In consequence the long-term future of the Port of London is not bright. It is clear that under changing world conditions, efficient operation is essential and the Port of London Authority cannot rely on a high rate of subsidisation.

The London Docklands

An important consequence of the closure of so great a part of the London docks has been the need to redevelop an extensive tract of inner London, mainly on the north bank of the Thames, covering 2,200 ha and stretching from Tower Bridge to Barking Creek. The London Docklands contained not only docks, but waterside industry, extensive gas manufacturing plant, and housing for the workforce (Fig. 19.5). Since 1945 not only has employment in the docks contracted severely, but also employment in manufacturing industry. Obsolete plant, and little room for redevelopment or expansion, has caused either the closure of many firms or their movement out of the area. Unfortunately, the application of regional policy has until recently prevented industrial regeneration in the South-East, so that the Docklands area has faced in an acute fashion the problems of the inner city referred to in Chapter 12.

In an attempt to remedy this situation, and to plan and co-ordinate the development of what must be one of the most attractive industrial zones in the whole country, a special Docklands Joint Committee has been created. This is composed of representatives of the G.L.C., the London Boroughs of Tower Hamlets, Newham, Southwark, Lewisham and Greenwich, and the D.O.E. Following the publication of the London Docklands Strategic Plan (1976), improvements have been set under way for transport, housing, environmental quality, and industrial development.

The meandering of the Thames makes communications within Docklands very difficult. The area has been poorly served by public transport, and road congestion is particularly acute. Under the plan, rail services are being enhanced by

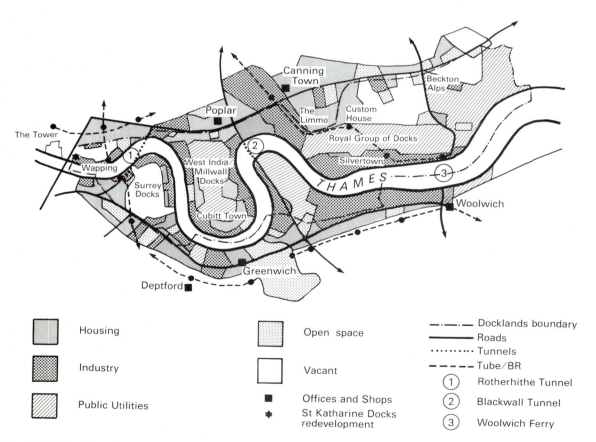

Fig 19.5 The London Docklands

improvements to the East London, North Woolwich and (eventually) the Jubilee line. While major improvements to the A 13, and a new tunnel under the Thames between Beckton and Thamesmead will take longer to materialise, a number of smaller improvements to the existing road network have already been approved for completion by 1985.

The 55,000 inhabitants of Docklands currently occupy 19,000 housing units. Almost one-third of these units need replacement or rehabilitation, but the Strategic Plan envisages the building of 23,000 dwellings, which will provide for a doubling of the present population. It is intended to up-grade shopping and community facilities accordingly, and provide a further 140 ha of public open space. Provision of advance factories has been rapid, with almost 40,000 m² being provided by 1980, and the Docklands area is being vigorously promoted in the E.E.C. and in Japan. As Beard (1979) has pointed out, the estimated cost of developing Docklands (£2,000 million at 1976 prices) is formidable. Such a sum is viewed with alarm by peripheral regions, yet the country as a whole cannot afford to lose the prime potential of such a location.

Water Supply

The country's water budget was described in Chapter 3 and attention was drawn to the fact that the south-eastern part of England was likely to suffer water shortages in the future. At the beginning of this chapter reference was made to the 17 million people living in the South-East Region and to its economic growth. This demographic and economic expansion, together with the improvement in social conditions, is bound to put stresses and strains upon the region's water resources. Higher standards of living require some 300 litres per capita per day and, as this water demand increases, so will the domestic supply need to be increased; municipal needs will also grow to meet the needs of waste disposal, street cleansing, fire-fighting services, etc.; agriculture is likely to require increased amounts for irrigation purposes; and industry will demand more water both in processing and as a cooling agent. It would seem there will be no escape from the need to find greatly increased volumes of water.

At present London's water supply is provided by three main sources: (i) Deep artesian wells which tap the Chalk aquifer beneath the overlying clay. Although the yield is declining as a result of the increasing demand, the artesian bores supply about 10 per cent of the total needs. (ii) The Thames itself, upstream from London, the abstracted water being filtered and stored in large reservoirs such as the four at Staines and the four near Walton-on-Thames. (iii) The string of reservoirs in the Lea Valley which stretch all the way from Waltham Abbey to Walthamstow. Gregory (1974) writes, "the predicted population expansion indicates a potential deficiency of some 5,000 million litres (1,100 million gallons) per day by the end of the present century." How, it may be asked, is this deficiency to be made good? The more immediate solution is to exploit further the two principal sources of supply – the groundwater resources and surface storage in reservoirs. The Thames Water Authority plan to meet half the deficiency from groundwater sources beneath the Chalk and pump it into the Thames, from which it would be directly abstracted. In the long term, however, it may be necessary to import water from outside the region, transferring more water from river to river by a measure of environmental engineering. Such a scheme is already in operation – from the Ouse to the Colne. Yet another possibility is to adopt desalinisation if sufficiently economic methods could be adopted.

Tourism

The growth of the overseas tourist trade to Britain grew from six and three-quarter million in 1970 to twelve million in 1977, Jubilee Year. The majority of overseas tourists visit London during their stay in the U.K.: often they visit nowhere else. It was estimated that Britain earned £3,000 million in foreign exchange from tourism in 1977, of which around £2,400 million was spent within the country and some £600 million on fares to Britain. This meant that Britain was earning the equivalent of £8 million a day from overseas visitors. It will be clear that many sections of the community benefit from this injection of additional wealth that foreign tourism brings; moreover, if we take into consideration the multiplier effect of this expenditure, then the value of foreign tourism to the country is much greater.

Major disadvantages include the fact that, especially during the summer holiday season, too many crowd into London. One complaint is that the great numbers of visitors emphasise an already existing congestion and lead to increases in prices. It is doubtful whether the latter complaint can really be substantiated and probably life would be more expensive without the tourists. The chief disadvantages are above all the problems of congestion, accomodation shortages, employment and conservation. The great influx of tourists in summer exacerbates congestion on the capital's thoroughfares and underground system. A more serious objection to the growth of London as a tourist centre is that houses and flats in the centre of the city are frequently turned into hotels, thereby aggravating the already acute housing situation. A further complaint is that the tourist industry especially its hotel and catering side, employs large numbers of foreigners who compete with the indigenous population for jobs and accommodation. Such foreign labour, while enjoying all the social benefits of our national social security system, sends a high proportion of its earnings back home as remittances. Another disadvantage is that native provincial visitors to London find it difficult to secure accommodation in town because accommodation has been booked by, or for, foreign tourists. Another important issue is the problem of conservation, since the flood of summer tourists means that London's ancient buildings, historical monuments, parks and other places of interest must bear the impact (in terms of wear and tear, litter, disfiguration, vandalism, etc.) of the tourist. Finally, the greater the influx of foreign tourists, the greater the inconvenience and loss of amenity and facilities for those resident in London.

The Outer South-East

Sir Patrick Abercrombie's Greater London Plan (1945) and the Greater London Council Plan (1969), though differing very significantly in both their data and approach, had one important feature in common: they agreed that neither Greater London nor the rest of the South-East region could be planned in isolation but should be the subject of joint comprehensive planning. Both saw the whole of the South-East as, essentially, a single functional region. As Keeble (1972) remarks, the "various formally dissimilar parts – the built-up areas of Greater London, the surrounding commuter towns, the rural areas of Kent, Hampshire, Berkshire, Essex, the south coast ports – are initimately linked by regular if not daily flows of people, goods and information". Nevertheless, there is variation within the South-East. Taking the region as a whole, although the boundary between the Outer Metropolitan Area and the Outer South-East is more or less arbitrary, towns in the Outer South-East tend to be rather larger, and to have a greater measure of independence, e.g. Colchester, Southampton, Bournemouth and Oxford. These urban centres are separated by appreciable rural tracts in which agriculture is significant. Towns along the coast from Poole to Folkestone have developed important interests in tourism and recreation, and have become significant centres of retirement migration.

The apparently relentless spread of development outwards from London has been admitted by successive policy statements since the Abercrombie Report. In 1970 the publication of the *Strategy for the South-East* envisaged rapid expansion on the fringes of the Outer Metropolitan Area, and even beyond (Fig. 19.6). In contrast to the major and medium growth areas, development was to be restrained to protect open country in areas of high agricultural or environmental value. At the time the Strategy was drawn up, there was every indication of vigorous growth, particularly in the Southampton-Portsmouth area. Over the 1960s this had emerged as the fastest growing sub-region in the country, and indeed the 1970 White Paper on local government reform suggested that the area should be designated a Metropolitan County. Succeeding years, however, have proved that the growth projections for the South-East were exaggerated. A subsequent review of the Strategy, published in 1976, highlighted some of the changes that had taken place:

(i) Resources for development in the public sector were less available;
(ii) Population was likely to remain stable at 17 millions (or possibly even decline slightly);
(iii) Household composition had changed markedly in favour of small households of one or two persons.

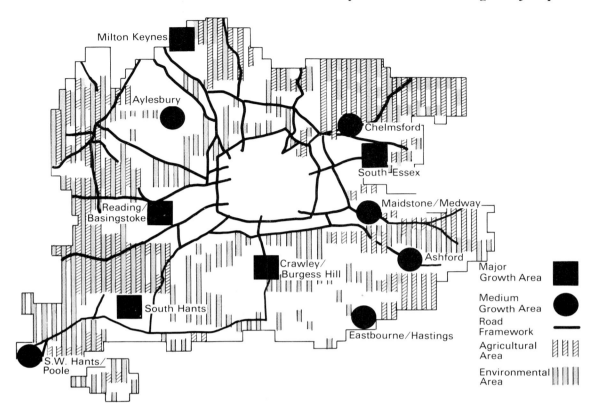

Fig 19.6 Main Spatial aspects of the Strategic Plan for the South-East, as approved in 1971

In view of these changes, the commitment to growth has been reviewed, and it is now expected that only the S. Hants., Crawley and S. Essex growth areas will come anywhere near their expected level of expansion.

It is interesting to note in the review the comment that, though the economy of the South-East is healthy by comparison with the rest of Britain, it is mediocre by comparison with some other regions in the E.E.C. We have described the Metropolitan Core Area as containing regions of expansion, but such a term is only relative. The South-East has significant long-term problems. It is by no means self-sufficient in energy; the growth in the tertiary sector which fuelled its recent expansion is not likely to continue; and the need to sustain an adequate level of economic and social well-being in the inner Metropolitan Area must divert development from other parts of the region. This will reverse the outward flow of recent years, and there is no doubt that policies based upon confident expectation have now been replaced by ones of cautious flexibility.

EAST ANGLIA

The East Anglian economic planning region is a rather different area from that traditionally known as East Anglia. Historically, East Anglia was separated from the rest of the English Plain by the marshy flatlands in the north-west and the forest belt in the south-west, and this relative isolation helped to give the region a distinctive identity of its own. Today, although the region has no well-defined boundary on the landward side, there is no escaping the fact that East Anglia has a geographical character and personality which puts it apart. The recognition that East Anglia had an individual character led to its separation from the

239

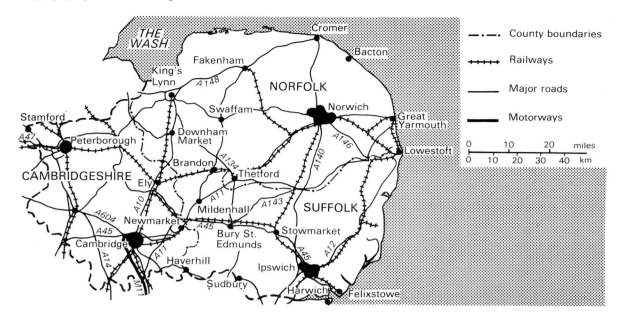

Fig 19.7 East Anglia—major towns and communications

area contained in the South-East Study 1961–81 (Fig. 19.7). Nevertheless, the region lacks homogeneity and is subject to strong external influences from the south, and Thomas has referred to, "the split personality of the region".

Physically East Anglia is a region of subdued relief, for even the Chalk of the East Anglian Heights, which forms the backbone of the area, does not rise to more than 120 metres (400 feet). The lower-lying areas to the west and east of the Chalk uplands are lower Jurassic beds and Quaternary deposits respectively. But it is not so much the solid geology or variations in elevation that give regional variety in East Anglia: rather it is the occurrence of superficial deposits that are significant in producing sub-regional differences and distinctiveness. Over much of East Anglia, regional diversity arises from differences in the character of the deposits of glacial drift: for example, in the central part of the region, High Norfolk and High Suffolk, medium to heavy boulder clay occurs interspersed with gravels and brick-earth. In the north and north-west is an area of gravelly and sandy drift called the 'Good Sands' region. In the north-east is an area of glacial loams giving light, easily worked and generally very fertile soils. In the south-east coastal belt, the area known as the

East Suffolk Sandlings, are gravels, sands and loams which yield light soils. In the centre-west (the Little Ouse basin) is a highly distinctive area known as the Breckland, where a thin deposit of sand lies on top of the Chalk to give an extensive area of dry heath; and, finally, in the extreme north is the Cromer Ridge, an end moraine 24 km (15 miles) in length, averaging 7 to 9 km in width, and over 60 metres (200 feet) in elevation. (Fig. 19.8).

Apart from the above areas which owe their differences largely to glacial drift deposits, there are five other regions having a peripheral distribution: the Chalk Downland in the south-west; the Fenland, of which two parts can be recognised – the silt fen near the coast and the peat fen further inland; the Greensand Belt lying east of the silt fen, which has produced broken hill country; the alluvial coastal plain of north Norfolk; and the Norfolk Broads in the east, where large-scale peat working in medieval times created shallow hollows which subsequently became inundated to provide a maze of inland waterways.

Climatically this is the most 'continental' part of Britain with its cold winters, relatively warm summers, low precipitation and a rather high amount of sunshine. With mean July temperatures

240

Table 29: East Anglia statistical data, 1978

	CAMBS.	NORFOLK	SUFFOLK	TOTAL EAST ANGLIA
Area (km²)	3,404	5,368	3,797	12,576
Persons per km²	165·8	125·7	155·0	145·4
Agricultural area	2,896	4,205	3,050	10,157
Total population (in '000s)	564·3	674·7	588·4	1,827·4
Live births (per '000 pop.)	12·3	11·7	11·9	11·8
Deaths (per '000 pop.)	9·6	12·2	11·0	11·0
Employees in employment (in '000s)	210·1	246·0	213·3	669·5
Percentage employed in:				
1. agriculture, forestry and fishing	6·7	7·7	5·7	6·4
2. manufacturing	27·8	28·9	31·7	29·2
3. construction	6·4	6·7	6·2	6·5
4. gas, electricity, water	1·4	1·7	2·4	1·8
5. service industries	58·3	55·5	54·5	56·1
Numbers unemployed, July 1978 (in '000s)	10·4	15·4	11·1	37·1
Unemployment rates percentage	4·8	6·0	5·0	5·3
Car and van licences (per '000 pop.)	294	303	289	295

Source: *Regional Statistics*, 1979

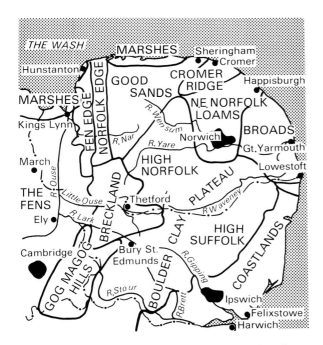

Fig 19.8 Agricultural regions of East Anglia

rising above 15·5° C and the January mean falling below 3·5° C, giving annual ranges of 12° C or more, this is the most extreme part of Britain. In winter and early spring there is a marked tendency for East Anglia to come under the influences of continental high pressure conditions which give rise to cold and bitter east winds. While spring is often delayed, the winter frosts are helpful for they break up the soil in readiness for ploughing. Precipitation is low, between 500 and 630 mm, with a slight summer maximum. The late winter and early spring months are normally noticeably dry, but early summer brings convectional showers; both conditions contribute greatly to successful grain cultivation. October is characteristically the wettest month. The mean daily average of sunshine is 4·5 hours, although the eastern coast south of Great Yarmouth exceeds this. During the summer months the average daily total of sunshine is 6 hours.

Agriculture

The visitor to East Anglia is immediately struck by the evident agricultural prosperity of the region. The beginnings of this agricultural prosperity go back to medieval times when sheep raising became important and East Anglia became famous for its production of raw wool. Upon this wool there developed a famous late medieval textile industry whose prosperity is reflected in the very fine churches of the market towns and villages. Similarly, it was not inappropriate that the Agrarian Revolution should have at least some of its roots in East Anglia and nearby areas during the eighteenth century.

Although the fortunes in farming have varied over the past two hundred years, tillage has always been important and more than half of the region is under arable. The Fenland excepted, this is the most highly tilled region in Britain today and around 6·5 per cent of the workforce is employed in agriculture, a proportion much above the national average. Over the western parts of East Anglia large farms with large fields are characteristic. In more recent times hedges have been quite ruthlessly uprooted to create enlarged fields which offer opportunities for mechanised working matched nowhere else in Britain. Unfortunately, the destruction of the hedgerows has led to a measure of soil erosion – sometimes serious – by wind action.

East Anglia's agriculture makes a vital contribution to the nation's food supplies for it has about one-fifth of the area devoted nationally to barley, wheat and potatoes, half of the total sugar-beet acreage, and about a quarter of the fruit and vegetable acreage. Grain is the most extensive crop, for about one-third of all the arable land in East Anglia is under barley (grown mainly for malting and as an animal feedstuff), wheat which covers about one-fifth of the area, and oats which are also commonly cultivated. Although potatoes, vegetables, orchard fruits and small fruits are fairly widely distributed, there is an emphatic concentration in the Fenland area, in North Norfolk and in the south-east where proximity to London has encouraged intensive cultivation. The area under pasture is relatively small, hence the number of cattle is not large and that of sheep is very low indeed. In contrast, pigs are fairly numerous, there being nearly half a million of them. Poultry, reared for eggs and as table birds, are also numerous.

Industry

Until the Industrial Revolution, East Anglia was the most important manufacturing region in Britain. Its lack of energy resources, however, led to its eclipse by the coal-rich industrial districts of the Midlands and the north of England, and it is only recently that local industry has shown much vigour. A great proportion of local industry is associated with *food processing* but, apart from some larger concerns such as Reckitt & Colman and Birds Eye, most of the firms are small. Typical are such activities as flour-milling, malting, brewing, sugar-refining, fruit and vegetable canning. Flour-milling is widely spread and found in all the larger centres. Barley is the basis of the malting industry which at one time was found in most East Anglian towns. The processing has become mechanised with the result that the smaller malting houses are gradually closing down. The introduction of sugar-beet cultivation in the region in 1913 has given rise to a seasonal processing industry and there are factories at King's Lynn, Ely, Bury St. Edmunds and Ipswich.

Engineering is the most important industry. Though closely associated with the production of agricultural machinery, it has gradually widened its range of products. The old-established firm of Ransome in Ipswich became one of the largest companies in the country manufacturing all kinds of farm and horticultural machinery. Engineering is also a notable industry in Norwich. In addition the manufacture of metal fencing and wire netting, has developed in response to the needs of local farms, and two Norwich firms now produce about half the entire U.K. output.

With the decline of the textile industry in Norwich, the city turned to the manufacture of footwear in which there was a remarkable expansion and until recently the industry employed around 9,000 people in about a couple of dozen factories. Cheap foreign competition has seriously affected the industry during the past few years, there have been cutbacks in production and many firms have had to close down. The coming of motor transport and the electricity grid fostered a wider development of industry in the region and some towns have developed newer industries: e.g. photographic equipment at Colchester, electric equipment at Chelmsford, the working of synthetic fibres at Braintree, and the manufacture of fertilisers and cement at Harwich.

Since agricultural employment in East Anglia has always been much above the national average, the unemployment and distress caused by mechanisation has been correspondingly severe, with North Norfolk suffering most. The food processing industries are principally employers of female labour, so that the main shortage of jobs is for men. Accordingly, there is a need for more industry, especially labour-intensive industry, which would help to reduce male unemployment.

Tourism

Each year East Anglia attracts some 10 million visitors who spend around £100 million. They do not all confine themselves to the coastal resorts, for many of the larger towns such as Norwich, Cambridge, Ely and Bury St. Edmunds, and many of the smaller picturesque towns and villages, such as Kersey, Lavenham, and Long Melford, attract numerous visitors, who in summer stretch accommodation beyond the limit. The coast and the Broads, however, are the major attractions, at least in terms of numbers. Of the coastal resorts Yarmouth is the most important, attracting about half a million visitors a year, but

Fig 19.9 Boats at Sutton Staithes, on the Norfolk Broads. Generally, the Broads in high season are highly congested—an example of a facility which is becoming over-exploited

there are numerous small resorts such as Hunstanton, Sheringham, Cromer, Southwold and Aldeburgh.

A specialised aspect of the tourist trade is sailing and cruising on the Broads. The Broads comprise some 320 km (200 miles) of intercommunicating inland waterways based upon the rivers Waveney, Yare, Bure, Ant and Thurne, although many of the channels and wide stretches of shallow water are the handiwork of man – the outcome of the excavation of peat in earlier times. Large numbers of holiday-makers come to the Broads every year – in some seasons the Lowestoft-based firm of Hoseasons has no fewer than 250,000 customers for its Broads fleet, and its riverside and seaside bungalows – and the region's popularity grows annually (Fig. 19.9). There are some 2,000 cabin-hire craft and 8,000 privately owned boats. The increasing popularity of Broadland is creating an environmental problem, for the area's space, beauty, peace and quiet, and wildlife are being threatened.

The real threat to this unique area, however, probably comes less from the accelerating numbers of visitors and craft as from the insidious side-effects of the use of the waterways, e.g. power-driven craft churn up the bottom mud which kills off fish and steadily chokes the vegetation which provides a habitat for wildlife. Meanwhile, spillage of oil and other pollutants poisons the water, to the detriment of fish and fowl alike, along with the drainage of massive amounts of fertiliser from the surrounding arable lands. In an attempt to meet the dilemma of overcrowding, it has been suggested that the Broads should be enlarged by the reopening of 40 km (25 miles) of abandoned waterway; this would not only ease the congestion elsewhere on the Broads but would bring the tourist trade to Aylsham, Bungay and North Walsham. Closer supervision of casual private boat-owners and perhaps the banning of certain types of undesirable water craft should be considered, for it is important that the livelihood of the local people should be protected since they largely depend upon the £10 million or so spent by holiday-makers. Tourism has brought a substantial measure of prosperity to an area which half a century ago was one of great poverty, but has also helped to generate a need for co-ordinated planning and development for the Broads. This need was met in 1978 by the formation of the Broads Authority.

Transport

One of the most serious problems facing East Anglia is the lack of an adequate communications infrastructure. This is particularly apparent during the holiday season when traffic throngs the roads and has to compete with commercial carriers on an inadequate road system. There are poor road (and railway) links in the region and heavy commercial vehicles are obliged to use sub-standard highways in the absence of an adequate trunk road system. Plans for the region, embodied in the so-called 'Strategy Network' of trunk routes, look extensive on paper but are slow in being implemented. Until recently the main activity involved by-passing towns to relieve the centres of heavy commercial traffic. However, the M 11 – the region's first motorway – on completion will link up with other major routes to facilitate rapid traffic movement to the coastal areas.

East Anglia has the highest car ownership per head of population of any region in Britain, but this is from necessity rather than indulgence and even then there are many who cannot afford personal transport. Ordinary working people have a daily problem of travelling by a completely inadequate public transport system. Thirty or so years ago, when the population was more especially based on agriculture and was comparatively static living in self-contained communities, buses and local trains were reasonably good. But with the drastic cuts in the train services and the reduction in bus services, human mobility was also reduced and unemployment exacerbated. Many former farm labourers, who would be prepared to commute to employment, are unable to do so unless they are car owners.

Following the transport economies suggested by Beeching in 1963, savage cuts were made in the East Anglian railways and now there are only two main north-south lines in the region. The railway links between London and major centres such as Ipswich and Norwich are good though they fall short of the standard usually set by British Rail's main inter-city services. The other line runs from London via Bishop's Stortford to Cambridge, from whence it continues northwards via Ely to King's Lynn. Cross country travel is difficult and the closure of so many railway lines has left many communities isolated from the towns.

Regional development necessitates good communications for the movement of both people and goods, but there seems to be a lack of any integrated transport plan in the region. Many communities are isolated, industrial development has hitherto been inhibited by the inadequate road system, and East Anglian ports do not function as well as they might since the journeys from the industrial Midlands to the coast are slow and difficult. It is not surprising that the overall transport provisions are a matter of great dissatisfaction to local authorities, industrialists and businessmen. The urgency of the problem was recognised by the Government when the Norfolk County Structure Plan (1979) was criticised for a lack of a comprehensive programme for communications (though its other proposals for increased industrial employment and better housing were applauded).

The Future

Agriculture has long provided the mainstay of the East Anglian economy and played a dominant role in the region's prosperity, and in the provision of employment. It seems likely that farming will continue to be of vital importance, although it will require less labour as the industry continues to mechanise and modernise. There is thus a need for an increasing amount of industrial employment to make good the agricultural wastage. Although local politicians, public servants and businessmen have appreciated the necessity of an injection from industry, industrial development has fallen short of what is needed for a variety of reasons. First, the region has been loath to develop heavy industry since this would be likely to disfigure the countryside. Secondly, increased tourism development, for which the region is well suited, is often considered to be in conflict with agriculture. However, this is not necessarily so and it should be considered as merely another facet of the economy bringing money and employment to the area. Thirdly, industrial development has been handicapped and held back by the inadequate transport infrastructure, although much small industrial development has taken place recently. Fourthly, because of the dominance historically of agriculture, labour has a restricted range of skills to offer and this, no doubt, has militated against the development of a more varied economy and especially of jobs for the male population.

THE EAST MIDLANDS

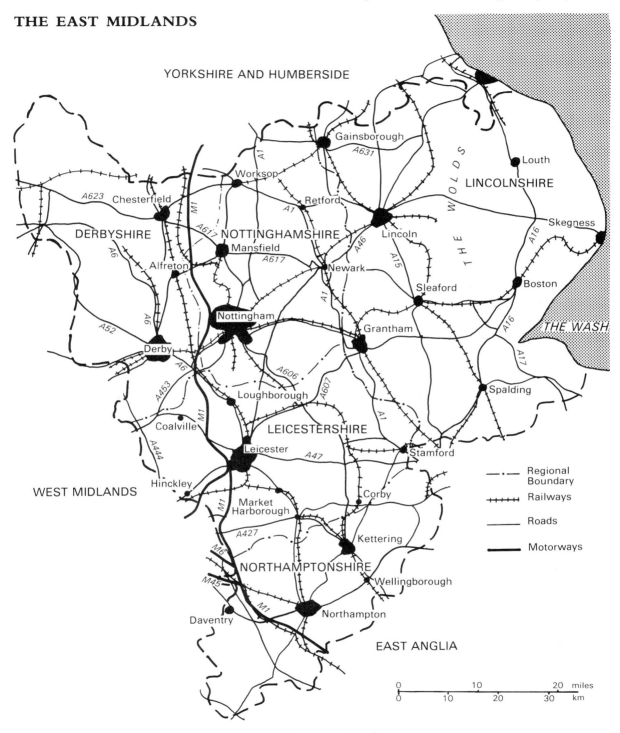

Fig 19.10 East Midlands—major towns and communications

The East Midlands economic planning region comprises, for the most part, the eastern portion of the Midlands Plain with a part of the Jurassic uplands and, beyond, the lowland parts of South Lincolnshire (Fig. 19.10). Although the term Midlands Plain is often used, it is something of a misnomer for it is by no means all flat and featureless: in the East Midlands, between the Rivers Tame and Soar, the hills of Charnwood Forest rise up to 274 metres (900 feet), while to the south-east are the Northamptonshire Uplands. The Midland Triangle as a whole is largely underlain by rocks of Permo-Triassic Age, notably New Red Sandstone and Lower Lias rocks. However, in the East Midlands, ancient volcanic rocks have broken through the Permo-Trias to produce Charnwood Forest, while in the south-east are clays and clayey limestones of the Lower Lias which belongs to the Jurassic, and in the basin of the Soar are extensive deposits of boulder clay. Clearly, therefore, both geologically and topographically, there is a considerable measure of internal physical diversity within the East Midlands.

In part because of this internal physical diversity but also because of powerful influences outside the limits of the region – the metropolitan influence in the south, that of Birmingham to the west, and of Sheffield in the north – the East Midlands region is somewhat lacking in coherence. However, the region has certain advantages which help to counteract this disadvantage; these are:

(i) its central location in England lying astride major national communications routes: the M1, the A1, and major north-south railway lines;

(ii) its diversity of resources which include high quality agricultural land, ample water supplies, coal, iron ore, limestone, sand, gravel and fireclay, and other raw materials to support extractive industries;

(iii) its broadly based economy, including a varied and prosperous agriculture, and a wide variety of industries ranging from engineering and electronics to textiles, hosiery, footwear and leather goods;

(iv) its fairly evenly spread urban settlements of moderate to small size, with no single city large enough to dominate the whole region, as does Birmingham in the West Midlands;

(v) its spatial environment variety and diversity, and wealth of resources, offer considerable opportunities for future developments in the region.

Agriculture

Farming varies considerably between the different sub-regions of the East Midlands. Fertile soils are located on the Eastern Lowlands, on the good quality land of the Midland Plain and on the dip slopes of the Jurassic and Magnesian Limestone outcrops; the poorer land is associated with the Millstone Grit, the Coal Measures, the thin, gravelly soils of the Bunter Sandstones (clearly reflected in the presence of Sherwood Forest), and Charnwood Forest. As a result of these differences, three main contrasting areas are recognisable: intensive arable cultivation with horticulture in the north-east and east (Nottinghamshire and southern Lincolnshire), mixed arable and livestock rearing in the south (Leicestershire and Northamptonshire), and dairying with pigs and poultry in the north-west (Derbyshire and Nottinghamshire).

A high proportion – some three-quarters – of the land in the East Midlands region is agricultural: this amounts to 10 per cent of the agricultural land of England and Wales. Substantial quantities of cash crops, chiefly wheat, potatoes, sugar-beet and green vegetables, are produced and, in fact, the region has some 15 per cent of the total acreage given over to these crops in England and Wales. The low rainfall and high amount of sunshine favour intensive crop growing in Lincolnshire where some 80 per cent of the farmland is under arable, especially wheat on the clay soils and barley on the lighter soils. It is worthy of note that it is in the Eastern Lowlands that agriculture is most significant in terms of employment. In addition to the chief cash crops mentioned above, an element of diversity is introduced into the characteristic farming pattern by the production of flowers, bulbs, soft fruits and specialised vegetable crops. For example, bulb growing and flower culture are produced on the light soils in the vicinity of Spalding; early potatoes are grown near Boston; and carrots are cultivated near Newark.

In the north-west and west, i.e. Derbyshire, Nottinghamshire and Leicestershire, dairying is the main farming activity and is often accompanied by poultry rearing, notably in Nottingham-

Table 30:   East Midlands statistical data, 1978

	DERBY	LEICS.	LINCOLN	NORTHANTS.	NOTTS.	TOTAL E. MIDLANDS
Area (km²)	2,631	2,553	5,915	2,367	2,164	15,630
Persons per km²	340·7	326·2	89·6	217·1	450·1	239·7
Agricultural area (km²)	1,911	1,997	5,174	1,913	1,535	12,530
Total population ('000s)	896·5	832·7	529·8	513·8	974·1	3,746·9
Live births (per '000 pop.)	11·3	12·8	11·5	12·8	11·4	11·9
Deaths (per '000 pop.)	12·3	10·4	12·1	10·5	11·0	11·3
Employees in employment (in '000s)	360·2	345·4	184·1	197·8	409·2	1,496·8
Percentage employed in:						
1. agriculture, forestry and fishing	1·2	1·1	10·4	1·6	1·2	2·4
2. engineering and allied industries	21·7	17·2	13·1	18·1	12·5	16·6
3. other manufacturing	22·6	28·2	13·9	24·8	20·7	22·6
4. construction	5·3	4·9	6·2	4·6	5·3	5·2
5. mining, gas. electricity, water	6·6	4·1	1·6	1·3	12·8	6·4
6. service industries	42·6	44·6	54·8	49·5	47·5	46·8
Numbers unemployed July 1978 (in '000s)	20·6	18·2	13·2	10·7	26·2	88·5
Unemployment rates (percentage)	5·3	5·4	6·8	5·2	5·6	5·6
Car and van licences (per '000 pop.)	197	261	289	254	251	246

Source: *Regional Statistics*, 1979

shire which is the leading producer of poultry in the Midlands. Milk production also led to cheese-making, especially in south Nottinghamshire and north Leicestershire, where stilton was produced. Although no longer dependent upon local supplies of milk, there are many dairies, especially in the Vale of Belvoir. Stilton cheese is now mostly factory-made at Melton Mowbray. In southern Leicestershire and north Northamptonshire stock raising, especially the fattening of beef cattle and sheep, is the chief enterprise.

The varied pattern of land use has given rise to a number of agricultural industries as, for example, cheese-making at Melton Mowbray, food processing at Boston and Wisbech, the making of potato crisps at Lincoln, and the refining of sugar-beet.

Industry

In discussing the industrial character of the East Midlands region two important points may be made: the first, and perhaps the most striking feature, is the wide variety of its extractive and manufacturing industries; the second, is the concentration of the heavy industrial zone roughly astride the M 1 in the western half of the region.

The variety of industries stem to a large extent from the diversity of its raw materials – coal, iron ore, limestone, gravel, fireclay, leather, etc. Notwithstanding a drop in coal production and a decrease in the number of miners, the region continues to be responsible for about one quarter of the national coal output. There are two coalfields: the Derbyshire and Nottinghamshire field which extends from Chesterfield to the Trent, and the much smaller Leicester field which flanks Charnwood Forest. Although the western collieries of the Derbyshire and Nottinghamshire field are largely exhausted there are large reserves in the concealed field and two new collieries have been opened, Cotgrave colliery (1964) and Bevercotes (1965) a fully automated colliery. In the eastern basin of the Leicester field, thick seams lie close to the surface but the coal is rather low grade; even so, it is being increasingly worked in modern mines around Coalville. Mention must also be made of the new coal deposits discovered in the Vale of Belvoir but their exploitation is opposed by the local farming fraternity and environmental preservationists, for the Vale is an area of great natural beauty (Fig. 19.11).

With the gradual exhaustion of Britain's iron ore deposits, increasing attention has been paid to

Fig. 19.11 Vale of Belvoir, Leicestershire. Local conservationists have felt strongly that such tranquil beauty will be destroyed by the development of coal mining in the neighbourhood

the low grade iron ore of the Inferior Oolite of the Jurassic rocks. The Northamptonshire ironstone contains only about 32 per cent iron and is phosophoric, but it is present in large quantities and can be mined cheaply by open-cast methods. The development of the iron and steel industry in Northamptonshire was a twentieth century development and grew up at Kettering and Wellingborough, and more recently at Corby (although it had two blast furnaces as early as 1914). The East Midlands region produced about 7 per cent of the total British production of pig iron and some 4 per cent of the steel, chiefly in the form of steel strip and steel tubes. Under the plans for reorganisation in the British steel industry, steel-making at Corby is to cease. This has had a profound effect upon the town, which was specifically enlarged to cater for the steel works, and populated by workers deliberately drawn from contracting regions (particularly Scotland).

There are various branches of the engineering industry which is widely spread throughout the region. Agricultural machinery is made at Newark, Grantham, Lincoln and Derby; constructional machinery at Grantham, Lincoln and Leicester; hosiery and textile machinery at Nottingham and Leicester; automobile and aero-engineering at Derby; bicycle manufacture at Nottingham; and bell-founding at Loughborough.

The textile industry has a long history in the East Midlands, and with the importance of sheep and the woollen industry, it existed almost everywhere in medieval times. Cotton manufacturing had appeared by the mid-eighteenth century in Derbyshire and Nottinghamshire; mills existed throughout the valley of the Derwent as far north as Edale, and in a belt from Hucknall to Worksop. The hosiery industry was a domestic one which at first was confined to the area north of Nottingham to Sutton-in-Ashfield; but in the 1870s it became a fully mechanised industry and concentrated itself at Mansfield and Sutton-in-Ashfield on the coalfield. Factory framework knitting is now confined to the small centres of Long Eaton, Ilkeston, and Heanor in the Erewash valley. Lace-making on frames became famous in Nottinghamshire, and when an adapted Jacquard loom was introduced a lace curtain industry developed. A silk industry focused itself on Derby. More recently, when artificial fibres were introduced, Spondon became a centre for rayon goods. Further south, in Leicestershire, hosiery and knitwear goods have become concentrated at Leicester and Hinkley, and about two-thirds of Britain's hosiery factories are now to be found in and around Leicester.

The region claims some 40 per cent of the national footwear industry, located in the southeast at Northampton, Wellingborough, Rushden and Kettering, and in the centre of the region at Leicester, Barwell and Earl Shilton. Low cost imports have eroded the British market for footwear, resulting in the closure of some factories, redundancies in others and widespread short-time working.

Diversity in the East Midlands region has long been a force making for stability, although not all parts have been able to maintain their traditional prosperity. Unemployment in some of the traditional industries, such as footwear, hosiery and lace, has created problems particularly in the smaller specialised towns. But even in the main manufacturing belt of Derby, Nottingham and Leicester there have been difficulties; for example, Nottingham's hosiery industry has been badly affected and Leicester has suffered the closure of Imperial Typewriters and the Stibbe hosiery machinery factory. Nevertheless, because of the wider spread of trades, unemployment figures are less than the national rate. The propects for growth in employment are probably best in engineering and the electrical industries, and in the service industries.

Problems

Authorities generally are agreed that the East Midlands region will enjoy fairly steady economic growth, although it is unlikely to achieve the dynamism which its neighbour the West Midlands enjoyed until its recent economic downturn. It is also anticipated that the East Midlands will continue to increase its share of the country's population. In spite of local difficulties, centred particularly on the hosiery and footwear industries, the economic prospects are reasonably promising. But the region has some problems which require attention.

First, industry tends to be over-concentrated in the western part close to the M 1 – in Nottingham, Derby and Leicester – and in the south in and around Northampton. The Chesterfield-Worksop and the Alfreton-Mansfield areas have been proposed as new growth zones, while some see growth possibilities at Grantham, Newark and Retford along the axis of the railway and the A 1 M. Such developments would help to give a more balanced spread and possibly a greater diversification of industry. Secondly, in many parts of the region there is a substantial element of dereliction to be clearly seen in the coalfield areas, where the iron ores have been extracted by surface mining in south Lincolnshire and Northamptonshire, and where gravel and sand have been excavated, especially in the Trent valley. Much of this spoilt land could, and should, be redeemed. The pressures on the environment and the need for careful physical management is also clearly manifest in the Trent valley, where giant power stations have mushroomed with their heaps of coal, cooling-towers and mesh of transmission lines, to create a depressing landscape.

The lowland areas in the east of the region form a rather neglected rural sub-region in contrast to the urban-industrial zone in the west. The Eastern Lowlands sub-region is characterised by its sparse population, its low density of small, and often dispersed, rural settlements, and by continuing depopulation, although the former Holland County Council made efforts to stabilise the rural economy. Agriculture is the mainstay of the economy of this area, especially in the eastern coastal area. Lincoln and Grantham are the chief centres of manufacturing but further east there is heavy reliance upon primary activities.

THE WEST MIDLANDS

The West Midlands economic planning region comprises the counties of Staffordshire, Shropshire, Hereford and Worcester, and Warwickshire (Fig. 19.12). The West Midlands region has very considerable physiographic variety. The real core of the region is the low plateau, around 122 metres (400 feet) on which Birmingham stands. This is surrounded by a collar of lowland which gives access in the north-east to the Vale of Trent, in the North-west to the Cheshire Plain and in the south-west to the Severn estuary. Beyond this collar of lowland lie upstanding hills: a portion of the southern Pennines in the north; the Wrekin, Long Mynd, the Clee Hills and part of the Black Mountains along the Welsh Marchland zone; and part of the Cotswolds in the south-east. This rather complex physical character denies the region any real geographical unity and there is a dichotomy between the Birmingham

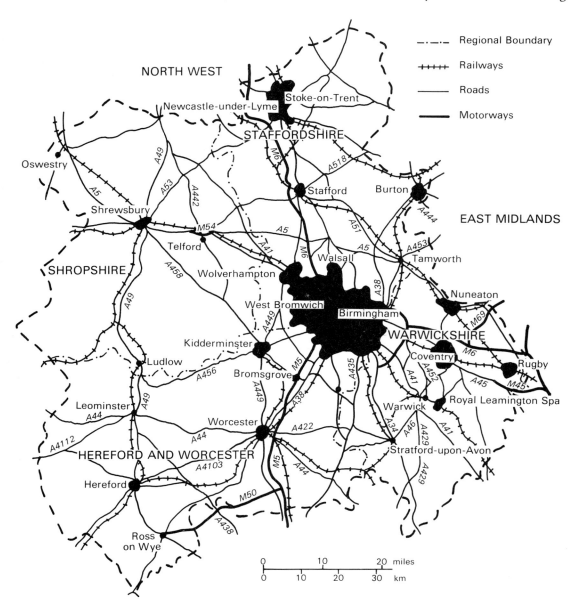

Fig 19.12 West Midlands—major towns and communications

conurbation, the Coventry region and the Potteries on the one hand, and the rural west and south on the other. This gives the West Midlands region, like its neighbour the East Midlands region, a split personality.

In addition there are two further underlying factors we should note. First, the diversity of the physical landscape has had very significant influences: the uplands which in general encircle the region have meant that access to the area has been channelled through the breaks in the surrounding higher land. From the agricultural viewpoint the variety of landforms and soil types has offered a basis for agricultural specialisation, e.g. arable cropping, dairying, fruit-growing, market-gardening, and sheep-rearing. The physical variety, too, provides a wealth of recreational opportunities within a short distance for the urban dwellers of the West Midlands region. Secondly, almost from the start of its industrial growth two spatial factors have been a continuing stimulus to the region's economic development: (i) its central position in England and Wales, making it an excellent centre for the distribution of its varied manufactured products; and (ii) the progressive development of a communications infrastructure

– eighteenth century canals, nineteenth century railways, and twentieth century motorways – which converge in the West Midlands and give it unrivalled inter-regional accessibility. Finally, the West Midlands during the present century, and especially from 1945 up to the energy crisis of 1973, enjoyed vigorous economic development. Growth industries flourished and there has been a relative absence of stagnant or declining activities. However, since the impact of the energy crisis, the West Midlands conurbation in particular has run into difficulties and begun to share the problems which are afflicting the national economy as a whole.

Birmingham and the Black Country

Birmingham (population 1,084,600) the regional capital, lies east of the South Staffordshire Coalfield but is the major manufacturing centre on the plateau. Extending northwards and westwards are Walsall, Wednesbury, Wolverhampton, West Bromwich, Smethwick, Oldbury and Dudley, along with other smaller centres, which collectively form the Black Country. The metal trades

Table 31: West Midlands Statistical Data 1978

	HEREFORD & WORCS.	SHROPS.	STAFFS.	WARWICKS.	WEST MIDLANDS*	TOTAL WEST MIDLANDS.
Area (km²)	3,927	3,490	2,716	1,981	899	13,013
Persons per km²	153·5	103·4	366·0	235·7	3,036·6	396·7
Agricultural area (km²)	3,164	2,867	2,009	1,604	194	9,838
Total population (in '000s)	602·7	360·7	994·0	467·0	2,729·9	5,154·3
Live births (per '000 pop.)	11·6	12·0	11·6	11·2	12·0	11·8
Deaths (per '000 pop.)	10·6	11·0	10·7	10·3	11·0	10·8
Employees in employment (in '000s)	217·2	122·7	372·7	135·5	1,338·0	2,186·1
Percentage in:						
1. agriculture, forestry and fishing	6·0	6·5	1·4	2·4	0·2	1·5
2. engineering and allied industries	19·5	21·7	16·2	26·3	39·5	31·7
3. other manufacturing	15·0	9·2	28·9	9·8	9·1	13·1
4. construction	5·0	6·1	4·8	5·2	4·7	4·9
5. mining, gas, electricity and water	1·7	2·9	6·1	3·4	1·6	2·5
6. service industries	52·9	53·6	42·6	52·9	45·0	46·3
Numbers unemployed, July 1978 ('000s)	13·4	9·9	21·7	9·9	93·2	148·2
Unemployment rates, percentage	6·0	7·6	4·7	n.a.	7·1	6·7
Car and van licences (per '000 pop.)	295	295	251	247	259	263

* Note: this column refers to the metropolitan county.

Source: *Regional Statistics*, 1979

proliferated in this area in the nineteenth century, turning out a wide range of small metal goods including tools, scissors, nuts and bolts, locks and keys, tubes and general ironmongery. Gradually an element of specialisation began to emerge but generally expensive, high-quality, and preferably small items which would meet transport costs were developed, and this kind of product is very characteristic to this day.

Car manufacturing has a long history in the conurbation, although it is concentrated at Birmingham, where are British Leyland and Talbot. The difficulties of the car industry in the wake of the energy crisis has struck at the heart of the West Midland's affluence since its problems have had repercussions for other firms, such as Dunlop, Lucas and Triplex, which are closely associated. Since the car industry is essentially an assembly industry, firms making component parts are necessarily affected by the problems of the motor vehicle firms. Foreign competition and internal disputes have aggravated what was already a very difficult situation and British Leyland, as is well known, has been kept afloat only by the massive injection of public funds.

Rodgers (1972), commenting upon industrial changes in the Black Country towns, has said, "two superimposed patterns of contrast can be seen: the traditional local specialisations in distinctive branches of metal processing, and a manufacturing geography of more recent origin keyed to the degree to which lighter assembly industries have penetrated the sub-region. Traditional interests have died hard in the Black Country". Unfortunately, the older as well as the newer industries have suffered in a period of economic recession, for lower levels of industrial investment affect the demand for the products of the machine tool industry before any other sector. The region really needs lighter industries which would widen the base of its economy.

In the south-west, in Dudley and its surroundings, which is much concerned with the making of machine tools, there is an emphatic traditional industrial structure of numerous small units; in contrast, in the north-west, in Wolverhampton and district, there has been strong progress towards industrial diversity and a much higher proportion of the workers are to be found in larger units.

Birmingham is, by a very considerable lead, the largest town in Britain outside London. A major factor in its growth has been its command of the communications networks since the eighteenth century. Today the city has spread outwards to cover an area of 208 km² (80 sq. miles) and displays fairly well-marked concentric zones. Four main zones may be distinguished: (i) the inner city, including the central business district with its towering office blocks, shopping centres, New Street station and inner ring roads (Fig. 19.13). It is dominated by numerous small firms and workshops mostly concerned with traditional activities, such as the jewellery and gun trades, but also contains various newer light metal-working industries; (ii) the surrounding decaying zone of congested housing and factories in the districts of Highgate, Ladywood, Lee Bank, Nechells Green and Newtown, all of which are now comprehensive development areas undergoing clearance and replanning for new development; (iii) the middle zone, represented by Selly Oak and Strichley, containing old localised industries and characterised by nineteenth century terraced housing; and (iv) an outer zone of vast housing estates which have devoured extensive areas of agricultural land which hitherto surrounded former village settlements.

Beyond the inner factory zone, manufacturing zones radiate outwards along the major lines of communication and it is in these zones that the city's larger factories such as heavy metal working firms, electrical engineering works and the great assembly industries, e.g. car plants, are located. To the south-west, beyond Edgbaston and Moseley, lie the Cadbury works at Bourneville and the huge British Leyland plant at Longbridge. Birmingham, as a major manufacturing centre, a great commercial focus, an important communications hub, and possessing two universities and a cathedral, is incontestably the regional capital of the West Midlands.

The Coventry sub-region

East of the Birmingham plateau, between the upper Tame and the Anker, and extending from Tamworth south-eastwards through Nuneaton as far as Coventry, is the East Warwickshire coalfield. It is concealed except in the north and north-east where a small band of it is exposed. The field covers some 390 km² but the seams have been much broken up and, although thick in the

Fig 19.13 Birmingham city centre. The 19th century civic buildings are top left, the modern Bullring development middle right, and in the foreground can be seen the mixed office and small workshop zone characteristic of the city

north, become thin to the south. Coal output gradually increased from 1900 up to the outbreak of World War II when it reached a peak of 5·8 million tonnes; since then production has declined to around 2 million tonnes. The coal is mostly bituminous and is mainly used locally for domestic and industrial purposes.

Long before Birmingham became a place of even minor note, Coventry was a town of major importance. From the Middle Ages onwards Coventry has had a reputation as a manufacturing centre concerned successively with woollens, silk ribbon manufacture, watch-making, the produc-

tion of sewing-machines and the manufacture of bicycles. In 1896 the city became the home of the first British commercially-produced motor-car, and a decade later the new industry already had a workforce of 10,000. The original textile tradition was maintained by the rayon industry established by Courtaulds at the beginning of the present century. A characteristic feature of Coventry's history has been its readiness to abandon declining industries and to adopt new ones.

The rapid modern growth of Coventry as an industrial centre was closely associated with technological developments, especially the internal combustion engine and the applications of electricity. Today, the city has a population of 334,000 and a wide range of industries which include the manufacture of motor vehicles, tractors, aero-engines, machine tools, electrical equipment, television sets, synthetic fibres and plastics. However, Coventry, like Birmingham, has begun to feel the effects of the recession. The machine tool industry, one of the staple trades in the city, has recently run into difficulties and Alfred Herbert Ltd., the largest machine tool firm in the West Midlands, had to be rescued from insolvency by the government in October 1975.

No account of Coventry would be complete without some allusion to the wartime air attack which wrecked the city centre. The devastation required the complete replanning and re-building of the town centre which made Coventry a model for much city centre reconstruction in other parts of the country.

In contrast to Coventry, the ancient cathedral city of Lichfield has retained much of its former character. By-passed by both canal and, until later, the railway, Lichfield failed to industrialise on the large scale, and it maintains the air of a prosperous market town rather than of an industrial centre.

North Staffordshire and the Potteries

In the south-western corner of the southern Pennines lies the North Staffordshire coalfield, the seat of a very distinctive area long known as 'the Potteries'. The area is topographically broken as a result of the heavily faulted and folded Coal Measures and the erosive activity of the head-streams of the upper Trent which have carved out narrow valleys. It was in this broken country that the pottery industry emerged and eventually became localised, to such an extent that four-fifths of all pottery workers in the country are domiciled in the area. The Potteries virtually monopolises the British ceramics industry and it is not unlikely that it produces more pottery than any other area in the world. Such a narrow industrial base would normally give cause for alarm, but such is the success of the industry that the Potteries, long regarded as being more vulnerable to recession than the rest of the West Midlands region, currently has unemployment rates among the lowest in the region.

The industry is an important employer of female labour, especially in the decorating and finishing branches.

The original six centres of the pottery industry were amalgamated in 1925 and given city status as the County Borough of Stoke-on-Trent. Nearby Newcastle-under-Lyme, which rejected amalgamation with Stoke at that time, is chiefly a residential and shopping centre. There are two other towns in the area away from the coalfield that have important functions: Stafford and Crewe. The former is an old, and originally walled, town which is the county town of Staffordshire, with footwear manufactures and electrical engineering industries. Crewe, in contrast, was a small village in a rural area until the coming of the railways when three lines converged here and a marshalling yard was established. Crewe is essentially a railway town for it also became the centre of a railway works. More recently, the town has attracted a variety of light industries to it. In the far east of Staffordshire is Burton-on-Trent, the largest brewing centre in the country.

The Rural West and South

Standing in marked contrast to the Black Country and the Potteries with their congested, industrialised, urban features, are the extensive rural areas of the Severn valley and the Welsh Marchlands in the west, and the Avon and Hereford lowlands in the south of the region. The diversity of the physical landscape, the varied nature of the soils, and climatic differences offer opportunities for variety in the agricultural economy of the western and southern parts of the West Midlands region.

In east Shropshire and north Worcester, arable crops tend to dominate; this is reflected in the large farms and their mechanised methods of cultivation. In the higher lands of the Welsh border country and Hereford, farming is dominated by livestock enterprises: sheep on the hills, cattle for beef production in Hereford, though dairying has now become much more important. Although in the West Midlands region as a whole under 2 per cent of the population is engaged in agriculture, in the far west of the region the figure rises to over 30 per cent in some areas. In the rural western fringes of the West Midlands, i.e. in Shropshire and Hereford, which lie removed from the English megalopolis, rural depopulation has long been endemic and continues to be so. There are few large towns and Shrewsbury (population 85,000) and Hereford (population 47,800) alone are centres of importance being the urban focus of large farming areas and significant agricultural markets. Both of these towns have food-processing industries and engineering activities. There are also a number of small, widely-spaced, attractive towns, such as Much Wenlock, Ludlow, Leominster and Ledbury, functioning as minor marketing centres. The historic town of Ludlow, once the administrative capital of Wales, is now a great tourist attraction.

On the eastern edge of the Plain of Hereford is the outcrop of Pre-Cambrian rocks of the Malvern Hills, and beyond is the Plain of Worcester, an extensive and rich agricultural area, part under grass but mostly under arable and orchard fruit. The chief arable crops are barley, wheat, sugar-beet, potatoes and vegetables, and orchard fruits such as apples, pears, plums and cherries. Stock-farming is varied in its character, although dairying is of growing significance. In this rich and highly attractive rural area, settlements are few, widely scattered and mostly small. Worcester (population 74,000) is situated at what was once the tidal limit of the Severn and is the chief town and market of a very productive area. It has engineering, porcelain and glove-making industries.

The Plain of Worcester merges into the Vale of Evesham (Fig. 19.14). Mild, moist, relatively frost-free and sheltered, the Vale is one of the most important horticultural and orchard areas in Britain. Brussel sprouts, cauliflower, beans, peas, onions and asparagus are grown in large quantities, while the area is also famous for its orchard fruits, especially cooking and eating apples, plums and cherries. Small fruits are not of any particular note, apart from currants. Throughout the Vale are a number of small, attractive market towns, e.g. Tewkesbury, Pershore and Evesham, which have industries based upon the farming activities of the area, as, for example, fruit and vegetable canning, jam-making, brewing, soft-drinks manufacture, cheese-making, etc.

In the extreme south-east of the West Midlands region is a group of small towns – Warwick, Royal Leamington Spa, Kenilworth and Strat-ford-upon-Avon – which are of special interest because of their historical background and tourist

Fig 19.14 Avon Valley, near Evesham, Worcestershire. Orchards line the gentle slopes of Chadbury and Craycombe Hill, with mixed arable and pasture land along the river

attraction. Warwick (population 16,000) occupies a site fortified from Saxon times, and with its fourteenth century castle and fifteenth and six-teenth century buildings, it has become a tourist attraction. It is the county town of Warwickshire and a market centre. Farming is the chief local activity but is has some small manufactures of farming implements and motor engineering products. Some 8 km north of Warwick is Kenilworth, with its ruined castle and priory, which has tended to become a residential town, although it has some industries mainly associated with agricultural and automobile engineering, and the making of caravans. Leamington (population 43,000) became famous as a spa but now has become involved in the manufacture of motor-car parts. Stratford-upon-Avon (population 16,750), largely because of its association with Shakespeare and its memorial theatre, has grown into a major tourist centre but it still has a market, is concerned with brewing and produces gloves, chemical products and metalware goods.

Conclusion

It must be conceded that the West Midlands region is a very diverse area, parts of which are highly industrialised and heavily urbanised while other parts are essentially rural and thinly populated. Given such disparate geography, regional affinity is much less keenly felt than in many other regions. Industrially, the West Midlands has enjoyed a long period of success and prosperity, and the region has consistently maintained unemployment rates that were well below the national average. Although there were hints of industrial difficulties prior to the energy crisis of 1973, it was that crisis together with foreign competition in the motor car industry and problems in the machine tool industry, which precipitated the present problems. The unemployment rate has thus risen to a figure on average higher than the national rate – 6·7 per cent compared with the national rate of 5·2 per cent (1977). Many of the major companies in the region, e.g. British Leyland, Chrysler (now Talbot), Norton Villiers Triumph, and Alfred Herbert Ltd. – all important employers of labour – ran into difficulties and had to seek government help. The near total collapse of the motor-car industry has struck at the very heart of the West Midlands prosperity, for the problems of that industry have washed over into other industries such as those supplying components for the car assembly plants. Strained labour relations have aggravated the industrial problem within the West Midlands conurbation and warnings have been given that the area is well on its way to becoming a 'grey' area.

The fundamental causes of the current problems of the West Midlands are not easily isolated. Perhaps the region has relied for too long on the metal trades and the motor vehicle industry; perhaps, using the expertise gained in the past, the area should have invested in new technology-based industries; perhaps private and public investment has been insufficient to maintain the region's industrial vigour; and perhaps, too, the government should have relaxed some of the tight industrial controls to foster greater flexibility and diversification.

References

Manners, G., Keeble, D., Rodgers, B., and Warren, K., *Regional Development in Britain* (John Wiley & Sons, 1972).

The U.K. Space, House, J.W., (ed.) 2nd edition (Weidenfeld & Nicolson, 1977) Chapter 1.

Brown, A.J., *The Framework of Regional Economics in the United Kingdom* (Cambridge University Press, 1972) Chapters 1 and 2.

Chisholm, M.D.I., (ed.) *Resources for Britain's Future* (Harmondsworth, 1972).

Carter, A.H., and others, *An Advanced Geography of the British Isles* (Hulton Educational Publications Ltd., 1974) Chapters, 7, 9, 10, 11.

Wood, P., 'West Midlands leads the downward trend', *Geographical Magazine,* Vol. XLLX, No. 1, October 1976, pp. 2–7.

Blacksell, M., 'Places for Leisure: pressure on the Broads', *Geographical Magazine,* Vol. LI, No. 2, November 1978, p. 88.

Norwich and its Region, British Association, Norwich, 1961.

Hall, P., *London 2000* (Faber, 1971).

M.J. Wise, 'The Birmingham-Black Country Conurbation in its Regional Setting', *Geography,* Vol. 57, April 1972, pp. 89–104.

M. George, 'Land Use and Nature Conservation in Broadland', *Geography,* Vol. 61, July 1976, pp. 137–142.

East Anglia Regional Strategy Team, *Strategic Choice for East Anglia* (H.M.S.O., 1974).

West Midlands Economic Planning Council, *The West Midlands: Patterns of Growth* (H.M.S.O., 1971).

Beard, N., 'London Docklands: an example of inner city renewal', *Geography,* Vol. 64, 1979, pp. 190–195.

South-East Joint Planning Team: *Strategy for the South-East,* (H.M.S.O., 1976).

20

Peripheral Regions

The affinity of the western regions of Britain has been remarked upon by several writers. While South-West England, Wales, Scotland and N. Ireland may have little in common in the public mind, except as places to go on holiday, the geographer has long been aware of their considerable physical and cultural similarities. Along with their peripheral position in relation to the British heartland in lowland England, these distinctive physical and cultural characteristics underpin a range of related structural problems. Before proceeding to a closer examination of regional problems within these areas, then, let us set out, briefly, their common context.

While Britain's position off the western shores of Europe disposes towards a certain economic disadvantage, the westerly location of these peripheral regions makes for downright remoteness, not only in European but also in British terms. Although much of Wales and the South-West of England are within 300 km of London, their topography is such as to make communications with the English lowlands circuitous and sometimes difficult. No part of Scotland is within 400 km of London, the majority of its population live beyond 500 km, and the great mass of the Highlands lies over 550 km distant. In American terms, of course, such distances make for neighbourliness rather than separation. Why, then, should they make such a difference in Britain? The reason lies in the distinct physical make-up of the peripheral regions that we noted in Part One, drew attention to in Chapter 18 and which we can summarise as a matter of relief, rainfall and resources.

Environmental Background

Scotland, Wales and the South-West of England are all largely made up of highland masses, often with ancient crystalline intrusions at their heart. In the South-West stand Dartmoor and Bodmin Moor, in Wales the Cambrian Mountains, and in Scotland we find both the oldest of rocks and the newest of tertiary lavas in the North-Western Highlands. These mountain masses, whether formed into monotonous erosion surfaces, or dissected by glaciation and faulting into deep highland valleys, are not the likely site for a congenial human environment. Combined with the high annual rainfall – the extreme North-West of Scotland has an average of 5·5 hours of rain a day – and generally low temperatures, this obdurate relief bears poor soils. The very cold and wet regimes of Snowdonia and the Cairngorms support Raw Mineral Soils and Peaty Rankers, while on areas like Dartmoor, Central Wales and most of the uplands of the Borders and North-West Scotland, Acid Peats, Peaty Gleys and Peaty Gley Podzols are the rule. Only in the marginal lowland areas are more welcoming soils found – Brown Rankers, Acid Brown Earths and Non-Calcareous Gleys. Equally, while the surface of these areas offers little potential for intensive agriculture, their constituent structure does not now offer much in the way of mineral wealth to provide an industrial base. Even the coalfields on their fringes – in the Scottish lowlands, South Wales and Somerset – possess, with a few exceptions, the least viable mines in the country. In N. Ireland, hill masses are almost always in sight, and even in the lowlands features of glacial deposition render level ground extremely rare, and make soils very variable. Almost all of N. Ireland's soils are of recent origin and immature. However, amongst this apparently unrelieved economic gloom lies the most magnificent scenery in Britain, which offers enormous potential for tourism and recreation, particularly since these regions also possess a very distinctive cultural geography.

The Celtic element of our cultural history has been less diluted by Anglo-Saxon migration and influence the further west and north we go. While traces of a Celtic heritage were discernible in much of central and northern England during the Middle Ages, they remain obvious today only in Wales and Ireland, though apparent in Cornwall. In Scotland, Celtic influence is strongest in the most remote regions, but a distinctive national culture which derives at least its dress from the mid-Victorian revival of interest in the Highlands, pervades even the Anglicised and industrialised lowlands. In both Scotland and Wales the nationalist movement has been a factor of growing importance for almost a hundred years; in Cornwall the emergence of *Mebyon Kernow* and a revived interest in the jurisdiction of the ancient Stannary Parliament points to at least an ember of separatist sentiment. Devolution apart, this cultural aspect of the peripheral regions is an important attribute of their distinctiveness, for it helps to encourage regional cohesion and a perception of issues which is often different from that of Whitehall and Westminster. In N. Ireland, of course, cultural distinctiveness led to devolved government in 1920, and the consequences of political separatism continue to provide a major problem.

Land-use

While the configuration of relief in these regions is provided by the highland masses, the pattern of the landscape is dominated by the disposition of rough grazings and improved farmlands. Overwhelmingly these regions are the home of pastoral farming, either on *hill farms,* where 95 per cent of the pasture is in the form of rough grazing, mainly for a breeding ewe flock, or else on *upland farms* where at least 30 per cent of the pasture is rough grazing, and where store cattle are likely to be dominant. As we have already seen, however,

these are regions of marked rural decline. Part of the problem is the inherent infertility of such areas. Apart from N. Ireland and the South-West, and some coastal locations, a major problem is the shortage of the growing season. In the worst areas, farmers may have to provide winter fodder for seven months in the year, as well as having to contend with acid soils deficient in phosphates and nitrogen. In contrast to the lowland farmer, the range of choice open to the upland grazier is very limited. On the other hand the regions *are* suited to sheep farming in particular, especially in Wales and Scotland. Thompson noted that, "if there is a future for the sheep industry within the Common Market then a future for sheep in the hills and uplands is assured". To achieve that assured future, however, output must be raised and more rough pasture improved. Jones contends that about one-quarter of the rough grazings in Britain are improvable, and points to the fact that about 25 per cent of the hills and uplands of Wales have been improved by ploughing and reseeding between 1952–77. Equally, much of the sheep industry needs to be restructured to provide far fewer small farms. Jones suggests that *upland farms* should be at least 100 ha, with about 450 ewes and 30 beef cattle; and that *hill farms* should cover at least 2002ha to carry 1,000 ewes and 30 breeding cows. Of course such a policy naturally leads to further depopulation and the chain of problems which we noted in Chapter 14.

The peripheral regions are also characterised by the other major land uses of the uplands: by forestry, by water catchment, and by the barely productive deer forests (1,100,000 ha) and grouse moors (303,000 ha).

Industrial Employment

Although South Wales, the Belfast sub-region, Central Scotland and the Bristol sub-region are significant industrial areas, they all lie outside the axial belt of population concentration and industrialisation. In both Central Scotland and South Wales, restructuring of the industrial base away from the Victorian staples of coal and steel has been particularly difficult and long drawn out. In these districts high levels of unemployment and the low level of environmental conditions associated with declining heavy industry have long been familiar. Similarly both areas have experienced massive government investment in the form of industrial aid and the provision of improved infrastructure, particularly through the road programme. Because the industrial revolution had a less direct impact upon the South-West the situation is rather different, yet there are still some surprising similarities. Opportunities for employment in manufacturing industry are still restricted, especially away from Severnside; unemployment levels are higher than the national average, and far too many towns are overdependent upon one major employer.

In consequence we can see broadly similar social movements taking place. There is a tendency in all

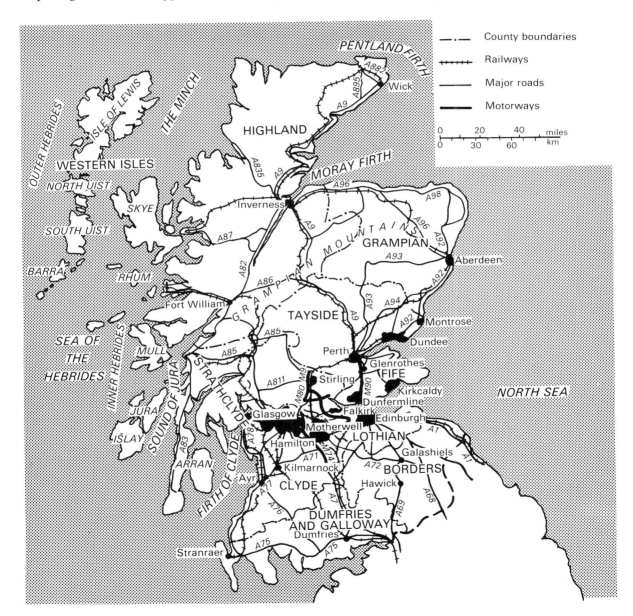

Fig. 20.1 Scotland—major towns and communications

these regions for persistent out-migration of young people, whether from the countryside or from industrialised areas, most apparent in Scotland and least apparent in the South-West. As a result the population structure is tending towards the older age bands, a process which is speeded up in parts of the South-West and Wales by the marked in-migration of retired people.

SCOTLAND

Scotland is the largest of all the regions in terms of its area, occupying almost one-third of Great Britain, yet it has only 9·3 per cent of the population and so is the most sparsely populated of all (Fig. 20.1). But what regional variations there are! Scarcely anywhere else in Europe is there such a

Fig 20.2 Edinburgh: Scotland's national capital, but second city, Edinburgh has a vivid townscape. To the right the Old Town straggles down the High Street from the Castle. To the left, across the now-drained Nor-Loch, the orderly New Town was begun by James Craig in the mid 18th century

thinly populated area as the Scottish Highlands, yet Glasgow is the most grossly overcrowded city in Britain. On the western coasts of the Highland Region are to be found the last vestiges of peasant farming in Britain, while to the east and south multi-million pound investment programmes are in hand in the most modern petro-chemical industry in the world. While Edinburgh can truly boast of being one of the cultural capitals of Europe (Fig. 20.2), social deviance and delinquency measured by levels of alcoholism and crime rates in neighbouring Strathclyde have been amongst the highest in Britain.

As we cannot hope to be comprehensive in this section we shall highlight four issues that have a specifically regional dimension: (i) the role of the Highlands and Islands Development Board, (ii) the impact of North Sea oil exploitation, (iii) industrial readjustment in Strathclyde, and (iv) the challenge of the Borders.

Highlands and Islands Development Board

Ever since the Rebellion of 1745, Governments in England have been aware of a 'Highland problem'. Subsequent land clearances by Scottish and English landlords alike considerably worsened a problem of rural poverty which was already endemic in the region. Massive out-migration to the industrialising Scottish lowlands, and beyond to the Dominions during the nineteenth century, was nothing very new to the Highlands. But still the problem remained, as a residual population tenaciously maintained a living of sorts based upon part-time farming and fishing. When the Highlands were rediscovered by fashionable taste during the mid-nineteenth century, clan, tartan and croft became the romantic symbols of the 'essential' Scotland, a world away from the grimy towns that constituted the real heartland in the industrialised Central Valley. Since then, despite the fact that crofting was a grossly uneconomic way to derive a living, attempts have been made to secure the Highland population and the Highland way of life. The Crofters' Act of 1886 and 1892, and the Taylor Commission of 1954, were each aiming to maintain a way of life which was thought to be desirable, even if its exponents were condemned to near destitution. Thus there were still over 20,000 crofts in the Highlands by 1971, supporting part time employment, usually not more than two days work per week, for about 16,000 workers. In the western districts, where crofting remains, incomes are made up partly from fishing, tourism and forestry, but mainly from welfare benefits (Fig. 20.3).

Fig. 20.3 Croft near Bernisdale, Isle of Skye. Built of immediately available materials, the crofter's house and its nearby peat-stack mark the near-peasant economy of the western Isles

However, crofting only accounts for a small proportion of agriculture in the Highlands, and is mainly limited to the poorer land along the western sea lochs and the islands, where 30 per cent of employment is in any case related to the fishing industry. Much of the land remains part of a series of vast estates, largely maintained for shooting purposes, so that the interests of the small farmer, whether tenant or crofter, have in some cases been a secondary consideration. Farming is solidly pastoral. Out of 36,260 sq. km only 24,000 ha were given over to the production of grain in 1977, largely for the whisky industry, and there were more than eight times as many sheep as people. With a sparse population, few towns – none except Inverness having more than 10,000 people – the area has suffered in an acute form all the problems discussed in Chapter 14. Between 1921 and 1971 population fell by 13·6 per cent, almost 1,000 per year, unemployment was usually twice the average for Scotland and locally often very much worse.

It was in this situation that the Highlands and Islands Development Board (H.I.D.B.) was set up in 1965 with what on paper appeared to be very wide powers to purchase land, direct investment and encourage initiatives across the whole range of economic activity. In the event the Board has not proved to be the bureaucratic overlord that some feared, and can claim some success for stimulating new employment and securing existing jobs. In a sense its path had been smoothed by the North of Scotland Hydro-Electricity Board which was set up in 1943 to produce electricity for the scattered communities of the region, not just as a basic service, but as a means of improving the standard of living, attracting industry and stemming the out-migration of young people. In the event its main achievement was the provision of electricity, but at least that resource was available for new developments sponsored by the Development Board. What then has the Board achieved? In *agriculture* the results have not been startling. This is not surprising given the poor conditions and an unwillingness on the part of many crofters to engage more readily in the communal schemes which would alone make possible the practice of a more efficient agriculture. When almost every crofter and small farmer insists on having his own tractor and implements, then it is not surprising that almost 50 per cent of the capital input in crofting regions is tied up in machinery that is barely used – capital which could be directed towards other ends. (The equivalent figure for capital expenditure on machinery for Scotland as a whole is 28 per cent.) In 1977 the Board spent £800,000 on assisting farms, and where the expertise of the Board has been utilised farm productivity has been rising at about 10 per cent per annum. The Board's main successes have been of the research and development type, with particular interest in increasing yields for dairying, the growing of soft-fruits and the improvement of beef strains. The development of bulb production in the Outer Hebrides was an interesting venture, but perhaps most innovative of all has been the successful domestication of deer for venison on the Rahoy estate.

The reinvigoration of the west coast *fishing industry* has been one of the Board's success stories. Building on the success of a training scheme initiated in 1958, the Board invested £3·5 millions between 1965 and 1970, underpinning some 1,699 jobs mainly in the Outer Hebrides. In the Isles up to 30 per cent of employment is fish related, and the development of multi-species fishing has proved particularly significant given the uncertain future of the herring, formerly the major catch. Investment in training and boat purchase is now being followed, in partnership with Norwegian interests, by a major landing and fish drying facility at Breasclete on the Isle of Lewis, for the supply of 5,500 tonnes of dried fish per annum for markets in Scandinavia, Italy and East Africa.

While *tourism* has been an inevitable area of the Board's interest, it is in the encouragement of *manufacturing industry* that the Board has hoped for most success, although not much was achieved until the advent of oil-related industry. The Board has been willing to encourage the establishment of any industry in the region, and the undoubted growth in industrial employments can be grouped into craft industries (e.g. glassware, ceramics, precious metals, and high quality knitwear) light industry (particularly small component electronics, on the Orkneys, on Skye and at Wick) and capital intensive industry centred on northern Caithness, and the Moray lowlands. In Caithness the Board's interests have centred around the Atomic Energy Authority's developments at Dounreay, near Thurso. During the 1950s experimental work at Dounreay transformed the local economy with an influx of highly skilled workers and new houses which acted as a catalyst for other new developments. In 1966 a prototype fast breeder reactor was established, and now that the experimental period is coming to an end, the Development Board is anxious to retain this highly specialised and high income workforce, rather than see twenty years' worth of expansion be reduced to a few hundred maintenance staff. Along the Moray Firth the completion of the Invergordon aluminium smelter for British Aluminium in 1971 was seen as a major breakthrough. It employs about 800 workers, at the cost of very considerable public investment, and now forms part of an astonishing transformation of the Moray Firth due to circumstances beyond the knowledge of the Development Board of the 1960s – North Sea Oil. This has transformed the Highland economy far more than the H.I.D.B. could have ever dreamed, even though the Board has directed £38·4 millions into the local economy between 1965–77, and attracted a further £57 millions from private investment.

North Sea Oil

The pattern of discovery of oil reserves in the North Sea has already been outlined, and its importance for the whole British economy is obviously very significant. The physical impact of the discoveries, however, has been most marked in Scotland, and we can conveniently list three main regional issues: *platform construction, platform servicing,* and *downstream activities.* With the first discoveries of North Sea Oil in 1969–70, it was clear that a new deep water technology would be needed to exploit the finds, and the subsequent construction of the massive platforms needed for the drilling rigs made a dramatic impact (Fig. 20.4). The first two construction yards began work in 1972, and both made an immediate local impact. Dorman Long reclaimed an old colliery site at Methil in Fife, and Highland Fabricators established themselves on the otherwise lightly populated Nigg Bay on Cromarty Firth. While the Methil yard could call upon a local labour force, and make use of existing infrastructure, the yard at Nigg required the provision of all the necessities of life for a workforce which soon totalled 2,500. By 1973 a further yard had been opened at nearby Ardesier, drawing on Inverness and Nairn, and within two years further deep water yards had been established on the west coast to provide the

huge concrete platforms, at Ardyne, Kishorn and Portavadie. A controversial proposal to establish a yard at Drumbuie on beautiful Loch Carron had been turned down earlier after a stormy planning enquiry. A further yard was later established at Hunterston. Kishorn faced similar infrastructure problems as Nigg, though on a smaller scale, but the remaining yards could make use of the facilities offered by Clydeside. In addition, the construction of modules required to house workers and plant on the platforms provided work at Leith, Dumbarton and Burntisland, while the

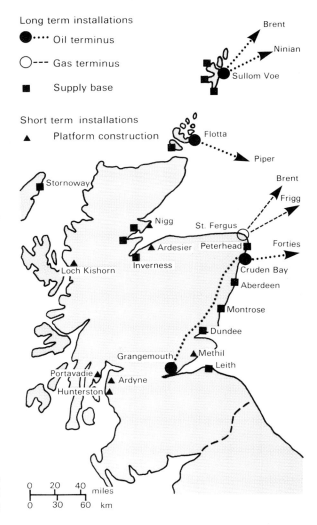

Fig 20.4 Oil and natural gas industry in Scotland

modernisation and re-equipment of B.S.C.'s plants at Belshill, Coatbridge, Cambuslang and Motherwell allowed the supply of the greater part of the well casings and steel tubing needed for the U.K. sectors. Unfortunately, this is all rather a once-and-for-all market, and the sudden gains in employment in each of these areas are unlikely to be sustained far into the 1980s.

A much more stable addition to local employment has been provided by the *supply industry* needed by the off-shore platforms. From the very first, Aberdeen, with its existing large harbour facilities and Dyce airport, became the major base. By 1975 special support bases and regional headquarters had been set up for six major oil companies, serving over twenty platforms. The flood of planning applications placed the property market under enormous pressure. House prices rose to levels comparable to the South-East of England,

while office rents in the town centres became more expensive than prime sites in central Edinburgh, Scotland's office capital. From Aberdeen development spilled over to Dundee, and later to Montrose and to Peterhead, where the former fishing port was transformed into a major supply base. All of these developments, of course, have transformed the employment situation in the Highland and Grampian regions, particularly the latter where, despite considerable in-migration, the unemployment rate has approached zero. There are, however, important side effects, for the sudden availability of high paid employment makes for labour difficulties in the traditional, but low paid, jobs in farming, forestry, fishing and boat building.

The major impact of downstream activities will first be felt in the early 1980s. The first on-shore handling facility was established at Cruden Bay,

Fig 20.5 Shetland—Construction of Sullom Voe terminal on Calback Ness

near Peterhead, passing oil through from the Forties field to the Grangemouth refinery in Central Scotland, later joined by the gas terminal for the Brent field at nearby St. Fergus. Gas from here services an area from Inverness to Lancashire, and an ammonia plant has received the go-ahead at St. Fergus. In the Orkneys an oil terminal has been established at Flotta, but the biggest of all is the £672 million Sullom Voe terminal in Shetland, which will eventually handle well over half of Britain's oil needs (Fig. 20.5). By virtue of the 1974 Zetland County Council Bill, Sullom Voe is owned jointly by the Shetland Islands Council, thirty-two oil companies who laid out the capital investment, and B.P. as the operator and constructor. It is expected that tankers of up to 300,000 tons will eventually be able to receive products from the site. However, in spite of the aspirations of the H.I.D.B. for a share of the petro-chemicals industry which is expected to flow from the oil finds, it is likely that most of the major downstream development will be established further south. Shell/Esso are to build a £435 million gas processing and petro-chemical complex on a greenfield site at Mossmorran in Fife, and further investment by B.P. and I.C.I. at Grangemouth may well top £1,000 million.

Such huge investments seem astonishing, yet this is a highly capital-intensive operation and the end result is far fewer jobs than we might imagine. At Mossmorran, for instance, only about 400 permanent jobs are envisaged. The major difficulties at this stage of exploitation lie in the huge numbers of men that are required for construction work – over 4,000 at Sullom Voe, for instance, when the total Shetland population is only 20,000. These massive intrusions cause considerable disruption to the local labour market, and often result in more unemployment. As labour is drawn from local low-paid jobs, then mechanisation is often the immediate result – so on completion of the major project there are few old jobs left to return to, while a proportion of the migrant labour force may remain to swell the register of the unemployed. Estimates of the numbers of workers that are employed in oil-related occupations must be treated with great caution (Table 32). Clearly the numbers *directly employed* will fall as the construction phase ends, but it is hoped that the numbers of those *indirectly* involved, and through the multiplier effect, will rise for some further years. This is certainly to be hoped, for Strathclyde alone is

Table 32: Total numbers directly employed in North Sea Oil activities, 1977

Highland	7,400
Shetland, Orkney and Western Isles	700
Grampian	11,500
Tayside	1,600
Fife, Central and Lothians	2,700
Strathclyde	3,100
TOTAL:	27,000

Source: Dept of Energy and Department of Employment

likely to have lost up to a quarter of a million jobs between 1971–1981, and one of Scotland's major difficulties is the matching of the loss of jobs in Strathclyde, and West Central Scotland, with new oil-related opportunities demanding different skills that might be available in other regions. Meanwhile northern Scotland can thank the oil industry for at least improving its communications with the rest of the U.K., through the upgrading of both rail and road links to Inverness and beyond, and for giving the region a sudden and dramatic shot in the arm.

Industrial Readjustment in Strathclyde

As we have already noted the great majority of Scotland's population is to be found in the central valley which extends from the Clyde to the Forth, including parts of the Strathclyde, Lothian, Central, Fife and Tayside Regions. However, almost half of Scotland's population is located in the giant Strathclyde Region, which centres upon Glasgow, and includes the major industrial towns of the nineteenth century. Consequently the decline of the older industries has had a more concentrated effect here than anywhere else in Scotland, with the result that unemployment has been high (10·7 per cent in July 1977), the physical fabric of the environment is urgently in need of renewal, and as we noted in Chapter 16, social deprivation is amongst the most acute in Britain (Fig. 20.6).

The region's fortunes were largely built upon the *iron and steel trades*. The iron industry had become established in the Clyde by the end of the eighteenth century, but only rose to prominence

Fig 20.6 Glasgow—So close to the open spaces of the Highlands, Glasgow's crowded city centre is marked by 19th century tenements, and beyond, the tower blocks of City Council redevelopment. In the foreground is the University quarter

after the introduction of the 'hot blast' in 1828. By this method the ores of the Lanarkshire coalfield could be utilised for a range of metallurigical products. Glasgow's growing colonial trade during the eighteenth century had made it a major international port by this time, with associated shipbuilding and repairing, so it was almost inevitable that the shipbuilding trades became a major outlet for the iron and steel industry. After the exhaustion of the Lanarkshire iron ore in the last quarter of the nineteenth century, Motherwell in particular rose to prominence using imported ores in Siemens open-hearth furnaces, and Clydeside became Britain's premier shipbuilding area, located downstream at Clydebank, Dumbarton, Port Glasgow and Greenock.

Today these industrial leaders are only a relic of what they were. Mid-Lanarkshire has had to face particularly severe contraction in the coal, steel and heavy engineering trades. Geological conditions have always made coal mining difficult in the region, but productivity in the Scottish coal industry is consistently lower than the average for Britain, which renders its future less certain than it might otherwise be. To help in this regard, in 1978 the Government allocated to the South Scotland Electricity Board an annual subsidy of £5 million to maintain coal burn. A planned investment programme of £30 millions will help to modernise existing pits, but most new developments will probably take place further east in the Lothians.

Shipbuilding on the Clyde has consistently proved to be a very political subject, and still today, in the face of a world-wide recession in shipbuilding, about 50,000 jobs depend directly or indirectly upon the yards. On the upper Clyde the government has poured about £100 millions into preserving what is now Gowan Shipbuilders (a division of British Shipbuilding) totally redeveloping the Govan and Scotstoun yards into one of the most modern in Europe. Other yards include Yarrow (Shipbuilders) which specialises in naval craft, and at Port Glasgow and Greenock the five yards which make up Scott Lithgow, employing 8,000 workers, and which alone of the Strathclyde yards has involved itself heavily in the off-shore oil market. The heavy engineering industry as a whole, however, has generally failed to take advantage of the oil market, apart from the examples mentioned earlier.

As for steel making itself, Scottish losses have been even more worrying than in the coal industry – about half the total British loss in 1977 – and the industry can only look forward to a period of sustained contraction, with the one bright spot being the expansion of the new Ravenscraig plant to an annual capacity of 3·2 million tonnes, along with investment at Hunterston. The development at Ravenscraig was initially for the motor industry, diverted by the government away from the West Midlands in the 1960s in the hope of shoring up the industrial structure of Strathclyde. The two plants involved are Chrysler/Talbot at Linwood and Leyland trucks at Bathgate, but productivity has remained low at both plants largely due to industrial relations difficulties.

What then of readjustment? While the labour force has expanded only slowly over the last thirty years, due to persistent net losses by migration, there has been a rapid rise in the numbers involved in the *electronics industry*. Scotland has achieved enormous success in this direction, largely through American led investment programmes, so that Scotland now possesses one of the greatest concentration of electronics companies in the entire world outside the United States. The numbers employed now exceed those in coal mining, and it is felt that this offers the real basis for industrial diversification. A particular shortage at the moment (1980) is in firms making components, and in local research and development. However, it is hoped that the presence of an array of universities

and technological institutes will help to rectify at least the latter. The only cloud on the horizon would seem to be the rapid penetration of the electronics industry by microprocessors, and the extent to which the Scottish industry will be able to adjust.

In all these industries, regional aid from the government has been absolutely vital. Government spending on regional assistance to Scotland has increased considerably over the last decade. In 1964–5 the total was just over £10 millions, by 1970 it was almost £100 millions, and in 1976 was over £200 millions. Altogether Scotland has received about 30 per cent of the aid distributed under the 1972 Industry Act (up until 1977), plus, of course, aid through normal government channels in rate support, etc. On the ground this shows itself not just in new factories and new industries, but in improved communications, town centre development programmes, the massive increase in council house building referred to in Part Three, and in agricultural benefits. In an attempt to reduce the congestion in Glasgow, four new towns were designated – East Kilbride (the most successful) and Cumbernauld within Strathclyde, Glenrothes in Fife, and Livingston in Lothian. However, one of the major problems for Glasgow is that the shedding of labour in this way has also been accompanied by the shedding of the newer industries that she herself needs for her own regeneration; indeed, it may well be that more radical proposals are needed to really deal with the problem of unemployment in inner Glasgow. Thus in 1976 a £150 millions plan was announced by the Government to rehabilitate Glasgow's East End, and in 1978 the District Council announced a £56 millions plan to revitalise one of the worst areas of deprivation in Maryhill.

The Borders

Like the Highlands, the Borders is a largely rural area, with few large towns and relatively little industry. The region has chiefly been famed for its sheep rearing and local high class woollen industry. Unfortunately, both these are low-wage industries. At April 1976 the average weekly wage in this area for men aged 21 and over was only £59·1, compared with a Scottish average of £71·6. Between 1951 and 1974 population fell by about 12 per cent to 99,000, giving losses both in the rural areas and in the small manufacturing towns. In farming the population is generally older than the norm in Scotland, and this lack of interest on the part of the young is causing concern. An interesting feature of the region is that unemployment tends to be below the average for Scotland, and that in fact there is a labour shortage in the area. This is a function not just of low wages, but of losses by migration, particularly of the young, and also of mechanisation in farming, which has resulted in a loss of female labour as rural-based male labour has been shed from the region. The problem that is faced in the region, then, is one of making the area attractive to the younger age bands of the population by diversifying the industrial base, and the provision of better social facilities especially in housing. Unfortunately the attraction of new industry is not easy when labour is not plentifully available. In addition, the region is not well served for communications, particularly since the Carlisle-Edinburgh line was closed under the Beeching proposals.

However, there has been some success in the attraction of a range of small light industries. Between mid 1975 and mid 1976 there was a net population gain by migration of 900, which after natural decline left a modest gain in the total. Most of the credit must go to the efforts of the local authority and the Scottish Development Agency in attracting new industry and providing new factory accommodation. Over 1976–7 an ambitious plan for converting existing mills in Hawick and Selkirk suffered some delays, but additional factory space is increasingly being provided in this manner. The concomitant to additional employment opportunities is the provision of new houses, and this is seen as a major target, particularly in Tweedbank, Hawick and Galashiels. Overall, then, the problem is rather different to other parts of Scotland, and in general is being resolved favourably. In the process the balance of population is shifting eastwards as the hill country continues to shed population, the mill towns hold steady as new jobs have replaced losses in textiles, and towns such as Kelso and Eyemouth experience modest growth.

WALES

Despite five hundred years of Anglicisation, the distinctiveness of Wales has persisted. Yet as with

Scotland there are marked regional differences, not just in the form of such obvious contrasts as between southern Pembroke – 'little England beyond Wales' – and Snowdonia, but important structural differences. North Wales and South Wales look respectively more towards North-Western England and the South-West/West Midlands, than towards each other, while Mid Wales remains as something of a cultural and economic island (Fig. 20.7). Unlike Scotland, which continues to have a natural population gain but a net migration loss (4,800 in 1975–6), Wales has a natural loss yet a net migration gain (5,500 in 1975–6). This fact is highlighted by the ageing character of Wales's population after years of sustained migration loss, and the growing increase of retirement migration particularly from the North-West.

North Wales

North Wales's connections with the North-West are strong and indissoluble, and characterised by institutions such as the North-West Electricity Board which covers an area from Aberystwyth to Appleby. Nowhere are those links more strongly felt than along the coastline from Prestatyn to Pwllheli. There, but particularly along the north coast as far west as Llandudno, considerable numbers of retired migrants from the North-West region have made their new home. Perhaps they had spent several holidays in the area, for this is the other aspect of the invasion of North Wales by North-Westerners in particular. Few areas in Britain have seen such a complete transformation of their coastline by caravan parks as North Wales (Fig. 20.8). Between Colwyn Bay and the Dee estuary, around Red Wharf Bay in Anglesey and along the southern shores of the Lleyn Peninsula there were over 200 caravan parks established by 1965. As caravans offer by far the great majority of overnight accommodation in Wales, their role for the tourist industry is important; but their distribution represents a significant planning problem, not least because of the deleterious landscape effects of clusters of vans, and because of the servicing arrangements that are necessary in the holiday months. Planning policies have generally favoured the concentration of caravans into large and compact sites, particularly on the coast, rather than a rash of haphazardly arranged small clusters.

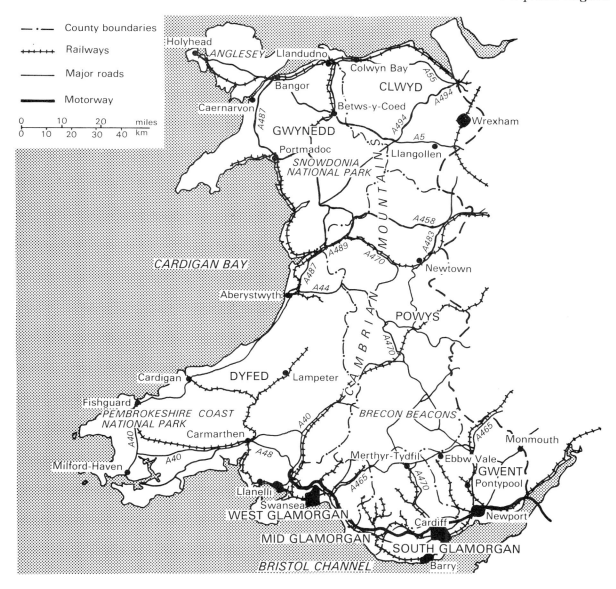

Fig 20.7 Wales—major towns and communications

Pryce suggested three stages in the development of caravan sites: pioneer, expansion and saturation. The North Wales coast had already reached saturation by 1965, with individual sites attaining the size of small towns during the main holiday months, with a wide range of shops and entertainment facilities. In appearance these services reflect the character of the caravans rather than indigenous architecture, so the total landscape impact is altogether exotic. Inland, the impact of the caravan is less concentrated, and reflects the earlier stages of Pryce's model.

Industrial links between the North-West and North Wales are more apparent in eastern Clwyd, in the broad arc of the Flint and Denbigh coalfield, between Oswestry and the Dee estuary. A scattering of industrial concerns herald the fringes of the main axial belt mainly in the engineering and

269

Fig 20.8 Prestatyn, North Wales. Caravan parks and holiday camps stand between the town and the beach·

textile industry. The Shotton plant of B.S.C., threatened with closure many times over the last decade, has finally succumbed to rationalisation, and with the decline of the coalfield little remains of the former industrial base. However, the area has kept its head above water with important investments by Pilkingtons glass fibre and Monsanto chemicals. The potential of the southern shores of the Dee estuary for major overspill of Liverpool does not appear to be likely to be realised in the immediate future.

Western Clwyd, as with the interior of Gwynedd, has experienced sustained population decline associated with the loss of jobs in agriculture. In Gwynedd the decline of the slate quarrying industry was a severe blow to the industrial fortunes of the area, and seemed to point to the hopelessness of vigorous life in the interior of the region. Two developments have helped to counter the mood of pessimism that undoubtedly settled on the area in the late 1960s. The first is the success of *Antur Aelhaearn,* a craft co-operative involving the whole village community at Aelhaearn, which

has not only achieved modest economic success but more importantly rekindled a spark of hope for indigenous industrial developments. The second is the very reverse of *Antur Aelhaearn* – large, capital intensive, high technology developments, for the North-West Region of the Central Electricity Generating Board. Britain's first pumped storage scheme at Blaenau Ffestiniog was opened in 1963, with a further new scheme at Dinorwic. At Trawsfynydd the first commercially operated nuclear power station in Britain was one of the early generation of nuclear stations, using water for cooling from an artificial reservoir created for the earlier Maentwrog hydro-electric scheme. A larger and more advanced nuclear station is also located at Wylfa in Anglesey, while the recent construction of an aluminium smelter has also injected additional employment opportunities. The impact of the smelter was carefully monitored in this respect, and as noted in Scotland, the construction stage made for severe dislocation in the local labour market which continued for some time after completion.

Mid Wales

The two new counties of Dyfed and Powys represent the rural heartland of Wales, with significant sections of the population retaining the Welsh language. Although the 1971 census revealed a wedge of Anglicisation through the Severn-Dyfi routeway, this area of inland, rural, upland Wales is the undoubted repository of the Welsh language. Welsh speaking has progressively declined over the last century but such a large area of linguistic separatism is unique in Britain. Language apart we can pick out two regional issues in this area: *water supply* and *rural development*. The flooding of Welsh valleys for English water supply purposes has long been an emotive subject, and both the West Midlands and parts of the North-West are supplied from the region. The present strategy of the new Regional Water Authorities is to use reservoirs not as huge cisterns, but as regulators for the flow of water down rivers for abstraction in their lower reaches. Reservoirs in Mid Wales form an important part of this system (20.9). Lake Vyrnwy was established in the last century for conducting water to Liverpool, but for the North-West in general a new reservoir, Llyn Brenig, plus the Alwen, Llyn Celyn and Llyn Tegid reservoirs are used to feed the Dee, from which water is abstracted near Chester. Water for Birmingham is piped from the Elan Valley reservoir complex; but plans to enlarge Craig Goch reservoir would allow regulation of the flows on the Wye and the Severn, and (by means of a transfer scheme between the Wye and the Usk) supply water to South-East Wales, as well as meeting the needs of the Severn-Trent and Welsh Water Authorities for the foreseeable future. In addition, of course, the increased recreational use of these reservoirs is of considerable importance, particularly to the West Midlands.

The close proximity of a rapidly expanding West Midlands conurbation and a steadily contracting rural population in Mid Wales led in the 1960s to a proposal to develop a linear new town between Newtown and Llanidloes, with an eventual population of 70,000. Such a proposal was clearly over-ambitious, particularly considering the remoteness of the area, and was subsequently modified to double the population of Newtown itself to 11,000. This plan fits much more harmoniously into wider plans for Mid Wales on the part of the Development Board for Rural Wales and its

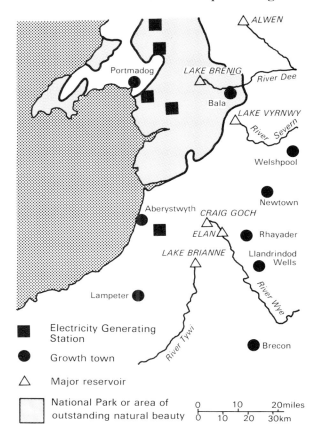

Fig 20.9 Regional development in Mid Wales

predecessors. These plans which are generally designed to arrest regional depopulation by attracting industry into the small towns in the area have already had some success. Altogether 5,000 new jobs in manufacturing industry have been created, the majority for men, so that a population decline from 197,600 to 183,500 between 1951–71 was turned into a rise to 188,900 by 1975. The strategy has included the designation of nine growth towns (Fig. 20.9) with a second tier of twelve centres termed 'key towns', which should be encouraged to grow through the normal processes, without dilution of the Growth Towns policy. (Critics have argued that this second tier is largely cosmetic). The hope is that development will be mainly from the local area, rather than by the attraction of firms from outside, and that the manufacture of tourist items in particular will become more significant. The strategy adopted is worth comparing with that advocated for the Borders region in Scotland.

South Wales

The problems of South Wales have attracted a great deal of attention from both policy-makers and academics alike. But the problems associated with massive contraction of the coal mining industry and a strong reliance on heavy industry remain, despite the great efforts that have been made towards diversifying the industrial structure, renewing the urban fabric and improving communications. The general characteristics of the South Wales coalfield are well known, with the main basin scored by deep valleys which formerly allowed relatively easy access to the shallower coal seams. The valleys have been the scene of marked loss of population. To the south the Carboniferous measures give way to the gentler Lias and Keuper Beds of the Vale of Glamorgan. These low lying areas have been the locus for most, but by no means all, modern development. As a result the population of the central and eastern valleys has fallen by about seven per cent since 1951, while the population of the coastal belt has risen by twenty per cent over the same period.

The decline in the coal industry has been remarkable. In 1921 there were over 215,000 jobs in coal mining. By 1976 that figure had fallen to a mere 31,000, with losses of 40,000 since 1960 alone. There were 118 pits operating in 1960, but only 52 in 1970. The full impact of such changes has been most acutely felt in the upper valleys. In the upper Afon valley, for instance, prior to the 1960s there were thirteen pits active, keeping a population of about 10,000 in almost full employment. A railway line brought in additional labour and there was strong community spirit. By 1971 the last pit had closed and the population had shrunk to 8,650. Without the coal traffic, British Rail removed the railway line, so there was no hope of the inhibitants using it to commute out for jobs. Car ownership was low at 33 per cent, so the population had to rely on an inadequate bus service which did not coincide with the shift system operating in Port Talbot, the obvious source of alternative employment, and the whole community has had its vigour torn out. The physical fabric decays, most higher order public

facilities are only available 18 miles away in Port Talbot, and weekly social security payments amount to over £20,000.

In the steel industry, inland locations were becoming progressively less viable as local sources declined during the nineteenth century, so that already by 1918 the only remaining inland works were at Dowlais and Ebbw Vale. Both have now closed, although tin plate works remain at Ebbw Vale. Thus the steel industry in Wales is now exclusively concentrated on the coast where there has been heavy investment, associated with rationalisation. Thus from a scattering of sixteen steel works in 1950, only six remained in 1979, at Llanelli, Port Talbot, Cardiff (East Moors), Pontypool and at Newport. At Llanwern (Newport) and Port Talbot the plants are integrated with associated blast furnaces, the blast furnaces at Briton Ferry and Ebbw Vale having since closed down (Fig. 20.10). Tin plate works are now solely located at Ebbw Vale, Trostre and Velindre, instead of the 38 separate plants which existed in 1950.

Under the 1979 rationalisation plans, Wales will be the hardest hit region. In any event it is intended that the labour force in South Wales should be reduced by over 11,000. The contraction of steel making also implies a loss of jobs in coal mining, and other sectors of the South Wales economy, so that the provision of alternative sources of employment has become even more urgent.

In the face of such significant changes, regional policy assumes a critical significance. It would have been physically impossible to have stemmed the outflow of population from the region, and to have provided an equivalent number of jobs for those lost in coal and steel. It is remarkable that upwards of 80,000 jobs have actually been provided since 1945. It would not be true to say, however, that there has been a clear regional strategy, and many writers have commented on the lack of consistent direction in this regard. The essential difficulty has been to maintain the balance between taking advantage of opportunites in the coastal belt, with particular reference to Severnside, and maintaining a momentum of development in the older inland industrial communities – without wasting effort in those locations which are clearly not suited to modern requirements for either residential or industrial functions. Thus regional policy has steered light

Fig 20.10 Llanwern Steelworks, South Wales. The massive integrated plant at Llanwern on the Severn coast, threatened with closure in 1979 and now operating on a considerably reduced scale

engineering and electronics into valley centres such as Treorchy and Merthyr Tydfil, while large capital intensive and land hungry industries such as the B.P. refinery at Llandarcy, and motor manufacture at Llanelli and Swansea, are located in the coastal zone. The south-east of the region, between Cardiff and Newport, is clearly the most attractive location with an array of assembly industries and light manufacturing which has given the area a very diversified structure. With the likelihood of increased opportunities in the service sector, particularly with more government functions being carried out from Cardiff, the area is relatively buoyant. Unfortunately this has led to fears that this is at the expense of the valleys, an example being the abandonment of the proposals for new town development at Llantrisant.

THE SOUTH-WEST

In some respects the South-West of England (Fig. 20.11) is a much more advantaged region than Scotland and Wales. The easterly districts are sufficiently prosperous not to qualify for regional aid, and indeed the areas closest to Bristol and to Bournemouth have experienced very rapid development over recent years: therefore, they do not conform to the general pattern that has been described in this chapter. West of Torbay, however, we can see the familiar pattern of high levels of unemployment, losses of population from the countryside and limited job opportunities in the towns. Three themes are explored as typifying the region – tourism, the specific problems of Cornwall, and growth in the Bristol sub-region.

273

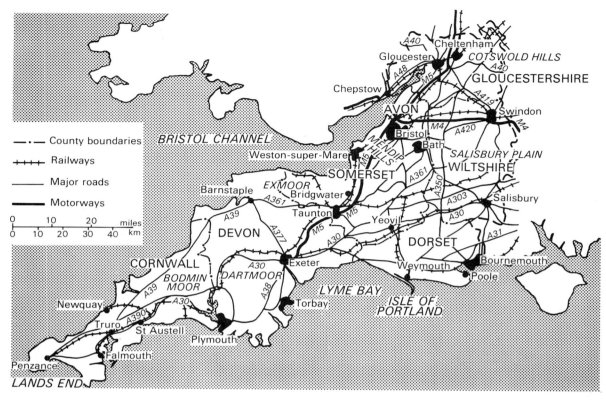

Fig 20.11 The South-West—major towns and communications

Tourism

A survey in 1973 pointed to the economic significance of the tourist industry to the South-West. About 8 million tourists visited the region, generating a net regional income of about £80–£100 millions. In Cornwall the net benefit was 80 per cent that of agriculture. All year round employment was provided for rather more than 60,000 people, with perhaps as many as three times that number being involved during the peak period. Eighty per cent of visitors came by car, mainly from the South-East and from the South-West itself, with a general fall-off further north with distance. Relatively few of the visitors were from overseas. About half the accommodation was of the self-catering variety, which has increased steadily over the last twenty years.

The problem, of course, is that the industry is extremely seasonal, and unevenly distributed. Consequently while some parts of the region

encounter relatively few tourists at any time of the year, others are almost totally overwhelmed for a few weeks in July and August. Ninety per cent of the tourists in the South-West are to be found in the coastal zone, with particularly high densities along the coast of North Cornwall, North Somerset, Torbay and Lyme Regis and Weymouth. Torbay itself receives 14 per cent of all visitors to the region. Such numbers clearly produce enormous problems of overcrowding, for it is just not possible to provide facilities to cope with a sudden peak of demand which only lasts for a few weeks. These areas are now regarded as saturated, and the hope is to divert visitors to alternative locations, without at the same time destroying the amenities of quieter locations. The same is true of communications into the region. The extension of the M5 to Exeter has smoothed the journey to the South-West for many visitors, but the A30 and the A38 westwards into Cornwall still produce bottlenecks at peak periods; yet the diversion of through traffic onto smaller roads would be counter-productive – in any case, the mass of Dartmoor makes this difficult.

The case of Dartmoor illustrates the point. Despite its huge expanse, the areas of real attraction for the tourist are really quite small and highly localised, along the Dart valley, and the 'honeypots' of Postbridge, Two Bridges, Widecombe and Haytor. Few of these places have adequate facilities to cope with the massive summer influx of cars and coaches, yet if such facilities were provided, they would lose much of their present attraction. Equally, to line the main roads across the moor with picnic places and car parks would destroy the quality of grim remoteness that the car-borne tourist wishes to enjoy, spoil the enjoyment of walkers who try to escape the motorist, and interfere with the extensive military use of the region.

A major challenge for the region is to channel the growth of the tourist industry, largely through land use planning controls, and to encourage the extension of the season in so far as this is possible, and so produce more full-time jobs and encourage the visitor to spend more by providing additional opportunities for active amusement. This last is much more a matter of entrepreneurial activity than public planning, but novel examples from south-west Cornwall include recent development of a seal sanctuary, a reconstructed tin mine and an aviation museum (Fig. 20.12).

Cornwall

The superficial attractions of Cornwall's physical environment are considerable. Much of the Duchy contains very attractive scenery, particularly along the coast, its winters are mild, spring comes early and the summer is often sunny. It is, therefore, not surprising that civil servants have asked to be de-centralised there and many workers have dreamed of being re-located to the region. Why then has this not occurred? The reason is simply one of physical and economic remoteness, compounded by a dispersed population unable to support the range of facilities and services demanded by larger firms and the heavier machinery of government. The problem of remoteness is not just a matter of distance from London – the furthest

Fig 20.12 Cornwall Aero Park, Helston. An example of the new style of leisure promotion for a public which increasingly demands sophisticated and informative displays

parts of the region are nearer both London and the Midlands than is most of the Central Valley of Scotland. But the attenuated physiography of the area reduces the 'all-round' connections that are possessed by more inland regions. This is aggravated by the poverty of most of the main lines of communication. No motorway, for instance approaches within 60 km of the county, and it has been estimated that road transport costs from Cornwall to the Midlands are 50 per cent higher than those from Development Areas in lowland Scotland, and 100 per cent higher than from Development Areas in Wales. Among the complaints of new manufacturers in the region is the difficulty of often being distant from markets, from sources of supplies, and from other industries, so that there are poor industrial linkages.

Notwithstanding all this, manufacturing employment has increased considerably since 1960, although this was from a very small base. There was still only 17·7 per cent of the workforce employed in manufacturing industries in 1975, compared with a regional average of 28 per cent. Unfortunately much of the new employment that has been generated has been in the form of low technology, small businesses and branch factory operations, often employing more women than men. Wage rates in both native and in-coming businesses tend to be lower than the national average, and with female activity rates still lower than the norm, household incomes are reduced. In consequence, less money is generally available in the local economy. It is interesting to note that most new businesses located in the region have been attracted by a combination of Development Area status, the high quality of the physical environment, combined with the high cost of land and labour in the South-East region from which they originate. Unfortunately many have found that local labour, though available, is not sufficiently skilled, and this is a function of both the low level of educational provision in the county, and the absence of a manufacturing tradition in the area.

In contrast, the 'indigenous' industries of Cornwall can be said to be *tourism, agriculture* and *mining*. We have already discussed the problems of tourism in the region as a whole. It provides regular employment for about 7 per cent of the county's labour force, and it is worth pointing out that the seasonality of the trade helps to smooth out the demand for energy, as well as demand in the building trades, which are needed for maintenance work in the winter, usually a slack time. Employment in agriculture and fishing stood at almost 7 per cent in 1975, the majority in agriculture. The natural fertility of the land is less than many might imagine; dairying is the chief occupation, and surprisingly only 1½ per cent of the cultivated land is devoted to horticulture, compared with a national average of 2 per cent. The proportion of small farms is higher than the norm, and this has considerable repercussions in terms of the bulk collection of milk. Small herds and difficult access raise the costs of milk production considerably, as well as reducing the potential for farm mechanisation and technical expertise on the part of labour.

Mining and quarrying employ about 10,000 workers, 85 per cent in china clay. The massive landscape intrusion of the china clay workings, particularly around St. Austell is well known, and the industry produces around 2·5 million tonnes each year, with a turnover in 1974 of £65 millions. Not surprisingly the industry is one of Cornwall's leaders. Employment in tin mining has become less secure in recent years, although mining for tin, copper, zinc and wolfram accounted for 1,500 in 1974.

In all of this, the population response has been complex. Migration both in and out of the county has been high, although the pronounced net losses of the 1950s and early 1960s have more recently been replaced by net gains. Those moving out have consistently been the young, in search of higher education and better wages. Those coming in have predominantly been the retired, so that Cornwall has a relatively large proportion of retired people – a fact of some seriousness given the very low level of health and social service provision in the county. During the 1970s there was an increased tendency for in-migrants to include all age-groups, a factor of some surprise in the face of low wages and high unemployment – up to 18 per cent in some districts in winter.

Lastly, we cannot leave Cornwall without making some reference to Plymouth, the sub-regional capital and the nearest centre for higher education and most higher order service functions (Fig. 20.13). Not without its own problems, its impressive civic redevelopment since damage in the 1939–45 war has been seen as a symptom of the city's determination to regenerate itself. Employment in the service sector is now very high – 9 per

Fig 20.13 Armada Way, Plymouth—Post-war redevelopment of Plymouth city centre has produced this formal boulevard, flanked by strictly functional shops and offices

cent above the average for the U.K. – but employment in the manufacturing sector is still dominated by the naval dockyards – about half the total jobs in manufacturing. Fortunately the loss of jobs as the dockyards have progressively contracted has been matched by new jobs attracted to the city, but there is still deprivation, with 19 per cent of the houses in the area being without at least one of the basic amenities.

Bristol and Severnside

The distinctive character of this area, and its structural coherence was recognised at the time of local government reform in 1972, when the new county of Avon was designated, incorporating parts of Somerset, Gloucestershire, and the historic County of the City of Bristol. Like Glasgow, Bristol benefited from its westerly position during the period of overseas expansion, and became a major port for the colonial trade. Its economic base consequently reflected this trade, as its manufacturing industry still does today. Chocolate manufacture, the wine trade, tobacco processing and flour milling are all distinguished staples for which the city has a high reputation. Unlike Glasgow, however, the city never developed the basic industrial trades associated with steel and coal, although some small coal reserves were available locally. In consequence the city has not had the difficulties associated with industrial readjustment over recent years, and indeed in contrast has experienced considerable expansion, based partly upon its estuarine location. Although its deep water facilities have been very limited, and until the recent completion of the new facilities at West Dock general handling for container traffic was inadequate, a series of chemical and metallurgical processing industries developed along Severnside north of the city. These relied upon the local importing of non-ferrous ores, and phosphates, sulphur and potash, for the manufacture of agricultural fertilisers. The inadequacy of the port facilities is highlighted by the large I.C.I. plant receiving its principal feedstock by overland pipeline from Fawley. In addition, however, the area also has the benefit of the presence of B.A.C. and the Bristol engine division of Rolls Royce. The aircraft industries in fact increased their employment from 16,000 in 1951 to 27,500 in 1961. During the 1970s about 12,000 of these workers were involved in the Concorde project, but despite fears that the conclusion of the project would mean a run down of the labour force, a successful move into space technology and servicing work for the American airforce has maintained high levels of employment. As if all this success was not enough, Bristol has also benefited from a rapid expansion in office industries, due particularly to policies of decentralisation from London. The insurance sector especially has grown, both in Bristol and in other neighbouring towns such as Cheltenham and Gloucester. With a distinguished university, a polytechnic, and a further technological university at nearby Bath, the area has also taken part in the rapid expansion of higher education over the 1970s.

Clearly this represents a quite different picture from all the other areas we have examined in this chapter. Between 1961 and 1971 the total number of persons employed in Great Britain declined by

2·1 per cent. In Avon the number actually grew by 6·4 per cent, and despite a net loss of manufacturing employment over the period, the county increased its share of the national manufacturing labour force. Its service industries, too, increased more rapidly than the national average. Rapid development of this kind has led to expansion of the built-up area, and the necessity to delineate green-belt policies to prevent the creation of a totally suburbanised axis between Bristol and Bath. Equally the high levels of employment and sustained prosperity of the area has led to difficulties on the part of the older industries of the town, when they have wished to expand and redevelop their own premises. Considerable pressure, for instance, was applied to Imperial Tobacco to move to an Assisted Area, and it was only with difficulty that permission was obtained for the firm to redeploy itself within Avon. However, Avon is very much the exception in a region which suffers considerably from structural employment problems. Far more typical is West Somerset where unemployment in 1978 even in July was 6·3 per cent; where the majority of firms employ less than 10 people, and school leaver unemployment is acute.

NORTHERN IRELAND

Of all the peripheral regions, Northern Ireland is farthest removed from the mainland metropolitan area, as much by ethos and culture as by distance and the Irish Sea. However we perceive the nature of the links between the various parts of the British Isles, the fact remains that Northern Ireland is heir to a rather different cultural history from mainland Britain. To this must be added the fact that in European terms Ireland is an off-shore island of an off-shore island, poorly endowed, moreover, with natural resources. Unlike Wales and Scotland, for instance, it has few energy resources and little mineral wealth. Although it is less mountainous, and more amenable to agriculture than Wales and Scotland, its agriculture shares the disabilities of South-West England as regards land quality and farm structure; but the province does not have the warm summers of the South-West, and is less able to sustain successful harvests of grain crops. More importantly, however, its domestic market for all goods is small, and connections with other markets are

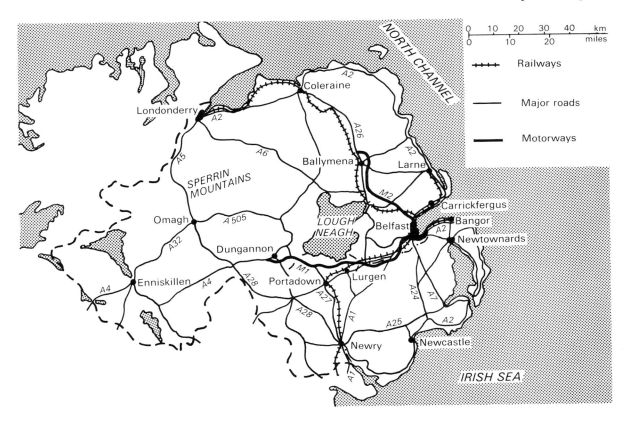

Fig 20.14 Northern Ireland—major towns and communications

hampered by the sea crossing. In many respects the problems of N. Ireland hang upon its location and poor resource endowment, and although an explanation of the political problems of the area is very complex, such an explanation inevitably has its roots in these two geographical aspects (Fig. 20.14).

Political Problems

The relationship between Ireland and mainland Britain has been uneasy since at least Viking times. Because of Ireland's proximity, Anglo-Norman kings came to regard Ireland as a natural extension of their domain, but it was not until the tempestuous years of the sixteenth and seventeenth centuries that English political domination became pervasive throughout the majority of the country.

Unfortunately this was at a time when political affairs were closely associated with religious affiliation. The distinction between rulers and ruled, therefore, became marked as nowhere else in the British Isles by a sectarian as well as an economic divide. Although there were notable exceptions, the landlord class was of mainland extraction and therefore non-Roman Catholic, while the tenantry was predominantly made up of native Irish who remained staunchly Roman Catholic.

To this generalisation has to be added a profoundly important spatial variable. The ancient province of Ulster had always been the most resistant of the four provinces of Ireland to English infiltration; its people the most fiercely independent. Mainland occupation of the province, therefore, was associated with considerable bitterness and strife, and achieved under English landlord direction mainly by poor colonists from

279

neighbouring Scotland. These colonists were Presbyterians, who were at the time of an uncompromisingly Protestant disposition. Over most of Ireland the English Protestants were a small landholding minority. In Ulster the mainland settlers became a majority along the main points of entry in the eastern counties and along the Bann and Foyle lowlands, occupying similar agricultural holdings to the native population, and competing with them for new land as population expanded during the later eighteenth and early nineteenth century. Because capital often lay in the hands of colonists of mainland origin, the Protestant tended to be advantaged both on the land and in the growing industries. Commerce and industry in the North thus came to be directed by the Protestants, although the labour force on both the land and in the expanding linen and marine engineering industries was made up of both Protestants and Catholics.

During the nineteenth century, agitation for Home Rule increased in Ireland, but was resisted by the Protestants, particularly in Ulster. The result was the partition of the country into two states in 1920, and the creation of a Protestant dominated enclave occupying the majority of ancient Ulster, with a capital city and local Parliament in Belfast. In the face of continued hostility from many remaining Catholics (now a minority), and uneasy relationships with Eire, the Northern Ireland Protestants undoubtedly felt vulnerable and attempted to secure their hold on public life by electoral manipulation. Although there were real signs that emnity was at last being overcome during the early 1960s, extremists on both sides of the cultural divide were more than ready to exploit old fears and past grievances when the civil rights movement began in Northern Ireland in 1967–8. As a result, civil disorder increased to such an extent that the Northern Ireland Parliament at Stormont was first prorogued in 1972, and then disbanded. Direct rule from Westminister was imposed, and a large military presence installed. Despite the undoubted wish of the vast majority of the population for peace and security it has not been possible to restore devolved government, although local government has been reformed. The result of this unrest has undoubtedly had a major impact upon the economic vigour of the province (and of the rest of the U.K.) and upon the social well-being of the community as a whole.

Social Cleavage

In contrast to the rest of Ireland, Roman Catholics account for only slightly more than one third of the population in Northern Ireland, and are predominantly in the former western counties of Londonderry, Tyrone and Fermanagh, and the southern parts of Armagh and Co. Down. It is in the urban areas, though, that sectarian division is most marked, particularly in predominantly Catholic Londonderry, and predominantly Protestant Belfast. The social geography of Belfast has been extensively studied over recent years, since Emrys Jones's seminal work in 1960. In common with many other British cities, Belfast shows considerable variation between socially desirable and socially less desirable areas. Again in common with other large urban areas these are arranged in rough sectors or swathes that extend outwards from the city centre, each sector whether richer or poorer becoming more desirable away from the downtown area. In Belfast, however, the interest lies in the low-status sectors, particularly to the west, where religious polarisation has been particularly marked. Religious segregation is much less apparent in the higher status sectors.

Over recent years two trends have been apparent. As new housing estates have been built on the periphery of the built-up area since the early 1960s, these sectarian zones have been extended outwards. As Boal (1971) has pointed out, this is largely a reflection of two factors. On the one hand the linear arrangements of bus routes has meant that, in moving out of the city, people have preferred to be along an easy line of communications from their former friends and neighbours – a factor of some importance given the low level of car ownership. On the other hand because the Roman Catholic community prefers to maintain its own schools, such schools (and churches) are located in predominantly Catholic areas. As a result Catholic families either buying or renting a house generally prefer to be near to a Catholic school, particularly a primary school, and a church. Sectarian distinction is thus perpetuated. A second trend is that, as civil disorder increased during the early 1970s, there was a marked tendency for residual Catholic or Protestant families to move out of mixed neighbourhoods, into their respective majority areas. This is not necessarily from a thorough-going dislike of their former

Protestant or Catholic neighbours. In many cases such families were anxious because their children had to cross boundary zones to go to school, or that housewives had to shop in vulnerable local centres. Needless to say, such readjustment has been painful, and regretted by the majority of the population.

While such patterns are interesting geographically, they do raise important questions as to the well-being of the whole community. Social cohesion is generally regarded as a desirable objective, yet a major problem is presented in Belfast because much of the inner city area needs to be redeveloped, and the population housed, in the most harmonious manner. In 1978 almost one quarter of the 123,000 houses in the city were unfit, 25,000 of them in clearance areas in the central residential area. More than 44,000 houses lacked one of the basic amenities, and £130 millions has been allocated to house building programmes. The allocation of new houses to Protestants and Catholics is a very contentious issue, and there are conflicting views as to whether the long term future is best served or not by the construction of extensive new housing areas, occupied predominantly by one or the other of the religious groups. Housing is not the only problem in inner Belfast, of course, for the city shares the problems of many other large inner urban areas. Multiple deprivation is chronic in some areas, with juvenile male unemployment rates being as high as 45 per cent in some districts. In such an economic climate social unrest is inevitable.

Economic Problems

Northern Ireland's economic problems have a familiar ring. A generally low level of economic activity is accompanied by high levels of unemployment, which at 12 per cent in 1978 was almost double the average for the United Kingdom. Most employment is disproportionately concentrated into a few areas, notably Belfast, leaving the majority of the province a rural backwater, with low incomes, limited job opportunities and an ageing and declining population. Out-migration from Northern Ireland to the other regions of Britain, however, has been less than from Scotland and Wales. This is a curious characteristic which cannot be explained by the psychological

difficulty of 'crossing the water', as emigration from Eire to the U.K. has consistently run at a higher level. Busteed (1974) suggests that the differences between the two parts of Ireland may be a reflection of higher welfare benefits in the North, but this is unlikely to be the whole reason. An additional factor may be that the cultural links of Northern Ireland are greater with Scotland, and so there is less inclination to look towards England, the obvious source of job opportunities. However, this is unlikely to be more than a contributory factor.

All of the province's major sources of employment in 1945 have contracted to half their former size. Agriculture formerly supported 150,000 jobs, linen manufacture 50,000, and shipbuilding and marine engineering 22,000. On the other hand the main growth sectors have been in office employments which have doubled over the same period, but which have provided neither a sufficient number of new jobs, nor jobs of an appropriate kind for dispossessed manual workers. Consequently, as on the mainland, a policy response has been required to attract new industry and aid existing businesses.

Throughout the 1960s and the 1970s, there was specific government intervention in the aircraft and shipbuilding industries, although the long-term future for the latter is extremely uncertain. In the former industry Short Brothers and Harland, which lies outside the nationalised British Aerospace organisation, has increased its activities and now commands the market in a number of specialised components for civil and military aircraft and missiles. It is now the second-largest engineering employer in the province (after Harland and Woolf, Shipbuilders). This is one of a number of engineering brightspots which include among others a new bicycle manufacturing agency in Londonderry. It was felt that the engineering trades had turned a corner in the late 1970s, with a series of American investment decisions. (Foreign investment has been very low in the province since the start of the present disturbances.). The *DeLorean* car project at West Belfast will provide 2,000 jobs, a £10 million project by *General Motors* in East Belfast will provide another 600, and a further £10 million project by *AVX New York* to manufacture capacitors at Coleraine will provide a further 600 new jobs. However, these developments apart, the engineering industry in Northern Ireland is still too small to support the range of skills and technical capacity that a modern industry needs for self-sustaining growth.

The textile industry has been through an uncertain period. As the linen industry contracted, the expansion of synthetic textiles seemed to offer a ray of hope. All the major chemical combines were enticed to the province. Courtaulds, I.C.I., DuPont, Monsanto, and British Enkalon all responded to the lure of development grants, but the current massive over-capacity in the European fibres industry has cast a cloud over what seemed a promising future, and it is likely that most further investment will reduce, rather than increase, the number of jobs available.

In all of these developments, though, there is little doubt that in attracting new industry, Northern Ireland suffers from three major drawbacks. Two we have already referred to. First is the effect of perceived peripherality from the main centre of European economic activity and the additional transport costs engendered by the crossing of the Irish Sea (which can add between 10 and 20 per cent to unit costs). Secondly, although industry as such has not suffered very much from terrorist activity, the stormy political climate has been a strong disincentive to overseas investors. Thirdly, however, energy costs are very high. In 1978 electricity charges were 30 per cent higher than on the mainland, and a massive investment of public funds was made to write-off outstanding debts on the parts of the Northern Ireland Electricity Service, and to help keep further increases in cost to a minimum. Gas supplies are very limited, and are produced from imported petroleum. Thus gas supplies are more expensive than the natural gas available on the mainland, and there is considerable agitation for an extension of the natural gas grid across the North Channel from Scotland. In the event, however, it might be cheaper to write off the existing gas industry and convert exclusively to electricity. (Most domestic customers already rely on bottled gas).

Regional Disparities

The distribution of economic activity within Northern Ireland has been characterised by two features: (i) a declining, thinly populated and mainly agricultural zone west of the Bann, and (ii) an over-concentration of population and employment in the city of Belfast, itself suffering from an over-dependency upon nineteenth century staples and a housing stock of a similar date. In this respect the province has a problem similar to that of Glasgow and western Scotland, though on a smaller scale.

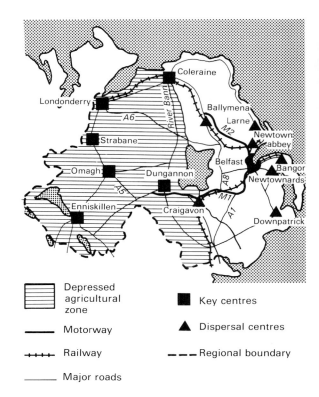

Fig 20.15 Regional Policy in Northern Ireland

Employment in agriculture is three times as high as on the mainland and this has produced a particular difficulty in the former western counties, where agriculture still employed up to one-third of insured male workers in some districts as late as 1978. These mainly Catholic areas maintain a high birthrate in spite of continued out-migration of young people. With agriculture likely to continue to decline as a source of employment, either additional jobs will have to be created in these areas, or further sections of the working population encouraged to migrate if higher unemployment is not to follow. As in Mid Wales, a 'key centre' policy has been designated with Enniskillen, Omagh, Strabane, Dungannon, Coleraine and Londonderry designated as the location for investment of capital infrastructure, and advance factory development. In addition road improvements have been carried through, including a motorway link from Belfast to Dungannon, and the underused railway link from Belfast to Coleraine and Londonderry kept open, though at a considerable loss (Fig. 20.15).

Londonderry has been seen as the major centre of attraction for these former western counties. Although located at the north-western extremity of the zone it is not well-placed to aid the former counties of Fermanagh and most of Tyrone. Indeed much of Londonderry's natural hinterland lies over the border in Co. Donegal, although this too is a poor area. Following the reform of local government in N. Ireland and the setting up of a Development Commission for Londonderry, considerable improvements have been made in the economic and social welfare of the city and the surrounding rural area. In 1975, for instance, Courtaulds received a grant of £5·6 millions from the E.E.C. for a new factory in Londonderry, and in 1978 the DuPont company embarked upon a $50 millions re-equipment programme in an attempt to secure the jobs of 1,600 workers in the synthetic fibres industry until the end of the century.

As we have already seen, on the mainland the policy response to over-crowded, badly serviced central area problems has been to create New Towns and overspill arrangements. Already in the early 1960s there was some modest movement of population of Belfast into new housing estates in the small towns around the edges of Belfast Lough. In 1963 the *Mathews Report* formalised and encouraged this trend by promoting small-scale dispersals of population over a rather wider area to the small towns of Co. Antrim and Co. Down, from Ballymena in the north to Downpatrick in the south. In addition a major out-of-city programme was initiated at Craigavon. This new development was strategically located alongside the M 1 and the Belfast–Dublin rail link, between the existing settlements at Lurgan and Portadown, south of Lough Neagh. Among a range of industrial concerns re-locating on the site, Courtaulds and Goodyear Tyre Co. are among the larger employers. The latter decided in 1979 to establish a division of its Research and Development Unit at Craigavon. High grade employments such as are created in research and development, of

course, are precisely the type that are being eagerly sought by development agencies in all the peripheral regions. Movement of population out of Belfast, however, has not been as popular as was hoped in the 1960s. The city has grown at a faster rate than was anticipated because out-migration has been so unpopular, and this seems to be because of social and also economic reasons, in that housing in the outer city areas, being new, tends to be more expensive than the older property in the city centre.

The longer term prospects for Northern Ireland are difficult to predict given the uncertain political situation. Relationships with Dublin and the rest of Ireland are an important aspect of the problem, which continues to prove contentious on both sides of the border. Meanwhile government in Westminster is obliged to take account of the clear wish of the majority of the population to remain within the United Kingdom; and consequently has to support the economy of Northern Ireland to the tune of £140 millions in employment support in 1978–9 alone, in addition to other Exchequer payments.

References

Law, C.M., and Warnes, A.M., 'The changing geography of the elderly in England and Wales', *Trans. Inst. Brit. Geogrs.*, N.S., 1, 4, 1976, pp. 453–471.

Turnock, D., *Scotland's Highlands and Islands* (OUP, 1974).

Manners, G., Keeble, D., Rodgers, B., and Warren, K., *Regional Development in Britain* (Wiley, 1972).

Smith, H.D, Hogg, A., and Hutcheson, A.M., 'Scotland and offshore oil; the developing impact', *Scottish Geographical Magazine*, 93, 2, 1976, pp. 75–91.

Fernie, J., 'North Sea Oil, a Review', *Department of Geography, Huddersfield Polytechnic, Occasional Paper No. 4*, 1976.

Pryce, W.T.R., 'Holiday caravan camps in Wales', *Trans. Inst. Brit. Geogrs.*, 47, 1967, pp. 127–52.

Rees, T.L., 'Population and industrial decline in the South Wales coalfield', *Regional Studies,* 12, 1, 1978, pp. 69–78.

Busteed, M.A., *Northern Ireland* (OUP, 1974).

Boal, F.W., in *Irish Geographical Studies,* edited by Stephen, N., & Glassock, R.E. (Queens University, Belfast, 1971).

Jones, E., *Social Geography of Belfast* (OUP, 1960).

21

Intermediate Regions

The three remaining economic planning regions lie in the North of England. They are given a certain common identity by the upland massifs which form the Lake District, the Pennines and the North York Moors, and by the problems which emanate from their rapid industrialisation during Victorian times. To this image of factory town, coal mine and moor-clad hills, needs to be added considerable stretches of improved pastures in the lowlands (and indeed some first class arable land) and a degree of positive environmental intervention unparalleled in the most other areas.

Environment and Land-use

The asymmetrical anticline of the Pennine chain forms a dissected upland extending from the Scottish Borders to the Peak District. Only rarely does it rise above 750 m, although extensive tracts lie between 300 m and 600 m, so it is not to be compared with the mountain fastnesses of the Scottish Highlands or North Wales. Much of it is capped with millstone grit clothed in peat, which combined with a series of structural and erosional plateaus gives a depressing monotony to the vista. This is greatly relieved by the series of gashes, more noticeable in the east than in the west, which make the Pennine Dales, from the South Tyne valley in the north to the Don in the south. To the west of the Pennines, the Lake District with its core of ancient rocks, and radiating finger lakes, offers a more spectacular scenery. To the east, the North York Moors display in a subdued form the topography of the Pennines, but on younger rocks of Jurassic age. All three areas, however, experience the problems associated with upland and hill

farming, and the pressures of large nearby urban populations. Afforestation is extensive in all three, while considerable tracts have been designated as National Parks. In contrast, as we noted in Chapter 7, lowland reclamation around the Humber and on the Lancashire mosses during the nineteenth century produced stretches of first class agricultural land, while the cretaceous Yorkshire Wolds support a rural economy much more evocative of southern than of northern England.

Economic Legacy

In all three regions the presence of extensive coalfields supported industrial development over the nineteenth century, but proved an Achilles heel during the first half of the twentieth. Today, the coal industry is only a faint shadow of its former self in the Northern and North-West regions, although the future in Yorkshire and Humberside looks relatively assured. Similarly the industrial structure that was built upon the power base of the coalfields has largely withered away. 'King Cotton' has been deposed in Lancashire, the Yorkshire woollen trade has been drastically reduced, whilst the iron and steel trades in the North-East and the North-West have been re-structured out of all recognition from their former importance and distribution.

With such an economic history it is not surprising that all three areas have a sad legacy of social and environmental deprivation. At the regional level most indicators show trends that are consistently below the national average, although as we saw in Chapter 16, there can be marked local variations. The North-East of England and West

Cumberland have had a consistent designation as areas in need of regional aid since 1934, Merseyside since 1945, and since 1972 the whole area has been under either Intermediate Area, Development Area or Special Development Area status. The economic problems of parts of the Northern and the North-West regions have sometimes matched the worst of conditions in Scotland and South Wales. In contrast, other parts, and much of Yorkshire and Humberside have fared much better, with unemployment rates often lower than the national average. Rodgers, for instance, remarks on the division of Lancashire between a prosperous west and a rapidly declining

east. Similarly, in Yorkshire and County Durham, the Pennine districts are generally relatively less prosperous than areas in the more open lowlands to the east, where the legacy of early industrialisation is not so pressing, and modern industrial development is able to make use of superior communications.

THE NORTHERN REGION

With a greater proportion of its area occupied by uplands, and industrial districts once based almost exclusively on coal, iron and steel products, and

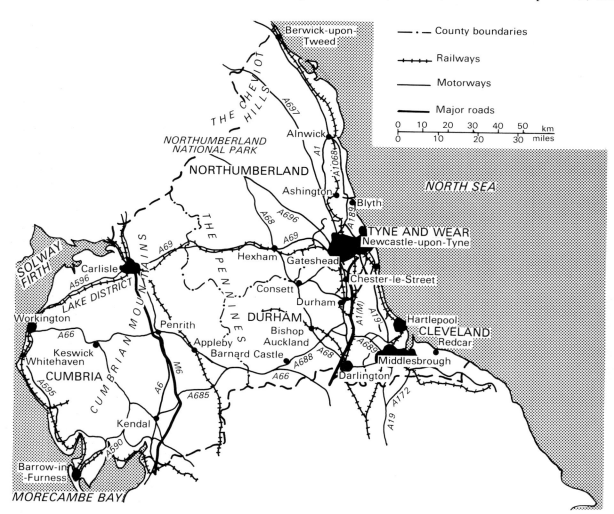

Fig 21.1 Northern Region—major towns and communications

more recently chemicals, the Northern Region shows the characteristics of a region in economic and social difficulty more acutely than any other region in England (Fig. 21.1). Straddling the Pennines it is a dichotomous region, not just because the major concentration of population is found on the eastern seaboard in Tyne and Wear, but because the Cumbrian massif, rather like Wales, while being a distinctive region in itself, tends to have a centrifugal rather than a centripetal effect upon movement. Thus, the northern and western districts may look towards Carlisle and, via the Tyne gap, east to the regional capital in Newcastle upon Tyne; but the south eastern areas naturally look towards the North-West region, with which communications, via the M6, are easier than the awkward crossing of the Sedbergh Fells to the North-East. In addition, the contrasts that we noted in Scotland between sparsely populated uplands and highly congested industrial districts are also present, while the unique attractions of the Lake District have generated one of the most important tourist developments in Britain. Regional consciousness is well developed on both sides of the Pennines, but particularly in the North-East where a distinctive dialect, a deep tradition of manual labour and a rich folk heritage have combined with a shared hardship in the years of depression to give a very strong regional self-image.

The North-East Industrial Region

We noted in Chapter 7 that the tidewater coalfield adjacent to the Tyne and the Wear played a significant part in the early development of industrial techniques from the sixteenth century onwards. Innovations in shaft mining and rail transportation encouraged the rise of the coal export trade, and the progressive enlargement of the worked coalfield. The development of the iron and steel trades was a major feature of the nineteenth century, using at various times ores from local Coal Measures, the Jurassic ores of Cleveland, Cumbrian and Weardale haemetites and imports from overseas. First the demand for iron rails for the railways, and then the demand for sheet metal for commercial and naval shipping fostered the iron and steel trades at an array of locations from the western periphery of the coal-

field at Consett and Tow Law, to estuarine sites on the Tyne, Tees and Wear. Inward migration was considerable until the 1920s, with not only agglomerations of population on Tyneside, Wearside and Teesside, but also a dispersed industrial population across the whole coalfield, from Amble on the Northumberland coast to the Gaunless valley south-west of Bishop Auckland. Beyond the coalfield, the extraction of lead, barytes, fluorspar and iron took the miner deep into the heart of the Pennines. In some senses, the decline of the area's industrial fortunes begins there, with the collapse of the lead mining industry in the 1880s and the initiation of an eastward drift of population which has continued ever since. The inter-war depression and the miners' strikes of 1921 and 1926 – a major blow for the whole region – hit the western parts of the coalfield particularly severely, and many mines became irretrievably flooded. Although the war-time demands placed upon the heavy engineering and coal industries, and the short-lived boom in the post-war demand for coal obscured the trend, the economic decline of the basic industries of the North-East was already under way by 1930. There are two major strands to this decline: (i) the problem of the coalfield, and (ii) the problem of heavy engineering, each with distinct geographical components.

(i) The *decline of the coal industry* can be expressed quite starkly. At the beginning of 1947 there were 225 working pits in Northumberland and County Durham. By 1964 there were only 105, and the industry entered the 1970s with fewer than 50, of which less than half were expected to survive into the 1980s. Employment has shrunk from more than a quarter of a million in 1913, to 119,000 in 1964, and to 38,000 in 1975. While closures have been experienced in all parts of the coalfield, the effect has been most pronounced in West Durham, where a combination of thin, largely worked out seams and small units made continued extraction quite uneconomic. A marked feature of the area was the rash of small settlements with population between 5,000 and 10,000, and with immature economies which depended almost entirely upon coal mining. In West Durham the pits were smaller but more numerous, and this reflected itself in a settlement pattern of small villages grouped around larger service centres like Stanley and Crook. In the east, however, larger collieries supported a more uniform scatter of medium-sized to large villages, though none that could be described as towns. The closure of the local coal mine, therefore, wiped out the *raison d'être* of many settlements. For a time the situation was eased by the bussing of miners to surviving pits in the eastern, concealed sector of the coalfield, but as collieries there began to close during the later 1960s the tenuous position of such settlements was highlighted. The dangers were foreseen as long ago as the 1940s by the Durham County Council. Its controversial 1951 County Development Plan outlined four categories of settlements, A–D. About one third of all settlements were in the D category, which were seen as having no long-term future. The intention was that population should be encouraged to move towards the more viable centres, where investment would be concentrated, and as 80 per cent of these D category villages were west of the A1 road, a very significant shift in the balance of population was envisaged. Events have largely

borne out the sense of such a strategy, and although the dormitory function of some of the smaller settlements in the west has become more significant than was originally envisaged, population in West Durham has progressively declined, and some of the smaller settlements, such as Waterhouses, have been almost entirely demolished. However, in the face of sustained local opposition the D classification was abandoned in 1978.

(ii) *Iron and steel making* was inevitably more concentrated, and since the 1930s steel-making has been confined to coastal sites at West Hartlepool, the south bank of the Tees, and at Skinningrove high on the Cleveland cliffs, plus one inland location at Consett, at 300 m possibly the highest steel making plant in Europe. Much of the region's output of steel was geared either to direct export or to the local *shipbuilding* and associated engineering industries. As early as 1913 these two industries accounted for over 125,000 jobs, over-

Fig 21.2 Steelworks, Consett, Co. Durham. With little alternative employment, the closure of BSC Consett has dealt a long-feared death blow to this town of 40,000

whelmingly concentrated on Tyneside, Wearside and Teesside. Although Tyneside was able to participate in the demand for heavy electrical engineering products as the electricity supply industry developed during the inter-war period, this did not offset the massive fall in employment in the shipbuilding trades, so that unemployment in Jarrow and Sunderland remained above 25 per cent until the sudden demand for naval vessels at the time of the 1939–45 war. By the mid 1950s, though, the shipbuilding industry was again experiencing a shortage of orders, partly as a result of strong competition abroad, so that the widespread loss of jobs on the western parts of the coalfield were being again shadowed by localised unemployment in the conurbations. In the 1960s almost 3,500 jobs per year were being lost in shipbuilding, so that by 1974 merchant shipbuilding in the area was employing only about 25,000 workers, and that largely due to government aid in reorganisation and modernisation, and the encouragement given to U.K. firms to place orders with domestic yards.

The reduction in demand from the shipbuilding industry clearly had repercussions upon local steel making, and although it continued to export and to supply other areas of the domestic market its rate of growth in the 1950s and 1960s was very slow (about 3 per cent per year). Since nationalisation in 1967, though, the pattern of the industry in the North-East has changed significantly. The first stage of change involved the closure of small plants at Hartlepool, Skinningrove and in Middlesbrough, which resulted in heavy job losses on Teesside. However, the ideal facilities of Teesside for the development of a modern steel industry have not been lost, and under the 1972 Ten Year Development Plan, South Teesside was intended to produce one-third of Britain's steel output. Substantial moves have been made towards this target, despite the recent contraction of the world market for steel. A new ore terminal was completed at Redcar in 1972, and steel making is being progressively shifted towards new plant there and at Lackenby. Iron and steel making at West Hartlepool closed in 1977 with a loss of 1,500 jobs, leaving only coke making and the plate mill on the north bank. Early in 1978 the new Redcar sinter plant was opened to feed 10,000 tonnes of blast furnace charge a day for new blast facilities nearby. The new basic oxygen blast furnace is one of the biggest in the world.

It was a surprise to many that in the Ten Year Plan for steel, plate and billet working were to be maintained at Consett, appearing to assure the medium term future of this isolated hilltop town. The 1979 rationalisation proposals, however, included the closure of the Consett works, which was a particularly bitter blow to a workforce which had increased productivity considerably over the preceeding two years (Fig. 21.2).

Regional Policy

The contraction of the major staples in the region has brought overwhelming problems, as in South Wales, and the way in which the challenge has been met deserved outlining as a useful case study (Fig. 21.3).

The North-East was one of the original areas to benefit under the 1934 Special Areas (Development and Improvement) Act. Although much that issued from the Act was of the nature of relief work, it did increase the rate at which the infrastructure of the region was up-dated, with particular regard to water supply and sanitation. More significantly the Act spawned the concept of *advance factories,* through the work in particular of the English Industrial Estates Corporation whose headquarters and major development was on a reclaimed site at Team Valley, south of Gateshead. (The Team Valley estate now employs over 20,000 workers in a range of manufacturing industries.) Other industrial estates were established in south-west Durham and south Tyneside. The region continued to be designated under the Distribution of Industry Acts of 1945 (amended in 1950), and 1958, and the Local Employment Acts of 1960 and 1963, but relatively little was achieved, despite the continued agitation of local interests. It was in fact, only with a direct political initiative in the face of rapidly deteriorating conditions in 1963 that the problems of the region were given an overview by government, with the so-called Hailsham Report of 1963 (*The North East: A Programme for Regional Development and Growth*). This introduced the new concept of a 'Growth Zone' where industrial development would be most likely to prosper. Its location, to the west of the A1 trunk road, largely reflected the Durham County Council policy of 1951, but in addition it pointed to the necessity of improving

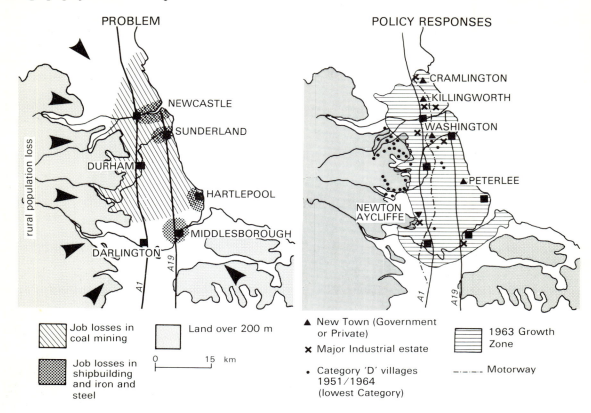

PROBLEM

POLICY RESPONSES

▨ Job losses in coal mining	▧ Land over 200 m
▨ Job losses in shipbuilding and iron and steel	0 ___ 15 km

▲ New Town (Government or Private)

✕ Major Industrial estate

• Category 'D' villages 1951/1964 (lowest Category)

▤ 1963 Growth Zone

━·━·━ Motorway

Fig 21.3 Regional development in North-East England

communications, housing provision, town centre redevelopment and reclamation. As a consequence of the report the two major trunk roads the A19 and A1 were upgraded, the partially re-routed and developed to motorway standard. In addition a new town was proposed at Washington, close to the A1(M) between Newcastle and Sunderland.

Two other *new towns* had already been established to act as centres of redevelopment. Only five miles north of Darlington, Newton Aycliffe was designated as a new town in 1947 to cater for the rapid development of an industrial estate as the successor to a war time munitions factory. The site has in fact proved very popular with industrialists, and the population target has been progressively reviewed upwards from the original 10,000 target to 45,000 in 1963. On the East-Durham coalfield, Peterlee was designed to serve a quite different function. It was designated in 1948 in an attempt to provide a truly urban facility for the scattering of large mining villages that

developed on the concealed coalfield mainly during the present century. During the early 1960s its future looked uncertain as mining employments contracted, but with the enhancement of the nearby A19 its prospects have become brighter. With their new town centres and (at Peterlee) futuristic architecture, the image of the two towns made a great impression on local thinking so that two new developments were undertaken, at first independently of government designation, to the north of Newcastle. At Killingworth Township, a comprehensive redevelopment area was designated as an overspill town for the Tyneside conurbation, but the slower rate of population increase has meant that the target population (20,000) is unlikely to be reached. Nearby Cramlington New Town (which was sponsored by Northumberland County Council, but to be built almost entirely by private developers) was afforded benefit under the Town Development Act (1952) by the Hailsham Report. In the event it has remained more of a dormitory suburb than as a locus for new employment.

The main thrust of regional policy, however, is to create jobs. In 1967 the whole of the main coalfield region was designated a *Special Development Area*. As a result, building grants of up to 35 per cent, loans towards the balance of building costs, rent-free periods of up to five years for advance factories, and special operational grants were available in addition to the benefits under the Industrial Development Act 1966 and the Regional Employment Premium. Regional development presently operates under the Industry Acts of 1972 and 1975, until the 1979 arrangements come into full operation in 1982. There is no doubt that

regional policy has proved of considerable benefit to the North-East in particular, and the Northern region in general. It is estimated that between 1963 and 1973 an extra 50,000 manufacturing jobs had been created in the Northern region by regional policy, 70 per cent of which had come from outside, but many of which were branch operations, often involving female labour or associated with massive capital investment. Employment in the service sector, traditionally weak in the North-East, has increased over the same period in line with national trends. There has been some 'topping-up' by the dispersal of some civil servants from London – only 2,600 between 1963–72, but with already established posts the Northern

Fig 21.4 ICI—Wilton Works, Cleveland. 800 ha were acquired by ICI in 1945 on th south bank of the Tees. The site now houses branches of the Petrochemicals, Plastics, Fibres, Organics and Mond Divisions of ICI

Region now has a greater proportion of head-quarters civil servants than any other region in Britain, except of course the South-East.

Lastly, we must take note of the very great changes which have taken place on Teesside as a result of huge investment (largely from government sources) on the part of the *chemicals industry*. With its strategic position and ample flat land, Teesside had already experienced massive development by I.C.I. and Monsanto, before the discovery of North Sea oil and gas turned the estuary into a major oil terminal. I.C.I. had invested more than £1 billion at Billingham and at Wilton by 1977: it contributes about £6 millions in rates, and in 1977 had a local wages and salaries bill of £119 millions (Fig. 21.4). One of its major new investments is a 500,000 tonnes a year ethylene plant, commissioned jointly with B.P. Superficially the technological transformation of Teesside is abundantly impressive, yet its economy remains immature. It relies on a bulk-reducing economy, which is still the subject of massive labour rationalisations, producing semi-finished goods which provide more employment in other regions. Despite the proliferation of industrial estates, this is a comment which can be

applied to the region as a whole. With unemployment still running close to double the national average, the North-East is far from being delivered of its problems, but one can only conclude that the situation would be very much worse were it not for the considerable assistance received by the region since 1963.

Cumbria

The popular image of Cumbria lies in its rural heartland, but the majority of the county's population is to be found, as in the North-East, on a relatively confined coastal strip, with concentrations around Barrow, Whitehaven-Workington, and Carlisle. These concentrations were the result of the boom in coal and haemetite extraction which hit the area following the introduction of the Bessemer process in the mid-nineteenth century, and as in the North-East these industries are now but faint shadows of what they once were. In 1977, the industry was reduced to one mine at Whitehaven, which although it employed 1,200 workers, had an uncertain future. The mining of iron ore ceased

Fig 21.5a Windscale and Calder Hall works of British Nuclear Fuels, Ltd

Fig 21.5b Buttermere, in the Lake District. One of the most popular tourist areas of the country, it is nevertheless an area of declining employment

in 1968; closure of the steel-making plants at Workington and at Millom soon followed, leaving the area with only the rail production plant at Workington, and the plate industry at Barrow to supply the Vickers shipyards. Barrow-in-Furness is a classic example of a company town, and even today Vickers employ half the town's workforce. For many years the yards have specialised in naval engineering, and their immediate future is assured. Nevertheless the weakness of relying on one major employer has been appreciated for many years, and a number of firms have been established recently – in textiles and drugs – to provide much-needed female employment. The arrival of Bowater-Scott (paper tissues, etc.) – making use of existing timber importing facilities – and of Sovereign Chemicals, has helped to provide alternative male labour oppor-

tunities. The major problems, however, have been encountered on the former coalfield area, where a depressing environment coupled with extreme remoteness did not help in tempting new industries to the area. Two major growth points have been established at new industrial estates between Maryport and Workington, and between Workington and Whitehaven, and these have been modestly successful, but unemployment continues to run at significantly above the national average. Consequently, local views on the desirability of having a major nuclear installation at Windscale tend to be very mixed (Fig. 21.5a).

A greater contrast between the grimy shipyards in Barrow and the open fells of the Lake District could not be imagined (Fig. 21.5b). To the visitor the Lake District seems to show many signs of prosperity with its gift shops, hotels and restaurants. As an attractive area it has received considerable numbers of retired migrants, there are many second homes, and not a few very wealthy industrialists who have established homes particularly in the Windermere area. The consumer market has been very buoyant for many years, house prices are above the regional average, and unemployment lower, yet the area still has significant problems. Between 1963 and 1975 the Lake District uplands lost 26 per cent of all full time labour, mainly from farming. Although farming still employs 15 per cent of all active males, over 80 per cent of farm labour is provided by the farmers themselves. Similarly slate quarrying, which employed over 1,200 workers in the 1950s, notably in Langdale, Borrowdale and Coniston, is now reduced to 300 workers. The provision of 200 jobs in forestry is just no substitute for such losses. The result has been the now familiar decline of population in the rural areas in the interior of the Lake District, with a corresponding rise in both employment and residence at the peripheral towns, particularly at Kendal and Ulverston. The post-war boom in tourism has brought a series of problems in its wake. Although 3,000 jobs are provided by the industry, a large proportion of these are for females, and many are taken by itinerant workers from other parts of the country. Meanwhile congestion both on the roads and even on the fells has raised the question of whether entry into the National Park area should not be regulated by some means, if the essence and charm of the area is not to be bludgeoned away either by over-use or modification to accommodate the rush of visitors.

The Rural Pennines

In many respects the North Pennines are a continuation of the hill country that extends all along the boundary between Lancashire and Yorkshire, and they deserve consideration as a whole. In contrast to the Lake District, the rural Pennines have experienced a loss of jobs and continued out-migration, without a corresponding increase in tourism. Apart from a few 'honey pots' along Hadrian's Wall, the North Pennines have remained a relatively undiscovered area. Further south the Yorkshire Dales National Park is used mainly for recreation from the built up areas of Lancashire and Yorkshire, rather than for longer-

stay tourism, although there has been an increase over recent years particularly of foreign visitors.

However, although the Dales are scenically attractive, they are not particularly productive. Full-time male labour has declined by 29 per cent in the Cumbrian Pennines between 1963–75, and farming remains the dominant activity over the whole area. Unfortunately topography, soils and climate all combine to make farming difficult, and the emphasis is on livestock rearing of sheep and cattle, with a tendency towards dairying in the lower dales and in districts close to the main built up areas in the North-East, Lancashire and Yorkshire. A study of the uplands within the former West Riding revealed that the average size of holding was only 25 ha, plus roughgrazing, and 80 per cent were smaller than 600 standard man days – a higher proportion even than in Scotland. Upland farmers are caught in a difficult position. A poor environment and small units inevitably make for low income and low incentives. Because they are mainly producing store livestock, they are dependent upon the willingness of lowland graziers to buy their finished product, who in turn depend upon market price for butcher meat. To encourage investment, therefore, a long-term confidence is needed which has just not been provided. An additional means of improving the position is to encourage the restructuring of farm holdings. This was one of the major aims of the North Pennines Rural Development Board, which covered an area from Wharfedale to the Scottish border, but it had only a short life (1969–71), and the task still remains to be accomplished.

Forestry becomes progressively more important from south to north in the Pennines. Between the industrial areas of Lancashire and Yorkshire, atmospheric pollution is such as to render tree growth uneconomical (over 150 microgrammes of sulphur dioxide per cubic metre). In the Yorkshire Dales forestry is not a major land use, and much of the woodland is under private ownership rather than in the hands of the Forestry Commission. In the North Tyne Valley, however, Britain's largest forested area is to be found, and Northumberland has over 60,000 ha of woodland altogether.

Quarrying is an altogether more important industry, with perhaps half as many employees as agriculture. Output includes roadstone, sandstone and gritstone, particularly for crushed aggregate in the south Pennines. The most controversial quarryings, though, are for limestone – on the Great Scar limestone on the fringes of the Yorkshire Dales National Park, and at Eastgate in Weardale, and around Kendal. Apart from the visual intrusion into areas of great scenic beauty, the extensive production of dust that accompanies cement making, and the pounding of local roads by heavy lorries have both produced complaints; yet the value to the local economy of better-paid jobs than either farming or forestry cannot be denied.

THE NORTH-WEST

The sorry decline of the former staple industries of the Northern region has its counterpart in the contraction of the *cotton industry* in the North-West (Fig. 21.6). Less than two generations ago 25 per cent of Britain's export account was made up of cotton products, providing employment for over half a million workers in Lancashire alone. Today, though not extinct, the Lancashire textile industry employs only a tenth of that labour, cotton is a minor constituent of an industry that uses a range of artificial fibres, and cotton imports have exceeded exports for over twenty years. The reasons for this change of fortunes are well known. First, a rise in cotton textiles in Third World countries eroded Lancashire's export market, followed by a penetration of the home market as the weakened industry was no longer able to maintain its technological advantage. Under-capitalised and over-manned, the Lancashire cotton industry was unable to face the free-market competition of the 1950s, and mills and jobs fell disastrously – almost 200,000 jobs and over 500 mills between 1951 and 1960. The policy response was significant. The government produced the Cotton Industry Act (1959) to re-shape the industry. Compensation was offered for the scrapping of outdated machinery, so enabling employers to either rationalise or release their capital, and grants were made for re-equipment. Almost half the plant – both looms and spindles – were removed, but little unemployment resulted as workers were themselves leaving the industry as fast as they could. As the industry moved more and more into artificial fibres, then so it came to be increasingly dominated by the chemical giants, and indeed be seen as an off-shoot of the chemicals industry. As a result I.C.I. and Courtaulds now dominate the industry, whose locational characteristics are derived as much from the suitability of individual premises for larger working units and the presence of appropriate machinery, as from any so-called 'geographical' factors.

The Lancashire cotton industry was the major market for the local *coal industry,* but decline here had already set in quite independently of the contraction of demand for fuel. The field suffered from a complex geology so that mining operations have been scattered across a discontinuous zone stretching from Burnley in the north to Widnes and Manchester in the south, with a centre of activity around Wigan. Contraction since the 1930s gradually reduced mining to a relic around Burnley and the southern edge of the field between Salford and Widnes. Here, massive investment had produced a string of 'super-pits' by 1960, but the still unpredictable geology, as well as labour difficulties, has resulted in further closures, so that fewer than ten mines now survive.

Grey Areas

With such serious industrial collapse, severe unemployment could be expected in the zone of textile towns along the western margins of the Pennines, where the cotton industry established itself during the nineteenth century. With their rows of terrace houses and huge mills, towns such as Oldham and Rochdale, Darwen and Burnley were epitomised in the paintings of L.S. Lowry and form a fitting backdrop to industrial misery. Yet this has not in general been the case, at least in so far as unemployment is concerned. Instead, population losses by migration have more than made up for the decline of the cotton industry. Young workers in particular have left the towns in droves, leaving an elderly population, which is in many cases not capable of maintaining its present size into the next generation. Not all young families have left, of course, and work is still required by those that remain that are below retirement age. This need for employment has been provided by a remarkable re-occupation of many of the former cotton mills by a variety of small industrial concerns, providing almost two-thirds of the jobs lost in cotton (Fig. 21.7). By no means all the mills have been used in this way – some were too old and insecure, and multi-storey premises are often not suited to

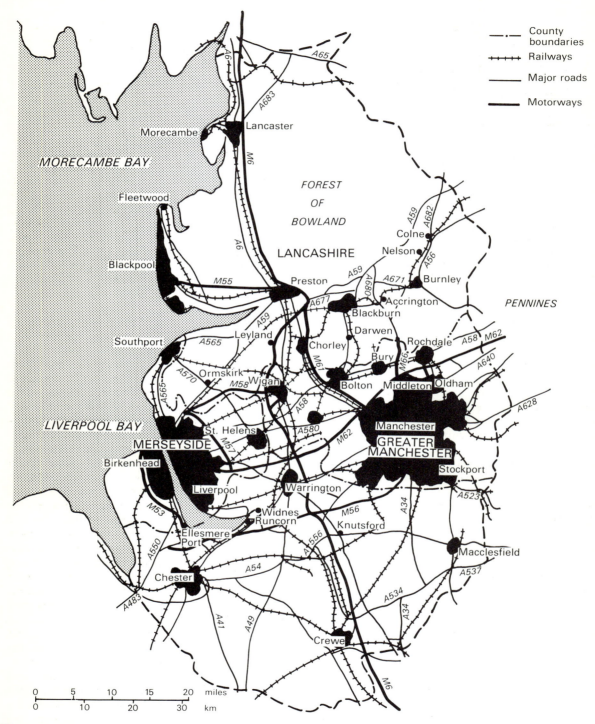

Fig 21.6 North-West—major towns and communications

Fig 21.7a and b   Re-occupied cotton mill, Rochdale, before and after. The re-occupation of former cotton mills has been an important aspect of industrial survival in eastern Lancashire.

conversion – but many are, with the result that some factories are now divided between half a dozen employers. The new industries are often labour-intensive, requiring little expensive plant – indeed the very reason why they are established in second-hand premises – and often offer more employment to women. This is not necessarily a bad thing as female employment was particularly vulnerable in textile closures. On the other hand, wages tend to be low, with the result that although unemployment rates may not be high, the level of prosperity is relatively low, and the industrial structure is not one that inspires a great deal of confidence.

It was factors such as these that led the government to initiate the investigations of the Hunt Committee which reported in 1969 on intermediate or 'grey' areas. The textile towns on both sides of the Pennines can be regarded as typical of such areas. While unemployment is not very high, wage levels within the existing industries tend to be below average. The physical structure of the towns is often outworn because both town centres and housing were created during the later decades of the nineteenth century. Industrial dereliction is a commonplace as empty mills decay, canals become choked with rubbish and spoil heaps gently

erode. Situated in hilly country the roads are frequently inadequate for modern traffic densities, and particularly for large articulated lorries, while the railways which formerly served industry and town alike have been removed under rationalisation. As a result, aspiring, better-educated and higher skilled people tend to migrate leaving a residual population bereft of their talents. With only low-paid jobs available, in-migrants tend to be from the New Commonwealth so that social strain is added to inadequate economies. However, because the areas do not have high rates of unemployment, assistance under regional policy is not available, and indeed footloose industry that successfully outgrows its nursery in the converted mill may be tempted by the benefits available in Development Areas to move away itself, taking its enhanced job prospects with it. With no such incentives, low unemployment, and low levels of skill, plus the structural inadequacies of the physical environment, it has proved very difficult to attract any new mobile industry into such areas. We can see, therefore, that not just the rural Pennines, but also the urbanised fringes are shedding economic activity, although this is often a relative rather than an absolute trend. They are economically stagnant.

297

Merseyside

In contrast to the cotton towns of the Pennines, decline and attempts at rehabilitation could not have taken a more different path on Merseyside. Like Glasgow and Bristol, Liverpool rose to prominence as a major colonial port. As the cotton industry achieved its spectacular success, so Liverpool prospered as a result of both imports of raw cotton and exports of finished products. In addition it became the major port for the manufacturing industries of the whole of the North of England, and for the West Midlands, as well as acquiring an important share of the passenger liner traffic. Its port facilities were progressively enlarged over the nineteenth century, served by a massive labour force. Shipbuilding and repairing were natural concomitants, and additional specialist facilities for handling chemicals, minerals and foodstuffs were established at Bromborough, Garston and Ellesmere Port. As the major port of entry from Ireland, Liverpool attracted a constant stream of migrants, many of whom stayed because of the attractions of a plentiful demand for unskilled manual labour. Manufacturing industry, however, failed to develop in any great measure. Liverpool's employments were dominated by the port, its handling and initial processing industries, and the shipyards on both sides of the river. This failure to diversify cost Liverpool dearly as port requirements changed, and shipbuilding and repairing encountered fierce competition from overseas.

Liverpool's decline was heralded by the construction of the Manchester Ship Canal in 1894. This enabled Manchester to grow as an inland port at the expense of Liverpool, while the associated Trafford Park industrial estate, developed after 1896, attracted the range of manufacturing industry from which Liverpool could well have benefitted. The inter-war depression hit Liverpool particularly strongly, as both the shipbuilding and cotton trades suffered. In contrast, London, Liverpool's main rival, had a relatively prosperous hinterland during this period, and its steady expansion of facilities further eroded trade along the Mersey. By 1945, therefore, Liverpool was already in a precarious position, and in the succeeding twenty years the antiquated nature of its docks and handling systems, along with the mili-

tancy of its dockers made it less and less attractive for modern traffic. The liner trade was progressively eroded by developments in air transport, and this had an adverse effect upon the repair and refit trade, which was all but lost. During 1959–63, employment in the shipyards shrank by 32 per cent. In contrast there was some gain in the food processing industries over the 1950s in particular; and over the 1960s, considerable investment in chemicals at Ellesmere Port, Widnes and Runcorn. Unfortunately, while this increased, it did so with a smaller labour requirement, so that the overall trend in Merseyside's established industries was by no means healthy. In addition the area's problems were aggravated by a burgeoning population. Because the area has a high proportion of families in low-income groups, many of whom are Roman Catholics of Irish extraction, birth rates have been consistently high – around 20 per thousand until recently. A stagnating economy was quite incapable of dealing with such an increase, and it was only a strong current of out-migration, along with the note-worthy success of regional policy in attracting new jobs to the area, that prevented Merseyside's unemployment rates becoming catastrophic.

Merseyside has been designated as a Development Area since 1946 (and a Special Development Area since 1974). Of itself that has been of great help, even though it has drawn industry into the area from other parts of the region, but perhaps most significantly, it was an important factor in the decision of three of the major motor manufacturing concerns to establish additional plant in the are to cope with the rapid expansion anticipated in the demand for their products in the 1960s and 1970s. Ford at Halewood, Vauxhall (Talbot) at Ellesmere Port and Standard Triumph (British Leyland) at Speke (closed in 1978) all chose to establish assembly plants in and around Merseyside in the mid 1960s, so that by 1969, 30,000 new jobs were directly created, plus of course additional employment via the multiplier effect. Export facilities through the port and rapidly improving inland links through the M6, M62 and main line electrification, as well as an ample supply of labour, were all part of the location decision, of course; and the cumulative impact of such a massive increase in job opportunities in a high wage industry was enormous in the whole of the sub-region.

New Towns and Motorways

Economic growth on Merseyside cannot be divorced from the rapid changes that have taken place in the whole of south-west Lancashire and northern Cheshire. Partly as a response to population growth and industrial congestion on Merseyside, Skelmersdale New Town was designated in 1961, five miles to the north of the Merseyside conurbation, and Runcorn New Town was designated five miles to the south-east across the Mersey in northern Cheshire. In 1968 the decision was taken to designate the existing town of Warrington (strategically situated near the junction of the M62 and M56 with the M6) as a new town. A proposal to develop a Central Lancashire New Town around existing settlements between Chorley and Preston has not been proceeded with. Nevertheless the three established new towns, which have owed their success as much to their strategic location and to the movement of population and industry from the Pennine fringe, as to spill over from Merseyside, have proved key features of the rapid growth of the western part of the region (Fig. 21.8).

Three-quarters of Skelmersdale's population is in fact drawn from Merseyside and supported by a range of manufacturing industry, including plants belonging to Dunlop, British Oxygen Co., and Alcan. Unfortunately the town suffered a considerable blow in the mid 1970s with the closure of its two biggest employers – Thorn Electrical and Courtauld's. Twenty-five per cent of manufacturing employment was lost, and although there has been some recovery, unemployment still stood at 11 per cent at the beginning of 1978. Its original target population was 80,000, but in 1977 that was scaled down (to 60,000) in common with other new towns. The population now stands at 42,000 (1978). Unfortunately this reduction in the designated population has repercussions on the range of service and shopping facilities that the town can support, although fears have also been expressed that insufficient land is available for the provision of employment for a town of more than 50,000. Although the town's long-term future is perhaps not as exuberant as was once thought, there is no doubt that the creation of an attractive environment for both living and working has enhanced the quality of life in the region, and is much to be preferred to the vast council ghetto of Kirkby, Liverpool's former major overspill estate.

At Runcorn, an existing town of 28,500 was chosen as the nucleus from which a town of 100,000 would eventually develop. It was expected that its population would reach 70,000 by 1979, and this has not been very far off-target. Runcorn has been successful in attracting industry to its two major industrial estates, but its main significance is in the attention the town has paid to developing its internal transportation system, including a 'Busway' arrangement – a road system reserved for buses to provide a fast link between all parts of the town and residential districts. The existing shopping centre in old Runcorn has been supplemented by a completely enclosed and pedestrian-segregated 'Shopping City', utilising a major district heating system.

Less than ten miles away at Warrington, the existing town already had a population of more than 100,000 at designation, with an intention that it should grow to double that figure, although that is not now likely to be the case. Unlike the Special Development Area status enjoyed by the other two new towns, Warrington only has the benefit of Intermediate Area status. However, there have been suggestions that this has meant that new industry has been attracted to the area for 'natural' rather than 'artificial' reasons. Integration with the existing town had been less pronounced than at Runcorn, partly because of the difference in size between the two settlements. Industrial development has mainly been concentrated at peripheral industrial estates at Winnick Quay and Risley on the M62, and Grange on the M6, but a distinctive new approach has been the creation of Birchwood Science Park, a 30 ha landscaped area in which are to be set research and development type employments. A major employer already is the headquarters of British Nuclear Fuels and the UKAEA, Risley Reactor Group.

The other major symbol of massive public investment in the North-West is the motorway system (Fig. 21.8). Few areas of Britain are served by such a complex web of motorways. The major axes of the M6 and M62 are supplemented by the M61 and M63, M55 and M56, with a total motorway extent of almost 400 km. As a result most of the highly populated areas are within 10 km of the motorway system, except for the declining textile towns of the north-western Pennines, a factor

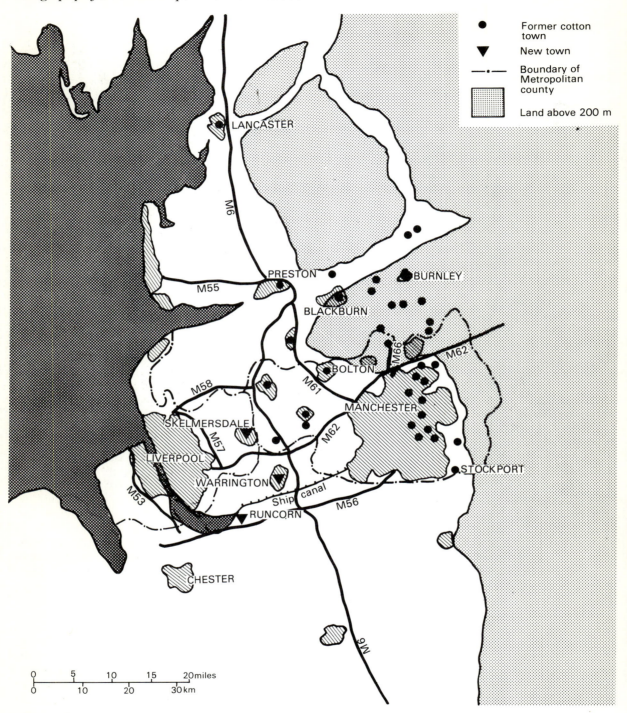

Former cotton town

New town

Boundary of Metropolitan county

Land above 200 m

LANCASTER

PRESTON

BURNLEY

BLACKBURN

BOLTON

MANCHESTER

SKELMERSDALE

LIVERPOOL

WARRINGTON

STOCKPORT

RUNCORN

Ship canal

CHESTER

M6

M55

M58

M57

M53

M61

M62

M66

M62

M56

M6

| 0 | 5 | 10 | 15 | 20 miles |

| 0 | 10 | 20 | 30 km |

Fig 21.8 Regional development in North-West England

Fig 21.9 The M62, at Scammonden dam, with Huddersfield in the distance

which underlines their relative deprivation. Thus growth in the North-West is strongly centred on the south-west of the region, leaving even Manchester in a difficult situation. Although the regional capital, and the scene of rapid developments in office-based industries over recent years, its economic structure is amongst the weakest of all the major cities in Britain. In many respects the city has two faces. Towards the south-west Greater Manchester is an area of generally prosperous middle class residential development and associated employment. To the north-east, however, the Pennine foothills are soon reached and the familiar characteristics of the grey areas become apparent. The inner city area has been decimated by population loss, clearance schemes and removal of industry, and it is with some justification that Manchester looks to the rapid developments in the New Towns to the west as the source of some of its industrial decline.

YORKSHIRE AND HUMBERSIDE

Our last region has a certain parallelism with the North-West. In both there is a major estuary, in both the Pennine interior whether rural or industrial is an area of economic stagnation and population loss, and in both cases the main zone of prosperity occupies a lowland corridor close to the

301

main north-south axis of communications. But there the comparison ends for Yorkshire and Humberside has neither New Towns nor Expanded Towns. Indeed, its level of per capita public investment has been lower (87 per cent of U.K. average) than any other region except the West Midlands. In many ways this is a paradoxical region, for although its level of unemployment is generally lower than the U.K. average, so also are its wage rates. While regional pride in 'Yorkshire' (a unit unrecognised by local government for nearly a century) is intense, many of the indicators of social well-being are relatively low. Health provision, crime rate and the proportion of chil-

dren staying on at school are all worse than the U.K. average. Average house prices may well be lower than anywhere else in the country, but that is probably a reflection of the large numbers of small, old properties in the industrial districts, and as much an indicator of ill-health than well-being. However, there are contrasts in the region, and local issues which we can see focusing upon the wool textile districts in West Yorkshire, the coal and steel industries mainly in South Yorkshire, and the peculiar problems of Humberside. We have already noticed the distinctiveness of the rural Pennines, but agriculture in lowland Yorkshire could not be more different.

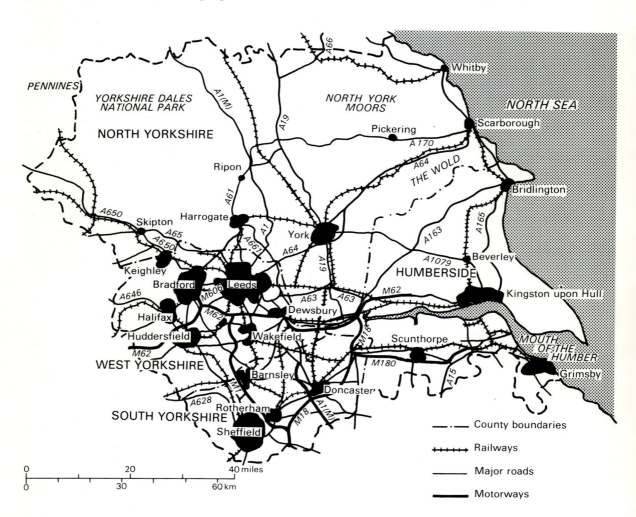

Fig 21.10 Yorkshire and Humberside—major towns and communications

West Yorkshire

One of the six metropolitan counties, West Yorkshire encompasses the conurbation which resulted from the rapid expansion of the wool textile industry in the last century. Although Leeds is the largest city, and the regional capital, Wakefield is the county town, with the larger towns of Bradford, Huddersfield and Halifax (and Leeds) mere centres of county districts. The wool textile trade, like the cotton trade, is now much smaller than it once was. At its peak during the late nineteenth century, the Yorkshire wool textile industry employed about 250,000 workers. As late as 1955 (a post-war peak) there were still 201,000 employees, but since then contraction has been rapid to only 59,000 in 1976, and probably less than 50,000 by the 1980s. Contraction in the industry has been eased by a government scheme under the 1972 Industry Act, through the 1974 Wool Textile scheme, which was to enable rationalisation on the lines of that of the Lancashire cotton industry in the previous decade. Many mills have subsequently closed, and considerable investment made on the part of surviving firms – over £100 millions from the government and normal market sources between 1972 and 1977.

As with the cotton industry, foreign competition has been the major source of the industry's decline, although changing fashion habits have also influenced the demand for the industry's traditional products of suitings, overcoatings and blankets. The heaviest losses have been sustained by the cheaper parts of the trade, and in the home market, but in contrast to the cotton industry, there is still a vigorous export market for high quality woollens, amounting in 1977 to over £390 millions. However, because there has always been a marked degree of local specialisation, contraction in the industry has been unevenly spread. In Huddersfield, and to the south and west, a traditional concentration upon the export market along with a spread of employment into engineering and chemicals has served the area well. In Bradford, a reliance upon the domestic market has meant that textile contraction has been more severe, but in the small towns which make up the Heavy Woollen District, in the heart of the conurbation, contraction has been catastrophic. Batley and Dewsbury, and their immediate neighbours grew to prosperity upon the manufacture of cheap heavy suitings, overcoats and blankets, using rag

wool or 'shoddy'. This is the sector of the trade which has been most adversely affected, and where the deprivation of a declining economic base has had its severest impact upon social and environmental structures. With severe competition, wage rates and investment have been very low. Many firms eventually closed, and their former employees forced to travel to work in the surrounding towns. On the other hand because of low wages and low morale, many skilled workers left the industry, so there were labour shortages which have been met only by the large influx of Asian migrants, who have been prepared to work in poor conditions in a declining industry. As the economic base has contracted, then so also has there been a decline in the community superstructure of housing, shopping, social environment and, not least, the revenue base of the local authority; so that a spiral of community decline is engendered that is difficult to reverse.

A similar situation has been developing for many years in the deeper Pennine valleys of the Calder and the Colne (Fig. 21.11). There, the problems of economic decline are aggravated by a dispersed population, poor communications and a difficult topography which have together conspired to give an impression of remoteness that is not altogether justified. Unemployment has been kept down by sustained out-migration of the area's youngest and most able members of the population. Attempts to re-invigorate the local economic base have been thwarted because of the low level of labour availability, and the simple fact that the area has never qualified for regional aid at a level higher than districts further east, around Leeds, where linkages with other industries are far easier, development land more suitable, and communications vastly superior. Under the 1979 proposals, all of West Yorkshire would be descheduled as an assisted area.

In the whole of West Yorkshire the brightest prospects for economic growth are to be found in Leeds. Despite the major blow of the collapse of a large part of the city's ready-made clothing trade in the 1970s (due to cheap imports from eastern Europe as well as the Far East), the overall base of Leed's economy is very wide. The city is a major centre for office employment and although there has been a marked decline in manufacturing industry since 1951, development prospects are assumed to be relatively good. Housing is amongst the best of all the major cities in Britain,

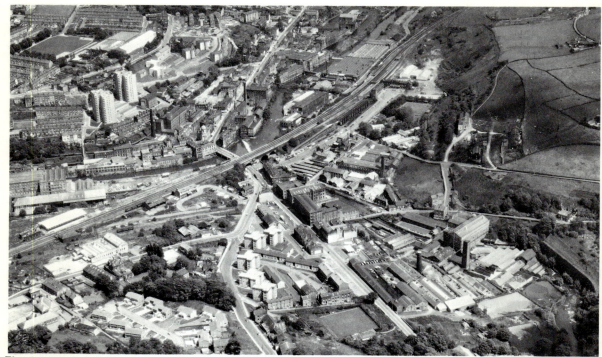

Fig 21.11 Sowerby Bridge, W. Yorkshire. Many of the textile mills lining the Calder and the Ryburn are now derelict, and much of the terrace housing is below modern standards. The proximity of the open hillsides and the provision of Council flats are among the brighter spots of this Calderdale town.

and its shopping centre is a major northern magnet. However, there are, even in Leeds, a few warning lights. Unemployment has been above the national average for some years, cut-backs in local authority expenditure have slowed the pace of inner-city renewal, and there are above-average proportions of derelict land which need attention.

South Yorkshire

The economy of many of the southern parts of the region – including some areas of West Yorkshire, North Yorkshire and Humberside – hangs upon coal and iron and steel. In contrast to other parts of northern England, however, both industries have an assured future, although there are local black spots and there have been anxious times. In the *coal industry* the trend in Yorkshire, as in other regions, was one of steady working down the dip of the seams; the closure of smaller and older collieries in districts which had witnessed the earlier development of mining; and the concentration of mining into fewer but larger units. Thus coal mining was virtually abandoned west of a line drawn between Leeds and Huddersfield by 1945, while by 1960 many of the former valuable coal mines between Wakefield and Sheffield had begun to experience closure. The exploitation of the concealed coalfield, roughly east of the A1 was largely a development of the twentieth century, but even here rationalisation around Doncaster was the harbinger of high unemployment and out-migration in the 1960s and early 1970s. It was the decline of the coal industry which led to the Barnsley-Doncaster districts being designated an Intermediate Area in 1969, three years before the rest of the region. Unemployment in older mining districts, such as Hemsworth between Wakefield and Doncaster, is almost double the regional figure, but the rate of reduction of the labour force has been much slower in the 1970s. Even then, however, manpower declined from 93,000 in 1967 to 65,700 by 1975.

Such a figure is likely to be the general level of employment on the Yorkshire coalfield for the immediate future, though in 1974 the N.C.B. hoped to raise production from 33 million tons to 45 million tons by 1975. Three major factors underlie this change in the industry's fortunes: the increased demand for coal in the new energy situation after the oil crisis of 1973; hopes for greater productivity; and the development of the eastward extension of the coalfield around Selby (Fig. 21.12). While all other parts of the coalfield foresee an expansion of their production without an increase in their labour force, the age structure of the Selby force means that there will have to be substantial recruitment of younger miners, as 40 per cent of the labour force was aged over 50 in 1975. Developments at Selby require 4,000 workers, some of whom are being redeployed from other collieries, the rest being made up of new recruits, set against unreplaced natural wastage in exhausted units further west. Thus, while the labour force remains roughly the same, the industry will experience a major eastwards shift during the 1980s. The market for Yorkshire coal is abundant and near at hand, with major power stations (including the double giants at Drax) and the iron and steel industry of Sheffield, Rotherham and Scunthorpe. The direct economic benefits of a stable labour force in the coal industry are obviously significant, particularly since the industry has moved steadily towards being a high wage industry. On the other hand, the environmental impact of expansion has raised some alarm, not least in the formerly tranquil (and agriculturally prosperous) area of the Selby extension.

As far as the *steel industry* is concerned the future is also less uncertain than for some other regions, because of the area's strong emphasis upon special steels. Sheffield/Rotherham is now the centre of B.S.C.'s special steel industry, output from which has been growing more rapidly than output from the steel industry as a whole, although the manu-

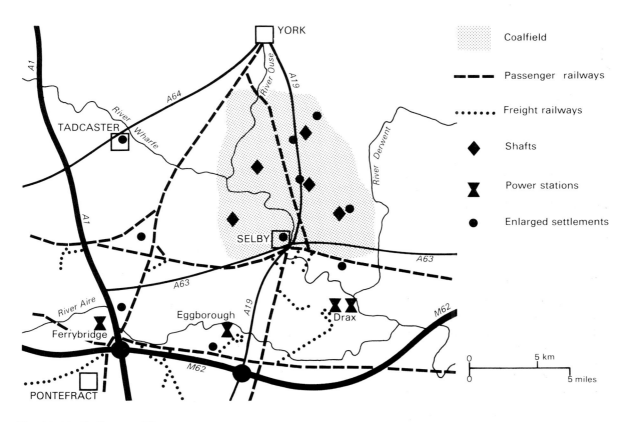

Fig 21.12 Selby coalfield

facture of cutlery, of course, has declined drastically in the face of competition from the Far East. It was anticipated that by 1980 the capacity of the area would be increased to produce about 3·75 million tons of B.S.C.'s total of 4·6 million tons of alloy steels per year, with considerable increases to the production capacity of stainless steel in Sheffield. On the other hand there would be reductions in labour if the non-alloy plants at Rotherham were closed down as part of general rationalisation programmes. At Scunthorpe the commissioning of the Anchor works in 1973 thoroughly modernised the pattern of steel making there, while the completion of the Immingham ore terminal allowed greater use to be made of foreign ores, rather than the local low-content Frodingham ores. However, as is so often the case, greater investment and more modern plant resulted in a reduction of the workforce, so that overall employment in Sheffield/Rotherham/Scunthorpe steel-making fell by almost 20 per cent between 1970 and 1975, to a figure of 70,000.

A pattern of employment which leans so heavily upon coal mining and the iron and steel trades, cannot be regarded as satisfactory. Female employments in particular are less available, and the range of job opportunities for the school leaver is narrow. Consequently there have been attempts to induce a wider range of industry to the area, promoting the motorway links via M1 and M62, good rail communications, availability of labour and prospects of exporting to Europe via Humberside. In the event, however, while there has been an expansion of office-based industries in Sheffield, there has been relatively little industrial diversification, except in the Doncaster sub-region where long-term growth prospects are probably good.

Humberside

During the 1960s there was a considerable body of influential opinion that the modern pattern of industrial growth should take particular account of the facilities offered by the major estuaries. Deep water for bulk transportation (particularly of oil), plus flat land for large-scale capital intensive industries, were regarded as the basis upon which could be established a line of downstream processing and manufacturing industries, which would in turn support an array of service industries and thus a whole new population. At first sight, Humberside appeared to be an ideal area for such development, particularly because it was close to the iron and steel base of South Yorkshire, the commercial expertise of the West Riding, and possessed a strategic location with connections across the North Sea to Europe. In 1969 the government published *Humberside – a Feasibility Study,* which explored the possibilities of establishing just such a pattern of growth. Communications with the national motorway system were to be improved by the completion of the M62, and subsequently the M180 along the south bank; and the decision to build the Humber Bridge was the symbol of a hoped-for interdependence of the two sides of the estuary. Local government reform in 1972 linked the two sides administratively by creating the new county of Humberside.

Ten years after the publication of the Feasibility Study these aspirations have not been fulfilled. The government decided not to proceed with the deliberate creation of large-scale developments on the Humber. In 1978 the decision to build the Humber Bridge was heavily criticised by a House of Commons committee, as production costs soared, and labour difficulties delayed its completion. Meanwhile, opinion on the south bank of the Humber against the new administrative arrangements has been gathering steady momentum. Far from being a dynamic growth area, unemployment stood at 10·8 per cent in the Hull area in February 1978, and 9·4 per cent in Grimsby, and in 1977 the area was lifted out of Intermediate Area designation to Development Area status.

It may well be that, in the long-term, Humberside's growth prospects are for better rather than worse, but in the short-term three trends have run against the area. First, population growth nationally has not been such as to require the creation of major new industrial and residential areas. Secondly, the economic recession forced such capital as was available towards more immediate short-term objectives, while thirdly the rapid decline of the fishing-based industries, following disputes with Iceland, Russia and Norway, has led to localised sectoral under-employment in Hull and Grimsby. Economic stagnation has been more marked on the north bank, where 10,000 jobs were lost between 1967 and 1978, many in light engineering. In the same period almost as many jobs have been gained on the south bank, largely through the development of petro-chemicals concerns – I.C.I., Laporte, Courtaulds, and Fisons among them. Increasingly, south Humberside has moved towards employment in heavy industry, and north Humberside towards employments in service industry, but on neither bank has there been the development of the manufacturing industry that the area needs to give it greater stability.

In some respects there is an interesting parallel with the case of South Wales in each of these three northern regions. In each case developments on lower more open lands towards the coast has inevitably been at the expense of inland (and often upland) locations where industrial growth was established in the last century. It is hard to predict what effect rapid estuarine development on the Humber would have upon the manufacturing industries of West Yorkshire; but the diversion of public funds from the support necessary in the Pennine valleys to the provision of infrastructure on the Humber would undoubtedly lead to a more

rapid demise in the Pennines. The same is feared to be the case in South Wales.

References

House, J.W., *The North East* (David & Charles, 1969).

Warren, K., *North East England* (O.U.P., 1973).

Centre for Agricultural Strategy (Reading) *The Future of Upland Britain*, Paper 2, 1977.

Humberside: a Feasibility Study (H.M.S.O., 1969).

Lawton, R., & Cunningham, C.M., *Merseyside: Social and Economic Studies* (Longman, 1970).

Freeman, T., Rodgers & Kinvig, *Lancashire, Cheshire and the Isle of Man* (Nelson, 1966).

Smith, D.W., *The North West* (David & Charles, 1969).

Batley Community Development Project, *Batley at Work,* 1976.

Manners, G., Keeble, Rodgers & Warren, *Regional Development in Britain* (Wiley, 1972).

Index